D1327399

de Gruyter Studies in Organization 39

Social Dynamics of the IT Field

de Gruyter Studies in Organization

Innovation, Technology, and Organization

This international and interdisciplinary book series from de Gruyter presents comprehensive research on the inter-relationship between organization and innovations, both technical and social.
It covers applied topics such as the organization of:
- R & D
- new product and process innovations
- social innovations, such as the development of new forms of work organization and corporate governance structure
and addresses topics of more general interest such as:
- the impact of technical change and other innovations on forms of organization of micro and macro levels
- the development of technologies and other innovations under different organizational conditions at the levels both of the firm and the economy.
The series is designed to stimulate and encourage the exchange of ideas between academic researchers, practitioners, and policy makers, though not all volumes address policy- or practitioner-oriented issues.
The volumes present conceptual schema as well as empirical studies and are of interest to students of business policy and organizational behaviour, to economists and sociologists, and to managers and administrators at firm and national level.

Editor:
Arthur Francis, Glasgow University Business School, Glasgow, GB

Advisory Board:
Prof. Claudio Ciborra, University of Trento, Italy
Dr. Mark Dodgson, Science Policy Research Unit, University of Sussex, GB
Dr. Peter Grootings, CEDEFOP, Berlin, Germany
Prof. Laurie Larwood, Dean, College of Business Administration, University of Nevada, Reno, Nevada

Finn Borum, Andrew Lloyd Friedman,
Mette Mønsted, Jesper Strandgaard Pedersen,
Marianne Risberg

Social Dynamics of the IT Field

The Case of Denmark

Walter de Gruyter · Berlin · New York 1992

Finn Borum is Associate Professor, Institute of Organisation and Industrial Sociology, Copenhagen Business School, Copenhagen, Denmark

Andrew Lloyd Friedman is Lecturer in Economics, Department of Economics, Bristol University, Bristol, Great Britain

Mette Mønsted is Associate Professor, Centre of Innovation and Entrepreneurship, Copenhagen Business School, Copenhagen, Denmark

Jesper Strandgaard Pedersen is Assistant Professor, Institute of Organisation and Industrial Sociology, Copenhagen Business School, Copenhagen, Denmark

Marianne Risberg is Research Secretary, Institute of Organisation and Industrial Sociology, Copenhagen Business School, Copenhagen, Denmark

With 28 figures and 19 tables.

⊗ Printed on acid free paper which falls within the guidelines of the ANSI to ensure permanence and durability.

Library of Congress Cataloging-in-Publication Data

Social dynamics of the IT field : the case of Denmark / Finn Borum [et al.].
    p.   cm. – (De Gruyter studies in organization : 39)
    Includes bibliographical references
    ISBN 0-89925-860-3
    1. Information technology – Denmark.   2. High technology industries – Denmark.   3. Corporate culture – Denmark
    I. Borum, Finn. II. Series.
    HC360.I55S63 1992
    306.4'2'09489 – dc20   92-19766
                             CIP

Die Deutsche Bibliothek – Cataloging-in-Publication Data

Social dynamics of the IT fielt, the case of Denmark / Finn Borum ... - Berlin ; New York : de Gruyter, 1992
    (De Gruyter studies in organization ; 39)
    ISBN 3-11-012981-7
NE : Borum, Finn ; GT

© Copyright 1992 by Walter de Gruyter & Co., D-1000 Berlin 30.
All rights reserved, including those of translation into foreign languages. No part of this book may be reproduced in any form – by photoprint, microfilm, or any other means nor transmitted nor translated into a machine language without written permission from the publisher.
Typesetting: Converted by Knipp-Satz und Bild digitial, Dortmund. – Printing: Ratzlow-Druck, Berlin. – Binding: Dieter Mikolai, Berlin.
Cover Design: Johannes Rother, Berlin.

Contents

Acknowledgements

The CHIPS project group would like to thank the Copenhagen Business School, the Danish Social Science Research Council, the Danish Council of Technology, and Bristol University without whose financial support it would have been impossible to carry out the project.

The Institute of Organisation and Industrial Sociology has given shelter – and a very pleasant one – to the project during its three years of existence.

We are indebted to the many Danish organizations and institutions that have participated in the project, and allowed the research team access to internal documents. We thank our many informants and interviewees for providing both information and ideas. We hope that this reader contains sufficient stimulating and useful feed-back.

We have benefited greatly from the comments of both practitioners and colleagues that participated in the CHIPS seminars, and from the "running commentaries" at the Institute of Industrial Research and Social Development and at the Institute of Organisation and Industrial Sociology.

Among our commentators we would like to thank in particular Niels Bjorn-Andersen, Frans Boch, Arthur Francis, Joan Greenbaum, Mary Jo Hatch, Geert Hofstede, Jens Horlyck, Kristian Kreiner, Peer Hull Kristensen, Jan Mouritsen, Bram Neuijen, Leif Bloch Rasmussen, Charles Sabel, Geert Sanders, Edgar H. Schein, Steen Scheuer, John Van Maanen, and Stephen Wood for commenting upon notes, papers and manuscripts.

We thank the Danish Social Science Research Council for permission to include the chapters I and V, Part A, and chapter VI, Part B. These three articles have earlier been published in a somewhat different version in "Technological Innovation and Organizational Change" edited by Finn Borum and Peer Hull Kristensen and published by the Research Council.

Copenhagen, July 1991

The CHIPS project group
Finn Borum
Andrew Lloyd Friedman
Mette Mønsted
Jesper Strandgaard Pedersen
Marianne Risberg

Introduction: Perspectives on the IT Field

1   The IT Field

In this collection of articles the information technology (IT) field in Denmark is analysed from several different perspectives. These perspectives reflect the different interests and backgrounds of the authors who came together to work on the CHIPS project at the Copenhagen Business School from 1986 to 1990. The authors worked as a self-directed group of colleagues. Differences in perspectives were discussed openly in order to understand the positions of the others without strong attempts at gaining converts. Eventually we came to see that the concept of the IT field could be used to embrace these different perspectives without requiring their melding or watering down. Rather what we have all learned to accept is the complexity of the IT field. We have come to appreciate the many forces driving, restraining and shaping the development of the field. While we each still favour different approaches, we have made no attempt here to adjudicate between them. Rather the field concept encourages the different perspectives to be developed and displayed without forcing their respective "value" to be measured or compared.

In the following sections of this introduction the IT field will be defined and the way we use this concept will be explained. We will then discuss the distinctive features of our empirical base, the IT field *in Denmark*. The Danish IT field is interesting because of certain of these distinctive features. We argue that most previous studies of IT specialists have been less careful to investigate distinctive features of their samples even though they have generally been drawn from a population as limited in size and geographic location as Denmark (that is, particular cities in the United States). Generalisation of our findings to the world IT field is likely to be no more dangerous than generalisation of earlier studies, as long as the distinctive features of the Danish IT field are appreciated.

Next, details about the CHIPS project are provided and this introduction ends with a very brief outline of the three parts into which the reader has been divided. A summary of the individual chapters is presented in the introductions to each of these parts.

What is the IT field? We define the IT field as that social space within which the structuring of institutions and people (in terms of their material positions and mental states) related to a broad bundle of techniques or knowledge resources commonly known as information technology occurs. It is the social space structured around the production, utilisation, and control of information technology. More specifically we focus on the aspect of the IT field concerned with the development, maintenance and operation of administrative computer-based systems or information systems.

People and material resources as well as institutions may be thought of as situated within the field. However they have a social existence in other contexts. The field does not completely enclose them, does not completely protect or separate them from other social contexts. As the actors and resources associated with the field are influenced by other associations and forces, so the field itself is altered. The field develops both in relation to these "external" contexts as well as through the interaction of agents and institutions "within" it.

The interaction of people and institutions within the IT field may be cooperative, as when groups within the field develop common strategies for advancing the field itself, but more commonly the internal dynamic arises from conflict within the field as people and institutions compete with the purpose of both getting their share of the field's resources (material as well as symbolic) and strengthening their position within that field. In this sense our view of the field accords with that developed by Bourdieu (Bourdieu and Passeron, 1970; Bordieu, 1984).[1]

Lewin was the first to introduce the field notion to the social sciences. Lewin defined a field as a "totality of coexisting facts which are conceived of as mutually interdependent" (1952, p.240). He worked with the concept of a force field in which an individual or social system is maintained in a quasi-stationary state as a result of the interplay between driving and restraining forces both within that social system and its setting. His primary interest was in how planned change to this social system could be achieved. He emphasised the need to appreciate both the social system and its setting, that is, the field as a whole.

Lewin's theory differs from ours in a number of ways. First, the orientation of Lewin's analysis is normative. It is intended to support an analysis of possible intervention strategies aimed at achieving a permanently higher performance level of the social system. We do not measure or judge the field's performance. Second, without active involvement of the analyst or the analyst's client, it is assumed in Lewin's analysis that the system would be in balance, in equilibrium, with respect to the forces influencing the social dimension of concern. We view the IT field as an inherently dynamic entity both because of internal interactions and because of continuous changes in the field's relation to its setting. Rapid growth of the field has itself stimulated rapid changes in the relation between the IT field and its setting throughout its history.

Using the concept of the IT field leads attention away from the usual things brought to mind by the study of information technology. Studies of information technology tend to be focused on technical aspects of computer hardware and software or with the effects on workplaces of the introduction of new computer-based systems. Instead our focus has been on the people who work with information technology. They can be producers, developers, operators, sellers or users of IT. They can also be mediators of IT, offering advice to prospective purchasers, acting as trouble-shooters and even providing a feeling of security to others who are apprehensive about their own relation to information technology.

We can think of the field as populated in different ways. The field may be thought of as comprised of organisations and studies of the nature of organisations and their interaction can provide valuable analysis of the nature and development of the IT field. Some of the chapters that follow focus on organisations, particularly on organisational cultures. However all people do not easily fit into one or other particular organisation and there are other groupings of people which can be discerned in the field. These other groupings have their own more or less independent influences on the development of the field.

We also examine the field in terms of communities, in terms of networks, in terms of actors *within* organisations, and by the types of strategies actors pursue for material advancement. These different perspectives, distinguished by different ways of grouping people in the field, lead us to explore parts of the field that would otherwise be neglected and to appreciate the role of certain groups or people that would otherwise be missed.

For example, with our community perspective we can focus on the systems programmers as a distinct, but limited, group in the field. They have their own technical culture which supersedes organisational boundaries. Other occupational groups in the field, such as applications programmers and operators, are more clearly contained within communities that coincide with a single organisation or communities which contain a distinct set of organisations.

Another example is our network perspective which leads our attention to the mediators of IT and to what may be regarded as the periphery of the IT field. Studying these people leads us to appreciate the way the IT field has spread at its "edges" and also the problems encountered by people at the periphery which have led to forces restraining the spread of the IT field at its edges.

The perspective based on strategies of the IT people allows us to appreciate dynamic aspects of the field in terms of different and changing itineraries of the individuals within the field without imposing a particular social entity or formal institution on the analysis. This can then be used to study the generation (and development) of social entities and institutions within the field. In particular we use this analysis to study the origins and development of trade unions in the IT field.

2   The Danish IT Field in an International Perspective

We focus on the IT field in Denmark, a country with interesting distinctive features. Even though the Danish context may seem exotic to some readers, we believe that this study of the Danish IT field is no more unrepresentative than other IT studies. Previous studies have been limited to regional studies of the position of IT specialists such as in Boston (Kraft and Dubnoff, 1986), or Silicon Valley (Larsen and Rogers, 1984). The readers of "Social Dynamics of The IT Field" can view it as another regional study on equal terms with these studies. The population of Denmark as well as the number of IT people in Denmark, is comparable to the numbers in one of the large American regional studies.

However, examining the IT field of Denmark allows several advantages over the regional studies. First, the Danish IT field is more confined than the IT field in a major American city, where the boundaries are more complex or "polluted" due to adjacent IT fields. Second, dealing with a whole nation allows us to match national statistics with our sample surveys and case studies. Third, dealing with a whole country makes it possible to speculate on the relations between specific national traits and the structuring of the IT field.

Several researchers have addressed the question of how national social institutions structure work relations, and by referring to two of these: Maurice et al. (1982) and Whitley (1990), we can spell out how our investigation contributes to the study of "national logics". In order to summarise important national traits which influence the IT field we will utilise the categories "state structure" and "state policies" from Whitley's "institutional structure dimensions". Maurice's "labour market relations", "educational system" and "work organisation" will be used to identify elements of the national logic emerging within the IT field.

2.1   Danish State Structure

The population of Denmark is 5 million, of which a third is concentrated in the Copenhagen area – historically the economic and administrative centre of Denmark. Cultural homogeneity goes hand in hand with a tradition for standardized public administrative systems. The development of the Scandinavian type welfare state has resulted in a large public sector which accounts for almost half of the national economic activity. However, the public sector only takes care of administration, control, infrastructure and services, and is not allowed to engage in the production of market commodities.

In this context information technology has made possible an expansion of centralised systems and the establishment of large data bases. Examples of large data processing tasks handled by the central systems are the Central Person

Register, the P.A.Y.E. (pay as you earn) tax system, the health insurance, VAT (value added tax), and automobile registration.

Thus, Denmark can be regarded as an environment which has favoured the utilisation of information technology. This is reflected in Denmark being number one in the world in "computing expenditures" expressed as percentage of GNP (0,56% against an average of 0,28% for the West European countries according to Hingel, 1986). The concentration of state administration and service industry in the Copenhagen area has resulted in the concentration of more than two thirds of the IT people there.

2.2   Danish State Policies

In relation to the emerging IT sector, the Danish State has been pursuing liberal economic policies. Regnecentralen and other Danish IT firms, as well as unions and other interest groups have argued for State support of Danish IT firms. However, the State has maintained the principle of not directly supporting specific firms in spite of arguments based on impending economic crisis and unemployment, as well as dependence on international suppliers. In line with this, the technological programmes launched in the late eighties have been devoted to furthering the use of IT within the public sector and within SMEs (small and medium sized enterprises), without directly supporting the suppliers of IT.

This may be an important explanation for the influential position gained by foreign suppliers in Denmark. They account for the major part of the hardware market, of which IBM's share alone is around 40% (Monopoltilsynet, 1988), and more than a third of the software market (OECD, 1985).

However, the policy decisions to establish the two large service bureaus of Datacentralen and Kommunedata to cater for software development related to state administration and the municipalities, have had fundamental effects upon the structuring of the Danish IT field. It has led to the creation of two very large IT communities which are ranked as number 13 and 17 among the world's IT service bureau (Hingel, 1985), and which account for one third of the national market for computer services and software. This has furthered the concentration of IT people in large organisations, and helps to explain why few large software houses exist in Denmark.

2.3   Labour Market Relations

A distinctive trait in relation to other countries is the Danish IT field's high level of unionisation. Some of the main factors producing this high level are the Danish tradition of high levels of white collar unionisation, competition between unions, and unemployment threats. In a Danish context, however, IT unionisation (67%) is moderate in comparison with the overall white collar level of unionisation (87%). For the IT field two factors reduce the level of unionisation: the favourable labour market and the affiliation with international suppliers, while two factors exert an upwards influence: the EDP-assistant education (a practical oriented education of a duration of 1 – 1,5 years) and the affiliation with the public and financial sectors.

2.4   Educational System

A variety of formal qualifications characterise the IT people. This is a consequence of the educational system not providing obvious candidates for the IT field during its early years, and the absence of established norms and traditions for the recruitment of people.

The public educational system was slow in responding to the emerging IT field. Suppliers started offering courses which later on were supplemented by independent schools and in-house courses. Computer science education was established at Denmark's Technical University and at Copenhagen University, but the number of candidates produced was modest. The main response of the public educational system has been in terms of the EDP- assistant education.

Even within the large organisations that have developed an internal for-malised education for planners, programmers, etc., learning-by-doing still appears to be the primary mode through which the IT people develop their competences. Our data indicate that these processes of skill acquisition resemble a craft mode of training. The more experienced IT specialists pass on their knowledge to the less experienced ones through collaboration on and supervi-sion of concrete projects. This apprenticeship system is controlled by the specialists, who form a relatively autonomous body, only partially submitted to the control of management.

2.5   Work Organisation

Concerning the *division of work* and the *autonomy* of the IT people, a comparative study of work organisation and industrial relations within IT in the UK, the Netherlands and Denmark (Friedman et al., 1987; Horlyck, 1988) revealed that of these countries Denmark represented one of the extremes. Denmark was the case with the least elaborated specialisation, the combined category of systems analysts/programmers being most common in this country. IT people performing the tasks of systems analysis and programming also had a higher degree of autonomy in their work than it was the case in the UK and the Netherlands. The cited study does not interpret these differences in terms of more and less efficient modes of organisation and management, but in line with the analysis of Maurice, Sellier, and Sylvestre (1982) as related to differences in local labour market conditions, structures, and cultural traits.

3   The CHIPS Research Project

The objective of the project has been to contribute to our understanding of the interaction between technological innovation, the formation of new occupational groups, and the restructuring of work organisations. Focus has been on the development of the Danish computing field (or IT field to use the more recent term of information technology from its initiation in the late fifties until today).

We focused on the occupational groups engaged in the development of systems and software, as well as consultants or advisors within the administrative IT field. This included the jobs of systems analysts/designers, consultants (inclusive of "borderline" specialists such as auditors moving into the IT field), systems programmers, programmers, and managers.

Our analysis of the formation of these new occupations was based on two different approaches. One was an analysis of the different strategies, individual as well as collective, the specialists have been pursuing in relation to the labour market. The other was an analysis of the development of the IT culture. This was interpreted from an organisational and an occupational community perspective.

The study addressed three aspects of organisational restructuring: changes in intra- and interorganisational relations, and the development of networks within the IT field. Intraorganisational relations are a question of how the new occupational groups are incorporated into the supplier and user organisations, and how the relations between these develop. Interorganisational relations focus upon changes in the relations of dependency between supplier, intermediaries and user organisations, while the network approach takes as point of departure the relations between actors and questions the importance of organisations as units of analysis.

4   Brief Outline of the Reader

The first part "Information Technology Cultures" approaches the IT field from a cultural perspective through analyses of different cultural entities: communities, organisations, and groups. The contributions direct attention to existing norms, values and beliefs, how they are generated, and the symbolic significance of what is normally taken for granted by the cultures' members.

In the second part "Actors, Networks and Organisations at the Edge of the IT Field", the dissemination of IT to small and medium sized enterprises is analysed. Also formal and informal mediators of IT to these enterprises are examined, including an analysis of the trade associations' role. Finally, a theoretical approach to network relations and the spread of IT at the periphery of the field is developed.

The third part "The IT People – Strategies, Skills and Careers" focuses on the producers and mediators of the technology. Both the individuals' labour market strategies, and management's strategies via-à-vis the IT specialists are examined. The Danish population of IT people and its development is depicted with regard to size, employment position, salaries, gender, educational background, and career patterns.

Notes

1   "The competition between the institutions are submitted to the specific logic of the field of
     legitimacy considered (i.e. political, religious or cultural).... The specific form of the
     conflicts between the institutions that strive towards the legitimacy of a given field is
     always the symbolic expression, more or less transformed, of the power relations that are
     being established between these instances within that field. These are never independent of
     the power relations exterior to the field (i.e. the dialectic of excommunication, heresy and
     contestation of orthodoxy in the literary, religious, or political history)" (Bourdieu and
     Passeron, 1970, p.33).

Part A
Information Technology Cultures

Introduction

"Culture" is the overarching analytical concept used to understand the structuring and properties of the Danish IT field in this chapter. Even though our stance in relation to much of the organisation culture literature is critical, we are convinced that culture provides an analytical perspective which is fruitful for understanding the structuring of the IT field.

The following five chapters focus on the organisations within the IT field: their history, their present characteristics, their interrelations, and their dynamics. The analyses encompass organisations acting as suppliers, users and mediators of IT. They are pitched at different levels of analysis: a field level (Chapter 1), an organisational and interorganisational level (Chapter II, III and IV), and an intraorganisational level (Chapter V).

Chapter I addresses two questions: how is the Danish IT field structured today, and what types of processes have produced this pattern?

In response to the first question seven different IT communities are identified. These embrace the majority of the IT suppliers and mediators, and most of the large IT users. It is estimated that 17.500 of the 25.000 IT people populate these communities.

The "community" term – which refers to different configurations of tasks, persons, and value systems – signifies that the present structuring of the IT field cannot solely be understood with reference to formal organisation hierarchies, but that clan-like relations are important as well.

Three of the communities coincide with the largest IT organisations in Denmark: IBM Denmark, Datacentralen, and Kommunedata. The other four reflect clusters which cut across the formal organisational borderlines: The Communities of the Danish Technical IT Suppliers, the Financial Sector, the Entrepreneurs, and the Systems Programmers. Of these only the Systems Programmers' Community reflects a pure technical culture. Thus this analysis does not support the existence of a single, unitary IT field culture.

The second question is explored by examining the genesis of the communities, and their interplay. Four sources of variation and convergence are identified: community initiation, domain adaptation, field interaction, and societal influence. These point to international, national, regional, sectorial, and occupational influences which, through complex patterns of interaction, have produced the present variety of cultures within the IT field.

Chapter II explores three examples of organisational cultures drawn from a small, a medium sized, and a large IT organisation. This in-depth study uses Schein's (1985) artifacts-values-basic assumptions scheme to produce a detailed insight into the cultural variations of the Danish IT field, and thus supplements the overview provided by the community analysis.

It is argued that the artifact level, when operationalised beyond Schein's model can become an important supplement to values as an indicator of basic assumptions. Furthermore basic assumptions need not form a completely coherent system, but may be more conflictual.

The three organisation cultures appear as quite distinct entities, endowed with different degrees of dynamism and coherence. This makes the understanding of the dynamics of culture important – a subject which largely has been neglected by the existing culture analyses with their bias towards stability and reproduction.

In Chapter III the theme of cultural dynamics is developed within a study of a merger case. The two quite different premerger organisation cultures, the merger process, and the resulting organisation culture are described. Four culture change models are derived, which differ as to origin of change, nature of change process, and preconditions for change. The models are labelled leadership, learning, intergroup, and local adaptation. Although all four models are relevant to the case, the leadership model and the learning model appear as the most significant for understanding the actual case.

Chapter IV further investigates learning and adaptation processes in three cases. Dynamic and complex environments create ambiguity with which the IT organisations have to cope. This makes it important to study actors' interpretations of the environment, belief systems, and relations between beliefs and action (individual as well as organisational).

A small enterprise case illustrates the crucial role of the entrepreneur's belief system, his responses to recruitment and growth, and the organisation's vulnerability to misfits between beliefs and contingencies.

For two large organisations, managerial beliefs and corresponding personnel practices are important for understanding differences in adaptability. In one case they contribute to organisational flexibility, whereas inflexibility results from the negotiated practices within the other large organisation. A supplementary source of resistance to change is identified in "main-frame thinking" which made it difficult to cope with the minicomputers.

Finally, adaptation is viewed in a resource dependency perspective, emphasising legitimation of practices in relation to the environment. An analysis of the force field around one of the large organisations illustrates how contestation of existing practice slowly results in a change of these.

Chapter V uses the differentiation and relative autonomy of the IT people as the point of departure for identifying organisational subcultures in IT firms. Four different types are identified: occupational, hierarchical, departmental, and imported subcultures. Of these the occupational subcultures of sales, systems development, and technical development (the systems programmers) possess substantial autonomy from management. Thus, the subcultures located within formal organisations are only to a limited extent submitted to the control of management.

Our subcultural analysis contests the corporate culture view of organisational cultures as managerial construct. However, it is possible for management to influence subcultures via manipulation of their ecological context in terms of recruitment of actors, socialisation, division of work, grouping of actors, and control systems.

In this light cultures identified at a specific point in time are regarded more as a truce between management and other groups, than as a crystallised social form.

Chapter I
Divergence and Convergence:
A Community Analysis of the Structuring of the Danish IT Field

Finn Borum

1   Introduction

Our investigation of the Danish IT field has revealed both differences and similarities in the forms and practices adopted by these organisations. The differences are perceived to be the result of institutionalisation processes that have occurred within this new, technology-driven organisational field since its emergence in the fifties. Institutionalisation is used here to denote two different aspects. One is the process through which organisational forms and practices gain legitimacy and acquire a taken-for-granted status within social systems. The other is the outcome in terms of institutionalised organisational forms and practices (see Scott, 1987b).

As no attempts have been made so far to carry out a field level analysis of the Danish IT organisations, the first objective of this chapter is analytical-descriptive: to produce a theoretically structured picture of the present institutional configuration of the Danish IT field. This configuration may be labelled a "variance type" institutional analysis (Scott, 1990). It focuses on the properties of institutions resulting from three decades of structuration processes. The variance displayed by the different communities – or clusters – identified within the IT field are captured by means of a "cultural paradigm". Following the reasoning of Selznick this analysis comprises both tasks (technique) and the value (belief) systems:"..'to institutionalise' is to *infuse with value* beyond the technical requirements of the task at hand" (Selznick, 1957, p. 17 cited by Scott, 1987b, p. 494).

The second objective is analytical-explanatory. In that respect we engage in a "process" type of institutional explanation (Scott, 1990), discussing the processes/forces which may have produced the present variance. Four different types of explanations are discussed. The first two address sources of variance, while the latter two account for tendencies towards convergence:

– community initiation, where the present properties of the communities are traced back to "genes" with which they were endowed at their time of birth;

- domain adaptation, according to which the focal IT community's specific properties are the result of interaction between the focal community and its ecology;
- field interaction, which focuses upon dissemination and influence processes between the communities within the IT field as causes of convergence of forms and practices;
- societal influences, according to which we understand important properties of the IT field as reflecting the influence of general forces which are not specific, and perhaps exogenous to the field in question.

These interpretations are necessarily speculative and incapable of producing a stringent causal explanation. First, this is because of the multiple sources of institutional forms and belief systems coexisting in Western society that concurrently influence emerging institutions. The processes studied are highly complex and multifactorial by nature. The second reason is that our analysis is based upon a variety of qualitative data and impressions which have been generated through an exploratory research methodology.

2   Dimensions of an IT Community

In this article the concept of "community" is used as a heuristic tool for understanding the present configuration and the historical structuring of the Danish IT field.

We define a community as one or more groupings of persons engaged in practical or scientific activities related to information technology. Such communities include both supplier and user organisations. These groupings of actors are knit together through relations that are both bureaucratic and clan-like (Ouchi, 1980). A community is identified by both in-siders and out-siders and by the delimitation of its field of activities. Within one community, several groups may coexist and these may differ in their degree of centrality, orthodoxy, etc.

The "community" represents a sociological approach to the study of IT people and to the development of informatics (the application of information technology). It is analogous to Kuhn's (1970) sociological approach to the study of scientific communities. The IT field may be regarded as equivalent to a scientific discipline, and IT communities as equivalent to different scientific schools. If only one school exists, the field is paradigmatic, but if several communities exist the field is either preparadigmatic or multiparadigmatic. Groups within a community correspond to scientific sub- schools.

Since the IT field includes application of information technology in many different organisational settings that may be only loosely coupled, and since it has been expanding rapidly, inter-community relations may be competitive, disjunctive or symbiotic. In other words, a "hard core" does not necessarily exist.

Our approach to the study of IT communities has been explorative and inductive. The main methods have been interviews given by informants, and studies of documents and secondary sources (see 'Data and Methods'). The different communities are treated more or less comprehensively – both as a consequence of the different importance which we attribute to them, and as a consequence of our qualitative and quantitative data not being equally strong in relation to the different communities.

The community analyses will encompass dimensions inspired by Kuhn (1970), Salaman (1974), Ouchi (1980), and Schein (1985). In order to provide input to a discussion of both variance and process, the dimensions cover both the actual value system and a brief historical account of the community:

- genesis
  (time of birth, aspects of the historical development);
- the persons
  (recruitment and qualifications, training and indoctrination, population size, itineraries);
- tasks, methods, and norms
  (task situation, methods, norms for problems to be considered, and repertoire of solutions);
- ideals and basic assumptions
  (values and belief system);
- relations to other communities
  (relations of influence and dependency).

3 An Overview of the Danish IT Communities

Our analysis begins with the most important international supplier – *the IBM community*. IBM accounts for about 40% of the hardware market in Denmark (Monopoltilsynet, 1988). Next we consider the important clustering of communities around large public sector service bureaus in terms of *the communities of Datacentralen (DC) and Kommunedate (KMD)* which have been strongly influenced by IBM.

Within the private sector, *the financial sector community* around banks and insurance companies is important, and leads to considering the importance of *the Danish technical community*. This comprises the Danish hardware suppliers, and Regnecentralen (RC) is used as an illustration of the interplay with the latter communities. From large organisations we proceed to the proliferation of small

Danish enterprises producing software and services, which are considered under the heading of *the entrepreneurial community*. Finally, we consider *the systems programmers' community*, which is the closest we have come to identifying an occupational community (Salaman,1974), cutting across organisational boundaries.

3.1   The IBM Community

Genesis

In 1950 IBM Denmark was established as a Danish subsidiary, producing primarily punched card equipment and typewriters. The introduction of the 7074 and 1401 series marked the transition to EDP in 1960. In 1970 the 360 series were introduced to the Danish market with a subsequent decline in punched card operations. At this time the practice of "unbundling" IT products emerged, i.e., a separate pricing for software, which had previously been included in the hardware prices. Important product innovations were the minicomputer in 1974, and the personnel computers (PC) in 1983.

Three important structural adaptations represent efforts to adjust the structure of IBM Denmark to better fit products and markets. The first adaptation involved the creation of a new division. In 1974 the General Business Group was introduced to complement the mainframe DP division. This new division was responsible for minicomputers and office equipment (other products, including typewriters). From about 1980 the sales of minicomputers and PCs and terminals were handled by different agents.

The present structure, established in 1982/83, was organised according to size of customer:

1. Large customers (subdivided into government, type of industry);
2. Intermediate customers (subdivided on a mix of geographical and customer type criteria);
3. Small customers (served via dealers, agents and mail).

While other large organisations within the IT field describe their structural changes as difficult, IBM reports theirs as unproblematic. In general, the historical development of IBM is described in terms of evolution, rather than in terms of critical events or turning points.

The Persons

Between 1950 and 1986, IBM Denmark had grown from a total staff of 40- 50 persons to 2.420, half of which were employed in marketing and customer engineering. Grouped according to formal qualifications, IBM's employees are today almost evenly distributed between high school diploma, non-graduate business education, non-graduate technical education, and graduates – mostly engineers and business economists, whose proportion has been increasing.

IBM's recruitment is based upon selection of young well-qualified persons without prior IT experience. New employees are subject to intensive internal training and indoctrination programmes for one and a half years. When training is completed, they become part of a yearly management by objectives system, which focuses on individual performance. The salary is fixed by the individual's manager in relation to performance, functions, and years of experience.

The salary system is determined by IBM, and unions do not participate in any negotiations, either in relation to collective agreements, or to individual contracts and salaries. Most IBM employees are non-unionised.

Tasks, Methods and Norms
IBM Denmark is a sales office. Its main task is selling hardware, software and services to the Danish market, but it also produces and distributes hardware and software to Danish as well as foreign markets. Accordingly, methods and norms for problem solving emphasise both a sales and an implementation approach to information technology. This is reflected in the internal educational system's emphasis on presentation and sales techniques. However, IBM consultants must be able to identify business tasks to be computerised and to assist the customers during the implementation process. This implies technical competences, and methods for analysis, design, and implementation of information systems. In line with this, IBM has imported and "translated" methods developed abroad. An example is the Study Organisation Plan (SOP) introduced in Denmark in the mid-sixties as the first effort to establish a coherent methodology for all the phases of the systems design process.

Ideals and Basic Assumptions
The officially stated beliefs comprise three basic components: respect for the individual, best possible customer service, and high quality. These are supplemented with four additional components: professional management, attention to stockholders' interests, fair treatment of suppliers, and responsibility to society.

These business beliefs are reflected in the writings of Watson(1963), Foy (1974), and Peters and Waterman (1982), and in Danish manuals and guidelines for IBM staff. They are also identifiable in "proper business practices" and the "esprit de corps" that are taught during basic training and reinforced via the systematic evaluation of the MBO (management by objectives) system which is used as a managerial tool.

Besides this "corporate spirit", individualism and career-orientation are central values. This is indicated by *the absence of unionisation* and the *high ambitions* of the persons recruited to systems engineering and sales functions. Management regards it as a private matter when an employee chooses to be a member of an union – but the level of unionisation is low according to our interviewees. This may be the result of recruiting very ambitious persons combined with individual performance appraisal, high wages and other benefits.

Relations to Other Communities

IBM's influence is not only confined to the specific hardware and software marketed, but also includes methods of analysis, systems development, and organisation of EDP-functions. In 1985, for example, IBM offered their customers a vast number of various training programmes. IBM's influence on the Danish IT field also extends to general managerial belief system concerning organisations and individuals.

IBM has played an important role in setting standards for hardware and software. This is reflected in both international standards and in competitors' utilisation of "IBM compatibility" as a sales argument. IBM is an important part of the Danish IT field. It provides a model against which the other suppliers – international as well as Danish – and IT communities react either with admiration or rebellion.

For many years, IBM has emphasised good relations with universities and other institutions of higher education. As an example, NEUCC (Northern European University Calculation Centre) at The Technical University of Denmark was started with a donation of an IBM computer. IBM also shows its interest in educational matters by being represented in various committees focusing on basic education and further training.

IBM also exerts influence on its environment through former employees: even though very few employees leave the organisation, they add up over three to four decades. Former IBM employees occupy important positions in both supplier or user organisations (the first managing director of Datacentralen was a former IBM employee, for example). Former IBM employees are perceived by many outsiders as still belonging to the "IBM-network".

Finally, two IBM customer associations "Share" and "Guide", and IBM employees' membership in professional associations are other means by which IBM interacts with its business environment. As an example, IBM is an important member organisation of Dataforeningen (The Danish Data Association – an association for senior computer specialists comprised of firms).

Thus the "IBM community" appears as a community that maintains a specific identity by buffering or sealing off itself from the environment. It influences and integrates with the environment via the different bridging mechanisms (Scott, 1987a, p. 181-194) mentioned above.

The communities of the Public Sector Service Bureaus

An international comparison makes Denmark number one in the world in "computer expenditures" expressed as a percentage of GNP (0,56% against 0,28% as an average for the Western European countries). A closer look at the Danish market reveals that around one third of the national market of computer services and software is controlled by the two big bureaus owned by and servicing the public sector: Datacentralen (the state administration) and Kommunedata (the municipalities). On a world scale these two companies are ranked no. 13 and 17, respectively, among the service bureaus (Hingel, 1986).

3.2   Datacentralen (DC)

Genesis

The idea of establishing a service bureau for the public sector emerged with the plans of a new P.A.Y.E. tax system in the late fifties. Even though the tax system was postponed, the idea of a public sector service bureau had taken hold – this led to the creation of Datacentralen in 1959.

During its first two decades, Datacentralen developed customised solutions to large data-handling tasks designed for and run on large mainframes. In the late seventies, when the minis appeared, DC was forced to adapt a new policy and to develop systems that could be run on the customers' own computers. Later on PCs were included in DC's repertoire, and today DC sells hardware (minis and PCs) as well as software, education and data processing.

Datacentralen has undergone several important structural adaptations in order to cope with external and internal contingencies. But in contrast to IBM these adaptations are described as difficult to implement. Throughout the sixties and seventies, the structural changes were mainly efforts to improve efficiency in the production and operation of information systems via changes in the internal division of labour, and the grouping of operators, programmers and planners. In the eighties, customer relations and economic performance came into focus. Following a McKinsey analysis, a major restructuration led to both the creation of profit centres and efforts to transform the management system.

The Persons

In 1988, DC employed a staff of 1800 people whose positions were distributed as follows:

managers	15%
systems analysts, systems developers and programmers	58%
operators	7%
specialists	20%.

Recruitment during the early years covered a broad range of qualifications, with a preference for experienced persons from the application areas. This included an important contingent of persons with a military background. Later the recruitment pattern shifted, and today the EDP-assistant (1 – 2 years of basic IT education) is the single most important category of employees (50% of newly recruited). These are primarily recruited for technical tasks. For most, DC is their first job experience.

The intake of academics, preferably with public sector experience, has been increasing. Today they account for 18% of the staff. They are recruited for customer-related consultancy tasks requiring knowledge about the field of application and communicative skills.

DC has developed its own internal educational system. Since 1988 the system has been based on an individual plan of education for each employee. On average 10% of an employee's annual working hours are to be spent on educational activities, primarily in terms of attending internal courses and, for systems planners, 3 months basic training.

Tasks, Methods, and Norms
During its first ten years in business, DC primarily focused the development, maintenance and operation of unique large and centralised public registers for large mainframes. Examples of these systems are a central personnel register, and a central register for motor vehicles. These systems require the processing of heavy loads of data. Also the data to be computerised (public registers) require high reliability and data protection.

This task situation led to the development of elaborate methods and norms for problem solving. At an early stage, Datacentralen introduced a strict division of labour between system planners and programmers and standards which these employees had to meet. Also the work process was regulated by a detailed phase model specified for systems development.

Other factors contributed to the development of these mechanistic traits. The size of the organisation, and its close relations to public bureaucracies may have made DC more receptive to control and regulation than other service bureaus. Furthermore, in the seventies, Tayloristic managerial approaches were proposed by several consultants and suppliers (see e.g., Brandon, 1963).

Throughout the seventies, these approaches created a tight and rigid system of standards and regulations which was so comprehensive that it was often circumvented (or freely interpreted) by the programmers who otherwise would have faced great obstacles to the construction of the systems and an intolerable degree of control.

In connection with the integration of planners and programmers into customer-based units in 1978, and the integration of the two groups into one – systems planners – in 1980, this system of control was significantly eased.

Furthermore, general developments within the field of information technology contested the initial mechanistic organisational principles DC had adapted. Minicomputers presented alternatives to the traditional, mainframe based and centrally run systems, and forced DC to adopt a new concept. This included the development of systems to be run on the customers' own installations and not at DC. This adaptation was described as very difficult due to resistance from both the computer specialists, and parts of DC's management. Apparently, a "mainframe production culture" had developed that resisted change, even though parts of the management were aware of the need for change. This problematic process of organisational learning and adaptation is further explored in Chapter IV.

Ideals and Basic Assumptions

The analysis carried out above emphasises control, which is also one of the five key values characterising the DC culture as summarised by Pedersen (Chapter II). In this analysis, which links values to basic assumptions according to Schein's (1985) model, "controllare necessere est" stands out as contradictory to "craftsmanship" and "no lay offs" which reflect a more humanistic value system. This may reflect a dissonance between a value system imposed on the community by environmental demands for safety (the motto of DC created in 1988 is "Safety, Service, and Coherence") and a value system developed by the community members.

The system of ideals and basic assumptions is quite different from that of IBM. First, the level of unionisation in Datacentralen is as high as 80%. The DC employees are organised in 6 different unions, and 9 collective wage agreements cover all employees with the exception of the 11 top positions. Prosa is by far the most important union, embracing 950 of the DC employees. Next, the "spirit of '68" seems to be quite influential – though not shared by the newly recruited. Thus DC is characterised by a "collectivist" orientation that is quite different from the individualistic, profit-oriented value system of the IBM community. This points not only to the impact of differences in recruitment-, training-, and remuneration practices, but also to the sectorial affiliation of IT organisations.

Relations to Other Communities

Although IBM and DC currently represent two different cultural systems, the two communities share a long history. DC's first two decades were characterised by very intimate links to the only supplier of hardware facilities – IBM. Throughout many years DC was dependent upon IBM's development competences and educational system, a dependence that was slowly reduced through the establishment of DC's own development and educational departments in 1965 and 1969. These intimate connections between IBM and DC resulted in very distant or perhaps troubled relations between DC and Regnecentralen (see the later section on the technical community), RC being the "rejected supplier".

A more detailed analysis of the development in relations between DC and IBM (Chapter IV) leads to the interpretation that the communities moved from social integration (with DC as the dependent party, as IBM controlled critical sources of uncertainty), towards more clearly defined boundaries between the two entities. Some indications of early social integration are that IBM supplied the first managing director of DC (who functioned as MD for 25 years), that IBM was the monopolistic supplier for DC until 1979 (at which time an Amdahl mainframe was bought), and that IBM consultants were being integrated into the work life at DC until the late seventies.

The rupture between the two communities is indicated by DC's shift to recruitment of MDs from the public sector, its policy of multiple suppliers, the strengthening of its own development competences, and the "expulsion" of the IBM consultants. The split also became manifest in the discarding of an MBO system that had been inspired by IBM's personnel management system – an action that resulted from employee pressure. In a resource-dependency perspective (Pfeffer and Salancik, 1978), this "drifting apart" of the two communities can be explained as DC's response to the demands of various influential interest groups constituting the ecology of DC. Among these influences unions are important. That is in contrast to their absence in the IBM community.

DC has influenced other communities by its turnover of personnel – a result of the restrictions imposed upon DC's wage policies, and the tight labour market. Thus, several former DC employees occupy high positions within both the public and the private sector. DC regards itself as a sort of "EDP- university" within the Danish IT field, since the capacity of educational institutions proved insufficient to supply the number of skilled employees required. Over time, DC has supplied quite a few computer specialists, primarily to internal DP-departments, to small software houses/consultancies, or to other smaller service bureaus. Only in a very few cases they have gone to IT suppliers.

DC also has an impact on the IT environment through the methods and standards it develops and the 500 annual courses offered both externally and internally. DC has been famous for its efforts to develop standards and methods. Also DC was very apt at developing the best "local" expertise in operating systems necessary to handle the IBM main-frames.

3.3   Kommunedata (KMD)

Genesis
Kommunedata originated in 6 different municipal service centres established in the fifties to solve tasks related to elections and taxes on the basis of punched card technology. In 1960, the centres were converted to IT (IBM 1401) and expanded into other aspects of tax, duties, social allowances, accounts, wages, etc.

In 1972, following the municipal reform in 1970, the data centres were merged into Kommunedata, which is a partnership between the municipalities (accounting for 75% of KMD's trade) and the counties' associations. This merger is described as the most important event in the history of KMD, and explains its geographical distribution as well as the current differences between the units. The merger was a problematic process in several respects, as the centres were rather different in size, economic performance, and culture.

In 1977, a consultancy (McKinsey) analysis of KMD led to the present organisational structure. Headquarters are located in Copenhagen, but all operations- and service activities (related to both standard systems and individual systems) are handled regionally by four data centres. The systems development activities are divided between six units, each taking care of all activities related to specific application areas. The units are situated in Jutland and in the Copenhagen area.

Today, KMD's share of the total supply of IT products and services to the municipalities is around 90%. Like DC, KMD sticks to the production of software for other suppliers' hardware in order to furnish the municipalities and the counties with total systems solutions.

The Persons

In 1972, when Kommunedata was established, the total staff of the six centres counted 560 persons. By 1986, the staff had tripled to 1685, expanding most rapidly from 1972 to 1979. In January 1986 the distribution of employees according to the function was: managers 8%, development 29%, user service 22%, production 17%, auxiliary functions 24%.

The "development" category is composed of two groups: (1) consultants or "product people" – academics or persons with a municipal background who carry out analysis and planning within application areas in collaboration with the customers, and (2) "constructors" – EDP-assistants, computer scientists, or engineers who take care of technical design and implementation of systems. The "production" category – mostly EDP-assistants and "autodidacts" – is responsible for the daily operations and the maintenance of the systems, and is a receding group.

As to qualifications, people with municipal education are the largest group (35%), EDP-assistants come next with 15%, while academics account for only 9%. This reflects KMD's recruitment practice of taking in people without any IT experience, and educating them through courses (many were external, for instance at IBM and DC) and practice. For some years EDP-assistants have been hired in "batches", and furnished with internal education. Around 1987 this recruitment practice was altered. Since 1988, KMD has recruited only people with 2-4 years of experience. Like DC, most of the employees of KMD are unionised: Prosa and HK (250 and 800) account for the majority of members, while 500 employees either belong to other unions or are not unionised.

Tasks, Methods, and Norms

In the mid seventies adaptation to the minis was problematic, as work methods, organisational structures and procedures were geared to standardised mainframe systems – as was the case for DC. The technical departments in particular were reluctant to accept the minis, and the municipalities began taking in minis via other suppliers. KMD thus, felt forced to go ahead with the minis and started with an accounting system in 78-79. This system turned out to be a success which made the shift from centralised batch-systems to terminal-based on-line systems possible.

The minis made it possible to produce solutions that better fit the needs and structure of the municipalities. The subsequent adaptation to PCs is described as unproblematic, as the main decentralisation lesson had already been learned in connection with the minis.

Servicing a larger number of customers and being characterised by a more decentralised structure than DC, KMD has focused less on standards. An interviewee, who in the mid-seventies shifted from DC to KMD, describes KMD as imposing less rigid documentation standards, and as using a much more floating division of labour between systems planners and programmers (this is reflected in the use of the term "constructors", which covers both categories and various combinations of the two). The present situation is marked by freedom to use whatever methods are regarded as most suitable for the specific project in question. This is a reaction to earlier practice that relied upon a standard method for all the development phases of a project which became too inflexible and costly in terms of documentation and had been circumvented. Recently a more simplified model of the development process has been developed.

Ideals and Basic Assumptions
KMD's birth produced an organisation of independent, geographically dispersed centres that had a strategic apex superimposed later on. Today, the different centres are described as possessing their own specific cultural traits – the result of history, different recruitment and personnel policies, and differentiation in tasks. Internally, people have a tendency to describe KMD as consisting of different organisations, and to point to differences between the Jutland (Aalborg) and Copenhagen (Ballerup) centres, and the Hospital centre. The first difference is described in terms of a Jutland versus a Copenhagen work culture and managerial style, whereas the Hospital centre has led a life of its own from the time of its establishment, facing harder competition than the other units.

The Jutland culture is described as a "pioneer" culture with close relations between customers and development. Also, it represents an attitude towards work that is more relaxed and informal, avoiding red tape and short-cutting formal communication lines. It is also more human (playful). But it contains a more authoritarian attitude and less "fuss-making" about political and managerial decisions. When decisions have been taken in Jutland they are accepted downward through the hierarchy, whereas in Copenhagen, the employees may continue to contest them.

A "group culture" and "horizontalisation" of KMD that was introduced by management in the period 1972-1980, resulted in a "social culture" with a proliferation of groups and committees, that reduced managerial power and decision making ability. This system was not quite compatible with the Jutland culture, and did not ease the relations between headquarters and Aalborg, in spite of many attempts to implement shared ideas and values. Since 1985, the present MD has delegated more responsibility to the regional managers, who at the same time were tied more closely to him. This has led to revitalisation of regional subcultures. The differences between the centres make the KMD community pluralistic, the different units taking colour from the spatial and sectorial contexts in which they are embedded.

Customer service is provided by consultants who keep in touch with the customers. The customers are municipalities and counties (there are 275 and 14, respectively) and there is a strong basic orientation of management towards them. This is reflected in both the structuring of the organisation, and the composition of staff. The environment of KMD is highly politicised, the board of directors and the customers both exert strong pressure towards increased focus on the customers. To maintain its monopolistic position as the sole supplier of IT services to the municipalities, KMD has to be highly sensitive to both customers and competitors. The municipalities have the option of buying services elsewhere, and are regularly approached by alternative suppliers. Management defines the need for more individual treatment of customers, to shift focus from systems to customers, and to a reduced emphasis on large systems and standardisation.

Relations to Other Communities
KMD entered the IT era with IBM equipment, and for almost a decade IBM was the sole supplier. This has changed, but IBM is still the single most important supplier of hardware, software, and knowledge as reflected in IBM's efforts to secure the continuity of the present product lines of KMD.

Former KMD employees have spread to other IT communities. If you want to be in a large organisation, you stay in KMD. Otherwise, you may shift to one of the smaller service bureaus within the Financial Sector Community or to the Entrepreneurial Community. Only a few KMD consultants have shifted to hardware suppliers.

Earlier KMD had a reputation among IT people as producing trivial batch systems, being bureaucratic, and not using PCs. Until a few years ago this image made it difficult for KMD to attract experienced IT people from other communities, even though KMD from our data appears to be less rigid than DC. This may explain the modest intake of persons from other communities – including those of DC and IBM.

3.4   The Financial Sector Community

Genesis
This community comprises large installations within the banking and insurance sector. As a consequence of the sector's large number of standardised transactions and means to invest heavily in technology, it was among the pioneer users within the private sector in the late fifties. In these early years, IT was located in

internal DP departments in the larger banks and insurance companies. These departments expanded heavily throughout the sixties, as a consequence of the application of IT to new areas, and the emerging concentration via mergers.

In 1962, the savings banks established a service bureau (Sparekassernes Data Centre, SDC) that today is one of the most important IT organisations (along with KMD and DC). SDC has a staff of about 500. In 1968 another important separate IT organisation (PBC) was established by the banks and savings banks to handle all transfers between accounts. Thus, the current organisational setting of IT specialists in this community is either that of IT departments embedded in user organisations, or of divisions or separate units with market-like relations to user units.

Even though the customer interfaces of banks and insurance companies are different one of the factors that has contributed to the emergence of this community is their similar task situation. They also share cultural traits as administrative, bureaucratic type organisations characterised by stability and traditions. However, during the last few years, both banks and insurance companies have faced a more dynamic and competitive environment. This has led to mergers and a tendency towards integration between the two sectors.

The Persons
The size of the financial sector's IT population is approximately 4.700, estimated to be split evenly between development and operation staff. Information from two important installations (one bank and one insurance company) indicates three patterns of recruitment and qualifications, of which the two first have been dominant,

(1) Recruitment "from the street" to routine jobs, with the possibility of advancing to operator, and later on to applications or systems programmers;
(2) Recruitment of bank or insurance employees to user liaison positions, and to systems development, from where they may return to user departments as managers. This category traditionally goes through an internal education of apprenticeship type.
(3) Recruitment of computer educated staff from IBM, service bureaus (among these Datacentralen), or universities to positions as systems programmers or systems developers. Most of these persons are either EDP-assistants, economists, or engineers. In particular persons with a long formal education may go into a managerial career.

Tasks, Methods, and Norms
The banks' and insurance companies' use of IT can roughly be described as occurring in three phases. During the first phase (in the sixties) internal accounting and portfolio administration systems were rationalised by means of batch processing systems on mainframes. Then, in the seventies on-line systems

were introduced. This led to integration of data entry tasks into the users' jobs by the installation of terminals in user departments and branch offices.

In the eighties, the development within the sector was characterised by extension of the on-line systems to encompass sales and customer related functions, and by the introduction of minis and PCs. Thus the overall development has been one from centralised main-frame solutions to decentralised IT systems, but still maintaining centralised and standardised "core systems".

The raison d'etre of this community is the application of computers to business and administrative needs, emphasising the development and operation of standardised systems capable of handling large amounts of data. Thus, implementation and reliable operation as opposed to technical sophistication and invention has been a basic orientation.

Methods and norms are concerned with craftsmanship: the practical solution of systems analysis and design. The "bibles" have been normative textbooks containing guidelines, for example, the Danish Syskon (methodology for systems analysis and design), the Swedish RAS (Riktslinjer för Administrativ Systemutveckling), and Yordan's methods.

However, due to the large size of the installations, and emphasis upon on- line systems and networks, quite a few technical IT specialists (systems programmers, database specialists, network specialists) work within this community. SDC (the large data centre of the savings banks) also possesses a certain development orientation reflected in its shifts between different hardware suppliers (Bull, SAAB-FACIT, IBM, Olivetti).

Ideals and Basic Assumptions
The IT people within the financial community have formed a subculture of young, well-paid persons who enter the organisations via path 1 or 3 above, make quick careers, and whose loyalty is to IT rather than a specific organisation. This is in contrast to the traditional bank/insurance culture of the somewhat older employees, who were more modestly paid, had slower careers, and were loyal to their company and the trade. These differences in many cases led to tensions between IT departments and user departments (see as example Borum and Enderud, 1981). However, differences seem to have been smoothed as a consequence of the transformation of the financial sector and the use of the second recruitment path mentioned above.

More than half of the IT people are unionised, either in sector affiliated unions (DBLF, DFLF, DSLF), in IT unions (Prosa), or in the unions of the academics (DJØF and DIF), (see Chapter IX for a further description of these unions). The level of unionisation is, however, below that of DC and KMD, and the role of the unions is quite different for operations (collectivist) and development staff (more individualistic). This reflects both the importance of collective versus individual negotiations for wage settlements, and the differences in educational background, career orientations, and prospects.

Relations to Other Communities
The financial community is mainly influenced by the IBM community, and by other suppliers. Apart from hardware, software and advice, influence also flows via the supply of persons to specialised or managerial positions. The DC and KMD communities exert a rather modest influence via the supply of actors, and certain links have been identified from the technical community (see below) to the large SDC data centre. The financial sector mainly influences the other communities through Dataforeningen, and by the migration of actors to the entrepreneurial community.

3.5   The Technical Community – Regnecentralen (RC) as an Example

The historical perspective on the IT field's development obliges us to move from the service sector into the part of the IT community inhabited by Danish companies engaged in production and development of computers (comprising hardware and software) that can be applied for administrative and industrial purposes. This community can be traced back to the initiatives of ATV (the Danish Academy of Technical Sciences – a body that can initiate new R&D institutions in collaboration between research institutions and industry). Thus, it represents a meeting place for practitioners and academics from The Technical University of Denmark.

Three organisations constitute this community: Regnecentralen, CRI (Computer Resources International), and Dansk Data Elektronik. The total number of employees in these organisations is somewhere between 1,500 and 2,000. We will use the oldest one – Regnecentralen (RC) with a staff of around 700 – as a key to understanding this community.

Genesis
RC started as a working group in 1947, and in 1955 it was transformed into an independent institution under the auspices of ATV. The objective of RC was to develop electronic calculators, and in 1956 the first Danish calculator (DASK) was completed. Later on this product was succeeded by GIER, RC 400, RC 3600, RC 8000 and micros (RC 45 and RC 39).

A dimension other than innovation – financial crises – is important for understanding RC and other organisations belonging to the technical community. RC has experienced seven important crises:

1963: 25% of the staff was sacked, but most of them were rehired after a reconstruction. However, at this occasion some went to user organisations.

1971: RC turned out to have lost the struggle against commercial suppliers that had started around 1963. As a result the "founding father" Niels Ivar Bech was dismissed, an event that triggered off the dispersion of the old core at RC. Many of these joined the emerging computing centres at the universities, or joined other industrial enterprises where their technical orientation was welcomed.

1979: Payments were suspended, RC reorganised into three companies, and the staff was reduced. This, however, did not solve the problems of acquisition of capital and enforcement of the management system.

1981: This led to ITT engaging into close cooperation with RC, providing the mentioned two types of resources.

1982: The service bureau section of RC with a staff of about 50 was sold to ØK Data.

1987: ITT sold its European companies, including RC, to the French ALCA-TEL.

1988: In the beginning of this year ALCATEL sold its RC shares to Danish Pension funds.

In september ICL took over RC by acquiring 50% of the shares for 70 million DKK.

The Persons

RC started out with a staff primarily recruited from the Technical University and from the University of Copenhagen. The first manager was a professor. The recruitment of academics continued until he was replaced. The first manager's successor – one of the grand persons of early Danish computing history – was Ivar Bech, a non-academic, who at an early stage recognised the potential of EDP for administrative purposes (see Svejstrup, 1976). During his regime, non-academics were recruited for business and administrative applications, and apparently the academics and practitioners were well-integrated for some years.

Throughout its development, RC has had intimate links to the technical research milieu and has recruited many researchers. This was facilitated by an early tradition of having many students from the Technical University working in RC as trainees. The itineraries of this community's specialists can essentially be described as movements between universities, suppliers belonging to the technical community, and users of their equipment. Most were recruited from the universities, and later on many returned there, as was the case of many RC-employees around the crisis in 1971. However, the picture became blurred by the recruitment of practitioners, and the strengthening of the community's commercial orientation in response to the economic crises. This has encouraged some engineers to migrate from this community to more stable ones.

In 1988, the total staff amounted to 800 persons, of which 110-120 were academics (60 engineers and 40 computer scientists).

Tasks, Methods, and Norms

Methods and norms for problem solving appear to emphasise invention, innovation and technical sophistication. A spirit of ingenuity is clearly traceable throughout RC's history, and is reflected in a way of working that is described as much less disciplined than that of other communities. The troubled history of RC (and of CRI) may indicate a tendency of the technical community to concentrate on technical sophistication and to neglect the important business issues of marketing and implementation.

Ideals and Basic Assumptions
Until 1962-63 a coherent RC value system existed emphasising technical creativity and invention. The underlying basic assumptions were either that by technological inventions man is able to control the environment and to improve society, or that as a research activity it has its own value and intrinsic rewards. This is in sharp contrast to the international suppliers' sales orientation that proved to be more efficient in the rapidly expanding market for IT.

The first time this value system was contested was in 1962, when it was decided to acquire a CDC mainframe for RC's service bureau operations. This implied taking in a new, externally developed philosophy in the shape of foreign software, resulting in internal controversies that continued throughout the sixties.

Around 1965-71, these basic assumptions were contested again by a newly appointed commercial co-manager to Ivar Bech. Their relations commenced harmoniously, but developed into antagonism. Instead of expanding in all areas, where technical expertise allowed for it, the new manager wanted to select expansion areas that could provide capital for the consolidation of RC. Around the crisis in 1971, this manager won out in relation to Niels Ivar Bech, who subsequently left RC.

RC's history and its crises reflect continued struggle between two competing orientations: innovation and commercialisation. This is reflected in the RC organisational chart from 1988, which shows two top managerial layers populated by persons of business expertise rather than of technical expertise.

Relations to Other Communities
The links between RC and the universities have been very strong. They are based upon an exchange of both technology and persons. This has led to an understanding of the uneasy relations between RC and the IBM community, where RC regarded the IBM donation of a computer to The Technical University as unfair competition, because RC was in the midst of installing a Gier computer at the University of Aarhus.

The "IBM salesmen" were also regarded as the winners in connection with the establishment of Datacentralen. The choice of IBM as supplier was experienced as the public sector's choice against the alternative to collaborate with RC. The appointment of a former IBM sales consultant as the first manager of Datacentralen was interpreted as the "IBM spirit" occupying Datacentralen.

This again led to tense relations between RC and Datacentralen, and RC was squeezed out of the public sector for many years. Until late in the sixties RC and Datacentralen did not collaborate – starting around the development of the SYSKON systems development methodology initiated by the Aarhus IT milieu. This gradually led to easier relations.

In general, RC employees have been active in relation to the creation of associations within the Danish IT field, for instance, the founding of the EDP Council in 1966, Datalogisk Selskab, and participation in IFIP, AIG, Dataforeningen, and in conferences. The participation of RC employees in computer associations as Dataforeningen and the dispersion of an important segment of the RC employees after the crisis in 1971 may indicate a commencing integration with the financial sector and public sector service bureau communities.

3.6   The Entrepreneurial Community

Genesis
This community comprises small organisations producing and selling data processing, software, and related services such as managerial or technical advice, and education. It was born in the early years of computing, and has been expanding throughout the seventies and eighties as the result of several factors being favourable to the entrepreneurial strategy.

First, the tight labour market and the expanding market for IT services have made user organisations willing to buy services from the market. Second, the unbundling of hardware and software and the international suppliers' subcontracting strategy have contributed to the creation of a separate market for software. A third factor is the increasing complexity of the market and IT applications, which creates niches for special services and products. A fourth important factor is that only modest capital is required to start a company since technological development has removed most barriers.

The resulting entrepreneurial community comprises organisations that are very different in size (from one man to more than one hundred employees) and in line of business. The lines of business vary from consultancies, business and systems analysts, facility managers, suppliers of total solutions, service bureaus, software houses, to programmers.

The Persons
It is possible to enter this community with many different formal qualifications, and a variety of competences acquired through practical experience – craftsmanship being described as a key to success.

Diversity is characteristic of persons within this community, but apparently a common background is employment in an organisation belonging to one of the other communities. The reason for leaving one of these communities may be related to one of the causes outlined above, but in several of our cases the triggering event has been the mismatch between employer and employee. The entrepreneur has, in most cases, left voluntarily because of dissatisfaction, need for more freedom etc., but in quite a few cases the entrepreneur's former organisation becomes one of his important customer.

Tasks, Methods, and Norms
The task situation of the entrepreneurial organisations is quite differentiated, as may be illustrated by the development of one of our case organisations. From 1976 to 1984 this organisation made three major product adaptations from data processing to body shopping (i.e., sale of man-power) to standardised software (Chapter IV).

Ideals and Basic Assumptions
The entrepreneurial organisation is a case of what Mintzberg (1979) labels a "simple structure". Fundamentally, the simple structure is characterised by the modest size of the organisation and the undifferentiated structure. Most employees report directly to the entrepreneur, who wants to be in control, and whose ideas and beliefs play an important role.

The managerial ideas in most cases represent a set of standard responses to challenges such as organisational growth, organisational structuring, new projects, and selection, retainment and development of employees. Based on our case studies, six basic values and beliefs seem to be predominant:

– A belief in a flat and small organisational structure;
– A belief in project organisation as a standard response to new tasks and contracts;
– The importance of careful administration of both the individual contract and the contract portfolio;
– The importance of careful selection of new employees to secure the right "chemistry";
– The emphasis on practical skills and craftsmanship, and disregard of formal qualifications;
– A belief in personnel development based on the individual's capabilities.

Relations to Other Communities
This community seems to fall into clusters, some of which are constituted by agglomerations of individual firms in the Copenhagen area. They form a network of subcontracting or co-producing firms, or a labour market. Other of these small organisations may be attached as subcontractors to one large firm. Often the entrepreneurs have developed their basic competences in a larger organisation belonging to the administrative or technical community.

This raises the question of the coherence of the entrepreneurial community. Is it indeed a community, or is it a lumping together of individuals and firms without interrelations who are more closely coupled to other communities?

We cannot answer this question definitively. However, two observations indicate the existence of networks between the entrepreneurial firms. The first observation is that several of the interviewed entrepreneurs are members of informal networks of "peers" that can be traced back to relations that have been established at an earlier phase of their professional career. The second is that there seems to be much job-hopping between the organisations although this might be explained in part by the average short life-time of these organisations.

However, it may be incorrect to perceive the many mini-size freelancees' organisations in the Copenhagen area as belonging to a community. Freelancing may be a life-style preferred by individuals who want to get out of the restrictions and rules associated with large, formal organisations. The free-lancees may be perceived as satellites to organisations within the above mentioned communities, but not necessarily constituting a community them-selves.

At present there is a tendency to merge and close down organisations which results in fewer and larger organisations. This may be due to the traditional emphasis upon individual software products providing an insufficient base for economic growth. Instead, there seems to be a move toward emphasis upon standardised software. However, the explanation behind this may also be that the recession in the Danish economy slows down growth within the IT trade, that was expanding until recently. Changed behaviour on behalf of some of the important customers also plays a role. Some public sector users have, for instance, reduced their demand for external consultants by entering into joint ventures with suppliers.

3.7   The Systems Programmers' Community

Genesis

In the first part of the seventies, systems programmers appeared with the introduction of more complicated operative systems, and the shift from batch to on-line data processing. The mainframes, and in particular the large IBM installations required employment of systems programmers – both for the development of new systems, and in order to secure smooth operations. According to Denmark's Statistical Bureau the number of systems programmers was 1,000 in 1986, and in general these people are employed in large installations. Horlück's survey (in Friedman et al, 1988) identified 382 systems programmers in 33 installations of a sample of 42. Based upon this it can be estimated that more than 100 Danish installations employ systems programmers.

The Persons
The individuals are either data-engineers, datalogs, or experienced programmers who solve very technical tasks related to operating systems, data transmission, etc. These specialists have been in demand for quite a few years and are extremely well paid. Many of them stay within this job category, and do not want to move into managerial or project responsibilities.

Tasks, Methods and Norms/Ideals and Basic Assumptions
Their basic orientation is towards technical sophistication and innovation, and they are the closest we come to an identification of a "hard technical core" of EDP specialists. Some of them are attached to research and development institutions such as the Technical University and DIKU, and to the association known as "Dansk Selskab for Datalogi". It is within this group that we have found the strongest tendency to regard oneself as a "specialist" – a term that in general is avoided by the IT people. It is also this group that other employees in IT organisations mention as representing IT specialisation – "bit-turners" or "techies".

Relations to Other Communities
The systems programmers apparently move rather freely between different organisations. According to the study of Friedman et al (1988) this is the case of the systems programmers working in IBM installations, whereas the specialists working with other suppliers' equipment are less mobile. The latter group faces fewer alternative job possibilities as the skills of systems programmers most often are tied to specific types of installations. As the large installations are located within different communities, the systems programmers represent a technical community that cuts across the other communities' boundaries. But their community represents an introvert universe which does not impose its norms and values on the other communities.

4   Discussion

4.1   Institutional Variance

Our explorative analysis has led to the identification of a diversity of institutional forms within the Danish IT field. These have been described in terms of seven communities which integrate technical, sectorial, and spatial cultural traits. They can be summarised as different configurations of persons, tasks, and value systems, which differ with regard to their internal coherence (see Table I.1).

IBM Denmark is a coherent community, clearly separated from both the other, smaller international suppliers, and the other Danish communities. IBM's recruitment practice and comprehensive internal educational system reflect a moulding of the IBM employees, which is much more far-reaching than that of the other communities. This heavy investment in training and indoctrination of employees is facilitated by IBM International's resources and corporate culture. IBM is dominated by a sales and profit orientation, and an emphasis on technical implementation, whereas the development orientation is secondary as a consequence of this function's location abroad.

In contrast, the *technical community* that comprises the Danish suppliers of hardware – Regnecentralen, DDE, and CRI – is much more oriented towards technical development, and is affiliated with Danish universities and research laboratories. But competition with the international suppliers has forced it to incorporate a sales and business orientation, which has led to an internal struggle between technical and profit orientation.

Datacentralen is an important community that qua its role as a centralised service bureau dealing with large scale public systems has been facing a stable task and resource situation. This has made possible the emergence of a coherent community around software development, systems operations, and user services. The affiliation to the public sector and the concentration of many IT specialists have led to the development of a culture with collective and craftsman-like traits. The public sector affiliation also contributes to explaining the organisational inertia of DC that has turned organisational change into a difficult exercise.

As a consequence of its genesis and task situation the *Kommunedata* community is internally differentiated, the differences between the regional cultures of Jutland and the Copenhagen area emerging as the most important ones. Our data do not indicate that Datacentralen and Kommunedata form one community. Instead, they seem to be more closely linked to their respective users via their different recruitments from the state administration and the municipalities.

The *financial sector* community has been moving from pioneer IT department within banks and insurance companies towards a concentration in either large separate IT organisations or large internal IT departments. This community is business and implementation oriented: user relations are an important dimension of the task situation. The resulting culture is characterised as dynamic, influenced both by the financial sector's changing trade culture and the other IT communities.

Diversity is pronounced within the entrepreneurial community which appears to be loosely coupled internally. It may be most correct to conceive it as divided into local communities, and to regard some of the entrepreneurs as "satellites" depending upon one or a few important customers to whom they are subcontractors or freelancers. However, our data indicate the existence of a set of values

Table I.1   Configurations of the Seven Communities Described

Community	Tasks	Persons	Value System
IBM Denmark (1950)	sales/profit service	high qualific. practitioners indoctrinated (2,500)	individualism ambitious corporate spirit
Regne- centralen (1950)	invention implementation sales	academics practitioners (800)	creativity research profits internal divide
Data- centralen (1959)	large systems design and service	EDP-assistants public servants (1,800)	craftsmanship collectivism control/safety coherent
Kommune- data (1970)	systems design consultancy service	municipal educ. EDP-assistants academics (1,700)	pioneering group orientation regional differentiation
Financial community (approx. 1960)	systems design (in-house) infrastructure rationalisation	practitioners clerks IT specialists (4,700)	craftsmanship- collectivism business- individualism mixed: firms and sectors
Entrepre- neurial community (approx. 1970)	systems design consultancy data power sales	all types few academics (5,000 ?)	entrepreneurship belief in simple structure split networks
Systems Program- mers' community (approx. 1970)	technical design and problem solving	IT specialists many academics (1,000)	technical sophistication specialisation split networks

(In parentheses: year of founding and number of individuals)

and beliefs that is quite different from those of the other communities in which the entrepreneurs have usually started their careers.

The *systems programmers' community* represents the only purely technical IT culture we have been able to identify. These technical specialists rotate around IT installations, without any particular affiliation to the communities or organisations in which these installations are placed. Their technical specialisation ties them to the installations, but they are able to move around – as long as the equipment originates from the same supplier. This community overlaps the communities mentioned above, and comprises actors who are regarded as different by the other communities' members.

In line with Selznick's reasoning (1957) these communities can be regarded as having acquired a status of institutionalisation in the sense that they have been infused with value beyond what is needed to cope with the technical task requirements. The combinations of tasks and value systems appear to be not completely arbitrary, but other combinations are not unthinkable. For instance, it might have been possible for IBM to perform its sales task with a more collective value system – but that would have necessitated different reward systems. It would also have been possible for Datacentralen to solve its systems design tasks with a value system of a less controlled and more collective-oriented nature.

Furthermore, even within the dynamic IT field these communities appear to be attributed value and a taken for granted status by our interviewees. Some of them also reveal considerable stability – again taking into consideration that we are dealing with a young field – as they have shown persistent patterns during a decade.

These communities do not include all organisations within the IT field, but only those belonging to clusters where our observations have indicated value systems of a certain stability and networks of a certain strength. Examples of excluded organisations are large public IT users, and small and medium sized private IT users.

4.2   Institutionalisation Processes

The variance analysis of the IT communities has not only produced a picture of stable patterns, but also of ongoing processes of institutionalisation. This is hardly surprising when we take into consideration that the IT field is only thirty years old. Our analysis has taken an arbitrary point in time as the entry point to address the structuration of the field – with the inherent risk of regarding the present situation as the outcome of a process, rather than only as a step in an ongoing process.

However, the descriptive analyses point to processes of institutionalisation which introduce both variation and convergence among the IT communities.

Community Initiation

This explanation makes us search for "genes" with which the community was endowed during its conception, and which can explain the important aspects of the present variance. Important examples of this can be traced in the cases of IBM, Datacentralen (DC), Kommunedata (KMD), and Regnecentralen (RC).

From its early years IBM Denmark has been the local sales office of IBM International. Research and development functions have not been located in Denmark. Thus the task orientation has been clear: sales, and the dependency on the IBM corporation has been strong. IBM Denmark has been furnished with both products and competences and concepts within marketing, accounting, organisation, and human resource management from the mother corporation. These US business attitudes and beliefs have been imprinted in the Danish office, as expressed in the attitude that individuals, and not unions, are the counterpart of the corporation.

Datacentralen's initial management team was derived from the IBM community. IBM Denmark supplied DC with its first managing director, hardware, important parts of its methodology and organisational thinking that were compatible with the task situation of DC: computerisation of large, centralised administrative systems. But IBM's personnel philosophy was, however, less compatible with the public sector's traditions for handling employee and union relations.

In contrast to Datacentralen, Kommunedata was born as regional centres which were products of local politics and local cultures. Even after these centres were merged into KMD, these regional entities continued to exert significant influence on both the structural configuration chosen and the value system.

Regnecentralen was created as a research and development based organisation with links to both research institutions and practitioners. Invention and creativity were early values which were compatible with the objective of product development. They were less compatible with the profit orientation which was later incorporated in order to compete with the international suppliers. This resulted in an internal conflict, which for many years made it difficult to implement internal transitions and to solve problems related to different segments of RC's environment.

Domain Adaptation

A second explanation of the variance between the different IT communities can be traced back to their interaction with different domains. Exposure to different domains has confronted the IT communities with different tasks and values. Hence, the communities' recruitment of actors, which differs considerably with respect to practical experience and level of formal qualifications, express adaptation to the community domains. The two extremes of IBM Denmark and the entrepreneurial community are examples of this.

IBM has not valued IT experience and has in stead emphasised formal, internal training and indoctrination of its new recruits. This may be a result of both the lack of relevant practical experience during the early years, and of pressure from the IBM corporation to adopt its US developed personnel practices. Higher formal qualifications are considered important for the shaping of new recruits.

The entepreneurial community, on the other hand, has valued outside experience because of its modest resources. However, higher formal qualifications are considered as irrelevant or potentially dysfunctional in relation to the domain: the issue is practical problem-solving and the customers do not value consultants with a theoretical background.

Datacentralen provides another example of domain adaptation producing variance: from its initiation the community was endowed with conflicting traits as described above. The potential conflict between the IBM and the public sector's traditions increased as DC grew and its centralisation became a stronghold of IT unions. Datacentralen thus offered an organisational arena for the processing of both political demands for a state technology policy, and political protests against the dominance of international suppliers and their union policies.

This led to the discarding of the IBM inspired Management By Objectives system, the expulsion of the IBM consultants from DC's premises, and the breaking of IBM's monopoly as a hardware supplier. This happened gradually through a laborious process and under pressure from the domain (described more detailed in Chapter IV). DC's recruitment of its last two managing directors from the public sector furthermore indicates supplier independency and that IT is regarded as being subordinated the public sector's raison d'etre.

IT Field Interaction

However, interaction between the IT communities also introduces a pressure towards convergence of organisational forms and practices. This happens through the exchange of actors, know-how, hardware and software which leads to the development of shared perceptions of proper practice. This includes methods for problem solving, division of labour, and structural arrangements.

In these respects the IBM community has been very influential throughout the history of the Danish IT field . From the early years of computing IBM has been one of the centres of expertise. As such it has been important as an educational centre, a supplier of (imported) methods, and IT persons for other communities. In particular, the financial sector community has been strongly influenced. IBM's present influence is expressed in its dominant market position and its role as a standard setter.

This has also been IBM's role in relation to the two Danish "giants" within public sector IT, and in particular to Datacentralen, which during the first decade was dependent on and socially integrated with IBM.

In the Danish context Datacentralen and Kommunedata represent a concentration of resources and IT competences that, after the early years of IBM dependency, has given them roles as possible counterweights to the international influence. DC particularly has been important as a centre for the development of methods and standards for mainframe applications. Both DC and Kommunedata function as important educational centres in relation to the Danish IT field, and have been important suppliers of actors to the financial sector and the entrepreneurial communities.

A recent example of IT field interaction, which seems to further convergence across previous boundaries and competitive fields, can be traced in the interaction between international and national suppliers. Thus, during recent years international suppliers have furnished Regnecentralen with capital and managerial methods, and IBM has become a partner in one of the offsprings of the technical community – the CRI software house. Parallel to this, parts of the entrepreneurial community have become sub-contractors of software to IBM and other international hardware suppliers.

This blurring of the previously clear boundaries between the international suppliers and the technical community has two aspects. One is a redefinition of the relations from pure competition to a mixture of competition and collaboration. The other is an increased uniformity of organisational and managerial principles. Some of the elements of the latter are the increased weight upon profitability, the introduction of a managerial apex on the top of the technically oriented organisations, the introduction of profit centres, MBO systems, and efforts to develop corporate cultures.

Societal Adaptation

Some of the convergence tendencies are not specific to the IT field but originate from the society in which this field is embedded.

One example is the diffusion of specific organisational forms across sectors and fields by consultancies in which McKinsey has played an active role as disseminator of the divisionalised form and the profit centre concept in Denmark. Datacentralen and Kommunedata are examples of important IT organisations, in relation to which McKinsey has acted as a consultant by implanting these forms. Other examples of the influence of consultancies are traceable within the financial sector community – as reflected in the concentration of former internal IT departments into self-sustaining profit centres. These organisational forms represent efforts to cope with increasing external pressures in terms of market competition and contestation of the economic performance of the large institutionalised organisations.

This convergence of managerial practices (by Scott, 1987a, termed "institutional isomorphism") between the communities cannot solely be attributed to the influence of consultancies and the international suppliers. It also reflects managerial fashion (Mintzberg, 1979) and shared rationalised myths about appropriate managerial techniques (Meyer and Rowan, 1983, pp. 340-363) that are disseminated through different sectors (Child, 1988). Facing dynamic and complex environments, the IT communities are receptive to new managerial and organisational ideas.

5   Concluding Comments

Our analysis has shown that the IT field is subject to different types of institutionalisation processes which introduce both divergent and convergent forces of influence. These mixed influences explain the development of different IT communities, the traits of which reflect general societal and field influences, as well as initiation and domain adaptation processes specific to the different communities.

The strands woven together are highly complex and do not produce simple conclusions. While "community initiation" as an example for four of the IT communities does provide a certain understanding of the subsequent institution-alisation processes, it only points to potential directions they may follow, and to potential dilemmas which may or may not be evoked by the historical development.

Another example is the question of the international suppliers' influence which has often been raised in light of their dominance within the IT field (Monopoltilsynet, 1988). Our analysis has identified some of the mechanisms through which international suppliers – in particular IBM – have influenced the institutionalisation of values and organisational practices. However, our analysis of the four types of institutionalisation processes points to complex processes which illustrate how the international suppliers also adapt to their local domains and are subjected to more general influence.

Thus, although the internationals' influence on the Danish IT communities is and has been strong, the communities are flavoured by international, national, sectorial, and local cultural traits. The communities are dynamic: our analysis has dealt with important aspects of the existing communities' historical development, but leaves them in the midst of a phase of transition.

Chapter II
Organisational Cultures in Information Technology Firms

Jesper Strandgaard Pedersen

1 Introduction[1]

Since about 1980, when the concept of culture has appeared on the scene of organisational sociology, numerous articles and books have been published on the subject[2]. However, compared to the relatively vast number of theoretical contributions addressing the issue of culture, a strikingly low number of empirical studies have been conducted. The reason may be that it is time-consuming and no straight forward task to conduct empirical studies of culture in an organisational context. The problems that scholars and students interested in studying organisational cultures face concern questions like: what is culture; how do you study this fuzzy concept; and what phenomena should you look for? A large number of methodological questions and problems quickly turns up concerning the study of the relatively intangible phenomenon called culture.[3]

In the book "Organisational Culture and Leadership – A Dynamic View" (1985), using the framework of Kluckhohn and Strodtbeck (1961), Schein has presented his views and suggestions concerning the concept of culture and how to study it. This article departs from this theoretical framework, reflecting on its strengths and weaknesses in relation to empirical research. The discussion is based on experiences derived from a study on information technology cultures (Pedersen and Sorensen, 1989) and the results from three case analyses are presented in this article.

The purpose of this article is twofold. The first purpose is to investigate information technology cultures at an organisational level and, in this context to address questions concerned with the stability/dynamism and homogeneity/ heterogeneity of organisational cultures. The second purpose is to conduct a theoretical discussion of organisational cultures extending Schein's theoretical framework.[4]

2   The Proliferation of Organisational Culture

Since about 1980, the concept of culture has been linked to the study of organisations. A wave of scientific literature on organisational culture has been published. Titles such as "Corporate Cultures" (Deal and Kennedy, 1982) and especially "In Search of Excellence" (Peters and Waterman, 1982) have sold millions of copies all over the world. Well-known scientific publications such as Administrative Science Quarterly and Organisation Studies have produced special editions on "culture" and "symbolism" (ASQ, No. 28, 1983 and Organisation Studies No. 7, 1986). The social science concept of culture has proliferated and been widely adopted within business and society at large. Today, it is not uncommon to hear people talk about "the culture I work in", whether they are public or private sector employees. The normative message of having "strong" cultures has been communicated in business journals (e.g. "Business Week" cover story, "Corporate Culture: The hard to change values that spell success or failure" (1980), and Fortune Magazine (March, 1982) had a "Corporate Cultures" section). The cultural approach incorporates a surprising number of scattered findings as regards organisations. It proposes novel ways of depicting organisations (Morgan, 1986) and creates new challenges for researchers concerning methodology and theory building. The linking of culture to the study of organisations has been accorded importance ranging from a paradigmatic shift to nothing new. However, whether you are a fanatic "believer" or a "skeptic", it is almost impossible not to be confronted with the concept of culture.

3   A Cultural Perspective on Organisations – What Does It Mean?

The topic of organisational culture is confusing and most writers use different definitions, different methods of determining what they mean by culture, and different standards for evaluating how culture affects organisations (Alvesson and Berg, 1988; Pedersen and Sorensen, 1989; Schultz, 1990).

The cultural perspective is still in an *embryonic stage*. At least some of the confusion and disagreement may be attributed to the fact that this perspective, is still in the phase of concept and theory building – generating more data and new models primarily on the basis of empirical studies (Alvesson and Berg, 1988).[5]

In spite of the above mentioned differences on conceptual definitions, research methods and standards for evaluating how culture affects organisations, a certain "core" of basic agreement concerning organisational culture can be observed. A common basis of agreement is that culture is viewed as a *"social construction of reality"* (Berger and Luckman, 1966) and is further described as possessing cognitive and interpretive properties. Culture is seen as a *social phenomenon* (Deal and Kennedy, 1982) located in the minds of human beings and is created and activated through cognitive processes (sense making, interpreting, legitimating and so forth). The majority of the literature on organisational culture also agrees, that it is a phenomenon, which cannot easily be grasped as it is portrayed as "hidden", "unconscious", "taken-for-granted" and exists as a kind of *"tacit knowledge"* (Louis, 1985; Schein, 1985; Molin, 1987). Culture gets *empirical representation* through manifestation in a variety of cultural forms; for example in artifacts like rituals (Deal and Kennedy, 1982; Beyer and Trice, 1987; Kunda, 1991), myths (Christensen and Molin, 1983; Molin, 1987), stories (Clark, 1972; Martin et al., 1983; Wilkins et al, 1991), jargon and jokes (Hirsh and Andrews, 1983; Hatch and Ehrlich, 1991), or physical settings (Berg and Kreiner, 1987; Hatch, 1987; Gagliardi, 1990) and in organisational work practices and routines (Bodker and Pedersen, 1991). Thus, the various definitions of culture, in one way or another, assume a linkage between culture and organisational *behaviour* to exist. The notion of culture as something, which is shared, likewise seems to be a common perception, that runs through the literature. The disagreement is limited to discussion about how widely shared the culture is. The question often can be boiled down to whether the author is subscribing to a unicultural view or a multicultural view, when dealing with the issue of organisational culture. Nevertheless, in both cases culture is defined as the sum of what is shared and, in the former case constituting a corporate culture and in the latter case subcultures (see Chapter V for a more elaborate discussion of the unicultural and the multicultural view). As to the *implications of culture*, a variety of outcomes have been listed in the literature. Some examples are, "anxiety reducing" (Schein, 1985), "controlling" (Van Maanen and Kunda, 1989), "identity providing" (Deal and Kennedy, 1982), "socializing" (Van Maanen and Barley, 1985), "sense making" (Christensen and Molin, 1983), "problem solving" (Schein, 1985), and "coordinating" (Pettigrew, 1979). Here also a common base of agreement seems to exist. Some of the implications have already been mentioned more or less explicitly above, but can be summarised to a view of culture as creating *continuity, identity, control and integration*.

Concerning the question of *culture change* and *the dynamics* of this process, culture has generally been depicted as a relatively stable phenomenon, largely self-sustaining and self-generating, resisting change, with a consequent tendency to stabilise and preserve the status quo. Some researchers have viewed culture to be continually, but slowly changing in progressively smaller ways. This continuation and permanence of the culture is often explained in terms of the particular culture being *passed on from one generation to the next*, through processes of socialisation, learning, imitation, or other forms of transmission via social interaction. In relation to this it is interesting that the agreement within culture research is fairly strong concerning the connection between culture and continuity. That is to say, even though cultures are recognised to change, they are seen as *changing very slowly* and surprisingly few suggestions have been offered regarding the dynamics behind culture changes.

4   A Dynamic Model of Culture

For the present study, the cultural model presented by Schein (1985), "Organizational Culture and Leadership – A Dynamic View", has been chosen as the theoretical framework for a cultural analysis of three information technology firms.
Schein is one of the few, "rare" writers of cultural theory, who has tried to establish a framework for the study of culture and provided elaborate guidelines and methods for empirical research.

Thus, Schein's work appears to be one of the most promising attempts, so far, concerning the balancing of theory and guidelines for methodological approach. In his book Schein explicitly states that the term "culture" should be reserved for:

"..the deeper level of basic assumptions and beliefs that are shared by members of an organisation, that operate unconsciously, and define in a basic "taken-for-granted" fashion an organization's view on itself and its environment. These assumptions and beliefs are learned responses to a group's problems of survival in its external environment and its problems of internal integration. They come to be taken for granted because they solve those problems repeatedly and reliably." (Schein, 1985, p. 6).

The key-concept of this definition is *"basic assumptions"*, because they, in Schein's terms, are to be viewed as the *essence of culture*. According to Schein, they have to be distinguished from *"artifacts"* and *"values"*, which are to be regarded merely as manifestations only reflecting the surface levels of the organisational culture.

Schein has developed and described his ideas and perception of culture in the model below. As the figure shows, he operates with three levels of culture in his model:

The idea of the model is that you begin your analysis at the two upper levels of cultural manifestations – at the levels of "artifacts" and "values" – and interpret their meaning through careful examination. You start on the surface level with the culture's manifestations because that is where you are able to obtain some data on the organisational culture. By interpreting and examining "artifacts" and "values" and their attached meanings, you get deeper and deeper

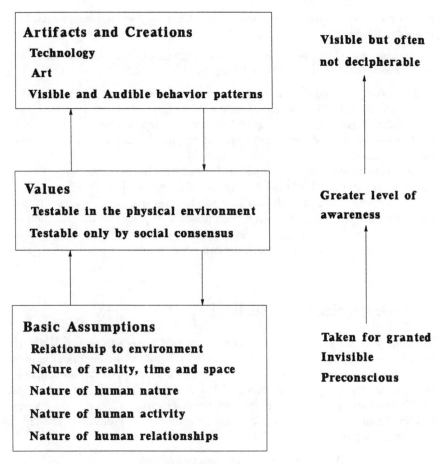

Figure II.1   Levels of Culture and Their Interaction
             (Source: Adapted from Schein, 1980, p. 4.)

into the culture, along the lines of the "basic assumptions", ending up trying to infer and establish the underlying cultural paradigm that ties it all together.

Operationalisation of Schein's Model
Although Schein, to my knowledge, is one of the few authors, who actually presents elaborate directions for conducting a cultural analysis, his model still lacks some important conceptual definitions and a "translation" in order to be workable. This is especially true concerning the levels of "artifacts" and "values", which Schein does not seem to care that much about as he provides

almost no information on their content apart from very general statements. For instance, Schein refers to the level of "artifacts" as :

"...the constructed physical and social environment, which includes technology, art and, visible and audible behaviour patterns." (Schein, 1985, p. 14).

This is a fairly general definition of "artifacts", which does not lend itself easily to an operationalisation or direction for cultural research. A "revised" and "translated" version of Schein's model of culture is depicted below. This revised model is the basis upon which the present empirical study and analyses have been conducted.[6]

The lines around the artifactual and value levels are deliberately drawn continuously, as these levels are viewed as *indicators* of culture, whereas "basic assumptions" are drawn with non-continuous lines due to their character of *deductions*. In this study, it has not been possible to place "myths" unambiguously and, hence, this category has been placed outside the model as they often serve as a kind of mediator between the two upper levels.

5   Description of the Study

The empirical part of the present study was conducted over a three month lasting period from mid August to mid November 1986, in three different organisations within the information technology industry. All three companies differ concerning age, size and the tasks they handle. They also face very different contingencies. Names and non-essential details have been changed or left out, in order to protect the anonymity of the participating companies and informants. The three companies studied are:

(1) "Advice", a small, start-up IT consultancy company
(2) "Total", a medium-sized, middle-aged (ten years old) software house,
(3) "Datacentralen", a large, mature service bureau, with more than thirty years of experience.

The three IT companies represent three different profiles within the Danish IT field (cf. Chapter I): "the small IT consultancy firm" (Advice), "the medium-sized software house" (Total) and, "the large service bureau" (Datacentralen). The idea of this sample has been to gain cultural insight and investigate the framework in three very different types of IT organisations. The three companies are interesting because they reflect different stages in an organisation's life-cycle. According to Schein (1985), Advice is in a stage of "birth and early growth", Total is in a stage of "organisational midlife" and Datacentralen is in a stage of "organisational maturity". Data for the present study were collected from various sources using a *hybrid methodology* based on a qualitative

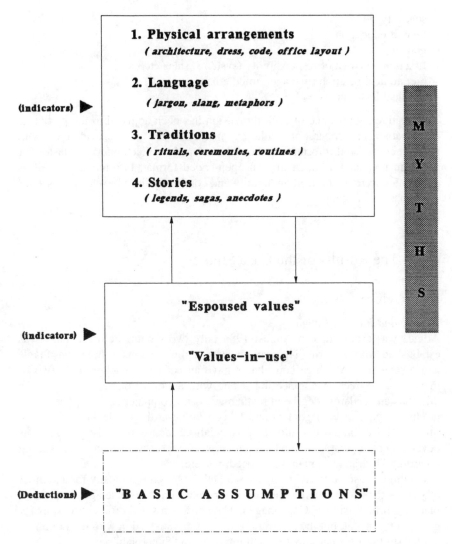

1. Physical arrangements
(architecture, dress, code, office layout)

2. Language
(jargon, slang, metaphors)

(indicators) ▶

3. Traditions
(rituals, ceremonies, routines)

4. Stories
(legends, sagas, anecdotes)

M
Y
T
H
S

"Espoused values"

(indicators) ▶

"Values-in-use"

(Deductions) ▶ **"B A S I C   A S S U M P T I O N S"**

Figure II.2   Operationalization of Schein's Model
(Source: Pedersen and Sorensen, 1989)

approach. Data rest on three main sources: Formal interviews, observations and archival studies. In depth interviews with 31 organisational members[7] were conducted and efforts were made to secure representativeness by taking into account the following dimensions when selecting informants:

- seniority
- type of education
- gender
- function and area of responsibility (systems, sales etc.)
- hierarchical position (manager, middlemanager, staff)
- physical location.

The relative significance of each dimension has been adjusted to the particular organisation in cooperation with an "insider", who also provided us with preliminary general information about the informants. Each interview lasted for about an hour and a half, using an open-ended format. Informants as well as companies were guaranteed anonymity and confidentiality in exchange for their participation and cooperation.

6 The Results of the Case Studies

6.1 Advice

History and Field of Activity
Advice was established in August 1986 only two months before contact was established with the firm. The firm consists of four persons – three consultants and a secretary. All three consultants have an academic background. Two of them have degrees in engineering – one with a Ph.D. degree, too – and the third has an academic degree in mathematics and computer science. The firm's product is general management and IT consulting at the top level in organisations. Advice offers consulting in specialised areas such as: IT systems development, operational analysis and optimisation, management consulting regarding IT strategies, planning procedures, etc.

All three consultants had formerly worked in the same company for a number of years – their former employee was "Superplan", a major management and IT planning firm outside of Copenhagen. The consultants had different reasons for going independent, but the general reason was dissatisfaction with the diminishing possibilities for participation and influence in "Superplan".

Advice is anxious to present the corporate image of three neutral, independent, highly qualified and educated experts who base their cooperation with the customers on confidence and trust and they deliver their "product" by participating in problem solving processes. The firm is doing pretty well – among other things due to the fact that the consultants have taken over some customers from their former firm "Superplan". Presently, Advice has one big client and a few smaller ones. All customers are quasi-public companies and government agencies that often compete with private firms.

The Culture in Advice
Artifacts

Advice is situated in a big two-storey house with an attic, big windows and a garden. The villa is built on a secluded little by-road, surrounded by other patrician houses. There is no noise and you almost feel as if you are on an excursion to one of the better off areas north of Copenhagen. Nonetheless, the villa is situated fairly centrally in Copenhagen. There are no signs, flags or other kinds of more spectacular symbols telling about the firm apart from a tiny brass plate with the company's name and logo.

The two oldest consultants, who are in their late thirties, give the impression of mature "sixty eights" and the dress code seems to be shirt, pullovers, and jeans or corduroy trousers – much like the "programmers' outfit" that can be observed elsewhere in the IT industry. The youngest consultant was dressed somewhat more in the "eighties" style, wearing a "sales people" uniform with jacket, tie, white or blue shirt. This gave a first impression of tolerance in Advice because these "deviances" seem to be accepted or at least not regarded as important.

The language code consists of a mix between a consultancy code of "process", "clients", "strategies", "consulting" and an analytical-abstract level of explanation. No signs of "trouble shooting" consultancy language were heard. Apart from the language code mentioned above, jargon or nicknames seemed almost non-existent. For example, the traditional, masculine IT language and metaphors that have been observed among programmers and operators in other IT firms (confer the two next cases) were not found in this firm. Furthermore they did not seem to use any technical jargon in the sense of traditional IT abbreviations. They appeared pretty polite when they addressed each other and you might describe the language as somewhat dry. The language code in Advice was characterised by an academic language code "dotted" with terminology from consultancy.

All the stories recorded in Advice are primarily related to and extracted from their professional lives as consultants. The consultants have a lot of stories about their former employee – "Superplan"- and about other consultants who have produced "empty" solutions – very costly to their customers.

Values and Basic Assumptions.

In Advice three key-values were identified: "High education – high spirits", "We want to make proper consultancy" and "Equal influence on working conditions". In the figure below, the relation between these values and the basic assumptions have been depicted.

In Schein's terminology the culture of Advice and the relationship to the environment is characterised not by dominance or harmony but by what you could call optimistic submission – that is to say – they have found a niche and thrive on it.

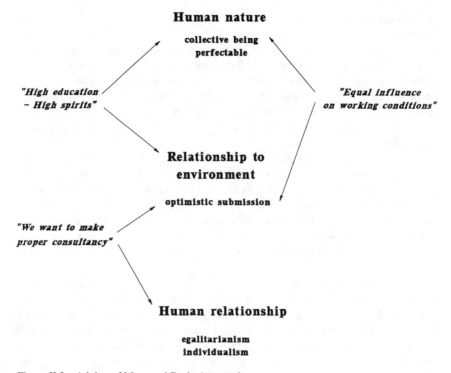

Figure II.3   Advice – Values and Basic Assumptions
              (Source: Pedersen and Sorensen, 1989)

A basic assumption concerning the relationship to the environment of Advice was found, which can be formulated as follows:

"In Advice we will survive and grow because we are highly educated and qualified and because we profile ourselves in a specialised area".

This assumption is related to the (academic) value of "High education – high spirits". This value is closely interrelated with the consultants' self-perception of being highly qualified and therefore able to "Make proper consultancy". There also seems to exist a basic assumption in Advice about Man as a collective being and an assumption about egalitarianism as the best way of social organising.

The assumptions about "egalitarianism" are related to the consultants' value of having "Influence on your own working conditions". The assumption concerning "egalitarianism" is reflected in the way the consultants have organised their mutual economic relations. They throw all their earnings in one pot and share it equally.

The basic assumption about "Man as a collective being" is not derived from the character of the day to day activities in the company, because the consultants exercise a strong individualism in occupational matters and they do not have much contact with each other during the day. "Man as a collective being" is reflected in their vision of the future and in their attitude toward future colleagues in their statement, "We want to take new people into partnership on equal terms – like in a commune". The institutionalisation of collectively oriented values in the partnership contract is a valid indicator of how important they regard these values and that they are shared by the members.

An assumption about man as perfectible also seems to exist. Human beings are seen as being able to change and develop or to be developed, especially through "High education", which finally may result in "High spirits". This assumption seems closely related to the academic values in Advice. All assumptions mentioned above seem fairly congruent. They are telling about the foundation for the collective orientation as regards the social values.

The collective orientation of the social values are clearly not congruent with the strong individualism that is expressed through occupational values, for instance, the principal autonomy of each consultant in occupational decisions.

The Cultural Pattern

The culture in Advice is certainly an academic culture but the culture does not constitute a coherent system of assumptions. It is rather embedded in a variety of contradictions and inconsistencies, especially between strong occupational individualism contrary to the collective social values.

According to Schein, one should be able to explain or at least understand these inconsistencies by analysing the underlying cultural assumptions. The underlying assumption explaining these dualities might be that:

"Human beings are collective beings but they also possess the competence to take responsibility and are capable of governing their own jobs".

An attempt was made to conduct a full analysis of the culture in Advice according to Schein's model. However, Advice had only been established at the time of our study and had not had much time to create, develop or firmly establish unique values and norms of its own. Cultural values were primarily entailed and carried by the founders and in that sense the analysis is not as much a study of an established organisational culture, as a study of cultural founders striving to form a culture.

6.2   Total

History and Field of Activity

Total is a medium sized information technology firm, which produces and sells administrative IT systems. The basic concept or idea in Total is to be an "over-all supplier". This concept captures the philosophy of being able to accommodate a potential customer with every aspect of his or her needs with regard to information technology. To be more specific this means, Total must be ready to provide the customer with the necessary software (standard systems or special systems), hardware to run the programmes, peripheral equipment (tapes, fire safes, terminal tables, ribbons etc.), system support, technical service as well as education and training. The company's basic product is the administrative standard system "Power". Furthermore they also operate as dealers for a couple of large hardware suppliers.

The story of the company from the late seventies until today has been a story of *continuous development and expansion*. This is true from an economic point of view as regards turnover as well as the number of people employed (from less than 10 persons ten years ago to the present situation with 40-50 employees).

The structure of competence and the composition of occupations are marked by a mix of "software specialists", "hardware specialists", persons occupied with sales of the equipment and systems and, finally, persons handling administrative tasks (management, accounts, budget planning, type-writing etc.). The employees in Total have a lot of work experience but normally no formal education.

Over the years the company has built up rather a large group of regular customers (more than 100) and, hence, has a solid economic basis in terms of a relatively stable market. The organisational growth and development have been rather rapid and extensive in certain periods and, today, Total in some respects suffers from "growing pains". For example, the organisational structure in Total has emerged through a process of "budding" as new functions and departments, over the years, have been added to the existing ones in consequence of expanding the "over-all supplier" concept.

The Culture in Total
Artifacts
Total and its various departments are not located in one building, but physically separated in various locations. *The buildings* are well-kept without being showy. There are no big signs, flags or streamers, to catch the attention of potential customers. Inside, there is a small desk which serves as the reception area. From the adjoining rooms you hear data-noise from printers, keyboards and other equipment, and this "hardware" seems to cover half the space of the ground floor. People pass – apparently without noticing the "intruders" – and there is an atmosphere of activity, though it is not hectic. Similar to the exterior, *the style inside* is also characterised by being discrete, tasteful and functional – all things present are needed. As regards offices and office lay out, no apparent difference in size or decor was observed, which could give indications of status or hierarchy. Office lay out does not seem to be a symbol of status, it rather underlines the impression of equality and informality. People seem relaxed.

They do not use titles, they call each other by their first names, smile, talk and chat in a hearty and friendly manner. Their dress-code is informal and casual – i.e., no formal uniforms or ties. The informal "uniform" is jeans or cords, T-shirt or shirt (according to the time of the year) and in some cases a sweat shirt or pull-over. However, you can observe a tendency towards persons in sales offices and marketing functions, as well as employees in some of the administrative functions, being dressed more formally in, for example, white shirts, tie, jacket or suit.

The tone used among the organisational members is, as mentioned, hearty and free with a touch of impudence. A lot of *jargon, nicknames, jokes* and technical expressions fill the air (e.g., "big chief", "the virgin", "cobol-crushers", "guru-organisation", "sweep up shit from the disc" etc.). The language and ways of addressing one another among the IT people may, at times, sound rather tough and aggressive to outsiders (e.g., "Idiots", "amateurs", "nuts", "fatheads" and so on). Contrary to this the administrative staff and sales people were low on jargon (i.e., no prevalent use of nicknames, technical expressions etc.). Even though the language and jargon among the IT people seem tough and masculine, different artifacts reveal other features of the culture in Total. *"Corporate" traditions* in Total include celebrating company jubilees, a summer party, Christmas lunch, Easter gathering (with spouses) and a company trip to Germany. All of these are normal and widely used corporate traditions in Denmark. However, another tradition was observed which caught our attention: whenever an employee was to leave the company – no matter whether he or she left in anger, was head hunted or "pushed" out – it was a tradition that the company arranged a "farewell-ceremony" on which occasion the "prodigal son or daughter" is given a "farewell present". The "party" took place in the company facilities and, wine was provided. Both management, colleagues and customers were invited to say goodbye and thank each other for a nice time.

This tradition is a very precise illustration of another prevalent aspect of the culture in Total, showing that the company is also a place where you care about the individual. This somewhat modifies the rather tough first impression you get from the language code and jokes.

In Total formality is not valued. They do not emphasise or rely very much upon titles, formal education or "certificates". Instead they look at what people are capable of in practice. For instance, the top manager is respected because he is dynamic, persuasive and good at getting new ideas, and not because of his formal power.

Values and Basic Assumptions
The following six values were dominant in Total: "Treat people with consideration", "No lay offs", "Do not brag or play Mr. Know-all", "Promote yourself – the right way", "Get things done – the results count" and the myth "Ask before you do anything".

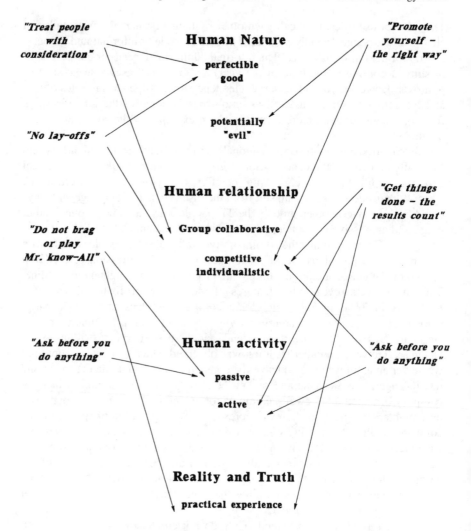

Figure II.4   Total – Values and Basic Assumptions
(Source: Pedersen and Sorensen, 1989)

The relationship between the six values and the various categories of basic assumptions are outlined below and can be described as follows:

The three "key-values" ("Do not brag or play Mr. know-all", "No lay offs" and "Treat people with consideration") reflect assumptions about human nature, such as human beeings as perfectible and good. For example, the general tolerance and patience with "newcomers" in particular, reflect the belief that human beeings are good at something and the reason for being unsuccessful is likely to be due to "misplacement" ("wrong job for a good man") or not yet possessing the necessary amount of experience.

These values also reflect an understanding of human relationships to be group collaborative and non-competitive. Concerning human activity the "right" way to relate to each other is perceived to be, if not passive, then at least not to be too active or self-promoting.

The "key-values" ("Get things done – the results count" and "Promote yourself – the right way") reflect a basic assumption about human relationships, viewing life as competitive and individualistic – a kind of "every man for himself". The "right" way to relate towards other individuals – the nature of human activity – is obviously to be active – to do things and take action. This is evident from the way the myth ("Ask before you do anything") is handled and, so to speak, "broken" by members of the group taking action.

Human beings are, perhaps, not regarded "hostile" by nature, but you had better keep an eye on them, due to the assumption that they are competitors (trying to promote themselves at your expense) and you have to check them out from time to time to see if they actually produce and do what they are expected to do (e.g., "profit centres" and economic orientation) – "the results count".

Thus, two aspects become clear. First, the various values are contradictory by nature, and it has not been possible to construct underlying assumptions, which could unite or dissolve the contrasting positions. Second, basic assumptions seem to gather around and form two separate value systems, which are mutually conflicting but internally fairly consistent.

The Cultural Pattern
These two value systems are seen as indications of a split culture consisting of two subcultures inscribed in a relatively weak overall cultural framework. The two groups (IT people versus administrative and sales people) are the central "carriers" of the two subcultures.

The subculture around the group of *information technology specialists* is dominated by a social group orientation, in spite of a tough language and a direct way of interpersonal confrontation at the artifactual level. A casual manner and extreme informality characterise this culture. This subculture is relatively open and friendly towards new persons, if they behave according to the language code, are informal and accept the "key-values" (especially "Do not brag or play Mr. know-all"). If you are once accepted and adopted by the group, you are fairly safe and it will take a lot to fall into discredit. Egalitarianism and practical experience are the dominant aspects of this subcultural pattern, together with an anti-authoritarian attitude. A prevalent aspect of the culture is group orientation. However, in certain matters, centred around their job function, a kind of professional pride or "shyness" was identified, as their jobs and methods were regarded private property and an individual matter.

The subculture among the *administrative staff and sales people* is dominated by an individual orientation. The culture is competitive and individualistic. Key guidelines are action, efficiency and productivity – "the shark ethic prevails.... eat the wounded" (Thompson, 1979). Consequently this group of persons also tends to be more willing to lay off persons, who do not show the expected results.

In this subculture ambitions are important, otherwise you will not get ahead in the system. An anti-authoritarian attitude is also dominant with the modification that persons with great power and charisma are likely to be treated with some respect, because they are capable of getting things done.

The Dynamics of the Culture

Looking at the history of Total, the split in culture is not that mysterious. Total has right from its start been based on systems development and has thrived so far on this strategy. The top manager and *founder* is a software specialist himself and, from time to time, still operates as project leader in the systems department. Total has no academic traditions, instead practical experience, entrepreneurial skills, good ideas and what has "worked", have been central elements in the success and rapid expansion which the company has experienced.

New groups of personnel have arrived at Total in the wake of the growth and expansion. Former dominance by (blue collar) information technology specialists is gradually being balanced by (white collar) sales and administrative personnel, who have their particular set of values and assumptions and code of conduct that is distinct from the group of information technology specialists. The cultural paradigm in Total is, thus, characterised by being divisive and split. The common base of reference or cultural pattern in which the subcultures are inscribed, are marked by a casual manner and high degree of informality at the artifactual level. Formal education, titles and "certificates" are not regarded as important. Practical experience and what you actually are capable of doing (the results), are what really count and unite the two somewhat different subcultural systems at the value level. Egalitarianism and a general anti-authoritarian attitude, are also dominant characteristics of the culture in Total and the only basic assumptions shared. Thus, the two subcultural systems are loosely coupled to each other, but internally fairly consistent. A common frame of reference, though relatively limited and weak, constitutes an overall cultural framework, which is capable of keeping the two contrasting subcultural systems together.

6.3   Datacentralen

History and Field of Activity

Datacentralen was founded in the late fifties with the explicit purpose of developing and carrying out data processing for the public sector (ministries, local and regional agencies, and other public institutions).[8] Today, Datacentralen is one of the main service bureau within the Danish IT field. Until now Datacentralen primarily has developed and maintained large, administrative IT systems for the public sector. Yet, Datacentralen has also handled technical tasks and IT services for enterprises within the private sector, and has furthermore provided IT systems for the international market. An issue in the development of Datacentralen's product profile has been the centralisation of computer capacity, which has inhibited local applications of IT systems at municipal and local institutions. The technological development and user demands have, though, forced Datacentralen to start working on decentralised IT systems (micro- and minicomputers). But Datacentralen's main income still derives from the large, centralised mainframe systems.

Datacentralen's formal organisation has been subjected to major structural changes during recent years. Until a few years ago the company was a functionally divided organisation with a systems department, a programmer department and an operation department. In 1985, following the new trends of service management and profit centres, the company went through a major reorganisation, guided by the service concept – "The Customer in Focus". Datacentralen was divisionalised and split up into a number of customer centres. By the end of 1986 Datacentralen employed about 1500 people. The balance between staff with some kind of formal IT education and the "autodidacts" (i.e., groups with no formal IT education) seems to be changing. During the last couple of years, the most important occupational group with a formal IT education now has become the "EDP-assistants".

A problem in Datacentralen regarding future development is the high turnover of personnel. The average turnover is about 15%, but in some centres as high as 25%, and in some project groups as high as 50%. Due to its status as a quasi-public company Datacentralen is not able to pay competitive wages. The result is often, that for example "EDP-assistants" leave for a private company, after two or three years, having obtained expertise in a given area of IT during their time at Datacentralen.

The Culture in Datacentralen
Artifacts
Datacentralen is located in the neighbourhood of Copenhagen. But you have to know the exact address because no signs or other physical directions tell you that you are approaching Datacentralen. The area is surrounded by a barbed-wire fence and you immediately associate it with a military camp. The building, which is withdrawn from the road, is enormous. There are many parking lots but apparently no kind of reservations. The place is characterised by anonymity and discretion as regards displays. At the main building neither signs nor flags or other items indicate who lives there. After passing two sets of doors, you enter the reception area. The light is subdued and the decorations remind you of a hotel lobby with modern art on the walls – all in all tasteful and discrete. By

know you have forgotten the barbed-wire fence but soon recall it when your purpose of visit is checked and you receive your numbered identity card. You are not allowed to "sneak" around alone – the colour of your identity card apparently says so – and you are "escorted" around the building. These arrangements were for "security" reasons, it was explained. The atmosphere in the building is characterised by silence and calmness. No shouting, loud laughter or hectic activity were observed in the corridors. Time clocks and an extended use of timetables for reporting of hours spent on particular activities, were examples of artifacts, which gave the first impression of control and bureau-cracy.

People in Datacentralen are informally dressed, in spite of the formal "Hotel lobby-like" atmosphere and the tasteful decorations described above. People placed higher in the hierarchy wear shirt, tie and sometimes a jacket, but in general the staff wear the traditional, casual "IT uniform" (i.e., jeans or cords together with a sweatshirt or shirt). The language code in Datacentralen is a bit rough, impudent and follows the technical macho code. Technical jargon consists of "shit" and "crap" metaphors, similar to the language code among the IT people in Total. Furthermore much of the jargon relates to drinking, girls, the former and present General Manager and technical issues. In general, the academics who were interviewed were low on jargon (nicknames, sayings, etc.) when compared to the IT people.

Corporate ceremonies in Datacentralen are first of all the celebrating and staging of major historical events. Examples are Datacentralen's twenty fifth anniversary and the celebration of "fidel" employee, having his or her company jubilee. The party club "Relax" is the main club and all employees are born members. "Relax" organises big employee-gatherings of various kinds (sports, fishing, wine-tasting, etc.). The patterns and the amount of the ceremonial and ritual activities in Datacentralen varied according to the age of the IT staff and the attitude of the management of the customer centre in question. Social networks created by the different clubs seem to be important for continuing tradition in the company. These clubs have been built up over the years by the employees. They are one of the mechanisms through which the culture is maintained and new members are socialised, for example, to traditions of spending time with colleagues outside working hours.

Datacentralen was "rich" on stories and they seemed to center around three themes : Bureaucracy, Managers, and Failures and Disasters.[9] They seem to be another important mechanism, through which the culture is maintained at Datacentralen.

Values and Basic Assumptions
Five dominant values were identified: "Controllare necesse est", "You do not fire people – stay and you shall be rewarded", "Big is beautiful", "Craftsman-ship is a cornerstone" and "Union membership is important". In the figure

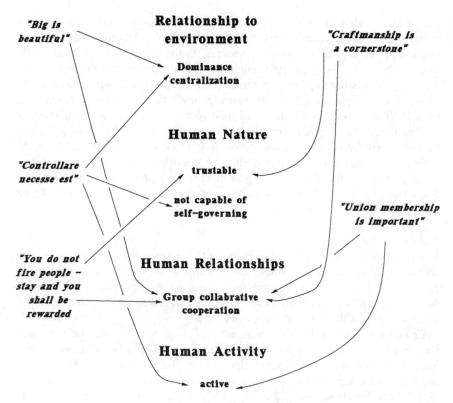

Figure II.5   Datacentralen – Values and Basic Assumptions
(Source: Pedersen and Sorensen, 1989)

below, the relationship between these five values and the categories of "basic assumptions" has been depicted.

This figure appears to signify some interesting aspects. First, the general impression one gets about the values is that they seem to be fairly consistent when one views their underlying premises. They are relatively consistent about the nature of human relationships as regards being cooperative and group collaborative. For example, a promotion practice rewarding the "fidel" employee who stays with the group (the company), is in accordance with this assumption. The group orientation is reflected in the values about "Big is beautiful", "Union membership" and "Craftsmanship". Concerning the nature of human activity, the "right" way for human beeings to behave is seen to be active and is illustrated by the values about "Control" and "Union membership". These values indicate both that you cannot just let things happen and you have to do something (e.g., "get organised" or "exercise control"). This assumption is in accordance with what the corporate identity or self-perception (in Schein's terms "Humanity's Relationship to Nature"), where centralisation, size and dominance are regarded as positive features. In the way values relate to "basic assumptions", the only "genuine" contradiction appears around the values: "no lay offs", "craftsmanship" and "control". They seem to be based on contrasting views about human nature. "Craftsmanship" and "No lay offs" are based on a view of human beeings as good and trustworthy – it is just a question about finding the "right" job and providing persons with the "right" job conditions, then they will be responsible and productive. Opposed to this view, "Control" reflects an assumption of human beeings as not reliable or at least not entirely capable of governing themselves – you must keep their noses to the grindstone and let them at least feel they are under surveillance, otherwise they will not be productive.

The Cultural Pattern

Even though several attempts have been made, it has not been possible to find or construct an assumption, which could explain and make sense of these contrasting views on the human nature. Yet, when the content of the value about "craftsmanship" was analysed more thoroughly and taken into account, a deeper understanding of this contradiction was reached.

Embedded in the value of "craftsmanship" is a pride in the company and feeling of belonging – especially for the older generation of "Datacentralene-ans". They tend to regard Datacentralen as their "baby". They identify with and are loyal to Datacentralen and therefore they are inclined to accept controlling aspects coming from their "baby". Moreover, the value of control seems primarily to be for an external audience and secondarily for internal use, signified by the ritual character of these efforts. The various artifacts are meant to signal to an external audience – for instance users – "confidence", "serious-ness", "professionalism" and "high degrees of security", because of the confidential character of the information Datacentralen possesses. Career employment based on seniority and the value of "No lay offs", internally reduces the experience of control as something threatening your employment or career, because you know that only severe violation of rules will have effects.

Concluding on the cultural pattern in Datacentralen, the culture is most properly described as being coherent and consistent in spite of these minor inconsistencies. The cultural paradigm is characterised by traditional "blue-collar worker" features at the levels of artifacts, values and basic assumptions. Informality as regards dress code and a lot of technical macho jargon can be observed at the artifactual level. At the value level union membership, good craftsmanship and what works is important, whereas formal education is not recognised. Concerning basic assumptions a distinct group orientation is prevalent and perceived of as a dichotomy between "us" (the workers' collective) and "them" (the management).

The Dynamics of the Culture

The history of Datacentralen, the start up and the early phase in the fifties, has been strongly influenced by the recruitment of "practitioners" and "autodidacts" of various kinds.[10]

For almost thirty years Datacentralen has recruited IT people, and a historically changing sets of social values among generations of IT people can be observed in the company. In that sense Datacentralen can be understood as a social system, reflecting conflicts of values from a wider societal culture. The expansion of Datacentralen, during the 1960s and 1970s, naturally implied that many of the new employees were younger people embedded in the youth culture of "1968". Many of the "oldtimers" at Datacentralen belong to the category of students from that time. Today, the new "fuel" to sustain this culture primarily comes from the academics, who are recruited and reeducated through internal job-training in Datacentralen. These academics are often thirty years old or more, and have a value orientation similar to the "oldtimers" in Datacentralen. Often they have also tasted the sour fruits of unemployment and bad wages and are more likely to appreciate the working conditions, the existence of the union, and other important values enhanced in the dominant culture in Datacentralen. But they do not affect the overall demographics much. Furthermore, the recruitment pattern in Datacentralen has changed over the last five to ten years. A growing number of people with formal education, for instance, humanists with IT courses and especially "EDP-assistants" have entered the labour market and Datacentralen.

This seems to suggest that the balance between the "practitioners" and the personnel with formal education may be reversed over time. As Datacentralen continues to expand, the company has to recruit a larger and larger proportion of new employees among young IT people – children of the eighties who do not share the values of the oldtimers at Datacentralen. They seem, in contrast to the "oldtimers" traditional worker-manager dichotomy, to be carrying values of a more non-political craftsman culture, and tend to be more individualistic, not considering themselves to be members of a larger collective. The young IT peoples' shared understanding is marked more by an orientation towards job content and obtainment of qualifications, accompanied by a consciousness about their market value and career prospects. Some "oldtimers" see the different value orientation of the young IT staff as a severe threat to their dominant culture. However, this threat does not appear to be real because the young IT people are actually leaving the company after a few years whereas the "oldtimers" stay and maintain the culture.

7   Discussion

7.1   The Empirical Findings

Returning to the initial research questions concerned with stability/dynamism and homogeneity/heterogeneity, the results of the case analyses create a distinct picture of the cultural patterns of Advice, Total and Datacentralen, which is summarised below.[11]

In the case of *Advice* the analysis was not as much a study of an established organisational culture as a study of *cultural founders and an emerging culture*. The company did not conform to the theoretical demands of the "group" in "Scheinian" terms, where the group is seen as a presumption for the existence of organisational culture. It has not yet taken in new members in the organisation and therefore no processes of socialisation of newcomers and handing over cultural norms and values have taken place. On this basis the culture is identified as emerging and in the stage of being formed. Advice was seen as being in a stage of "birth and early growth". Nevertheless, this exercise shows that it is both possible and rewarding to use cultural analysis as a framework for the understanding of even young and small firms like Advice. As to the homogeneity in the cultural pattern some contradictions and inconsistencies were found between a strong occupational individualism on the one hand and the collective social values on the other.

In the case of *Total*, the analysis revealed that the cultural pattern consisted of two mutually conflicting, but internally consistent cultural systems. The culture in this case, was characterised by being split and *divided into two subcultures* inscribed in a relatively weak overall cultural framework. These subcultures seemed to be based on, or at least to follow, occupational lines. Concerning the issue of homogeneity, this case proved to be marked by cultural heterogeneity at the organisational level and by homogeneity within the two subcultures. With regard to the question of dynamism a tendency was observed towards a change in the relative influence between the two subcultures and therefore marked Total's culture as *changing*. Total can be seen to be in a phase of "adolescent transition" (Larsen and Rogers, 1984) moving from "birth and early growth" to "organisational midlife". The framework has proved to be quite useful, in as far as you are capable of identifying, constructing and describing the culture as consisting of subcultures.

In the case of *Datacentralen*, and in contrast to the analyses of Advice and Total, it was concluded that a dominant culture existed. A common cultural paradigm was identified and with regard to homogeneity, the culture was seen as fairly homogeneous. Concerning the question of dynamism, change and transition did not appear to mark the case, on the contrary continuation and stability seemed to be more dominant features of the culture. On the basis of the present

	'Advice'	'Total'	Datacentralen
Artifacts			
Physical arrangements	X	X	X
Language	X	X	X
Traditions	–	X	X
Stories	X	–	X
Values			
	'Equal influence on working conditions'	'Treat people with consideration'	'Controllare necesse est'
	'High educations – High spirits'	'No lay-offs'	'You do not fire people – stay and you shall be rewarded'
	'We want to make proper consultancy'	'Do not brag or play Mr. Know-All'	
		'Promote yourself - the right way'	'Big is beautiful'
		'Get things done - the results counts'	'Craftsmanship is a cornerstone'
	'Ask before you do anything		'Union membership is important
Coherent values?	Partly	No	Yes

Figure II.6   Cultural Configurations in Advice, Total and Datacentralen

analysis Datacentralen was described as a *fairly homogeneous and stable culture* in a stage of "organisational maturity".

The cultural analysis of the three organisations has revealed three *different cultural patterns* and each pattern possesses its own "unique" features. Organisations may exhibit similar cultural features and have elements in common, but the *particular composition and patterning* of these cultural elements characterize and form the uniqueness of a given organisational culture.

	'Advice'	'Total'	Datacentralen
Basic assumptions			
Human nature	perfectible	perfectible/good potentially evil	trustable not capable of self- governing
Human activity	–	not too active	active
Human relationships	egalitarianism individualism	cooperative individualistic /competitive	group collaborative
Relations to environment	optimistic submission	–	centralization and dominance
Reality and Truth	(higher formal education)	practical experience	(non academic)
Culture	founders	subcultures	Corporate culture
The Dynamics of the Culture	emerging	changing	stable

Figure II.6 (cont.)   Cultural Configurations in Advice, Total and Datacentralen

As regards the questions of homogeneity/heterogeneity and stability/dynamism it has not been possible to give an unambiguous answer as the findings were more complex. However, it seemed as if the younger and smaller firms – Advice and Total – were characterised by more dynamism and change in the cultural pattern than was the case with the relatively older and larger IT firm, Datacentralen. This is not so surprising. What is more interesting is that the dynamism and change observed in these IT firms were accompanied by heterogeneity in the cultural pattern. However, on the basis of the present data it has not been possible to specify or document further the nature of the relationship between homogeneity/heterogeneity and stability/dynamism with regard to dependent and independent variables.

7.2   A Theoretical Discussion

The Hierarchical Structure of Schein's Model
The hierarchical nature of Schein's model is rather obvious, although it is not stated explicitly. The model is hierarchical in the sense that, Schein treats basic assumptions as the essence of culture, whereas the other two levels are conceived of as mere manifestations and symptoms of the culture. Thus, the level of basic assumptions is perceived of as the "real" culture. Furthermore, the value level is viewed as "more" culture than the artifactual level, as values over time may turn into basic assumptions and, hence, culture – mediated by the cognitive transformation process. Whereas artifacts have the doubtful honour of remaining mere manifestations of culture. The model is, however, not hierarchical as regards the level of awareness as the value level exhibits a higher degree of consciousness than both "artifacts" and "basic assumptions".

The hierarchical nature is also sustained by the graphical presentation of the model, which shows no direct relationship between the level of artifacts and the level of basic assumptions. This seems to indicate that "artifacts" are related to culture ("basic assumptions") only indirectly through "values".

This is a clear indication of Schein's low priority of "artifacts" in a cultural context. The present study of organisational cultures – and other cultural studies (e.g., Martin et al., 1983; Hirsh and Andrews, 1983; Beyer and Trice, 1987; Molin, 1987; Gagliardi, 1990) – suggest that "artifacts" are very "rich" on cultural information and much more than mere surface manifestations. This implies, that Schein underestimates the importance of "artifacts".

This does not mean that you can obtain complete information and infer directly from "artifacts" to culture, as Schein correctly points out :

".. "artifacts" are easy to obtain, but difficult to interpret" (Schein, 1985, p. 14).

It is also important to note that meanings *do not exist* in artifacts. They are *assigned* to events and symbolic forms by people, who perceive and interpret their content and context, as Smircich (1983a) has pointed out. On the other hand, this does not justify the exclusion of "artifacts", as Schein does, by reducing the category to "surface level manifestations" and mere "cultural symptoms". At this point Schein neglects that "artifacts" are important means by which the culture is transmitted and communicated among organisational members.

The results from the present analysis did not suggest that "artifacts" should be placed in a secondary position. In the case of "Total" for example, many artifacts gave clear indications of the split culture in the organisation. For example, the dress-code of the information technology specialists was rather informal and casual, wearing T-shirts and jeans, whereas the administrative staff and the sales people had a more formal dress-code, typically wearing tie, white shirt and sometimes a suit. Another example is the language in "Total". The information technology specialists possessed a language characterised by an extended use of nicknames, technical jargon, metaphores etc., whereas the administrative staff and the sales people in general were very low on jargon.

The Transformation of Values into Basic Assumptions

Unfortunately, Schein is not very clear as regards the value level in his model. He briefly touches the issue of distinguishing between "espoused values" and "values-in-use", although he does not directly utilise the concepts. Schein provides us with very few directions about the nature of the value level apart from stating that values are debatable and at a higher level of awareness.

"Values" do not appear as homogeneous and consistent as Schein presents them to be. By not discussing the consistency problems some severe implications arise for the model. If one recalls Schein's model, one of the dynamics is, that "values" are transformed into "basic assumptions", when a solution to a problem seems to work repeatedly. In this way, the value level in Schein's model becomes very important for the model, because this level becomes the only "channel" through which "basic assumptions" can be altered and new cultural patterns are produced. In relation to this issue a problem is that Schein does not discuss how the agreement process takes place concerning this transformation process. Schein seems to take for granted that it must happen and that it is quite simple and obvious for the participants to judge and agree on whether or not a solution has worked well. Even from an individual psychological point of view, such a process of learning is very complicated and full of traps. This has been argued, for example, by March (1981) talking about "superstitious learning" and by Weick (1979) who argues that intention and action are often loosely coupled within a single individual. There seems to be no reasons to believe that learning processes are less complicated at an organisational level (cf. Orton and Weick, 1990).

In contrast to the perception of organisations as highly complex entities, Schein's view on organisations and learning processes is distinguished by political processes, ambiguity and loose couplings. If the latter perception of organisations is valid the process of transformation of values into "basic assumptions" becomes very complicated and doubtful.

Basic Assumptions: A Consistent System?

The last point to discuss regarding Schein's cultural model concerns his notion of "basic assumptions". The basic assumptions are defined as "the essence of culture". According to Schein when:

"...we do surface them, the cultural pattern suddenly clarifies and we begin to feel we really understand what is going on and why" (Schein, 1985, p. 21).

But rather than constituting a logically coherent system of assumptions, and consequently a cultural paradigm as Schein suggests, results from the present analysis indicate that the paradigms consist of a variety of apparently *contradictory* and *inconsistent* assumptions. This implies that conflicting values and contrasting basic assumptions can co-exist within a culture. The argument is parallel to Schein's own view on the possibility of conflicting "artifacts" and "values". Yet, it seems as if Schein does not dare to take the ultimate step, but "protects" basic assumptions from conflict and loose coupling.

One might likewise argue that "basic assumptions" are not as "universal", as Schein tends to perceive, but instead depend on time and context. Weick's reflections about the relations between attitudes and action (Weick, 1976), and the ideas presented by Cohen and March (1974) that events in an organisation seem to be temporarily related rather than logically related, sustain this argument, too.

Some of Schein's constructions and attempts to make sense at a higher level and, thus, restore "rationality", tend to be somewhat "artificial" and it can be questioned whether they "enrich" our understanding of the culture. By reducing observed inconsistencies and paradoxes to problems that are solved by "underlying" basic assumptions, a danger exists that crucial and complex features of the cultural patterns are oversimplified and lost. Therefore, it is debatable to assume – as Schein does in his model – that both human beings and social systems operate from one consistent base of assumptions.

8 Issues for Further Research

The present discussion obviously has some implications for cultural research. First, artifacts contain a lot of cultural information which clearly ought to be explored further. Detailed studies on specific artifacts ought to be carried out and, the characteristics of the various artifacts as well as their influence on the cultural pattern should be explored further.

Second, a discussion about the value level in general is needed – for instance, whether the value level is to be viewed as an independent category. If so, one ought to be able to define and specify the concept of values further than Schein has done already. This could, for example, be done by distinguishing between various types and dimensions of values, such as between "espoused values" and "values-in-use", "internal" and "external" values, "occupational" and "social" values, etc.

Finally, Schein seems to be caught in rationality and consistency as regards the concept of "basic assumptions". The notion of an underlying base of reference may prove right in some instances, but a search along the lines of loose coupling (Weick, 1976 and Orton and Weick, 1990) and ambiguity (Martin and Meyerson, 1988) may turn out to be more promising. So far the concept of loose coupling is neither very developed in conceptual terms nor widely used in empirical studies, and further cultural research could be enriched by taking this perspective more into account.

Notes

1   Several persons have contributed importantly to the emergence of this article. I would like to thank my colleague Jesper Steen Sorensen for good collaboration and co-writing on our book, "Organizational Cultures in Theory and Practice", (Pedersen and Sorensen, 1989). Many ideas in this article are results of this collaboration. I would also like to thank Mary Jo Hatch and Joan Greenbaum for helpful comments on previous drafts of this article. An earlier version of this article has been presented at 'The 3rd International SCOS Conference on The Symbolics of Corporate Artifacts' in Milano, 1987.

2   See Alvesson and Berg (1988) concerning the expansion of cultural research within organisational sociology.

3   See Jones (1989) on the problems of doing ethnography in organisations and, Siehl and Martin (1989) on measuring organisational culture.

4   See Schultz (1990) and Hatch (1991) as other examples of research extending the Scheinian framework.

5   It is beyond the scope and limits of this article to make a detailed account of the various positions and contributions within contemporary cultural theory as regards organisations. See, for example, Alvesson and Berg, 1988; Pedersen and Sorensen, 1989; Schultz, 1990 for more detailed presentations of the contributions to cultural theory.

6   The various categories of 'artifacts' have been qualified and defined further in Pedersen and Sorensen (1989). For example a given 'artifact' must fullfil certain criteria in order to be labelled, e.g., a ritual.

7   The distribution of interviews in the three companies was as follows: 4 interviews in Advice, 13 interviews in Total and 14 interviews in Datacentralen, were conducted.

8   See Pedersen (1991) for more details on the history of Datacentralen.

9   It is beyond the limits of the present article to go into detail with these stories. For more details see Pedersen and Sorensen (1989).

10   As opposed to Datacentralen other institutions within computer industry (e.g. Regnecentralen and NEUCC) were influenced by an academic milieu.

11   Source: Pedersen and Sorensen, 1989.

Chapter III
The Unisys Merger – Cultural Perspectives on Information Technology Firms in Transition[1]

Jesper Strandgaard Pedersen

1   Introduction

During the last decades a growing interest in the symbolic aspects of organisations has emerged within organisational research. Under very different labels
symbolic and interpretive aspects of social organisations have been studied and
discussed. In "Leadership in Administration" (1957) Selznick stated that, "to
institutionalize is to infuse with value beyond the technical requirements of the
task at hand", introducing such concepts as "Organizational Character" and
"Institutionalization" for the discussion of the phenomenon. "The social
construction of reality" (Berger and Luckmann, 1966), "Theories-in-use"
(Argyris and Schoen, 1978), "Enacted Environments" (Weick, 1979) and
"Organizational Paradigms" (Pfeffer, 1981) are other examples of labels that
have been introduced as conceptual suggestions for capturing the symbolic and
interpretive sides of organisations.

Nevertheless, the most recent and significant stream of contributions within
organisational sociology approaches and discusses the symbolic aspects of
organisations in terms of "organisational culture" (e.g., Pettigrew, 1979;
Hofstede, 1980; Smircich, 1983a; Frost et al., 1985; Schein, 1985; Meyerson
and Martin, 1987; Alvesson and Berg, 1988; Gagliardi, 1990).

Even though the culture literature represents a fairly heterogeneous body of
research, some areas of agreement have been reached. One of the areas of
agreement seems to be that organisational cultures provide stability and
continuity (Pettigrew, 1979; Louis, 1983; Frost et al, 1985; Schein, 1985; Molin,
1987; Schultz, 1990).

Change in organisational cultures has as often been dealt with as a question of
planned change and management intervention, a perception which also draws on
a view of culture as securing continuity and stability. Culture is seen as a
preserving force that management has to consider and deal with when transformation and change is required in an organisational setting. In spite of this overall

tendency to emphasize culture as a preserving force, other contributions have, however, more or less explicitly pointed at forces that could create culture change.

The purpose of this chapter is to improve our understanding of the dynamics of culture change. This will be done by analysing a case of organisational change and transformation. The case study will describe and examine a merger process – the Unisys merger – from a cultural perspective. The Unisys merger is an example of the impact of a world wide merger on a local subsidiary and, the study will focus on the Danish subsidiary of the Unisys corporation. Four models of culture change will be presented, each suggesting certain dynamics and forces to be important for the understanding of culture change. The post merger cultural pattern will be analysed by applying the four models in order to identify some of the forces and dynamics behind the culture changes.

2   The Unisys Merger – a Case of Culture Change

The Merger from a World-wide Perspective

Unisys is a fairly young, *international information technology firm* (hereafter IT firm) headquartered in the US. It is a result of the recent merger between two relatively large international IT companies, Burroughs and Sperry, both based in US. These two companies started the merger process during fall 1986 and, they formally merged in January 1987. Since this merger, the new company, Unisys, has become one of the largest IT firms world-wide with a 10 billion dollar turnover, offices in more than 100 countries and around 100.000 employees. Technically, the merger was "a hostile takeover", as Burroughs US bought Sperry US.

The Unisys merger was a horisontal merger (i.e., identical products and same or different markets). This type of merger typically "can seek to consolidate operations and thus serve two firms clients with little more than one firm's resources", (Walter, 1985, p. 311-12). Napier (1989) refers to this type of merger as "collaborative" and states that synergy is a major motive in this merger type. Consolidation as well as synergy seemed to have been major motives behind the Unisys merger, as can be seen from the following.

The *espoused philosophy* behind the merger appears to have been based on the perception that the competition within the IT industry is becoming increasingly tougher and the idea that "bigger is better",

"You have to be big (a 10 billion dollars company is explicitly mentioned) within the IT industry today in order to survive in the long run"
(Source: Company material and business journals).

Apart from this general notion ("bigger is better"), three related reasons for the merger have been given:

1. Greater credibility among customers effected by size;
2. Increased profitability as a result of rationalistion and common cost base;[2]
3. Complementarity concerning markets and client bases geographically as well as by industry/sector

(Source: Merger consultants and company material).

Together with the aim of corporate diversity, corporate growth, consolidation and synergy are some of the most common reasons for mergers and acquisitions (Napier, 1989; Nahavandi and Malekzadeh, 1988), so in this respect, the Unisys merger was not different from other mergers and acquisitions.

The Principles for the Merger

Even though the merger technically has been a hostile takeover, Burroughs US stressed very early that they did not regard the acquisition of Sperry US as a conquest. Instead of the traditional subordination of the acquired company, Burroughs US stated that they wanted to form a new company based on the ideas of equality and partnership. This was contrary to most mergers and acquisitions where the typical pattern regarding related mergers has been that the acquirer has imposed its own culture and practices on the acquired company (Sales and Mirvis, 1984; Walter, 1985; Nahavandi and Malekzadeh, 1988).

The guiding principles, behind the formation of this new company as well as the merger process as such, have been stated to be:

a) Partnership (not a conquest)
b) Unity (one company)
c) Meritocracy (the most successful wins)
d) Dispatch (move fast)

(Source: Unisys Merger Consultant and company material).

Apart from being one of the largest mergers in international business, the Unisys merger was also interesting because it seemed to be a merger between two companies that appeared to be as different as day and night. When rumours about a forthcoming merger started to circulate, owing to this difference, the possible merger between these two companies was regarded with some scepticism by the IT industry and business in general as indicated by various articles in newspapers and business journals.

Unisys DK – a Danish Subsidiary

The Danish Unisys subsidiary is a relatively large IT company, in Danish terms, with about 250 employees and an annual turnover of around 65 million US dollar. The Danish office is a sales office regarding hardware and a production firm concerning software. On the software side it produces and develops specific software systems for customer applications on top of the sale of standard software packages. Unisys DK resembles the majority of the subsidiaries of international IT companies located in Denmark.

In Denmark the merger has been considered a success. Industry specific journals and general business journals emphasise the economic benefits from the merger. For instance, compared to the aggregated results of the two commpanies from the year before the merger, a 20% growth was experienced the first year after the merger. Furthermore the Danish subsidiary has shown the highest growth rate among the Scandinavian Unisys firms. This apparent financial success is noteworthy as it is claimed that studies show that between 50-80% of all mergers are financial disappointments (Marks and Mirvis, 1986). As to the disadvantages resulting from the merger, the turnover of personnel is reported to have been relatively high in the first year after the merger (16% of which half were involuntary).

Background of the Two Merging Companies

Burroughs DK
Prior to the merger, Burroughs in Denmark, was the smallest of the two merging companies with about 80 employees. Several observations indicate that it was a company, if not in crisis, then a company with many problems.

Burroughs was not doing very well from an economic point of view, as they were losing market share and facing stagnation in business volume. Six years ago the two companies had been equally large, but, at the time of the merger, Burroughs in Denmark was half the size of Sperry. Burroughs had tried to cope with this stagnation by adopting a *cost reduction strategy*.

Burroughs also seemed to have had a *management problem* and had experienced a rapid turnover of General Managers. Over the years, the average seniority of General Managers in Burroughs has been 2 years, resulting in a lack of continuity and stability in management. Another indication of this management problem was that the Danish subsidiary, for a certain period of time, had been under *"Swedish Hegemony"*. This means that Burroughs in Denmark was controlled by Scandinavian regional management team, located in Sweden, where each and every function had an external, Swedish boss. This created a lot of tensions and problems between the Danish management team and the Swedish management team. The period when they were under "Swedish

Hegemony" is surrounded with an aura of embarrassment and the employees are definitely not considering it a glorious period in the history of Burroughs.

Burroughs has traditionally recruited management from inside the organisation by promoting competent IT systems people to management positions. Some informants claimed that this had been part of the reason for the management problems. As one informant stated it,

"Management consisted of competent systems people, but they could not manage or organise... The General Managers (who were recruited from inside) were never available. The last General Manager (recruited from outside) was okey, the second last was invisible and was fired. The third last was a Swedish General Manager, appointed by headquarters. He was very unpopular, and quickly returned to Sweden."

From an organisational point of view Burroughs appears to have been a rather *centralised organisation*, characterised by an elaborate hierarchy (a 7- link chain of command between Burroughs DK and US headquarter was mentioned) with extensive use of *formal procedures* and rules (e.g., MBO had been utilised and was claimed to have worked in Burroughs). Moreover the organisation had been *tightly controlled* by elaborate planning and reporting systems, leaving limited room for autonomy and individual decision-making. An informant described Burroughs as,

"Very centralised with a seven-link chain of command from country level to US headquarters. Salaries were to be approved by two levels above the country level, which from time to time made it difficult to solve local problems."

A tradition also existed in Burroughs for separating systems people and sales people organisationally in separate, functionally based units. As regards business practices Burroughs was described as a kind of technical leader (compared to Sperry), but with almost no or very little efforts made concerning Public Relations (PR). Burroughs was depicted as rather anonymous, discrete and with a low profile concerning external communication, spending almost no money on advertising and image-building (in line with their cost reduction strategy mentioned earlier). Instead, Burroughs appeared to have valued control and formalisation. Consider the following statement from a former Burroughs employee:

"Another difference between the two may be that in Sperry they were used to quite a lot of autonomy and almost no control, whereas Burroughs were more tightly controlled through reports etc., which I personally find necessary, because of the need for information about what goes on."

The language in former Burroughs mirrored this value of control and formalisation. Jargon and metaphors used were drawn from a "bureaucrats' world" where "reporting", "planning" and "control" were frequently used concepts and seen as an integral part of work routines. Sometimes the jargon also had a military flavour ("getting my troops in line", "I will get honour and glory", etc.).

Control and formalisation were considered natural and necessary – a fact of life – and were reflected in norms about "sticking to the rules".

Sperry DK

In Denmark, the former Sperry, with about 160 people employed, was the larger of the two companies at the time of the merger. In contrast to Burroughs, Sperry was doing well, in economic terms, as their business volume was expanding. Their business volume had doubled over the last three years before the merger and the number of employees had been growing steadily again after a major crisis in the mid 1970s that resulted in a massive lay-off of personnel (25-50%), referred to as "The Black Friday".[3]

Part of the financial success which Sperry has experienced since then was attributed to a change in orientation and identity. Sperry was claimed to have changed, in the mid 1980s, from a technical orientation to a market orientation. This change took place in connection with a new product line and is portrayed as a shift from sales of hardware to sales of solutions, or in other words from being an IT firm in the IT industry to becoming a sales firm in the IT industry. Sperry's strategy since then can be characterised as an "improving sales" strategy with a focus on results.

Sperry has been described as a *horizontal organisation* with only 3 layers between Sperry DK and the Sperry headquarters in the US. A tradition existed in Sperry for structurally integrating sales people and IT systems people in market based units.

Organisational life in former Sperry appeared to have been hectic, chaotic and at times somewhat frustrating, and less structured and formalised than in Burroughs. As a specific example, one informant mentioned, that MBO had been introduced and tried, but did not work in Sperry (in contrast to Burroughs where MBO apparently worked together with other reporting systems). *Extensive autonomy* in decision-making was reported to have dominated the daily routines in Sperry (e.g., you had a greater discretion in hiring and setting salaries compared to Burroughs).

A variety of *social clubs and social activities* among the organisational members was an important part of organisational life in Sperry. Social contacts and personal networking were valued as means to achieve your goals. The exchange of information and social control stemming from these mutual activities may be seen as substitutes for more formal coordination and control systems.

Information and openness internally and externally were valued among Sperry employees and managers alike. The existence of an internal newsletter mirrored this value and a reputation for being good at Public Relations (PR) and getting information out of the organisation sustained this, too. The General Manager and his management style were explicitly mentioned by several informants as an example of the openness and information which characterised the former Sperry.

In line with this emphasis on openness, it was regarded "natural" to make mistakes and take risks. The problem would be to hide mistakes and not admit it, with the consequence that they became disasters later on. This value for openness and information can be seen as the organisational response and way of regulating the extensive autonomy confronted in an organisation with few formal control measures. Like mistake and risk, chance and luck were also considered and recognised as a fact of life. This is, for example, reflected in the verbal forms used which are dominated by a player's jargon and metaphors ("A-chain/B-chain, Co-jockey, Scoring positions", etc.).

Differences and Similarities

The former Burroughs appears to had been dominated by an orientation towards formal policies, directions, rules and procedures with extensive use of planning and reporting – organisational life is described as "structured", as summarised in Figure III.1. below. In contrast to this the former Sperry seems to had been dominated by a target and day-to-day orientation. At times it was a very hectic and frustrating organisation to work in, but also with an emphasis on people, informal contacts and networking across the formal hierarchy (see Figure III.1.).

The former Burroughs and the former Sperry appear to differ concerning their view on *uncertainty*. Sperry seems to be relatively comfortable with uncertainty and to regard it as a positive and dynamic factor – a fact of life and a challenge. Burroughs, on the other hand, conceives of uncertainty as a potential threat which has to be fought, avoided or minimised.

In spite of these differences, the two companies were also similar with regard to certain features, as summarized in figure III.2.

These two companies were apparently quite different along several dimensions and therefore it seems surprising that they managed to merge. The following citation from an informant illustrates very well the surprise for insiders surrounding the announcement of the forthcoming merger.

"The merger of Sperry and Burroughs was quite unexpected, but after the first astonishment and anxiety a very exiting process."

The process of post-merger integration that was to follow concerned different types of integration. These are procedural integration (accounting systems, appraisal systems etc.), integration of physical assets (product lines, production systems, technologies) and, finally, socio-cultural integration, which according to Shrivastava (1986, p. 65-66) is the most critical type of integration. The following section describes the merger process, which these two seemingly different companies have gone through in their attempt to transform and integrate themselves into a new company.

	Burroughs	Sperry
Power Base	Acquirer	Acquired
	Small (DK)	Large (DK)
	Stagnation Phase	Expansion Phase
Internal Org. Traditions and Routines	Control and Formalisation	Autonomy and Informal Networking
	Planning Orientation	Day-to-Day Orientation
	IT Management	Non-IT Management
	Separation (IT/Sales people)	Integration (IT/Sales people)
	Bureaucracy Metaphor	Players' Metaphor
External Business Practice	Cost Reduction Strategy	Improving Sales Strategy
	Centralised Org. (7 links DK-US)	Horizontal Org. (3 links DK-US)
	Low profile	Public Relations

Figure III.1   Overview of the Two Merging Companies

Both firms:
– were US based
– had a common background in IT
– emphasized job security
– had prior experiences of external control

Figure III.2   Similarities

The Merger Process

Technically, the merger was a *hostile take-over* wherein Burroughs US had acquired Sperry US. A take-over like this typically creates a superior-inferior relationship between the two parties involved (Sales and Mirvis, 1984; Walter,

1985; Napier, 1989). But as Burroughs did not view Sperry as a conquest and, instead, stated that they wanted to build a new organisation based on partnership, unity and meritocracy, a different situation was created. However, for that reason, the merger was viewed with some scepticism and uncertainty by Burroughs employees in Denmark.

Even though Burroughs DK technically was the acquirer, it was put in a rather *awkward position*, owing to the fact, that it was only half the size of Sperry DK and had been less successful than its merging partner. Therefore Burroughs DK could easily foresee a situation in which it was to play an inferior role in the forthcoming merger because of the meritocracy principle guiding the process of what to select from the two former organisations concerning management, staff, administrative systems, etc.

The meritocracy principle, thus, installed a more complex and reversed form of superior-inferior relation between the two companies. A former Burroughs employee has expressed it the following way,

"Regarding the merger we were very proud to begin with having "bought" Sperry. But the next day it was a new situation as the philosophy was to let the best/bigger of the two in each country be in charge. At that point in time, we experienced the situation as subordination and here the information is essential for the organisation."

The news about the merger was announced from the US headquarters by the chairman of the Unisys Corporation (the former Burroughs chairman). In line with the meritocracy principle, the General Manager of the former Sperry was selected, by US headquarters, to be the General Manager in charge of the formation of the new company and the further *management selection process*. The General Manager from the former Burroughs decided to leave the company as a consequence of this decision.

A commonly experienced problem in (horizontal) mergers is redundancy of personnel, especially at high levels – the *"Two-of-a-kind-problem"* (Sales and Mirvis, 1984; Marks and Mirvis, 1986; Napier, 1989). The newly appointed General Manager of the Danish subsidiary also faced this problem when he selected the next level of managers (13 candidates for 7 positions) after a two months selection process during fall 1986. During this period several full day seminars, held away from the firms, drove this selection process. The result was that former Sperry managers got four of the seven management positions. Former Burroughs managers occupied two positions and the last manager was hired from outside. Two of the four downgraded former Burroughs managers left, whereas the two downgraded former Sperry managers stayed. All downgraded managers were offered positions as vice-managers according to the principle that all Sperry managers got Burroughs vice-managers and the other way around, to represent both former firms at the management level.

A 10% *cut back in personnel* was announced from US headquarters in connection with the merger, equivalent to 22 persons in Denmark. This was made effective before moving together. In Burroughs as well as in Sperry, this problem was solved by what was referred to as "soft methods", meaning early retirements, voluntary job-shifts, notice many months in advance, etc. A statement from a former Sperry employee about getting rid of "stowaways" and "dead wood", nevertheless indicated that some people were laid off in Sperry. However, what seemed to be of importance in relation to these cutbacks was the *timing*. The cutbacks were implemented *prior* to the integration and as such perceived as belong to the history of the two former firms and *not as a part of* the history of the new company (Pedersen, 1991).

Three months after commencing on the merger the new management was put in place and all departments had been merged. Management in Denmark had decided that personnel from each department should move to one location even though the new building, which Sperry already had under construction, was only five months ahead. This decision of moving the departments together physically was mentioned repeatedly as being very important for the further integration of the two companies.[4]

In the creation and integration of the new company a new name for the firm had been chosen by US headquarters, after an internal, world-wide competition, that brought 30.000 proposals. A *grand ceremony* and PR event with a press conference, including direct phone connections abroad, was made out of the announcement of the winning name, sent in by a systems consultant from US. From the point in time where the new name was announced, the two pre-merger firms were consequently referred to as "the *former* Burroughs and the *former* Sperry", indicating that the two companies were to be regarded as "dead" and belong to the past. With regard to physical-material artifacts provided by US headquarters, the new logo and company colour have been mentioned as symbolic means of importance for the integration of the two companies during the merger process.

The Post-Merger Unisys Culture

The post-merger cultural pattern in Unisys appeared to be fairly homogeneous and was marked by a distinct influence and continuity of former Sperry's work-practices, values and beliefs. Post-merger life can be characterised as *"a modified Sperry world"*, as an informant expressed it.

The former Sperry managers dominated the management team, and former Sperry principles concerning organisation and administration have been adopted (e.g., the integration of sales and systems people). Likewise corporate social activities (e.g., social clubs and corporate newsletters) were continued from the former Sperry. The cultural tradition for being *extroverted* and conscious concerning image building through PR, commercials and other forms of advertisement, also originated from the former Sperry belief system. Another expression of the *belief in information and communication* continued from

Sperry was evident concerning internal communication, where *honesty, openness and truth* are the keywords, as expressed in the norm "if something is going wrong, you'd better tell about it". With regard to Burroughs's influence on organisational routines more structure, control and formalisation was reported to being implemented after the merger.

The post-merger culture is highly *oriented towards results*, reflected in the way status and prestige is determined and in the associated language. Consider, for example, the following description of how you get status and prestige.

"The activities that produce visible results give status. We have an A- chain and a B-chain....If you want to get on the A-chain, then you have to get involved and get into scoring positions, that is to take customers ashore."

The result orientation is a continuity of former Sperry beliefs and is further nurtured by the demands about financial performance and reports imposed upon the subsidiary from the US headquarters. But, maybe more importantly, it is also internally sustained by the value of *self-determination*, expressed in the widely shared belief following.

"As long as our financial performance is good and we live up to our targets, then we will keep our autonomy."[5]

Another consequence of the result orientation was that the company had to lay off people as the IT industry in Denmark stagnated. This practice was presented as new and was to a certain extent seen as both embarrassing and touchy, as it challenged a deeply rooted value of *job security*, which seems to be shared by both former Burroughs and former Sperry employees. A change in recruitment practice away from hiring IT oriented personnel and towards recruiting and employing personnel, preferably with higher education and some kind of professional background, is another example of change which is going on in Unisys.

The *corporate identity and self-perception* in Unisys DK is that of being "a small piece in the big game", and being a part of an international corporation. Consider, for example, the following statement which also reflects the result orientation mentioned above.

"It is celebrated when Unisys DK attains its target. The company is very result oriented. Unisys DK is only a small piece in a conglomerate of 100.000 persons."

The subsidiary's identity and perception of the external environment in the form of the international corporation is somewhat ambiguous. On the one hand, the external relation is offering the subsidiary some benefits in the form of increased *credibility*, resources and potential for survival in the IT industry ("Bigger is Better") and, thus, is associated with job-security. On the other hand, the Danish subsidiary also experiences the international corporation as constraining the subsidiary by way of financial obligations, general rules and procedures that are not geared specifically to meet the conditions of the Danish IT field. For example, budgets are imposed on the subsidiary, which do not allow for the present market situation. The whole system is affected when the budgets are exceeded. It is in relation to the latter experience about being controlled, that we shall understand the self-perception of being "a small piece in the big game" and the more comforting belief that "as long as our financial performance is good and we live up to our targets, then we will keep our autonomy". Unisys's DK culture can be summarized as:

– Belief in information and openness
– Orientation towards results
– Emerging control and formalisation
– Belief in self-determination
– Value job-security
– Corporate identity – a small piece in the big game
– Improved credibility ('Bigger is better')

Figure III.3   Overview of the Unisys DK Culture

The incorporation and integration of the two former cultures into one fairly coherent frame of reference is still going on. First and foremost the cultural pattern and the daily routines and practices are a continuation from the former Sperry. However, some new practices and values are also emerging. The question, therefore, is how to understand the dynamics of culture? What are the processes and forces behind culture change? In the following the dynamics behind cultural continuity and change will be explored further in theoretical terms before returning to the merger case.

3   Culture Change Models within Organisation Theory

Even though the culture research seems to have reached some level of consensus regarding a number of issues, culture researchers appear to differ concerning the question of the dynamics of culture change (Pedersen, 1991).

One issue is focused on the homogeneity of the cultural pattern and the degree of rationality regarding the process of change. Here, one body of research tends to view this as a *calculated* process through which organisations learn what solutions to a given problem work and which do not. Solutions are learned and stored in the organisational "mind" as knowledge, for example, in cultural forms, routines or standard operating procedures. This body of research has a

		Internal	External
Image	Calculated	Leadership	Learning
of			
culture	Compromised	Intergroup	Local Adaptation

Figure III.4   Origin and Location of Forces

tendency to present a unicultural view on organisation cultures, which emphasises integration, consensus, congruence and consistency.

Another body of research is more skeptical concerning the rationality behind this kind of learning processes. The outcome is not viewed as "solutions" but rather as *compromised responses* that are likely to be inconsistent, random and dysfunctional. These responses are as often seen as constraints for optimal and functional action ("myths", "superstitious learning", "hypocrisy", "institutionalism", etc.). A multicultural perception of organisations is typically depicted by this body of research and with an emphasis on differentiation, conflict and inconsistency.[6]

Another issue that divides the various researchers is the location of the forces that trigger off and affect culture change. Here, one stream of research looks for and finds the primary occasions and forces for change in the *internal* organisational context, whereas another stream of research is more occupied with the role of the *external* environment as the prime cause for change.

The following are suggested as dimensions of culture change models:[7]
Below, each quadrant will be treated as a separate model with its own distinct features and dynamics. The models will be elaborated and a more detailed explanation will be presented. All four models are based on the assumption that various degrees of tensions and contrasts in different areas of organisational life generate dynamics and forces of change.

The Leadership Model (internal and calculated)
According to this model, culture change is viewed as a result of a leadership process (e.g., Clark, 1972; Pettigrew, 1979; Pfeffer, 1981; Peters and Waterman, 1982; Deal and Kennedy, 1982; Gagliardi, 1986; Kilmann, Saxton and Serpa, 1986; Robbins, 1988).

In this model the tension is between the management and the employees – as often the individual (the "star" or "father figure") versus the collective. Leadership is seen as the prime source of renewal. The role of *the founder* is one suggestion which is often emphasised as important for understanding the present organisational culture (Schein, 1983). According to this view, the present cultural pattern is seen as a reflection of the values and beliefs of the founder and leader (e.g., Watson in IBM, Olsen at DEC, Jobs in Apple, Bech at

Regnecentralen, Olsen at Datacentralen, Rovsing at CR-84). A change in the values and beliefs of the founder is assumed to affect a change in cultural pattern for the entire organisation according to this perspective.[8]

A variant of this management-centred view is the emphasis put on *second generation charismatic leaders*. Such individuals are formal leaders, often Managing Directors (CEOs), who were not involved in the actual founding of the company. Instead they thrive on *symbolic management* and change the organisational culture through their actions (e.g., Carlzon in SAS, Treybig at Tandem, Iacocca at Chrysler).

In both of the versions the leadership-centred model depicts culture as marked by homogeneity, clarity, congruence, coherence, consistency and integration (Meyerson and Martin, 1987). Culture is portrayed as an instrument to achieve specified goals and through which to exercise control, thereby implying a strong element of calculation and intention. Organisations are seen as *having* cultures in contrast to a view of organisations as *being* cultures (Smircich, 1983b). Consider the following passage from Robbins (1988) as an illustration of this line of thought:

"The actions of top management also have a major impact on the organization's culture. Through what they say and how they behave, senior executives establish norms that filter down through the organization about whether risk taking is desirable; what appropriate dress; what actions will pay off in terms of pay raises, promotions, and other rewards; and the like." (p. 213)

The leadership model focuses on a single (or a few) central actor(s) exercising vision and direction and, the mode of explanation is based on the forces of dominance, loyalty and acceptance.

The Learning Model (external and calculated)
A second attempt to explain the dynamics behind organisational culture is the learning model, which emphasises the *collective experience of success and failure* as a process causing changes in the cultural pattern. The tension in this model is between the existing solutions based on past experiences and the new problems that the organisation faces. This model presents culture change as a result of a collective learning process in relation to problems and critical events. Culture is seen as a product of historical experiences. Changes in the external context (critical incidents, crises, etc.) create situations where new solutions have to be worked out in order to cope with these problems.

The idea of this model is that the *members* of a particular organisation face some problems and respond to them in the form of solutions worked out collectively. By processes of trial and error, experiential learning or selecting from a pool of standard operating procedures, the members are expected to learn from experience and in this way a cultural pattern is formed and changed. The cultural pattern is seen as a storage of knowledge based on accumulated experience (e.g., Argyris and Schoen, 1978; Dyer, 1982; Christensen and Molin, 1983; Lundberg, 1985; Schein, 1985; and Levitt and March, 1988). Culture in accordance with this perception is built on ideas about calculation and a certain degree of intention. According to this view, the cultural pattern changes when a solution to a problem is experienced by the members as no longer working and a search for alternative solutions is started (e.g., when a myth is "broken" by a consecutive row of experiences contradicting the central message carried by the myth). Consider the reflections on culture provided by Schein (1985) as an example of this line of thought.

"There has to have been enough shared experience to have led to a shared view, and this shared view has to have worked for long enough to have come to be taken for granted and to have dropped out of awareness. Culture, in this sense, is a learned product of group experience and is, therefore, to be found only where there is a definable group with a significant history." (Schein, 1985, p. 7)

This model assumes more generally that organisations learn from experiences, from repeating actions that are associated with successful outcomes. The lessons from the learning processes are seen as manifested in, for example, myths, stories or codified in routines and procedures.

In contrast to the leadership-centred model, which was based on a single (or a few) central actor(s), the learning model operates with several actors – a group. The model is, furthermore, based on a consensual perception of the organisational learning unit, where information and experimentation are significant elements.

The Intergroup Model (internal and compromised)
A third set of driving forces described in the culture literature is concerned with *subcultural forms* (e.g., Martin and Siehl, 1983; Gregory, 1983; Sales and Mirvis, 1984; Van Maanen and Barley, 1985; and Louis, 1985). The intergroup model views culture change as a result of *cross-cultural contacts* and a competitive process, marked by compromises. The tension and driving force here rise from the clash between the various, *incongruent* and sometimes conflicting subcultural forms and their striving to become dominant within the organisation or, in some cases, merely trying to be able to maintain a culture of their own (for empirical studies of this phenomenon see e.g. Lysgaard, 1961; Borum and Enderud, 1981; Larsen and Schultz, 1984; Sales and Mirvis 1984).

A subculture can be viewed as a self-organising subsystem which only exists in relation to another cultural system – typically a dominant culture. The subculture reflects constantly on itself – it is self-referential. This is the only way it can identify and recognise itself and the surrounding cultural system of which it is a part. The following excerpt from Sales and Mirvis (1984) is an illustration of this view.

"Theoretically, culture change resulting from contact will stop when a form of acculturation is achieved that is fully acceptable to both groups and they arrive at a state of co-existence in which differences can remain without conflict." (Sales and Mirvis, 1984, p. 132)

The intergroup model operates with several groups of actors in contrast to the two other models, which either operate with an individual actor or with one group of actors.

The notion of competition between subcultural forms rests on an implicit and underlying assumption about conflict, differentiation and segmentation. Conflict is depicted as the primary force in the intergroup model and differentiation and segmentation are preconditions for the idea of conflict.

The Local Adaptation Model (external and compromised)

The fourth model, which points to yet another set of forces causing culture change, is not as complete and homogeneous as the other three models. Nevertheless, a certain core of common ideas marks these contributions and, according to this model, culture change is viewed as a result of a local adaptation process caused by changes in the external environment. The tension in this model arises from the difference between the dominant perceptions and values in the organisational setting and in the organisational environment.

One of the explanations for the somewhat incomplete nature of this model, is that culture research has been comparatively scattered and cautious when addressing the role of the environment and the extra-organisational dynamics, relative to the intra-organisational dynamics. Nevertheless, in the local adapta- tion model the external context plays an important role concerning the understanding of primary dynamics for culture change. The organisation is seen as being dependent on external support and legitimisation. In order to achieve external support and legitimisation the organisation needs to be in congruence with and adapt to the values, norms and expectations in its environment for example by imitating other organisations. Brunsson (1986) is one example of this line of thought.

"Organizations are dependent upon external support in some form, upon their environments' willingness to exchange money, goods, services or people with them. Some organizations may use force to establish these exchanges, but most organizations must demonstrate congruence with the values and norms of their environment in order to receive support." (Brunsson, 1986, p. 165)

However, the values, norms and expectations of the environment are not considered homogeneous or consistent, but segmented and inconsistent. These inconsistent values, norms and expectations in the environment are carried into the organisation and reflected in a variety of ways (e.g., internal segmentation, differentiation in outputs, localised adaptation etc.). In this connection loose couplings are viewed as an important safety device for adaptation, support and organisational survival.

	Leadership	Learning	Intergroup	Local Adaptation
Origin of change impetus	Interplay Leadership Org. members	Interplay Existing solutions New problems	Interplay Subcultures	Interplay Environment Org. groups
Process	Vision/ Direction	Experimen-tation	Competition	Imitation/ Adaptation
Precondition	Dominance/ Acceptance	Experience Information	Difference Conflict	Loose Couplings
	Loyalty	Consensus	Conflict	Segmentation

Figure III.5   Overview of Culture Change Models

Culture is perceived of as *compromised* in the sense that it is composed by intended as well as unintended elements and adjusts to its external context. This approach is represented by authors like Meyer and Rowan (1977); Pfeffer and Salancik (1978); Meyer and Scott (1983); Christensen and Kreiner (1984); Brunsson (1985) and (1986).

The model operates with several actors and is based on forces of localised adaptation, legitimisation and imitation. In figure III.5. the main characteristics and differences between the models are summarised.

The models and forces of culture change, mentioned above are not thought of as mutually exclusive or necessarily contradictory by nature, they may very well turn out to supplement each other. The four models are different with regard to their focus and emphasis as to depicting the prime sources of cultural change. That is to say, what distinguishes the four models are the different ways of depicting the forces of change – concerning impetus, preconditions and so forth – when examining the processes of culture change at the organisation level. In the next section the four models will be explored further by applying them to the merger case.

4   The Models and the Unisys Merger

In the case of the Unisys merger, we saw, that in spite of the rather dramatic nature of the situation and substantial unfreezing started by the decision to merge, features of both pre-merger cultural patterns could be identified after the merger. The post-merger culture was in particular reflecting a continuity of pre-merger Sperry's cultural practices and beliefs. The post-merger situation, though, was not marked by strong cross-cultural clashes or severe fights. In spite of continuity of pre-merger cultural practices and beliefs, new practices and cultural beliefs were also identified as emerging during the merger process. Several forces seem to have influenced the merger process as well as the actual post-merger outcome of this process.

The Leadership Model
At the international level, management in the US made some strategic decisions and developed principles for the merger (partnership, unity, meritocracy and dispatch), which were found to have had considerable impact on the process and outcome. Nevertheless, these principles obviously gave room for local interpreta-tion – they had to in order to be applicable in all subsidiaries. The General Manager and management at the Danish subsidiary level made a skilful and creative translation of these principles set up by the US leadership. By filling out the frame offered by the US headquarters, the Danish leadership made some important decisions concerning the merger that affected the outcome (e.g., incorporating elements from the two former cultures, minimising uncertainty and undermining resistance to change by extended use of information).

The definition of the situation as *"We-They"*, where people focus on differences rather than similarities, is a typical reaction in mergers and acquisitions (Marks and Mirvis, 1986). In the case of the Unisys merger, it seems as if the management of the Danish subsidiary managed to avoid a conflict that could easily have emerged in this particular situation because the two pre-merger firms were so different. Instead, the "We-They" definition seems to have been turned into an *"inside-outside"* definition of the situation. Thus, a key to an understanding of the Danish subsidiary, as stated previously, would be to conceive the new firm as *"a modified Sperry company in a Burroughs world"*. In the way that an outer "enemy" was created – the international Unisys Corporation at large – which then serves as a basis for concerted action by reducing internal conflicts. In this way the Unisys manage-ment in the Danish subsidiary seems to have "killed two birds with one stone" in the sense that they have avoided internal conflicts and turned an external pressure into a positive internal force.

The symbolic dissolution of the two pre-merger cultures, by consequently referring to them as "former" (regarding the two pre-merger firms as "dead"), has been another purposive action by the leadership aimed at sustaining the integration and formation of a new firm. The continuity of pre-merger cultural practices and beliefs in post-merger life in Unisys, however, questions how successful this attempt has been, even though we should not expect pre-merger cultural features to disappear over-night.

Apart from the principles developed by the US leadership and their local Danish interpretation, the integration of the two firms was furthered by other symbols provided by the US leadership like the new company name, the new company colour, the new company logo and a new company slogan, which all aimed at symbolising unity and newness.

Finally, the new building became a symbol of unity, too, but cannot be seen as a purposive action from the leadership, as the new building happened to be there at the right time, because Sperry had planned on expanding.

The Learning Model

Concerning *the role of learning*, we got a very illustrative example of how prior experiences and critical events in an organisation's history, can shape present practices and beliefs. Pre-merger experiences in the companies – "Black Friday" in former Sperry and "Swedish Hegemony" in former Burroughs – were found to have melted together and shaped several intertwined values and beliefs in the post-merger Unisys culture.

These prior experiences concerning external control and lay-offs sustained the idea of a new large company in which job security was seen as being secured ("Bigger is Better"). These pre-merger experiences of external intervention in the subsidiaries also supported the idea of the inside-outside view and external enemy, described earlier. The inside-outside view is intimately related to the orientation towards results and the belief in self-determination ("as long as our financial performance is good and we live up to our targets, then we will keep our autonomy").

Thus, the successful integration of the two companies could be seen as a consequence of the two pre-merger cultures for different reasons being ready and being able to see the possibilities in the new situation, created by the announcement of the merger. Burroughs's readiness to enter a new frame can be explained by the problems Burroughs had experienced prior to the merger (stagnation, management turnover, etc.). These problems made them ready for something new to happen.

Secured by the meritocracy and partnership principles, Sperry could foresee a situation where it would not be dominated by its merging partner, though Sperry technically was acquired by Burroughs and could fear that its job security and self-determination was threatened. Nevertheless, because of the principles Sperry was more likely to get influence over the new firm (it had been most successful) and benefit from the possibilities of being large (double the size of Burroughs).

The Intergroup Model

With regard to the role of intergroup clashes, the two pre-merger cultures, with their distinct cultural properties, could potentially have been another force influencing the process and the outcome. However, the analysis showed that even though these two pre-merger cultures were very different, no signs of direct conflict between the two pre-merger company cultures was observed. Intergroup conflicts between occupational groups (systems and sales) which are well-known from other studies of High-Tech organisations (e.g., Gregory, 1984; Borum and Strandgaard Pedersen, Chapter V), were observed, too, but likewise found of little significance in relation to other forces. The only cultural tension of significance was created through the inside-outside view, mentioned earlier. This tension was between the Danish subsidiary ("a modified Sperry culture") and the Unisys Corporation (dominated by Burroughs). However, this tension did not take the form of a clash, but appeared rather to resemble a situation in which the Danish subsidiary had to adapt to the new standards and norms of the Unisys Corporation. Therefore the tension is more appropriately described as a local adaptation process (see below).

The Local Adaptation Model
Concerning the role of the environment and local adaptation processes, the standards and norms of the international Unisys Corporation environment, as mentioned above, were seen as a force that to a certain extent influenced post-merger cultural practices and beliefs. The emerging formalisation and increased use of written reports were examples of that. However, it has not been possible to exclude that this formalisation is an effect of the organisational growth and increase in size following from the merger.

Furthermore, data did not indicate that loose couplings internally or other local adaptation processes externally had taken place. Perhaps, this can be explained by such processes developing only over a considerable period of time and will not emerge until the organisation is at a later stage in the cultural maturing phase.

Concluding Remarks
In the case of the Unisys merger, it must be concluded that the forces depicted in the *Leadership and the Learning models* have proved to be most significant in relation to this particular culture change process, whereas the Intergroup and Local Adaptation have been of minor importance. This implicates that with regard to the location of forces, the internal forces (Leadership) as well as the external forces (Learning) were found to be the important dynamics in the culture change. Though, concerning the nature of the process, the primarily calculated processes (Leadership and Learning) appeared significant in this case. It was a surprise that the Intergroup model did not prove to be prevailing as one would expect cultural clashes to be dominant in a merger situation like the present. With regard to the Local Adaptation model it was less surprising that the environment played a minor role as a source of change in the process, as this type of local adaptation process requires considerable time to develop, as mentioned earlier.

Another question raised within culture research was concerned with whether cultures change at all. The results from this study gave no simple or clear answer to this question. On the one hand, the continuation of the pre-merger cultural patterns, that was observed, sustains the predictions of existing cultural research that cultures to some extent constitute continuity and rarely change. On the other hand, culture changes and important dynamics behind these changes were identified, too. This seems to suggest that culture changes take place in organisations but not at a very rapid pace.

Notes

1   An earlier version of this article has been presented at EGOS Colloquium '89: "Theory and Practice of Organizational Transition and Transformation. Organization Studies Between Formal Theory, Institutionalism and Social Interaction". Berlin-West, July, 11-14th 1989.
2   Mainly by a 10.000 people cut off, estimated to save about 150 mio. dollars per year.
3   "The Black Friday" is a very interesting example of an organisational story, which apparently can be found in other companies (IT firms), cf. Martin et al (1983) and Wilkins et al (1991). See also 'Black Monday' in Ore-Ida (Waterman, 1987) and Martin (1988) reports of 'Black Tuesday' and other examples of responses to lay-offs in IT firms.
4   Concerning the importance of the physical settings see also Berg and Kreiner (1987), Hatch (1987) and Gagliardi (1990).
5   Walter (1985) mentions, too, that self-determination is a central value surrounding mergers and acquisitions.
6   This distinction is also recognised by Meyerson and Martin (1987) and by Martin and Meyerson (1988), who name these two views the 'Integration' and 'Differentiation' paradigms, respectively.
7   The dimensions are inspired by Scott (1981) and his division of theories into 'rational' and 'natural' systems on the one dimension, and 'open' and 'closed' systems on the other dimension.
8   A more critical view on role of the founder can be found in, "Founders and the Elusiveness of a Cultural Legacy" by Martin, Sitkin and Boehm, (1985).

Chapter IV
Organisational Adaptation and Learning within Danish IT Firms

Finn Borum

1 Introduction

Structural adaptations, i.e., changes in patterns of organisational behaviour, have characterised IT organisations. Some of the important forces behind these adaptations are the novelty of the IT field, the field's expansion, and the evolution of information technology itself.

Chapter I investigated adaptation in terms of institutionalisation processes at the IT field level. In this chapter the focus of analysis is adaptation processes at organisational level in order to specify in more detail some aspects of the previous "domain adaptation" analysis.

The organisational learning perspective focuses on the social unit's adaptation to its milieu, and views learning as a question of matching routines, programmes or procedures to situations. Furthermore, it emphasises legitimacy and appropriateness of behaviour in relation to situations and systems, rather than processes of rational means-end analysis and calculation (Levitt and March, 1988). In line with this the purpose of the following case analyses is to interpret organisational adaptation processes during which the legitimacy of behavioral patterns (i.e., rules of correctness or appropriateness – see Scott, 1987a, p. 286) is established, evoked, or contested, and potentially transformed.

A precondition for learning is an interpretation of the environment, of the relations between and the importance of domain elements, and of the effects of chosen lines of action. However, interpretations are problematic in situations of ambiguity and turbulence. And the IT field has been so turbulent that some of our interviewees expressed that they often had to cope with ambiguous situations which made possible different competing interpretations of series of events – of which all were plausible, but none refutable.

These experienced conditions of ambiguity make us use the March and Olsen (1976, p. 56-59) model of individual and organisational learning under conditions of ambiguity as a means to structure the subsequent analyses.

In this model the zigzags indicate attenuations of the "complete learning cycle". The first one represents factors blocking the individual's transformation

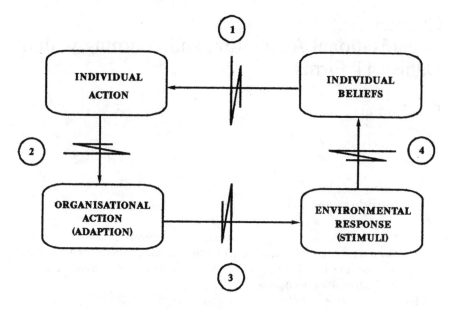

Figure IV.1

of new insight into (changed) individual behaviour. Examples of such cons-traints are role-definitions and standard operating procedures.

The second zigzag indicates disconnection between individual action and organisational action: the individual changes behaviour, but this does not have any effects on organisational action. At group, departmental, and organisational level no effects of the individual's action can be traced.

The third interruption points to a situation of organisational action in which no necessary connection exists between the organisational action and the response from the environment.

Finally, the fourth loose coupling represents ambiguous environmental responses that must be interpreted as to what happened, and why it happened.

For the current purpose of discussing organisational adaptation, only two minor modifications of the figure presented above are made – as indicated by the words in brackets. "Organisational action" is replaced by "organisational adaptation", reflecting our interest in changes of behavioral patterns, and "environmental response" is replaced by "environmental stimuli", as we regard environmental influences that cannot be labelled as responses to organisational action. After these minor adjustments the model will be applied as the common frame of reference for analysing three empirical Danish cases (SME, IBM Denmark, and Datacentralen, of which the latter two were presented in Chapter I). The three cases are, on some important dimensions, described in the data appendix to this chapter. The cases have been selected as types of organisations within the Danish IT field: small enterprises, international suppliers, and large Danish service bureaus.

2 Management Beliefs and Organisational Adaptation: The Entrepreneur's Organisational Preferences

The case of SME
The case focuses on the MD's (founder, manager, and principal owner) beliefs about appropriate organisational configuration, which have been guiding his responses to the changing ecology of the firm. This small organisation is a case of what Mintzberg (1979) labels a "simple structure", characterised by the modest size of the organisation and an undifferentiated structure. Most employees relate directly to the entrepreneur, whose ideas and beliefs play an important role.

Five important elements of the MD's belief system were identified. The first was *the belief in a flat and small organisational structure*. In fact, it was considered desirable only to have two levels: the boss and the subordinates. This structure was regarded both to secure tight control of operations, and to avoid a feeling of alienation among the EDP-specialists, who demanded a high level of motivation. However, it was not considered feasible to have more than twenty people relating directly to one man. In accordance with this principle, a major structural adaptation has been the creation of a new company when the number of employees passed this limit.

The second company was established in 1979 when only 15 professionals were employed, whereas the third company was established in 1985/86 when the total staff numbered 48. The companies were linked together by the mother company being a minority shareholder in the subsidiaries, and by the the MD interfering in all matters of substance.

The second important management belief was in *project organisation* as the standard response to new tasks and contracts. These were always solved by a project group headed by an experienced, trustworthy person who was responsible for scheduling and monitoring the project. However, the manager always intervened in larger projects (above 30.000 US$) and participated in a weekly meeting with all the project managers (3-4), and in a biweekly customer meeting.

The third important belief was the importance of a *careful selection of new employees*, who were interviewed by three different persons. Having the right "chemistry" is described as very important because of the flat organisation. Three task related elements of this "chemistry" were the ability to make quick decisions and implementations, and to resist customers' demands for extra services or additional products. The requirements for the more "hard aspects" of computing were rather vague, and boiled down to "some IT experience" (at least two years).

As to formal qualifications, "over-qualification" was regarded as a problem. Three "datalogs" (persons holding a university degree in computing science) had been hired, but "you can't use them", stated the MD. Some engineers had been hired, but most employees possessed no long, formal education. The most common background was EDP-assistant.

A fourth management belief was *employee ownership* as a means of attaching the employees to the company, and of reducing employee turnover. The remaining five of the original founders of SME were part owners, but apart from them less than 1/3 of the employees had accepted the offer to buy shares. The MD's explanation was that the employees could not afford it.

A fifth management belief was *personnel development* through education. No distinction was made between employees based upon their initial qualifications, and no strict division of work existed between programmers and analysts. Further education and development were encouraged, but the actual time spent on courses turned out to be modest: 1-2 weeks a year per employee.

A strong and coherent managerial belief system emerges from the case (identified in other Danish SMEs within the IT field as well – see Chapter I) which, given the manager's control of the firm, strongly affects organisational action. The MD himself explained this belief system as originating from his experiences of working within a management consultancy firm twenty years ago prior to establishing his own business. This managerial ideology represents a set of standard responses to challenges such as organisational growth, new projects, selection, retaining and development of employees. The major part of the structural adaptations made during the last 10 years can be explained by the MD's organisational belief system, which has remained constant in spite of three major product adaptations:

1976: Total shift from service bureau selling data processing to body shopping in terms of sale of programming manpower and related consultancy services;

1979: Inclusion of customised software development in the product line;

1984: Inclusion of standardised software in the product line. Since 1979 body-shopping has been reduced to a minor activity.

During the 1980s SME faced four severe crises:

1980: Economic crisis;

1984: A labour turn-over of 20% in conjunction with a period of important growth;

1987: Economic crisis;

1988: Economic crisis resulting in liquidation.

These shifts in product line, the recurring crises, and the final liquidation of SME in spite of an expanding market for IT services during the period considered, point to the dilemma of a strong belief system concerning appropriate organisation. On the one hand, the firm offers predefined and coherent responses to organisational growth and development. On the other hand, it relies upon a standardised pattern of response. The entrepreneur's beliefs imply standard organisational adaptations, which may be decoupled from the demands of the shifting ecology, and moreover constitute a self-referential system:

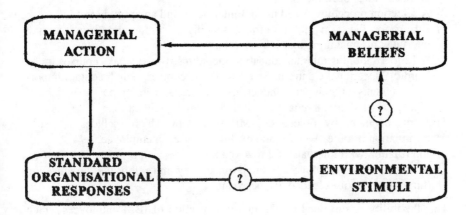

Figure IV.2

3 Individual Beliefs, Individual Action, and Organisational Adaptation: Flexible and Inflexible Bureaucracies

The Cases of IBM Denmark and Datacentralen (DC)
On the surface, the two organisations appear as large, bureaucratic organisations, which may prompt you to expect similar internal processes of structural change. This is not the case: Structural change is described quite differently in the two cases: as unproblematic in IBM, and as problematic in Datacentralen.

One important explanation is that the two companies operate within different fields. As a sales office IBM's performance can be evaluated on output criteria and adjusted to new products. Datacentralen, on the other hand, is committed to develop, operate and maintain large systems – tasks that require a structure somewhat similar to that of machine bureaucracy. However, there are other differences between the two organisations, which offer another explanation for the different experiences with structural changes.

In *IBM* structural change is facilitated by personnel policies, that emphasise both the recruitment of flexible actors and indoctrination of change as a core value. The main features of the personnel policies are:

1) Recruitment of highly qualified young persons without any prior career within the computing field. 28% of these have a higher education, and this proportion has been increasing.
2) A selection procedure based upon 3 interviews and an aptitude test.
3) Hiring for the firm and not for a specific position, and from the first interview promising regular job rotation.
4) A 12 to 18 months internal education including 10 two-weeks courses in the Nordic Educational Centre in Sweden. These courses, which contain important elements of company indoctrination, are a melting pot in which all newcomers are mixed regardless of their formal qualifications.
5) A management by objectives (MBO) system which includes a yearly formulation of objectives for and evaluation of each employee.
6) Job rotation with intervals of 2 to 4 years.
7) In no case are employees rehired once they have left the organisation (turnover has not exceeded 4% per year).

This flexibility is sustained by the non-unionisation of IBM-employees which supports the norm for individual as opposed to collective actions.

Datacentralen's personnel policies deviates from that of IBM on several issues. Firstly, the most important single basis of recruitment is EDP- assistants (a 1-2 years basic EDP-education aiming at programming and analyst functions), while academics only account for 18% of the total staff. Related to the third issue, employees are hired to specific positions, and are not led to expect frequent job rotation.

The internal education and management controlled indoctrination is not as powerful as that of IBM, and a MBO-system has only recently been reintroduced after having been abandoned in the seventies. Finally, there are several examples of former employees having been rehired, as experience from other companies is appreciated.

Besides the difference in personnel policies between the two organisations, the unionisation of DC's specialists contributes to explain the more difficult nature of structural change in Datacentralen: Prosa (a union of EDP- specialists) has held a strong position in DC, and has been reinforcing collective actions which, furthermore, were supported by a traditional high level of employee participation. This was explained as the reasons why a structural change in 1978, aiming at blurring the traditional strict division of work and physical separation between systems analysts and programmers, became a lengthy and arduous exercise. A structural change in 1984/85, on the contrary, dividing DC into seven customer based divisions, was rather quickly implemented. A contributing factor may also have been that a very modest part of the staff was affected by this change.

The Interpretation
In the case of *IBM* structural adaptations are facilitated by the organisational practice in terms of recruitment, indoctrination, and internal job rotation.

These elements altogether legitimise job rotation and gear the individual to expect frequent positional changes in the organisational structure. Furthermore, they create a notion of changes as being natural in a prosperous organisation. Whether the individual's shift of position is caused by standard job rotation or by a structural adaptation may, on this basis, not be perceived as important.

This organisational practice is consistent with the management beliefs reflected in the official personnel policies. This again may be explained as the Danish management's adoption and marginal adjustment of the corporate culture and sales objectives of IBM International, as disseminated from headquarters:

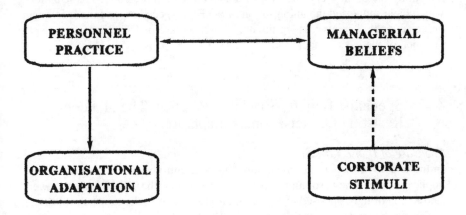

Figure IV.3

Datacentralen's personnel practice does not facilitate organisational adaptations. Employees are hired for specific positions and not for the firm as such. Hence, they are not led to expect frequent structural changes. In contrast, the impact of the public sector's task demands, norms and traditions have legitimised a structure in DC which is in keeping with the logics of machine bureaucracy.

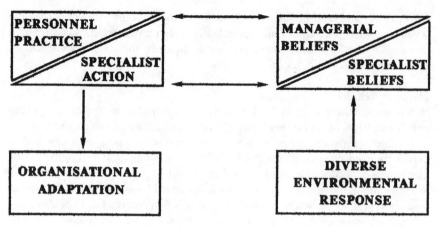

Figure IV.4

In relation to the specialists, the EDP-assistants and the staff recruited from the public sector have endowed the organisation with more collectivistic beliefs, which have supported the unionisation of the EDP-specialists and made frequent organisational changes less legitimate. Thus, the case of DC represents a "split version" of the basic model.

4   Specialist Beliefs, Specialist Practice: The IT People Resisting Organisational Adaptation

The Case of Datacentralen

In the late 1970s when the minicomputers were introduced and facilitated new applications and new solutions to known problems, the EDP-specialists were said to be strongly opposed to change their practice to fit the new possibilities.

During the sixties and the seventies the EDP-configurations were mainframes, and the systems developed were centralised solutions to be run on a service-bureau basis for the State agencies. Information technology in terms of mainframes formed the basis of a specific practice of the EDP-specialists, which essentially remained unchanged throughout almost two decades. The appearance of the minis in the late seventies introduced alternatives to the traditional mainframe based and centrally run system. DC was exposed to pressure to adopt a new concept, including the development of systems which could be run on the customers' own installations independently of DC. This product adaptation was described as very difficult due to both cultural and structural obstacles.

The specialists and parts of the managerial group regarded the minis either as irrelevant ("not proper EDP") in relation to the culture and competences of DC, or directly threatening to the organisation's survival. By designing and selling mini-solutions many employees felt that they were cutting off their noses to spite their faces, i.e., jeopardising the future survival and growth of DC. The *culture-bound resistance* to change was expressed in the specialists' wish to continue to develop mainframe based systems, and to pursue the established daily practices, methods, and specialisations developed in relation to this hardware technology.

Apparently the individual beliefs and the individual actions of the specialists were closely interrelated and formed a paradigmatic construct (Kuhn, 1970; Ritzer, 1975) resistant to external pressure. A paradigm in this context is defined as the normal practice of a group of specialists: what problems to undertake, what methods to apply, what types of solutions to produce, and the ideology (world-view) supporting that practice. What facilitated the development of a "normal practice" among specialists (analogous with Kuhn's (1970) concept of "normal science") seems to be a combination of Datacentralen's tasks, the technology available, and the presence of a specialist community.

The major task was to develop and implement large, centralised systems based on the mainframe technology of the sixties and the seventies. During these two decades, the IT specialists (systems designers and programmers) developed and refined methods and norms related to this task which sustained a belief in what "proper EDP" was about. This "specialist paradigm" was, furthermore, developed relatively autonomously of Datacentralen's top management, which at that time pursued a strategy of "responsible autonomy" (Friedman, 1977) in relation to the specialists.

Thus interpreted the model for basic learning in Datacentralen appears to be as illustrated below:

The *structural configuration* of DC had also been geared to the development and operation of large, centralised systems. Projects were managed by elaborate procedures which stipulated an array of phases that a systems development project had to run through. These project phases were enforced by means of approval procedures and documentation requirements. A strict system of control and security was applied to the test and operation of systems. This was a response to the nature of the systems – important central registers containing confidential information and requiring reliable operations and protection of data. Furthermore, a strict division of labour between system planners and programmers had been established and an elaborate set of standards had been developed, specifying requirements to the output produced by each of these categories.

Thus, organisational learning was based upon an encoding of experiences with mainframe solutions into the organisational structure in terms of routines and procedures. These were not geared to handle the development of smaller,

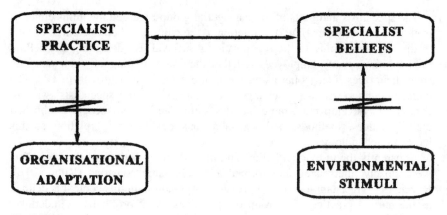

Figure IV.5

decentralised, minicomputer-based systems requiring less strict tests and operations.

The experiences of DC had been encoded into a culture and a structure antagonistic to the challenges and possibilities of the appearing minicomputers. Hence, DC was on the verge of being caught in a competence trap. External and internal pressures had to build up before DC engaged in the difficult process of learning and adaptation. This led to fundamental changes in the division of work and procedures – among which the rejection of the traditional division of work between systems designers and programmers was a key element. Another important element was the recruitment of new employees and the modification of their training and socialisation as prerequisites for the creation of a "mini culture" beside the "mainframe culture". A third element was the loosening of the established rigid standards for design and documentation of systems.

This adaptation resulted in learning processes which enabled DC to cope with the new challenges introduced by the PCs some years later. This "mainframe learning and unlearning" appears to have been a problem not only for Datacentralen, but for most of the Danish service-bureaus, which in general were slow at adapting to the minis and had great difficulties in doing so – and faced difficulties in adapting to the minis – and in some cases they did not survive the transition.

5   Environmental Stimuli and Organisational Adaptation: Reduction of Contested Interorganisational Dependencies

The Case of Datacentralen

As mentioned in Chapter I, Datacentralen was right from the beginning closely connected to one supplier (IBM), a dependency which was gradually reduced. The story runs as follows:

Prior to the establishment of Datacentralen, an investigation of data processing "needs and possibilities" within the State administration was carried out by an IBM sales consultant. This survey was a major premise for the establishment of DC. In 1959 this IBM consultant was appointed the first director of DC, and remained in this position for almost 25 years.

The first computer was bought in 1962 – an IBM mainframe. Through the first two decades (until 1979-80) only IBM equipment was bought except for some peripheral equipment (disc drives) and input-output media (tapes, discs, punched cards) which was purchased from other suppliers. The first break with this one-supplier concept was the purchase of an Amdahl mainframe. Later on orders for both minis and PCs were placed with other suppliers.

In 1970, DC established its own development unit and educational department. Both of these initiatives can be interpreted as efforts to reduce IBM-dependency.

The development unit of DC was intended to substitute the technical competence of IBM, which until then had controlled the formulation of DC's future demands, in that IBM had made the forecast of DC's future need for EDP-capacity, and spelled out the future feasible configurations. Likewise, DC in many cases was depending on IBM's systems engineers for software facilities to be installed or modified. IBM also had a regular office at DC's premises and systems engineers worked there throughout the sixties and the seventies. These IBM employees participated on equal terms with the DC employees in work-related and social activities. It was described as particularly important by some of our DC respondents to get out of this "development dependence".

IBM was also the main supplier of EDP-related education and courses, what also contributed to the integration of the two organisations. DC, however, had established some internal seminars that in 1970 formed the basis for the establishment of the educational department.

This story shows a change from two socially integrated organisations, with one party (DC) being dependent upon the other party, as the latter controlled critical sources of uncertainty, to a situation of more clearly defined organisational boundaries and reduced dependency of DC upon IBM's competence. However, our interviewees did not provide very good explanations of this change. There were good reasons for DC to rely upon IBM, as "security" and "service" were crucial issues for DC in its choice of supplier, having to guarantee stable operations.

The only overt explanations offered were that "IBM needed competition", and that Amdahl was able to offer IBM-compatible CPUs at competitive prices. These two explanations, however, appear to be insufficient rationalisations of decisions resulting from a long and laborious process, and do not at all explain why DC embarked on this complicated crusade. Why try to reduce supplier-dependency, when prices were not very important, when the supplier was extremely reliable, and due to its multinational mother corporation had a strong Research and Development department?

An Interpretation

The following interpretation of the structural adaptations made by Datacentralen explains these as responses to demands from the environment which contested the legitimacy of the traditional dependency of IBM Denmark. The analysis of the case is based upon a "resource dependence perspective" on DC as formulated by Pfeffer and Salancik (1978) as two basic assumptions:

(a) ".. that organizations survive to the extent that they are effective. Their effectiveness derives from the management of demands, particularly the demands of interest groups upon which the organizations depend for resources and support."

In line with this, "organizational effectiveness is an *external* standard of how well an organization is meeting the demands of the various groups and organizations that are concerned with its activities." (p.11). And "the effectiveness of an organization is a socio-political question" (p.11).

(b) ".. that to understand the behaviour of an organization you must understand the context of that behaviour – that is, the ecology of the organization." (p.1).

In line with these assumptions, the explanation behind DC's "liberation" from IBM will be sought in the demands put upon DC by the important interest groups constituting the ecology of DC. The ecology of Datacentralen can be outlined as in Figure IV.6:

(1) This relation has been commented upon at length by respondents from both DC and IBM, providing the initial picture of DC's dependence upon IBM presented above, and the integration of the two organisations.

(2) The other (potential) suppliers were characterised by their lack of links to DC, and non-significance as suppliers – Regnecentralen is an example (Chapter I). The potential suppliers, and in particular the Danish firms, had other ways of exerting influence. One was through the political parties, the other through the Government Department of Administration (Administra-

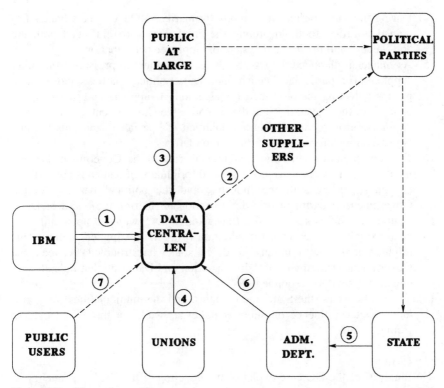

Figure IV.6   The ecology of Datacentralen

tions- departementet). In both cases the strongest argument for convincing these bodies of the necessity to intervene would be that if they did not, the State might in the future become too dependent on one single foreign supplier and suddenly find that no Danish alternatives had been developed.

(3) During the late sixties and the seventies the public in general was concerned about the multinationals' growing economic importance and influence through the technological development. The democratic control of multinationals was much debated, not only affecting the political parties but also DC directly. The latter in the sense that DC typically would recruit persons who were carriers of the "68-values" of democracy, anti-capitalism (see Chapters II and IX), anti-multinationalism, and anti- Americanism. During some years they created an interesting internal state of affairs. The position of managers was very weak whereas a number of newly established committees were attributed considerable power. In the same period, the internal climate shifted to outright hostility towards IBM and the local IBM engineers.

(4) During the same period, the unions (primarily PROSA – see Chapter IX) gained a strong foothold among the employees and reinforced both the "68-values" and the internal system of employee participation.

(5) As financial guarantee for DC the State was subject to pressure from other suppliers (in particular Danish industry), political parties, and interest groups reflecting the described forces amongst suppliers and the public in general. In the late sixties and the seventies the Government Department of Administration recruited external qualified IT specialists and thus became better equipped for exerting influence on DC.

(6) This interpretation attributes a significant role to the Government Department of Administration as processor and formulator of demands put forth by the public in general, the industry, and the political parties. As the Government Department of Administration is chairing the board of Datacentralen, it holds a strong position vis-à-vis DC, which it apparently has been exploiting to enforce the adoption of a "multi-supplier" policy. This might explain the relations at times somewhat troubled between the Government Department of Administration and Datacentralen indicated by one of our key DC respondents.

(7) The public users (the State, the counties, and the municipalities) may also have exerted influence on supplier policy as well, but this is not evident from our data.

Conclusion

This analysis of the DC case explains the reduction of the IBM-dependency as DC's response to the demands of various groups and organisations that were concerned with DC's activities, and upon which DC depended for future resources and support. Apart from the demand for smooth and secure data processing, these agents imposed another external standard to which Datacentralen had to comply: that of contributing to the creation of greater diversification on the supplier side. Or to put it more directly: to weaken the monopolistic market position of IBM in Denmark.

The process analysed covers the periods from 1960/65 to 1979/80. That it took such a long time for Datacentralen to adapt to this socio- political reality may be explained as a consequence of

- the time-consuming process of articulating demands and mobilising interest groups;
- the time-consuming tasks of processing demands through the political system;
- the slow process of building up organisational units with sufficient competences;
- the internal efficiency-standards (low costs and high security) that in the short run were contradictory to the external standards of effectiveness;
- management's weak internal position.

6   Discussion

The three cases of organisational learning and domain adoption exemplify how certain practices, which represent possible ways of coping with ambiguity and complexity, are pursued or adapted by organisations and groups embedded in a dynamic environment. The analyses can be summarised in terms of the organisations' external standards of effectiveness, the bases of legitimacy for organisational actions, and the implementation of organisational actions.

SME is the case of a small, entrepreneurial organisation which, in order to survive, primarily has to live up to economic standards of effectiveness. Legitimation of organisational actions is essentially a question of actions' congruence with the entrepreneur's belief system – which in this case is coherent and stable. Implementation of the manager's ideas is facilitated by the simple, owner controlled organisation structure.

In this simple structure, organisational learning coincides with individual learning in the sense that the inferences which the manager draws from his interpretations of experiences become organisational guidelines. Consequently, this type of organisation becomes dependent upon the owner's belief system – with respect to both the daily practices, and the domain adaptation. The small IT enterprise is vulnerable to shifts in the domain's demands and resources, and survival is a key issue – which was not the case of the two large organisations IBM Denmark and Datacentralen.

IBM Denmark is, as a sales subsidiary, primarily evaluated by corporate headquarters against economic standards of performance. Legitimation of organisational actions is, however, a more complex matter. Firstly, the corporation's belief system and practices have to be taken into account. Secondly, the Danish context is another source of legitimisation. IBM operates in a private sector, low-unionised context, which has made it possible for management to base its personnel policy and practice upon a firm-individual contract. This is furthermore compatible with the organisation's raison d'etre – sales – and the attitudes of the persons recruited.

In this case organisational learning becomes a system property in that specific patterns of behaviour, which are judged as more appropriate than others, are encoded into rules, routines or standard operating procedures and thus impersonalised (Levitt and March, 1988).

Finally, implementation within this large organisation is facilitated by the routines for training and indoctrination of the employees, which secure a "mental programming" in Hofstede's (1980) terminology. This has endowed IBM Denmark with a flexibility in spite of its size, complexity, and bureaucratic features.

Datacentralen has, in contrast, been facing a more complex ecology – a negotiated domain – within which several agents have strived to impose their standards of effectiveness. As a large, public sector affiliated IT organisation, Datacentralen became open to several discourses. Traditional economic performance criteria have not been important issues, but public technology policy related issues, which led to a contestation of its dependence on IBM as sole supplier. This initiated a long processing of demands and internal structural adaptations, before a multi-supplier practice was adopted.

Acting within the highly unionised public sector, limits are put to management's control in Datacentralen. In this context personnel policies and practices became issues of negotiation, and made it less legitimate to base contracts of employment upon a pure firm-individual model. The existence of a "specialists' collectivity" furthermore necessitated that managerial actions were perceived as legitimate in relation to the beliefs of this collectivity.

This divided internal power structure makes implementation of organisational changes in Datacentralen a more complicated affair than in the cases of SME and IBM. Furthermore the development of a "specialist paradigmatic practice" has been identified as another factor impeding structural adaptation, and complicating the transition from the "mainframe" era.

Thus, in the case of Datacentralen the structure and procedures regulate disputes between management and specialists and may be regarded as truces between units (Cyert and March, 1963). They have a political as well as an analytical aspect, in that they define both the relations of dependency and authority between units, and how to deal with operational matters.

The three cases thus reflect increasingly complex situations of organisational adaptation and learning – both with regard to the external standards of effectiveness, the bases of legitimation for managerial action, and the implementation processes.

Data Appendix

Name	IBM Denmark	Datacentralen	SME
Year of Founding	1950	1959	1974

Line of Business			
– Hardware	Ⓧ	X	X
– Software	Ⓧ	Ⓧ	Ⓧ
– Darta Processing (SB)	X	Ⓧ	
– Consultancy	X	X	X
– Education	X	X	
Number of Employees (1985)	2.288	1.404	48
Revenue (Mio. CR.)	4.823	603	–
Resources	Rich	Rich	Scarce
Resource Context	Buffered by international giant corporation. Market = private & public sector	Buffered by public agencies. Market = public sector	Submitted to the forces of turbulent private sector market

(Circles indicate major businesss areas)

Chapter V
Understanding the IT People, their Subcultures, and Implications for Management of Technology and Innovation

Finn Borum and Jesper Strandgaard Pedersen

1 Introduction

In this article, we investigate the work cultures of the IT people[1] in order to identify aspects of their organisational settings useful for understanding organisational flexibility and adaptation.

Having conducted cultural studies in Danish IT companies, we found cultural differentiation to be a dominant feature of these organisations. Thus, a subcultural approach to the study of organisational cultures in the IT industry appeared to be the most appropriate frame of reference for understanding organisational flexibility and adaptation.

After a critical examination of the corporate culture tradition a subcultural approach to the study of IT organisations is offered. A subcultural framework, based on Van Maanen and Barley (1985) and their concepts of "ecological context" and "differential interaction", is developed and explored in three case analyses. These results are confronted with the typology of subcultural forms by Martin and Siehl (1983) in order to examine the possibilities for managerial action. It is suggested that, once recognised, organisational subcultures ought *not* to be seen as a potential threat, as the corporate culture tradition has argued. On the contrary, subcultures should be seen as an important organisational source improving the capability for change and innovation in organisations.

2 The Danish IT Field and the Delimitation of Our Study

Other articles in this reader provide a description of the Danish IT field that shall not be repeated here. However, in accordance with some of the main characteristics and dominant features of the Danish IT field, we will select our cases so that they reflect these three characteristics:

– the dominance of the multinational corporations as suppliers of hardware;

- the concentration of IT services to the public sector in two large service bureaus;
- the proliferation of small and medium-sized organisations on both the user and the supplier side.

Our analysis is limited to people and organisations working with the development and implementation of IT software either within the service sector or for administrative purposes within production companies. The first reason for this focus is that this application area accounts for about 80% of total hardware and software utilisation in Denmark (Hingel, 1986). Furthermore, our previous research has focused on the administrative and service sector of society (Borum et al, 1989). Finally, it is primarily in software that Danish enterprises have a strong position vis-à-vis international suppliers.

3   A Cultural Perspective on the IT People

3.1   Corporate Culture – A Traditional View

The topic of organisational cultures has been a significant issue within organisational research since 1980. A major part of this research, normally referred to as the "mainstream" or *corporate culture* literature (e.g., Pettigrew, 1979; Ouchi, 1981; Athos and Pascale, 1982; Peters and Waterman, 1982; Deal and Kennedy, 1982; Kilmann, Saxton and Serpa 1986), presents a unicultural view on organisational culture. The normative "corporate culture" tradition regards a given organisation as having a single, dominant culture, shared by all members of the organisation. According to this tradition, culture is conceived as yet another organisational variable, with which it is possible for management to influence and control. The corporate culture tradition represents organisations as *having* cultures in contrast to viewing organisations as *being* cultures (Smircich, 1983). The founder and/or the leader of an organisation is perceived as very central in relation to the creation, maintenance and development of the cultural pattern, as expressed in the following statement by Schein (1985, p. 2):

"Organizational cultures are created by leaders, and one of the most decisive functions of leadership may well be the creation, the management, and – if and when that may become necessary – the destruction of a culture."

The "mainstream" culture literature further claims that organisational cultures provide their members with a frame of understanding that serves as a basis for concerted action ("the glue that holds the organisation together"). The culture is, however, not immediately accessible, but exists as a kind of "tacit knowledge" among the members in the organisation. Culture is manifested in and represented by a range of cultural forms such as rituals, stories, myths, jargon and heroes.

Culture, with its associated values and beliefs, is passed on to new "generations" of organisational members through this variety of cultural forms and practices. However, a process of interpretation and explanation must take place in relation to the symbols, practices and events, to which the organisational newcomer is exposed, before the content of the culture is revealed and the transmission process is completed. Thus, according to this view, culture takes on a socialising capacity by introducing new organisational members to the values and norms in the particular work setting. In this way culture, in more general terms, is found to provide continuity, control, identity and integration of members in relation to a particular work setting (Louis, 1980).

When the question is raised, "what can be done in order to influence the cultural pattern?", the suggestions for managerial action within this perspective would be to make the company values explicit and known by repetitive indoctrination and explication. Management should, for instance, carry out rituals underlining these values and beliefs, and exert symbolic management that expresses the same values and ideas via their own behaviour. This implies, for example, telling stories from the organisation's past, and pointing out role models or heroes in the organisation that exemplify and support the values and ideals which the company wishes to be dominant.

More or less explicitly, the corporate culture tradition also assumes that the cultural pattern and the various elements constituting this pattern, are coherent, consistent and clear, as some authors have pointed out (Meyerson and Martin, 1987). *Strong organisation cultures*, according to this view, are associated with a single dominant culture, which is shared by the organisational members who are seen as acting on the basis of the rules and prescriptions provided by the culture. As a consequence of this, the lack of a single, shared, integrating culture and the existence of subcultures, are referred to as reflecting a *weak organisation culture*.

Critics of the corporate culture tradition have stressed that it is "management-centric", holds a monolithic and harmonious view on culture, which is inaccurate and tends to overlook cultural conflicts and contradictions within the organisational setting (Martin and Meyerson, 1988; Gregory, 1984). Furthermore, the corporate culture tradition can be criticised for having a tendency to emphasise the more formal aspects of the culture such as corporate rituals, company slogans, espoused values and heroes. Thus, it neglects the work place culture, or "culture-at-work" (Christensen and Kreiner, 1984), that exists among organisational participants and may have much more influence on the practices and daily routines carried out in the organisation (Bodker and Pedersen, 1991).

Another argument against the corporate culture tradition is based on the observation made by Van Maanen and Barley (1985) that, "unitary culture is primarily an anthropological idea, while the notion of subcultures is predominantly sociological" (p.33). If this is correct, the transfer of the unitary, anthropological concept of culture to the field of organisations appears to be highly debatable.[2]

At best the corporate culture tradition, in our opinion, only high-lights certain parts of organisational culture and can be seen as a crusade against differentiation in that its main preoccupation is integration and uniformity. In this perspective management often ignores, or is at least inattentive to, the positive effects of the existence of subcultures in their organisational setting. This may be due to the fact that the majority of managers subscribes to the corporate culture perspective, which represents this unitary perception of organisation culture.

3.2   The Subcultural View

The issue of *organisational subcultures* has long been recognised within organisational sociology and the body of cultural research (Louis, 1980; Martin and Siehl, 1983; Gregory, 1983; Van Maanen and Barley, 1985; Meyerson and Martin, 1987). Nevertheless, apart from these contributions, the vast majority of the culture research has focused on the integrative perspective as presented by the corporate culture tradition described above.

If we claim not to hold a unitary perspective on organisation culture, but instead adhere to multiple cultures and a subcultural perspective, what does it then imply?

First, we will adopt Van Maanen and Barley's (1985) definition of subculture as

"...a subset of an organization's members who interact regularly with one another, identify themselves as a distinct group within the organization, share a set of problems commonly defined to be the problems of all, and routinely take action on the basis of collective understandings unique to the group" (p.38).

As to factors contributing to the genesis of subcultures, Van Maanen and Barley (1985, p. 33-34) stipulate two: *"ecological context"*, and *"differential interaction"*. The idea of "ecological context" is that a group's position can be mapped along physical, temporal and social coordinates such as division of work, autonomy and control, territory, and other groups, that together constitute an ecology that may make possible the emergence of a subculture. However, in order for a subculture to develop, "differential interaction" is also necessary, i.e., that the focal group in question develops intragroup relations that are stronger than the external relations. If these two conditions for the emergence of a subculture do *not* exist, then a subculture with a collective understanding, and a reproductive and adaptive capacity will *not* emerge (Van Maanen and Barley, 1985, p. 33-35).

We consider it necessary to elaborate Van Maanen and Barley's treatment of the ecological context, as it is neither logically exhaustive nor sufficient for the interpretation of our observations. We will consider the ecological context as the factors which create a situation that is more or less favourable for the development of subcultures. As such it comprises both properties of the individuals that are imported to the organisation, socialisation processes, and structural features of the organisation.

Ecological Context
a) The properties of individuals
   – qualifications
   – experience
   – age
   – gender
b) Socialization of new actors to the organisation
c) Division of work
d) The grouping of actors
   – physical location
   – structural clustering
e) The autonomy of the actors in relation to
   – management
   – customers/clients and other groups

The dimensions of the ecological context bear some resemblance with the design parameters of Mintzberg (1979), which is not surprising given the general nature of his classification. However, we find, that our approach differs from that of Mintzberg in that we are more analytical and less normative – see Mintzberg's dictum (p. 65) that "Design assumes discretion, an ability to alter a system."

As to the *collective understanding* which results from the ecological context and the differential interaction, we have operationalised it by means of Schein's (1985) distinctions between the levels of artifacts, values, and basic assumptions (Chapter II for the operationalisation of Schein's framework).

As to the *methods* applied to identify subcultures, we have regarded "differential interaction" as a necessary, but not sufficient condition for considering a collection of individuals as constituting a group. But in order to be regarded as a subculture, differences between the focal group and other parts of the social system have to be *manifest* through, for example, artifacts, norms, values, practices or other symbolic expressions. But it could also manifest itself through interpretations of artifacts and events that differ from that of the dominant culture or other subcultures. These are the indicators by means of which we have identified the subcultures in action.

	Occupational	Hierarchical	Departmental	Imported
Total	Systems/sales			
Unisys	Systems/sales			Sperry/Burroughs
Datacentralen		Mgmt/worker	'Old/new'	
IBM	Sales/systems		Divisions	
Kommunedata			Divisions	
RCI	Scientist/ Practitioner/ Marketing		Department	

Figure V.1   Overview of Observed Subcultures

4   An Overview of Organisational Subcultures in IT Firms

Applying the culture concept to a number of IT companies within the Danish IT field, we observed several subcultures to be co-existing in these organisations. It appeared, however, that the dimensions along which the various subcultures identified themselves as a subgroup and distinguished themselves in relation to other subgroups (or the rest of the organisation), were different. The most commonly observed types of subcultures are presented in figure V.1, and further explained in the text.

Occupational subcultures are clearly linked to the ecological dimension of "division of work"- referring to the nature of task performed – and is a widely observed basis for subcultures in the IT firms we studied. The most commonly reported subcultures based on occupational differences were the sharp distinction between *systems people* and *sales people*. In most instances the first group consists of the persons, who work intimately with the technology in-house such as operations, systems programmers, analysts/programmers etc. The latter group consists of persons primarily taking care of sales, marketing, sales related customer service etc. Apart from this difference regarding internal versus external orientation, a distinction between "we" who produce and "the others" who sell is prevailing. Other studies from the IT industry have found and described similar distinctions, for instance "Engineering-Marketing interface" (Kidder, 1977; Gregory, 1983; Larsen and Rogers, 1984).

Another type of subcultural form is the *hierarchical* subculture. This type of subculture is, in relation to the ecological context, constituted by the grouping of actors, and the relations of autonomy or control, and is based on the distinction made between *management and employees*, which we observed in some of the IT firms. This distinction is recognised within organisation research in general and in some studies referred to as the formal-informal organisation (e.g., Lysgaard, 1961), or "blue collar – white collar", "workers culture" (Wilkins and Dyer, 1987). This distinction is based on hierarchical position and may be sustained by the autonomy of the actors, for example, represented in the form of unions in the work setting, as was the case in our Datacentralen example.

Departmental subcultures point to other dimensions of the ecological context as the basis for subcultures – those of physical location and structural clustering. In some of the IT companies we studied, they appeared to be functionally based, for example, operations, systems, service, support and so forth. Whereas in other organisations they were based on divisionalisation, for instance, in terms of region, type of customer, product, market segment etc. In many instances, we observed that these departmental subcultures went hand in hand with physical segregation, which seemed to consolidate the subcultural identification. It is also important to mention that the existence of a department is not the same as the existence of a subculture. It may very well be that several departments share the same culture across departmental boundaries.

A fourth type of subculture appeared to be *"imported"*. This subcultural form is characterised by originating outside of the organisation, in other words it is brought into the organisation from the environment. In relation to the "ecological context", this type of subcultural formation is closely linked to "properties of the individuals" and the "socialisation of newcomers" in our previously presented framework. Imported subcultures are, for instance, found in cases of *mergers*, a situation that physically and/or structurally brings together two or more distinct cultures, which now have to co-exist, interact and form a new cultural pattern. This merger situation, is well described (e.g., Sales and Mirvis, 1984; Walter, 1985; Marks and Mirvis, 1986; Nahavandi and Malekzadeh, 1988; Dahlgren and Witt, 1988). One of our cases from the Danish IT industry is a merger between two firms with two very different cultural patterns.

Another type of "imported" subculture derives from different *educational institutions*. Such institutions shape actors outside of the organisation through the educational process, including indoctrination of certain values and beliefs, and training of certain practices. The organisations import these different, educationally generated traditions and sets of values by the recruitment of their students.

A third type of "imported" subculture emerges from different *organisational generations*. This points to the ecological dimension "properties of the individuals" in our framework, as a source of variation. In some of the IT firms that we studied, a boundary existed between organisational "oldtimers" and "newcomers". This phenomenon is also reported in other studies of IT companies (e.g., Dyer, 1982; Gregory, 1983 and 1984; Schein, 1985). In our cases from the Danish IT field, it appeared that the distinction made between "oldtimers" and "newcomers" often was also associated with a difference in type of education, which further supported the subcultural identity. "Oldtimers" were most likely to possess practical experience and have on-the-job-training, courses etc., whereas the "newcomers" typically had a formal computer education ("EDP-assistant" or some kind of degree in computer science). This may further imply that the two groups also use different technologies in their daily work (mainframes, minis, micros), which again support the subcultural identity[3].

Below we will examine three types of subcultures, drawing upon three different case organisations – Total, Datacentralen and Unisys – which have been introduced and described in more detail in the two previous contributions in this reader (Total and Datacentralen, Chapter II and Unisys Chapter III). We refer to these articles for background information on these three cases.

4.1   Total – An Example of Occupational Subcultures

Total is, according to Danish standards, a medium sized computer product manufacturer, which produces software and sells IT systems (including hardware) for administrative purposes (see Chapter II for more background information).

The cultural pattern in Total is found to consist of two subcultures inscribed in a relatively weak overall cultural framework (Pedersen and Sorensen, 1989). The two groups, around which these two subcultures are formed, are the group of information technology people (system, support, and technical service) and the group of persons with administrative, sales or marketing functions.

The subculture around the group of IT people is, in spite of a tough language and a direct way of interpersonal confrontation, dominated by a social group orientation. A casual manner and an extreme informality characterise the culture, too. The culture is relatively open and friendly towards new persons, if they behave according to the language code, are informal and accept the "key-values" (especially "Do not brag or play Mr. know-all"). Once you are accepted and adopted by the group you are fairly safe and you will be very unlikely to fall into disfavour. Egalitarianism and practical experience are dominant aspects of the collective understanding, together with an anti-authoritarian attitude. In general a prevalent aspect of the culture is group orientation. However, in certain matters centred around job function, we found a kind of professional pride or "shyness" as jobs and methods were regarded as private property and a matter of individual responsibility.

The subculture among the administrative staff and sales people is, on the other hand, dominated by an exclusively individual orientation. The culture is both competitive and individualistic. Members share a collective understanding that values action, efficiency and productivity. This subculture evidences a more formal dress code (shirt, tie and perhaps a jacket, when you meet with customers etc.) and tends to be less inclined to use jargon, nicknames and so forth. This group also tends to be less reluctant to lay off individuals who do not perform well and show the expected results. This subculture has a collective understanding that competition and ambitions are important, otherwise you will not get ahead in this system – the shark ethic prevails..eat the wounded (Thompson, 1979). An anti-authoritarian attitude is also dominant within this subculture, with the modification that persons with great power and charisma are likely to be treated with some respect because they are capable of getting things done.

One of the consequences of these two subcultural patterns is that different collective understandings have emerged in each subculture. This means that what is considered prestigious in one subculture, is regarded of no or little importance in the other subculture. Thus different values can be observed together with different status symbols. This is reflected in the reward system that comprises different motivational structures for the two groups. The group of sales and marketing people are working and rewarded according to a bonus system that reflects and supports individualism, ambition, and competition, whereas the systems people are rewarded according to a fixed salary system, in line with group orientation and egalitarianism.

This is not an exclusive finding in Total. Several other IT companies were observed to apply a similar differentiated reward system in relation to these two occupational groups. In Unisys, for example (presented later), it was reported that sales people were motivated by salary and found it prestigious to drive an expensive car, whereas system people found it more prestigious to be rewarded by a 3 weeks course in Silicon Valley in the US. In IBM this difference is institutionalised in the career system, in the way that people in IBM can choose between system engineering and customer engineering, after their basic training and indoctrination.

The cultural paradigm in Total is, thus, characterised by being divisive and split. The common frame of reference in which the two subcultures are inscribed seems to be marked by a casual manner and high degree of informality. Formal education, titles and "papers" are not regarded important, but practical experience and what you actually are capable of doing (the results) is what really counts and unites the two somewhat different subcultural systems. A certain amount of egalitarianism and a general anti-authoritarian attitude are also dominant characteristics of the culture in Total and are the only commonly shared beliefs. Thus, you may say that the two subcultural systems are loosely coupled to each other, but internally fairly consistent. A common frame of reference, though relatively limited and weak, seems to constitute an overall cultural framework, which is capable of keeping the two contrasting subcultural systems together.[4]

In this example of occupational subcultures, the division of work appears as a central dimension constituted by the "ecological context", which is important for the formation of these two subcultures. But other dimensions also contribute to the production of the two distinct subcultures: the grouping of the actors (physical location as well as structural clustering, as the IT people were located in their own buildings following the structural clustering), together with the different properties of the individuals (here sales oriented persons versus technology oriented people). The latter distinction apparently represents attitudes and value orientations that the persons develop prior to their recruitment to the IT organisation, and that are compatible with and reinforced by the reward systems applied by management.

The several ecological dimensions enforcing the two subcultures in the case of Total, explain both their development and their ability to co-exist. At the same time the Total case contributes to understanding why these two cultures, as shown in figure V.1, characterise many IT organisations on the supplier side. They emanate from a classical division of work, but are also rooted in individual properties and reinforced by management. This again helps to understand why these subcultures emerge even in organisations, as for example Unisys, where the two groups of actors are integrated in departments coping with different customer segments.

4.2   Datacentralen – An Example of "Hierarchical" and "Imported Generational" Subcultures

Datacentralen was founded in the fifties as a partnership between the Danish state, the municipalities, and the counties with the purpose of developing IT systems and carrying out data processing for the public sector – ministries, local and regional agencies, and other public institutions (see Chapter II for more background information on Datacentralen).

The cultural pattern in Datacentralen is characterised by traditional "blue-collar worker" features. By this we refer to informality as regards dress code and a lot of technical macho jargon that are observable in the organisation[5]. Union membership, good craftsmanship and workable solutions were regarded important by the members, whereas formal education is not recognised or valued (Pedersen and Sorensen, 1989). The collective understanding is dominated by a distinct group orientation among the IT people who have defined the situation as a dichotomy between "us" (the workers' collective) and "them" (the top management, who are separated and exists as a subculture).

When you look at the history of Datacentralen, during the start up and the early phase in the fifties, it was strongly influenced by the recruitment of "practitioners" and "autodidacts" of various kinds[6]. In the late sixties, the "spirit of 68" and the political orientation that followed in the 1970s made Datacentralen (as a quasi public institution) to a stronghold for the IT unions, that further sustained and shaped the "blue-collar" culture. This dominant "blue-collar" culture in Datacentralen appears, however, to be challenged by new values entering Datacentralen with new groups of IT people.

The recruitment pattern in Datacentralen has changed over the last five to ten years, and a growing number of people with formal education, for example, graduates with supplementary IT courses, and in particular "EDP- assistants" have entered the IT labour market and Datacentralen – the same trend which was explained in a previous section about the IT field in general. This implies that the balance between the "autodidacts"/"practitioners" and the personnel with formal education may be reversed over time. As Datacentralen continues to expand, the company has to recruit a larger and larger proportion of new employees among young IT people – children of the 1980s, who do not share the values of the old generation of Datacentralen employees. They seem, in contrast to the "oldtimers" traditional worker-manager dichotomy, to be carrying values of a more non-political craftsman culture and tend to be more individualistic, not considering themselves to be members of a larger collective. The young IT peoples' shared understanding is marked more by an orientation towards job content and obtainment of qualifications, accompanied by a consciousness about their market value and career prospects. One could say that for the "newcomers" union membership is an artifact they adapt to and not a value or belief, they have internalised; whereas to the "oldtimers" union membership is seen as reflecting and symbolising solidarity with the workers' collective. This is also evidenced in the observation that, while "oldtimers" exclusively believed in and advocated collective workers' strategies – like "trade unionism", "craftsmanship" and "professionalism" – the "newcomers" were more open towards the idea of pursuing more individual strategies – like "job hopping" (cf. Friedman, Chapter IX).

Some "oldtimers" see the different value orientation of the younger IT staff as a severe threat to their dominant culture. It appears nevertheless, as if the "oldtimers" culture maintains dominance. The reason may be that the "new-comers" ones are actually leaving the company after a few years, whereas the "oldtimers" stay. This is partly due to Datacentralen's status as a quasi-public company, which prevents it from paying competitive wages. The result is that the young "EDP-assistants" typically leave their jobs in Datacentralen after two or three years, having obtained expertise in a given area of IT.

Another explanation of the inertia of the old culture is that some of the academics, who are concurrently being recruited by Datacentralen, hold some values and a collective understanding similar to the "oldtimers" in Datacentra-len. Often they have tasted the sour fruits of unemployment and bad wages and, thus, are more inclined to acknowledge the importance of the unions and to accept other important values of the dominant culture in Datacentralen. But so far their numbers are not large.

The previous dominant distinction between management and "IT workers", resulting in management forming a kind of subculture in relation to the dominant "blue collar worker/trade unionist" culture, was based upon the values carried into the organisations by the individuals ("properties of individuals"). It was furthered by the division of work, the grouping of actors, and the employees' relative autonomy in relation to management – reflected in and sustained by the unionisation. However, this subcultural distinction and tension are blurred by the generationally based subcultures that reflect shifting social norms and values, imported into Datacentralen via the properties of new individuals in terms of qualifications, values, and norms. As the division of work has been altered towards more flexible forms, the grouping of actors has been modified into a profit centre structure, and a campaign has been launched to strengthen management's control. The old "IT worker's" subculture is thus put under pressure. In the long run, the result may turn out to be a transformation of the old subcultures of Datacentralen, and the emergence of subcultural patterns that resemble that of other IT organisations.

4.3   Unisys Denmark – An Example of "Imported Merged" Subcultures

The focus of the present case is on the Danish division of the Unisys corporation. Unisys is a fairly young IT firm, the result of a merger between two relatively large international IT companies, Burroughs and Sperry (see Chapter III for more background information on Unisys as well as Burroughs and Sperry).

The culture of the former Burroughs appears as an *administrative* and *procedural culture*, dominated by a collective understanding that values formal policies, directions, rules and procedures with extensive use of planning and reporting (organisational life is described as "structured"). This culture emphasises doing it "the right way". In contrast to this, the former Sperry seems to thrive on a *sales-marketing culture*, dominated by a target and day-to-day orientation. At times this culture is very hectic and frustrating to work in, but it also has a collective understanding that regards people, informal contacts and networking across the official hierarchy as important. The emphasis here is on achieving your goals and showing results.

In this case the subcultures are *not* constituted by division of work, hierarchy, generations, physical location or structural clustering. These two subcultures are *"imported"* as a result of the merger. This type of cultural clash in relation to mergers and acquisitions has, in recent years, attracted a great deal of attention (Sales and Mirvis, 1984; Walter, 1985; Nahavandi and Malekzadeh, 1988; Dahlgren and Witt, 1988). Such "imported" subcultures are products of different historical developments. Organisations facing different problems have, over time, developed different local solutions and built up different repertoires of routines and traditions.

These two quite different cultures emerged in organisations that in many respects were confronted with similar technical and market contingencies. This points to the importance of several of the dimensions of the ecological context. First, the separation of the two organisations, prior to the merger, created the potential for the development of different cultures. Next, the different groupings of actors into a hierarchical structure separating systems people and sales people (the tradition in Burroughs) and a less rigid, network-like structure encouraging team-work (the tradition in Sperry) introduced important sources of variation. These were reinforced by quite different managerial styles – direct control (Burroughs) and responsible autonomy (Sperry), and socialisation processes corresponding to these.[7]

After the merger, and prior to the interventions of management, these two cultures co-existed as "imported" subcultures, each with their own logic. Even after a series of well-planned interventions by management aiming at the creation of a new, unified culture, we were, however, still able to find traces of both of the pre-existing subcultures (Pedersen, 1991). This illustrates how persistent cultural patterns are, and that it is possible to have two different cultures co-existing in an organisation.

In our point of view, the co-existence of subcultures is possible, among other things because some kind of common, overarching frame of reference has been established. This new common cultural frame is expressed in a new name and logo, and in the physical integration of the two companies in a new building. These artifacts in themselves are only weak indicators of the existence of a culture, and do not create a culture per se. But in this case, they are attributed great significance by organisational members as symbols of unification and the change into a new organisation. It seems as if management (both at the international and national level) by creating these new artifacts, and by emphasising information to employees throughout the merger process, has furnished the employees with important means for the creation of a new, collective understanding.

In the relations between the two former cultures, and in particular the issue of post-merger cultural dominance, it appears that certain Sperry' practices have been continued and dominate the present activities in Unisys today. Yet, this dominance is not one-sided, as practices and cultural traits from the former Burroughs likewise can be found in the present Unisys culture. However, informants do not report any cultural clashes between these two apparently different cultures. It seems as if the emerging new organisation is characterised by a cultural pattern constituted by a dominant culture largely influenced by the former Sperry culture, co-existing with a subculture that primarily is expressing former Burroughs values and beliefs. It may be, however, that this observed cultural pattern represents a transition phase, and that in years to come these two "imported" subcultures will have transformed and integrated.

5   Implications for the Management of High-Tech Firms:
        Uniformity of Subcultures or Preservation of
        Differences?

As the preceding analyses have shown, the subcultures within IT organisations possess varying degrees of stability and are more or less clearly demarcated. Management has certain possibilities of influencing the ecological context of a given subculture via both the recruitment of actors, their socialisation, the division of work, the grouping of actors, and the choice of control systems. But management is not omnipotent. Our case studies indicate that at least the sales-, systems development-, and technical development subcultures have an important autonomy in relation to management. For one very technical group – the systems programmers – the subculture is largely outside the control of management (see Chapter I). This is both related to the nature of the tasks of these actors, and to a high turn-over of these actors between the firms. We have also identified collective understandings that seem to be occupationally based, as was the case for the sales consultants and the systems consultants. Thus, the subcultures are only partially within the control of the focal organisation and its management. To a large extent they are properties of complex actors, that develop competences by careers that cut across organisational borderlines.

In this situation management is facing the important strategic choice of manoeuvring between the two extremes of uniformity of subcultures via the creation of a corporate culture, and an acceptance or reinforcement of the subcultures. In our point of view, the different subcultures represent orientations and competences that are necessary for the solution of the complex tasks of systems analysis, development and implementation – and hence "invisible assets" in relation to the firm's effective and efficient performance.

Accordingly, the main problem of management is not to establish a strong corporate culture, but to differentiate and integrate (cf. Lawrence and Lorsch, 1967) the subcultures in order to cope with the complex task situation that a given organisation is facing. The differentiation is necessary in order to undertake the very different task elements in a competent manner, and the integration is necessary in order to achieve the necessary cooperation between the subcultures.

In some cases "isolation" and protection of a subculture may be the appropriate response – as is the case for some of the technically specialised subcultures. Thus, "corporate culture" can be regarded as a means to achieve a certain degree of integration, but not as the "one best way" of tackling problems experienced in relation to subcultures. On the contrary, a very homogeneous and coherent corporate culture may represent a threat to the organisation's capacity to solve problems and adapt, in the sense that differentiation of actors and the subsequent tensions and contradictions within the firm represent an innovative capacity.

However, in an organisational setting a given subculture exists in *relation* to a dominant culture or other subcultures, and can only be identified in this context. As a suggestion for a typology of subcultural forms and their interrelations, Martin and Siehl (1983), have identified three types of subcultures : "enhancing", "orthogonal", and "counter cultural".

The *"enhancing"* subculture is, in relation to the core values of the dominant culture, characterised by being more fervent than the rest of the organisation. In an *"orthogonal"* subculture, the members would simultaneously accept the core values of the dominant culture and a separate non-conflicting set of values particular to themselves. As regards the *"counterculture"*, some of its core values are in opposition to and represent a direct challenge to the core values of the dominant culture. A categorisation of subcultures according to this classification appears to be a useful procedure in order to sort out different situations, and to consider appropriate managerial actions.

Total is a case of two clearly distinct, occupationally based counter-subcultures – that of systems and sales – which co-exist within a weak overarching corporate culture. Several ecological dimensions tend to separate these two subcultures, and thus facilitate their co-existence. The existence of these two countercultures represents an important strategic concern for management in relation to future changes in the ecological context that may trigger off a higher level of conflict between these and, perhaps a need for a change in the balance between the two.

The case of Datacentralen can be described as illustrating two clearly demarcated countercultures, too, management versus a worker subculture of which the latter has been dominating. In this setting a new generationally based subculture is emerging that appears to be weaker, but orthogonal in relation to both of the other subcultures. This can be supplemented with external pressures on management and ongoing structural adaptations that tend to divide the IT workers' subculture. This leaves us with a diagnosis of the situation, where an important task of management will be to manage the transition of the identified three subcultures.

The Unisys case shows how management, forced to deal with existing orthogonal and "imported" subcultures, has the possibility of avoiding unproductive clashes between these. The key in this case appears to be the creation of an overarching culture, to which the preexisting cultures have positive relations, in the sense of points of identification (name, logo, physical integration etc.). The former "Sperry" subculture is enhancing in relation to the new, emerging corporate culture, while the former "Burroughs"'s subculture relates as orthogonal to this.

This leads to a perception of subcultures as being the "building blocks" of the future organisations – with the qualification that these elements in themselves are dynamic subsystems. However, from the perspective of management, in relation to innovation and change, differentiation in the form of subcultures seems to be much easier to handle. Subsystems can then be changed or subject to innovation without affecting other subsystems, as the various subsystems are loosely coupled (Orton and Weick, 1990). The challenge to management of innovation, therefore, is to pay attention to latent and emergent subcultures, not to eliminate them, but to utilise them as important sources of innovation. In the terminology of Orton and Weick (1990) the organisation, as a direct effect of loose coupling, then improves its requisite variety and its adaptability.

This proposed need for differentiation has to be combined with the changing demands faced by IT organisations over the last three decades. According to Friedman and Cornford (1990) the demands IT firms have been facing are shifting from hardware to software constraints, and then to constraints concerning user-relations. In this light, the relative openness of the IT field towards actors with a diversity of educational and practical backgrounds can be regarded as a viable response to the changing demands of IT application for administrative purposes. An early professionalization of the IT people combined with an emphasis on formal IT qualifications instead of learning-by-doing, or a tight managerial control of the IT people might have resulted in greater difficulties in adapting to the changing contingencies.

Notes

1   IT is used as an abbreviation for Information Technology throughout the article, and covers both hardware, software, and related services. In Europe this term has replaced EDP (Electronic Data Processing), DP (Data Processing), and computing.

 By IT people we refer to the people occupying positions within IT firms as operators, programmers, systems programmers, analysts/programmers, systems analysts or -planners, and systems consultants. In Denmark, these categories amount to about 30.000 persons.

2   See also Meek (1988), concerning some of the problems of transferring the culture concept from anthropology to organisation theory.

3   The same was found in a study of two radiology departments and the X- ray technologists and CT-techs, (Barley, 1987).

4   For a more detailed presentation of the culture in Total, see also Pedersen and Sorensen (1989).

5   See also Collinson (1988) for an interesting study on the relation between shop-floor humour, gender identity and working class resistance.

6   As opposed to Datacentralen, other institutions within the Danish IT industry have been influenced by an academic milieu, for example RCI.

7   See Friedman (1977) for more details on the concepts 'direct control' and 'responsible autonomy' and, Strandgaard Pedersen (1991) for a more detailed presentation of the differences concerning socialisation processes in the companies in question.

Part B
Actors, Networks and Organisations at the Edge of the IT Field

Introduction

In part A we concentrated on communities and organisations in terms of their similarities and differences, changes in their relative characteristics, their internal dynamics and interrelationships. In this part we concentrate on those who occupy positions between organisations and on groupings of people and organisations in the IT field who do not fit easily into a single community or a set of communities. Here we concentrate on the spaces between organisations and between communities. We examine mediators of IT functions, people and organisations which intercede between IT systems and traditional suppliers of IT on the one hand, and people and organisations at the edge of the IT field. We also examine the experiences and strategies of those which are most heavily dependent on mediators, the small and medium sized enterprises (SMEs – companies with 50 employees or less). Both of these groups are more likely to be regarded (and to regard themselves) as on the periphery of the IT field. Most are not full time IT specialists. Many regard IT as essential for adequately carrying out other tasks, but some are suspicious of IT and of providers of IT (particularly of traditional suppliers). In spite of their rather tentative relation to IT, these peripheral outposts of the IT field have been particularly dynamic in recent years. Throughout its history the IT field has grown at least as much by the introduction of computer-based systems into previously non-IT-using organisations as by new systems being introduced to existing IT users or by changes in implemented IT systems. The CHIPS project operated at a time when most new users were SMEs. We argue that the problems they and their advisors encountered as they approached the IT field were distinctive. These problems led to distinct responses at the periphery of the field in the late 1980s.

In Denmark this group of potential IT users is particularly large. SMEs account for 85% of Danish enterprises. In addition this sector of the Danish economy is well served by private and public sector advisors and intermediaries. There are specialists dealing with SMEs (trade associations, auditors, consultants, brokers and the Technological Information Centres) as well as informal advisors, including friends and relations, and the more general sources of information about IT (journalists, educators and, of course, salespeople). All can be viewed as providing a useful, but also a bewildering and potentially dangerous array of information resources to the owner-managers of SMEs deciding whether to adopt an IT system, which system to adopt and how to adjust their practices in order to benefit from systems being implemented.

Chapter VI analyses growth at the periphery of the IT field concentrating on the perspective of the SMEs. Their lack of in-house expertise and their inability to hire full time specialists to manage and carry out the implementation of IT have forced them to rely on external agents. They have found that these agents have been more concerned with selling and handling technical aspects of IT systems, rather than being oriented toward the implementation and adaptation processes. In consequence the implementation of IT for SMEs has often been a troubled experience, with clashes between the IT cultures arising from the centre of the IT field and the artisan nature of the SMEs.

The size of SMEs does not generally allow a strong division of labour for dealing with tasks beyond those directly related to servicing their prime markets. Traditionally they have had to rely on outsiders for specialist advice. This has been particularly important for financial management skills and has led to an expanded role for auditors in this sector. However IT threatens to replace many auditor functions. The danger of relying on auditors to give advice on IT systems when they have a vested interest in the result has pushed SMEs to other IT mediators. Other mediators are also difficult to rely on because many are not truly independent of particular suppliers. The general need for trust relations to be built up around advice on IT is discussed in this chapter and experiences of different sources of information and security in the mediation of IT are reported. The chapter ends with an evaluation of the many problems SMEs have encountered in their association with the IT field and recommendations for how this situation can be improved are offered.

Chapter VII investigates the role of the more than 200 Danish trade associations. Given the industrial structure it was expected that the trade associations in Denmark would play an important role as mediators of IT in relation to their SME members. However their role has been modest. Even though some of them have regarded IT as a base for expanding their activities and for attracting more members, few have established a service bureau solution or developed trade specific systems. The few cases of this are associations with artisans and small industries as members. Furthermore, with a couple of exceptions, only a modest proportion of members use the standard systems of their respective associations, where such are available. Thus the trade associations have experienced the strategy of systems development as both expensive and risky.

The major advantage from the members point of view is that the trade associations feel more responsible for the implementation process and educational needs than the traditional suppliers. They can also often negotiate better terms in relation to the suppliers than can their members acting as individuals. A major drawback, however, is that the members risk having to adopt a large systems package from the association and that this solution is not necessarily the best one on the market.

Chapter VIII is more theoretical and focuses on the overall networks which include both SMEs and their potential sources of information and security. A general model of network relations is developed drawing on three sets of analysis in the literature: social network analysis among individuals, the business network approach associated with work done at Swedish business schools, and relational contract theory concerned with repeated exchange relations. We develop the distinction between purposive linkages and potential linkages in networks relevant to computerisation. Purposive linkages are specifically made to gain access to information, services or materials relevant to computerisation. Potential linkages are formed for other purposes such as friendship or general business interests or hobbies.

Five case studies illustrate a range of experiences of SMEs in dealing with IT. The studies reveal the inadequacy of purposive networks and different ways in which potential networks are mobilised to compensate. These potential networks are not without problems and cannot be romanticised as providing a completely adequate "solution" to the short-comings of purposive linkages. Nevertheless, those SMEs with strong potential networks appear to be more likely to cope with the problems encountered during the introduction of IT.

Chapter VI
Small Enterprises Coping with the Challenges of Information Technology

Mette Mønsted

1 Introduction

The introduction of information technology to small firms has in many ways been troublesome and they have faced many of the same problems encountered by larger firms. The reason for focusing specifically on small firms is their lacking in-house expertise. Thus, the process and diffusion of technology to small firms should moreover be analysed as a social process of interaction.

Approximately 85% of Danish firms fall within the category small firms, i.e., firms employing less than 20 employees. These firms are typically characterised by their lack of specialised expertise. As a group they are more dependent on external assistance than larger firms and most of them have to rely on external experts, whose competences they are unable to assess. Therefore, the decision making process and implementation of IT is a good case for analysing the support of the network, the diffusion of a new technology, and how the problems encountered by user groups are handled.

The purpose of the study is not to evaluate the individual information system or configuration, but to assess how the implementation of IT is handled by small firms without "in-house" expertise and how it changes the division of labour. In this perspective the network approach seems to be fruitful for interpreting the use of advisers and specialists.

This chapter is based on interviews with 20 small and medium sized firms, up to 50 employees, within production and construction[1]. The firms selected are located around a provincial town in Western Sealand. Other interviewees are auditors, trade association officials, including the Association of Authorized Public Accountants, and small IT suppliers in regional centres.

2   Small Enterprises in a Danish Perspective

The issue of analysing the problems of introducing information technology to small firms may seem exotic. Danish industry is, however, strongly dominated by what is considered very small firms in a European context. Within manufacturing 83% of the firms are employing less than 20 persons; within construction the figure is 96%, and within retail 97% (1983).

The very small firms of less than 20 employees are qualitatively very different from larger firms. They are most often *run by the owner* who handles all the different roles of management.

The division of labour does not cater for specialists in all fields and the tradition seems to be to recruit mainly skilled labourers of the same skills as the owner. The generalised manager is the "expert at hand", and he rarely has immediate specialists to draw on. Therefore, small firms are highly dependent on assistance and expertise from outside the firm (Mønsted, 1986). The typical owner/manager of small manufacturing or construction firms have skills and interests in technical issues related to the production. But *they often lack both skills and interests in financial management*. Therefore, they are often highly dependent on persons who are qualified to deal with this issue, as for example, an accountant in the firm, or external experts such as the auditor.

In some very small firms the owner also handles the accounts. But more often (in approximately 30% of the small firms) his wife assists him in office work. She is often responsible for the accounts, whether she is a qualified accountant or not. The assisting wives have very different backgrounds. Most of them, however, are not qualified as business administrators or book- keepers, but are trained on the job by the auditor. Firms of more than 10 employees more often employ a clerk who is in charge of administrative tasks as well as the book-keeping. But all major economic decisions are left with the owner.

Small firms relying on external experts are rarely able to assess their complementary skills properly. Therefore, co-operation with external experts is often based on personal trust and recommendations by others. In order to avoid mistakes and to save time on searching for alternative information, small firms tend to build up networks of relatively permanent relationships through both formal contacts, i.e., customers, suppliers, colleagues, and informal relations, mostly friends, sports and sailing clubs, etc.(Mønsted, 1986; this reader Chapter VIII).

3 Motives for Introducing Information Technology

Small Danish firms within manufacturing and construction have, until recently, tended to let the auditor do most of the book-keeping, leaving only the cash book in the firm. Thus, the auditor to some extent functions as the external expert and service bureau.

The first introduction of administrative IT focused on the strong dependence on the auditor. The earliest systems were sold under the heading *"save the auditor"*, that is the introduction of administrative IT would make the auditor redundant and thus pay for itself. However, this objective is not always easily obtained. Transferring tasks from the expensive auditor to the firm may strengthen the autonomy of the firm, but does not in itself make the firm better equipped for dealing with financial issues.

Other motives for introducing IT have mainly been the opinion of others emphasising that "this is the future, and you may just as well start it now", or "the typewriter with a few lines of memory is more expensive than a PC so you may just as well jump into it". However, the need for administrative systems in small firms varies. For many, the investment is not profitable in terms of increased sales or profits. It may save time, but only after a long, and often very strenuous introduction period involving much extra work.

The benefit of introducing an administrative system is not only the possibility of processing invoices much faster. Qualitatively, it also improves the firm's access to economic data. The latter implies that data, which were earlier left to the auditor, were not always available when needed for planning. Now, the firms working with administrative systems have immediate access to these data in the firm and can thus produce figures for planning at any time.

A large number of small firms are interested in introducing IT, but have difficulties in finding the financial resources. Well over half of the small firms have not introduced IT, and a considerable part of them have no intentions of doing so. Their primary reasons for not wishing to introduce IT are either that the investment is not immediately profitable, or that they write very few invoices, as for example, sub-contractors, and thus do not feel a current need. An often used argument is that a standard system cannot supply the customer with the personal service which is so important in their field.

4 The Needs of SMEs and the Services Offered by the Suppliers

The suppliers saw the introduction of PCs into small firms as a chance to spread the technology and open up a totally new standardised market for IT. The suppliers, trade associations and auditors expected to penetrate rapidly into the market. However, the introduction of IT into small firms is different from that of larger installations where the requirements have been stated explicitly. Many of the small firms have not been able to specify their exact requirements and many salesmen have tended to sell much more comprehensive and complicated systems than required and to promise the customer "a rose garden". Furthermore, they have failed to give a realistic picture of the necessary amount of time to be spent on learning the systems. The first studies of the introduction of administrative IT in small firms revealed that the process had been extremely troublesome, and that some of the systems functioned poorly (Mønsted and Neergaard, 1986).

The needs of the SMEs can be divided into two fundamentally different types of situations.

a) The services demanded for the introduction.
   The level of knowledge of IT in the firm is often very limited and the role of the "IT specialist" is, together with the SME-owner/book- keeper, to specify the requirements often by using a mediator.
b) Service, maintenance and advice to firms using IT.
   Once the small firm has introduced IT, and perhaps even has developed some internal expertise, the role of the IT specialist is much more specific and technical.

These are very different profiles of suppliers, and with the tendency of small enterprises to maintain already established service relations, they cannot both be expected to be fulfilled. How these demands are met varies much from case to case. The main difference seems to be whether the consultant is very technically minded and mainly concerned with the technology itself, or he/she is an advanced user of the software and hardware simultaneously with being acquainted with the issues to be computerised.

Earlier, the more technical consultants and sales persons prevailed causing a lot of communication problems for first time adopters. Today, the two roles can be combined as the software has become more self-instructive. But in many cases the "techie" will expect the user to possess some basic knowledge of IT, though he may not himself have much knowledge about the application area, for example, accounting.

Currently there is a tendency for larger IT suppliers to combine the two roles and recruit people with different professional backgrounds related to the application area and then teach them the IT necessary for dealing with the customers. However, in many cases larger supplier firms are not very interested in servicing small firms which are thus referred to small suppliers. Therefore, the small supplier firms must, aside from the technical skills, also be able to communicate at different levels, understand the problems of the issues to be computerised and be capable of offering the necessary training during the introduction period. Thus integrating many aspects of computing in servicing small firms is demanding, but may be an opportunity for maintaining customers and securing the soundness of sales initiatives.

5   The Decision to Implement IT

The classical model of diffusion of innovation in Rogers's innovation theory attributes great importance to the roles of information, early adopters and opinion leaders for a wide dissemination of the technology (Rogers, 1962; Rogers and Shoemaker, 1971). Therefore, the functions needed in the different stages of computerisation change. The advanced users may need information and training that can only be rendered by a professional IT specialist. In the early phase, however, characterised by few adopters, information, training, advice, and recommendations are very important to the dissemination of technology. During the actual decision-making process in the purchasing firm, there is a great need for psychological safety and different types of experienced users are often contacted for advice, also outside the formal network.

Just as in other cases of new problems arising, small firm owners use their contact with colleagues, other consultants (e.g., auditors), and friends in order to find and assess relevant suppliers and relevant solutions. Most of them do not like the idea of being the first one to test out the technology, but will try to contact persons whose judgement they trust. The economic transaction of buying services and equipment is thus closely related to the evaluation of people trusted (opinion leaders), who are not financially benefitting from their choice.

Earlier research on small firms has shown, that the time span between the decision to have IT, and the decision of what to buy is very long (Mønsted and Neergaard, 1986). This long period is not spent on thorough assessments, but is characterised by preliminary examinations and much confusion. The possibilities are manifold, and frightening examples are plenty. The firm may well be stuck in this phase for a long time, unable as it is to evaluate the options and structures of the many and often contradicting information. The uncertainty is too overwhelming to get an overall picture of the market and make a decision.

A recent study confirms this long time-lag from the first interest and information meetings with suppliers to the actual purchase and introduction of IT. The period often lasts more than six months and during this phase the different types of network relations provide some help (see Chapter VIII). The informal network seems to be a way of screening the abundant amount of information from the suppliers, of finding relevant suppliers and of specifying some requirements.

The informal network is used to sort out information and reduce the feeling of uncertainty thus enabling the firm to act (Mønsted, 1990). This process of structuration is, however, based on other parties' evaluations rather than on the factual needs of the firm. Often solutions adopted by "very similar" firms are imitated. Another method of overcoming the problem of structuration is to adopt a gradual and "safe" introduction to IT; one solution could thus be to purchase a cheap "bamboo" PC and this way become acquainted with the technology and its possibilities and, hence, better capable of defining the specifications and requirements to the "real IT supplier". This way of introducing IT has proved successful in a few cases, but it was extremely time consuming.

6   The Implementation Process

Early adopters of IT were faced with many problems. Not only did they lack access to experienced users in their informal networks, but the first standard solutions were very inflexible. Thus the demand for programming expertise from the supplier specialists was evident. Also the technical problems were many: low capacity of hardware, poor or inadequate software and/or a malfunctioning printer. This created a demand for technical computing services from specialists who, however, did not possess any expertise in accounting and who were often incapable of understanding the requirements demanded. They were obviously much more *IT specialists, than support staff for new users.*

The marketed software has improved and thus the possibilities of acquiring suitable and more flexible standard software. Hence, the demand for specialists has changed and eased the need for instruction. As the programmes and systems as such have improved and become more flexible, the technical demands to sellers have declined. The ability to diagnose the combined problems of accounting, communication, and the technical solution becomes increasingly important to the competition between suppliers.

It is important to note that the small suppliers, who initially did programming, are now practically almost entirely engaged in selling and instructing, and hardly do any programming today. This is now the domain of specialised software houses. The availability of software packages with built in user instructions opens up new important aspects, as the user by following the instructions can learn how to exploit all aspects of the programme. Still, this requires some basic knowledge in and experience with IT, but not at the level of a programmer – advanced users may well take over this function. The problems arise if other more technical services are needed for maintenance or developing special functions, then the real technical experts are needed.

Most systems implemented by small firms are related to simple accounting and invoicing tasks. Very few have installed more advanced systems for financial management, stocks or tenders. The systems are fairly standardised but have undergone changes during the three years that the CHIPS research project studied the field and have thus improved considerably, especially in relation to the user support of the firm.

Introducing IT is not only a question of supplier-user relations, often it also involves other changes in the internal work processes and, hence, the skills needed. Furthermore, the division of labour between the firm and the external expertise has changed. Firms that earlier used the auditor as a service-bureau for book-keeping, most often handle the accounts themselves after having introduced IT. Thus, the process of computing is not only linked to the technology, but in many cases also to basic accounting problems.

In general the problems of implementation are due to the fact that information systems are not solutions in themselves, but rather means to solve problems. Therefore, different types of expertise are required to convert them into a useful tool.

7   Mediators of IT to SMEs

If the introduction of IT to small firms is perceived as a diffusion process, the early stages could be described as situations in which the firms introducing IT are opinion leaders with special characteristics, and at the same time as situations characterised by few available specialists and standard solutions. The customised service mainly demanded in the beginning of the 1980s was too expensive for the small firms. In this phase, the large installations were the interesting markets for the suppliers, and small installations had difficulties in finding the service needed. The "specialists" were interested in the technical aspects and were often incapable of communicating with the customer who had too little knowledge of the field to ask the right questions and specify his requirements. The probability of ending up with a satisfactory solution was small. There was every chance of the process being derailed by mistakes and problems.

With the introduction of the PCs in the mid and earlier 1980s the small and medium sized enterprises became an interesting market for the suppliers. Standard software was developed and a number of trade associations went into the field with the aim of diffusing new technology by developing a better and easier introduction to IT for their members. The many problems and the felt need for introducing new technology, paved the way for expanding the activities and engaging in the development of systems that met the specific needs of the members, as well as developing courses and a supportive structure for their members (Boch, 1989).

The other perspective of diffusion is that IT is just a means and is sold as any other type of machinery. But "the decision to change routines and formalise and standardise information processing may be much more difficult for the small firm, than the introduction of information technology itself" (Mønsted and Neergaard, 1986, p. 161).

Thus, the introduction of IT not only gives access to new problem areas and involves new expertise; it may also transfer job functions from an external expert to a non-expert in the firm. If this process is not supported, the result may easily be disastrous. It is no longer possible for the auditor to keep an eye on the firm's cash and deposits and to warn against crises due to lack of assets available.

The firm must be capable of handling the data, and time must be allocated to the process of learning how to computerise accounts. Furthermore, the users must thoroughly know the issues to be computerised – in most cases of small firms this means the principles of book-keeping. IT in itself is not a means to teach managers, secretaries or wives neither accounting nor book- keeping. The result is, of course, that technology is diffused, but the utility value remains very low. If the introduction is to succeed, it must be followed up by a learning process and supported by agents outside the firm.

The support structure of small enterprises during the introduction phase is different from that of large enterprises. Small firms often apply a combination of professional and non-professional advice and service (see Chapter VIII). The non-professionals are characterised by not possessing formal qualifications within the field; they are experienced users, fairly advanced users or perhaps merely other new users. During the phase of introduction it is most important to the SMEs that they have access to somebody whose skills and judgement they trust.

The announcement of problems to colleagues, customers or suppliers pro- vides access to alternatives or at least an important supplement to the IT supplier already picked. But it also tends to add to the IT specialists new groups of experienced users who may assist in a more "private" or informal way. Some of these are real IT specialists working as professionals. Others, however, are merely users who themselves have developed expertise in IT. Some of the early adopters of IT have had to develop certain skills, and even if this was not the purpose, they may be asked to play the role as specialists.

The group of people acting in the role of "IT advisor" is heterogeneous and their reasons for undertaking the role are several. Some may only occasionally act in the role, as they happen to be around when problems arise, i.e., teen-age children, who diagnose the problem by applying the method of trial- and-error and often have more general computing experience – and perhaps the "fearless approach" needed in the situation. Others are called among friends, customers or colleagues who have recently been through the problems themselves.

The "user specialists" have two important functions during the introduction phase. One seems to be related to recommendations on what supplier firms to choose, including specification of demands to the system, and in a few cases which system to choose. That is, the first search for advice seems to be related to: *Who to ask* in order to avoid repeating the problems others have faced. This demands assistance from people who are both experienced and able to translate the relatively vaguely defined problems of the application area, i.e., the needs of accounting and invoicing, into technical specifications.

The other function is related to the availability of a resourceful person, someone who can act as "trouble-shooter" when the system creates problems, and does not function as prescribed, or the introduction course or manual is not understood. Most of these problems are usually basic and simple and only require little knowledge and experience to be solved, and may be solved by slightly more experienced people.

The agents most often playing the role of mediator of IT are:
sales persons, auditors, consultants from trade associations, suppliers of courses, and from the informal network: friends and colleagues.

The more advanced trouble-shooters needed for more complex or technical problems are usually searched for through the same network channels, and not only through the formal supplier.

7.1 Sales Persons

From around 1986 the suppliers have very actively been trying to penetrate into the market of small and medium sized firms. In 1987 the interviewed firms told that they received telephone calls from suppliers or direct mail approximately once a week. This trend was confirmed by follow-up interviews in 1989 and in 1990. Currently, sales persons seem to compete on their ability to communicate with and understand the needs of SMEs. An important criterion for recommending suppliers is their ability to communicate with non-experts in everyday terms. Still, there seems to be a tendency to sell too comprehensive systems and to promise too much. The gap between what is demanded and the capacity of the system often gives rise to many problems in the small firms. The SMEs have often heard about cheap solutions, and may insist on a cheap solution, although it cannot meet the demands stated. The two parties inability to communicate and find solutions that meet the demands may very well constitute the basis for serious drawbacks. The sellers are often interested in getting a maintenance contract, but most SMEs find that this is too expensive and they expect the new machine to work perfectly without service.

The problems of communication are important for the understanding of SMEs' network of assistance. The support from the supplier may function satisfactorily and in many cases the "hot-line" seems to provide good support. But there are several cases of errors or misunderstandings, and to solve these the firms often avoid the sellers and try to find someone else whom they feel they can rely on. When the existing support is blocked in some way, either because of a lack of communication or because the supplier fails to meet the demands, the informal network is activated in order to find someone who can help solving the problems.

From the mid to late 1980s, suppliers have tended to promise too much service. Customers may refer to a supplier because of the perfect "hot-line", but if this is used excessively, the supplier might either be losing out financially, as this service generates no new income, or he might be forced to frustrate the expectations of the new customers.

Suppliers and customers seem to hold different expectations to services to be rendered due to different occupational cultures, i.e., the culture of artisan responsibility versus that of high salaried technical service; this different perception may constitute the basis for failures. Typically, the small firms try to find supplier firms which organisationally and culturally are similar to them-selves. A number of suppliers have specialised in certain trade specific solutions, and tend to sell via customers' recommendations using collegial references and informal networks.

Another clear trend is the emergence of local supplier firms. Many of the small firms are located in the regional areas of Denmark while most large supplier firms are situated in the Copenhagen area or in the large regional cities. Thus, when problems arise, the small firms often feel that the physical distance was too large and that it takes too long time to get the necessary service. By choosing a local supplier they obtain both easier access to service and a better service, the latter because a local dealer is more dependent on his reputation.

7.2   Auditors

Originally, the auditors were reluctant toward IT, partly because of experiences from other countries, and partly because of the initial sales- arguments: "save the auditor". However, most of them seem to have changed their attitude and now support IT. As a result they are asked for advice, and they often assist in outlining the chart of accounts as well as training the person in charge of the book-keeping. Very often two parallel sets of accounts are made for the first three months, one is made by the auditor and the other one by the firm itself.

The auditors often seem to recommend the standard trade-association solution if one is available. Or they recommend systems which they have adopted themselves or which they are familiar with through their clients. The increasing number of firms introducing IT has expanded the auditors' knowledge of systems and they may now be more inclined to recommend systems or suppliers, they know work well with other clients. The auditors are only to a surprisingly limited extent involved in the actual decision- making process or specification of requirements.

7.3   Trade Associations

Several trade-associations decided that IT was an entrance to the future, and saw their role in developing a standard system for their members. This way they could both play a role in the diffusion of the new technology and facilitate their members' introduction of IT.

The trade associations went into the IT field at a time when the PC had just been introduced (in the early 1980s), and at a time when the costs of developing software were very high. After a couple of years all of the trade associations' systems had to compete with other trade-specific systems which were being marketed. The most applied trade association solutions were pretty simple and had many standard alternatives. By the mid-1980s, it was difficult to see the rational need for continuing to develop new solutions.

Most trade associations possessed very little competence in IT when they started to engage in the issue and initiated the development of trade specific systems. Thus, most members asking for advice were referred to the supplier with whom the association had a contract. But right from the beginning all of the trade associations have emphasised the need for user-support, and they have established introductory courses in order to ensure a gradual and successful implementation of the IT solution. In the early phases this was only done by the computer firms, but the competitive situation has implied that more of the trade associations are involved in an evaluation and discussion of the systems.(For a further discussion of the role of trade association see Chapter VII).

7.4   Suppliers of Courses

The general educational system of evening classes also offers basic courses in programming and IT. Most of these are related to simple programming and "hands-on" experience rather than assessment of programmes. The courses offered both within the adult educational system and by suppliers provide an important source of information. They disclose some of the problems connected to IT and give the participants some practical experience and, as a side effect, offer the opportunity of establishing network contacts to skilled people and other users to draw on when necessary.

The users of IT in SMEs, who had participated in courses had very different experiences, and interviews with firms and institutions indicated that most of them spent much time after the course before they decided on a system. The experiences gained through the courses had made them aware of the many problems they might have to face and, hence, made them to more cautious and careful customers. Some of the interviewees clearly stated that the courses were their only relevant source of information which was not tied to any supplier or supplier interests and that they on the basis of this had felt encouraged to pursue the idea of introducing IT.

The trade associations' IT courses are closely tied to their own solutions. But IT is also introduced via other trade association courses, e.g., on accounting, financial management, tenders, and stock management.

7.5   Informal Network – Friends and Colleagues

Naturally, the early adopters of IT had very few experienced users to confer with and they were thus forced to rely on the sellers and IT people simultaneously with developing their own expertise. Very few of them knew anybody personally who was skilled in the field and whom they could ask for informal assistance.

It has become increasingly important for SMEs to be able to draw on the experiences of colleagues and friends, both in relation to sorting out the abundant amount of information from the suppliers, to choose an appropriate supplier, and to secure assistance if the formal network fails to function. The firms interviewed during the last period of the survey (October- November 1988) had all used contacts among customers, colleagues or other suppliers in order to identify a reliable supplier firm. Some of the firms asked for the type of configuration, but the most essential question in the purchasing situation seemed to be the one of finding a relevant and reliable supplier.

8   Networks of Assistance

The network approach seems to be fruitful for the study of how problems are tackled. Who are asked about what? Who are actually the "trouble- shooters" within the field? The pattern is very complex and dynamic. The role of different formal support structures seems to have changed, and the quality of the systems provided also seems to have improved during the period studied.

A few cases illustrate some of the combinations of formal and informal structures of support connected to the decision to purchase and introduce IT.

a) A carpentry firm wanted to introduce IT. The standard trade association solutions were not feasible and the introduction was delayed. The son of the owner and one of his friends supported the idea and promised to assist in the introduction phase. The owner then decided to buy a cheap PC and gradually become acquainted with the technology, supported by this informal assistance. This way of introducing IT was time consuming, but familiarised the owner with IT enough to introduce the larger system required for processing the necessary tasks.

b) The owner of a small electrical firm started to attend courses at the technological information centre two years before introducing IT. He assessed the trade association solution to be too expensive. The version aiming at small firms did not meet his needs for capacity and had a too small capacity for his purposes and the large version was much too complex.

He attended courses offered by the trade association in financial management, discussed alternatives with colleagues and asked for their advice. Through a colleague he finally found a suitable system serviced by a very small consultancy firm.

Once the system is bought a contact to a supplier is established. To supplement this a combination of formal and informal contacts may be drawn on when problems arise. The informal contacts are typical drawn on if the formal supplier fails to meet the expectations of the firm.

c) A small electrical firm had also contracted an agency for a heat control system. For a couple of years it had been working with a small IT accounting system. As the business expanded, the system proved to be insufficient. The firm contacted the supplier of the system who advised to buy a larger system, which it did. However, the hardware capacity was too low to handle the new system and the installation never functioned properly. The supplier firm had been paid and was very reluctant to render further services. A friend and customer (an auditor) of the owner learned about the problems and offered his assistance as he was familiar with the software. The problems were more complicated than he expected, but he referred to one of his friends, who was a skilled IT specialist and who managed to solve the problems.

To what extent a combination of formal supplier relations and more informal "expertise" is used depends on the complexity of the problem, i.e., whether the defined problem implies both technical and accounting practices. In relation to some problems the supplier may be the only one asked. But with other types of problems, the information is checked or evaluated by others as well, i.e., friends, colleagues, or the auditor.

9 Concluding Evaluation of IT in SMEs

From a strictly economic point of view it may not be neither very profitable nor rational for SMEs to invest in administrative IT. This is an argument often raised by some of the SMEs who do not want IT. Many SMEs have become hesitant after learning about the first adopters' difficulties. If the process of introducing IT is evaluated after the first six months, the failures are plenty. The overall experience is that it takes a long time to make the systems work satisfactorily. The use of software seems to be limited to, for example, book-keeping, accounts of creditors and debtors, and invoicing. Very few of the SMEs have introduced systems for financial management or stock management.

One indication of the problems of introducing IT may be deduced from a survey made by the steel employers' association (Jernet, 1984). One of the questions to new users of IT revealed the factors which the users found must be accomplished before the introduction of IT.

Procedures and systems to be computerised must be organised properly	63%
Data discipline, chart of accounts and number systems	31%
Describe tasks, make analyses and set up system requirements	18%
Knowledge, training, attitudes	15%
(Source: Jernet,1984)	

Figure VI.1   Factors which Need to be Accomplished before Introducing Computers

Many problems are created by the organisation's lacking capability of handling the important task of standardising and systematising data for IT. Many of these problems are often registered as IT problems, but they are actually caused by the firm's difficulties in standardiszing data and thus to facilitate computerisation.

What is actually characterised as a failure? If the machinery runs perfectly, the firms find the installation successful. But many firms discover shortly after the implementation that the capacity of the purchased system is too low, whereas others discover that the large and expensive system is only used for book-keeping. Some of the satisfied users will face problems later on. The apparently well fitting system may not be large enough or capable of coping with the complexity of tasks demanded later on. If a large system is purchased and only a minor part of it is used, or if a small system that works well now, cannot be expanded when necessary, then it is worth questioning whether the solution is satisfactory.

Regardless of the many problems encountered almost all of those having introduced IT are satisfied once the installation functions, that is when they have overcome the long period of introduction. Some may not have an adequate installation, but they are happy just to have a limited amount of information in-house and to have overcome the introduction.

This may reflect the expectations to IT. In the early phase the expectations from the "magic" of IT were greater, but they seem to have declined, and many are satisfied if the system does not create too many difficulties and facilitates the book-keeping process. Some firms would not have bought IT, if they had known the problems and the vast amount of time required. But the general picture is one of relief: it works and a lot of tiresome routine work, which earlier burdened them during week-ends, has become easier to handle. The cash book and the monthly or quarterly accounts were considered a burden, and many are now surprised how fast it goes.

The time saved may not be an argument for the profitability, as time often has no "price" when the work is done by the owner or his wife. But once the burden of paper work is lessened, the evaluation of the time saved is very positive, though it cannot be calculated in terms of money.

The feeling of having relevant economic data within the firm is a general positive statement, whether or not the competence to use these data is present. This may well be a "general statement", and it may reveal some mistrust in the auditors, and especially to the price of their services. Generally, the application of economic data is rather limited and primitive. Therefore, the criterion for good or bad solutions tends to become primitive and related only to whether or not it works. They do not comprise an evaluation of the unexploited possibilities of the system or of alternative solutions.

If the auditor is less used, also in connection with other issues than the book-keeping, then the change may be hazardous, as the occasions to discuss the accounts with a competent person disappear. The chance of having an early warning of critical trends may disappear, too. It is imperative with such a system that the firm internally has economic expertise at its disposal or has access to a system where this service can be used at a fairly regular basis.

The decision process and implementation of IT in SMEs have often implied serious cultural clashes between sellers and "techies" on the one hand, and the artisan culture of small firms on the other hand. The communication barriers are many and some of them resemble those of the large firms in the early phase of IT, but there are certain basic differences. Small firms cannot afford to employ an expert or buy customised software and are therefore continually dependent on a group of external consultants and suppliers, whose expertise they cannot really evaluate.

The combination of formal and informal networks seems to be important as a means of structuring the first uncertain periods of sorting out information. The combined network is suitable for seeking out "trouble-shooters" – both for simple problems in the introduction phase and for the more complex technical problems.

The reliance on the informal network and a basically non-professional assistance may lead to too much standardisation and too large installations in order "to play it safe". The choice of configurations is more based on the imitation of other social network contacts than on a systematic evaluation of the possibilities in relation to the needs. This way of evaluating solutions and options seems to be fairly common also when evaluating consultancies, technical changes and marketing relations. The feeling of insecurity while having to decide in an area where the firm has no capacity or knowledge, is comforted by using the informal networks. That means, it may in some cases offer some kind of security against a total misinterpretation, but it does not provide professional evaluation of competences.

Notes

1   20 small enterprises, 5 supplier firms of IT to small firms, and 2 auditors were interviewed. Apart from this, trade association officials, inclusive of the Association of State Authorized Public Accountants, have been interviewed.

Chapter VII
Trade Associations as Mediators of Information Technology to Small and Medium Sized Firms

Mette Mønsted and Frans Boch

1   Introduction

In 1984 the Danish Government launched a series of development programmes under the Technological Development Project with the purpose of diffusing knowledge of new technology to Danish firms, especially exporting firms, thus making them better equipped for competing in the international market.

Many of the first programmes aimed at speeding up the diffusion process and at furthering the application of information technology in products, processes, and administration. In the description of the programmes, the SMEs are mentioned as a special problem, though not the main target group.

Both groups of enterprises and individual firms were eligible for support if implementation of new technology was judged to have a diffusing effect. In an effort to speed up the process, it was considered important to identify potential agents /mediators. The Technological Development Project pointed to trade associations as potential mediators because of their rich contact to many small firms, organisations and training systems (Jernets Arbejdsgiverforening, 1984). Contact was established to several trade associations to discuss the possibilities and feasibility of new technology (Mønsted and Neergaard, 1986).

The purpose of this chapter is to investigate the role of associations as opinion- leaders in connection with the introduction and dissemination of new technology.

There are three main issues to be examined:
1) To map out the field of those Danish trade associations that are acting as mediators of information technology in order to describe *how* they have handled this role, *what* sort of IT *solutions they have produced* and *what strategies* they have pursued.
2) To use these findings to uncover some of the problems faced by the trade associations when acting as mediators of new technology.

3) To discuss from a member point of view some advantages and disadvantages of the IT solutions produced by trade associations.

If perceived as a model for diffusion of innovation, many trade associations have several properties facilitating the role of "opinion leader", i.e., advanced users and trustworthy persons (institution), who can diffuse new innovations (Rogers, 1962).

Our case studies and interviews provide clear evidence that the behaviour of large enterprises in relation to the diffusion/adoption process is different from that of small enterprises.

The structure of large enterprises is often more complex and they have more resources at their disposal making it feasible for them to employ IT specialists and, in some cases, establish their own IT department. Thus, the larger enterprise will, through its staff, be able to establish direct contact with the supplier of hardware and software.

In contrast, most small enterprises rarely deal directly with the technical specialists, most often they use a mediator. The introduction of IT to SMEs is dependent on different groups of mediators of IT, and makes visible the variety of "functions and roles of IT expertise".

The introduction of IT to an SME is not only a question of adopting new technology. It involves changes in existing work processes and a need for developing new skills. Furthermore, the introduction of IT often changes the division of labour between the firm and external expertise. After having installed IT, the small firm may prefer to do the accounts itself and no longer use the auditor as a service bureau for book-keeping – a decision which in many cases reveals basic accounting problems.

Many problems arise because information systems themselves are not solutions to problems but moreover *means* to solve problems. To be able to fully exploit the potentials of information systems it is essential to know the application area well.

The vision of trade associations as mediators is not new. In the early phase of IT, the Danish government formed a special council to investigate the perspectives of and barriers toward information technology. Its final report was published in 1974 (EDB-Rådet, 1975). The purpose of the report was to contribute to the debate about the utilisation of computers in a Danish context. A number of project groups counting experts from many fields was established with the task of producing a report on how the emergence of IT would affect their respective fields.

The group of experts who covered the use of IT in the larger industries paid particular attention to the trade associations and their mediating role. In a separate chapter on trade specialised IT solutions written by this group, the formation of trade specific service bureaus was mentioned as a new concept for the utilisation of IT in small and medium sized industrial enterprises.

Referring to a Norwegian survey (EDB-Rådet, 1975) the advantages of trade specific service bureaus, were, for example:
- to advance the utilisation of IT in small enterprises by up to 10 years;
- to make it profitable to invest in large IT installations (mainframes);
- to create an environmental effect through increased cooperation on the more operational level as well as creating better solutions through more expertise.

Furthermore, the Danish project group emphasised trade associations as mediators, that could unite the forces of the small enterprises and enable them to obtain the same benefits from information technology as the large enterprises.

"There are app. 3,500 Danish industrial enterprises, of these app. 800 use IT at some level. A large number of the remaining enterprises, which probably have a need, neither have the necessary expertise nor the financial strength for the transition to computerization. The trade associations carry a heavy responsibility to assist these enterprises in obtaining a reasonable benefit from the information technology." (EDB- Rådet, 1975, Vol. II, A-16. p. 2.)

The report was primarily concerned with the technical advantages of establishing trade specialised service bureaus, whereas the more sociological concerns about the trade associations' mediating role were only briefly touched upon. Thus in a short paragraph it was recognised that the affiliation between a potential trade specialised service bureau and the trade association could be problematic.

"Affiliation to the trade can be established in several ways. For instance as a department in the trade association, in co-operation with a research institution, or as an independent firm. Direct affiliation may have an adverse effect. The degree of freedom in a trade association being limited to areas of common interests." (EDB-Rådet, 1975, Vol. II, Section A-16. p. 1.)

One might add that enterprises which are members of a trade association may, although they operate in the same line of business, be quite different in terms of size and technology. Also, some enterprises may be highly specialised within the trade while others may be operating on the edge of the trade and/or overlapping other trades.

Furthermore, the interdependence between the members of a trade association is dualistic. While the firms within some line of trade join the association in order to pursue common interests of the trade, e.g.to exert political influence to the benefit of the members or to increase the overall size of their market, the same firms are nevertheless competing for the same resources. Thus the members of a trade association reside simultaneously in a symbiotic and a competitive relationship. (Pfeffer and Salancik, 1978). Consequently we realise that the role of the trade associations, acting as mediators of new technology, is ambiguous and potentially problematic.

2   The Diversity of Danish Trade Associations

The Danish trade associations could be expected to have common interests, but they actually constitute a very heterogeneous group. Depending on the trade, they each play a different role towards their members and are not, like the chambers of commerce in other European countries, powerful bodies. They are most often voluntary associations and, hence, forced to compete for members. Not all enterprises feel inclined to join a trade association and some may have different options. This is an important background for understanding why trade associations engage in new issues of interest to their members, and why some of them in the early 1980s undertook the role as mediators of IT as a means to ease their members' introduction to this technology and thus facilitate its diffusion.

Within almost any trade some sort of a trade association or federation exists. In Denmark alone, there are more than 200 trade associations ranging from construction, steel and iron, masons, carpenters, hairdressers and umbrella manufacturers.

What furthermore makes trade associations a problematic issue to deal with empirically is that they are not only formed at different levels; horizontally, vertically, and geographically. Also the objectives of trade associations vary tremendously from trade to trade.

Horizontally some trade associations are established within a narrow line of trade such as the electricians association (Elektroinstallatørernes Landsforening) which organises only electricians with a public authorisation, whereas other associations have established themselves within a broader conception of a trade, an example of this being the building trade association ("HO Byggefagenes Mesterforening"), which counts a number of different firms within the building industry: carpenters, painters, bricklayers etc.

Along the *vertical* dimension some trade associations are exclusively representing enterprises at one level, e.g., manufacturers, wholesalers or retailers, in a specific trade such as, e.g., plumbing. Examples are the Federation of Manufacturers of Heating, Ventilation and Sanitary Equipment (VVS Fabrikanterne) and The Danish National Federation of Master Plumbers, Heating and Ventilation Contractors (Dansk VVS Installatør Forening). Other associations include several vertical layers such as the Association of Manufacturers, Wholesalers, Importers and Agents in the Electrical Trade (Foreningen af Fabrikanter, Grossister, Importører og Agenter i El-branchen).

One of the major differences among the trade associations of the construction sector is, whether or not the association is a member of the employers' association, and thus responsible for collective bargaining with the unions. Some trade associations want to keep out of this, for different reasons.

There are several umbrella organisations, some of which are member of the employers' association, others are not. The Council for Small and Medium

Sized Firms (Håndværksrådet) is an umbrella organisation for many artisan and construction associations, that do not wish to become member of the employers' association.

While many trade associations were originally formed as social organisations, some have gradually undertaken to safeguard the general interests of the trade when facing a common threat. "The Association of EDP Systems Suppliers" (Edb Systemleverandørernes Forening), for example, was founded at a time when a number of failure stories began to have a negative effect on the general image of the trade. Accordingly, the association's objectives have been defined as broadly as:

1. to unite the trade;
2. to advance the views of the trade;
3. to develop and protect the interests of the members;
4. to promote knowledge about the trade (PR activities).

As Danish trade associations differ widely in regard to both level and tasks, we have, for empirical purposes, chosen to define trade associations broadly:

Any association or federation of enterprises within a trade established to pursue its members' common interests.

3   The Trade Associations as Resource Controlling Organisations

The formation of a trade association could be seen as a structural response to the establishment of extensive long term relations between a number of interdependent enterprises within a trade. In the process of establishing such long term relations each enterprise surrenders some of its autonomy to the trade association.

The raison d'etre of the trade association is to serve the interests of its members. But in doing so the association may well pursue its own interests and develop its own goals. This leads to two different interpretations of the behaviour of a trade association: As some sort of aggregated behaviour of all the members it represents, or as an organisation in itself with its own independent objectives.

As the associations degree of autonomy depends on the members, the association is likely to attempt to alter this dependence in order to gain a higher degree of autonomy. According to Pfeffer and Salancik (1978) dependency can be defined as "the product of the importance of a given input or output to the organization and the extent to which it is controlled by a relatively few organizations" (p.51).

The trade association may, however, pursue other interests different from those of the members. While it may, for example, be in the interest of the large firms in a trade to limit the number of members of the trade association in order not to constrict the common interests of the firms, it may be in the interest of the association to increase the number of members as a means to ensure a variety of income sources in terms of membership fees.

Therefore the analysis of trade associations should not only be tied to their role as interest organisations but also to their degree of autonomy and power base in relation to control of resources.

One important aspect of the autonomy of the trade association is the degree of competition it faces. In several situations competing trade associations exist, the most important ones are:

Firstly, an enterprise may operate on the edge of one or more trades and not belong exclusively to one trade. Hence, the enterprise may consider which trade association will provide the maximum benefits for the least costs, or the enterprise may even consider joining more than one trade association.

Secondly, within several trades two or more trade associations exist. This may be due to the fact that the trade associations define their scope of trade differently, in which case they may be overlapping, as is the case of the plumbing trade, where several associations are organising plumbers, either in collaboration with other plumbers and employers in heating and ventilation, or in collaboration with blacksmiths or other construction firms.

Thirdly, two (or more) trade associations within the same trade might be competing for the same members. An example of this is the trade of painters. In all cases of competition between two associations, one of them is a member of the Employers' Association, the other is not.

Jørgensen (1977) notes, with reference to Aldrich (1971), that the autonomy of an organisation is depending on how well it can defend its organisational boundaries. According to Aldrich (1971) control over the organisational boundaries can be characterised by:

1. The degree to which an organisation can control the members' access to the organisation.
2. The degree to which the potential members can decide for themselves whether or not to participate.

Here, we will regard the autonomy of the trade association as a result of the relative power of the association to exert control over access to the association and to what extent the members are free to join it or not.

Crossing the dichotomies of control over the participation exercised by potential members and the trade association 4 basic categories emerge.

		YES	NO
Potential member control over participation	YES	1	2
	NO	3	4

(Source: Jørgensen, 1977, p. 49.)

Figure VII.1   Organisational Control (trade ass.) over Access to the Organisation

A trade association's freedom to exercise control over the access of enter-prises within a trade will often depend on the competitive situation in which it resides. Most trade associations are in a competitive situation as they only represent a fraction of the trade and/or competing associations exist. Hence, they are not in a position to fully control the influx of new members.

Some associations (category 1) will only accept enterprises which they (the current members) consider to join the suitable association, trying in this way to legitimise their accept or refusal of new members by referring to professional criteria. An example of this is the Association of EDP-suppliers, which was established by a number of service bureaus and system houses when the trade faced increasing bad will due to a number of failure stories. In order to restore the image of the trade, it was decided that the association only accepts firms of legal and economic independence which are willing to comply with the collegiate norms and standards of the trade association. But the firm is free to join or not.

In category 1 and 2, enterprises within a trade may join the association(s) as they please. Some trades may stipulate some sort of formal requirement which the enterprise must fulfil to obtain membership; a certain formal education of the owner, an authorisation, or the like. In general, however, any enterprise which fulfils the formal requirements is free to join the association.

Most of the trade associations are in the very competitive situation of category 2. Membership is voluntary and the trade has no power of control. This is, for example, the case of the painters' association.

Category 3 represents trades within which membership of the trade associa-tion is compulsory as the association is authorised to issue license to operate within the field. None of the trade associations interviewed in this study fell within this category, but the situation may well occur in a trade characterised by market oligopoly. In this case it might very well be impossible for a firm to operate outside the trade association which makes membership of the associa-tion a must (in order to survive). Thus, the firms in the association could exercise control over access to the association whereas the potential member had no influence. In practice this is an unstable situation which is more likely to move into the next category, where the organisation may not control access, when a certain professional level is obtained.

Category 4 contains the trade associations of which membership is compulsory and cannot be controlled by enterprises operating within the trade. This may be due to legal requirements as in the case of the lawyers' association and the auditors' association. Or it may be due to the existence of an exclusive agreement which makes it impossible for enterprises outside the association to operate within the trade. A good example of the latter is the pharmacy trade, in which the pharmacies' association has a mutual exclusive agreement with the unions of pharmaceutists' (DF) and pharmacy assistants' (DATF).

Following this line of thought, we note how the trade association may develop its own individual goals in an attempt to reduce its dependency on the members. In this respect the mediation of new technology can be regarded as output from the trade association and as input to member organisations. Thus, the mediating function is also a means for the association to increase its members' dependency.

Given this background of trade associations and the role they play towards their members, a number of associations decided to develop standard IT systems for their members. By doing so, they could both play a role in the diffusion of new technology and offer their members a more protected introduction to the field. But this task could also pave the way for yet another competitive strategy for recruiting members. The ambitions seem also to be related to the self-perceived role of some of the trade associations: The more centralised and powerful they were (category 4), the more likely they were to perceive IT as yet another platform for an association attending to all its members' "interests".

4   The Trade Association Survey

To test out the types and strategies of different trade associations, a survey was carried out in 1987. The analysis, however, is not only based on the survey, but also on the following supplementary empirical data.

1. A questionnaire mailed to 150 trade associations (1987) that are members of: the Council of Small and Medium Sized firms (Håndværksrådet), the Federation of Danish Industries (Industrirådet) and the Danish Employers' Association (Dansk Arbejdsgiverforening), respectively (exclusive of employers associations which are locally oriented rather than trade oriented).
2. Interviews with 6 informants in 5 trade associations which have acted as mediators of IT to their members (1987-88).

3. Telephone interviews in 1988 and follow-up interviews in 1990.
4. Documentary data
   – reports, minutes from meetings
   – newsletters
   – sales material.

Of the 150 questionnaires 70 were returned. The questionnaires provides us with the following picture:

Questionnaires returned	70
Not applicable[1]	10
Subtotal	60
Trade ass, not working with IT	33
Trade ass., working with IT	27
Subtotal	60
Trade associations, which have worked with IT:	
From the survey	27
Interviewed associations	4
Others known	6
Total working with IT	37

[1] Associations which are solely employers' associations, employees' associations or trade associations with only one member.

Figure VII.2

The low number of trade associations (47%) which responded to the survey is somewhat disappointing, but not surprising. Many small trade associations are short of resources, some do not even have a staff or premises of their own and the questionnaire may have seemed irrelevant to them. Thus the survey is being biased having an overrepresentation of larger trade associations and mainly associations pursuing an active strategy on information technology.

The purpose is to find trade associations which play different mediating roles in relation to information technology, and not a general survey of trade associations. Other information seem to confirm, that trade associations, which have been active in collective solutions of IT for their members, are covered by the 37. Thus the 31 out of the 37 (84 %) is a quite high percentage coverage in the survey.

To the question of why they had not engaged in IT solutions for their members, the 33 trade associations answered:

1. No demand from the members	19	58%
2. Members too heterogeneous	4	12%
3. Both 1. and 2.	8	24%
4. Unanswered	2	6%
Total	33	100%

Figure VII.3

The high number of trade associations which do not view IT as part of their scope due to lacking demand from the members could, at a first instance, seem somewhat surprising.

However, the major part of these trade associations cover large industries of which relatively few members constitute the majority of the industry. One reason for these trade associations not having engaged in IT could very well be that their members have sufficient resources to deal with the matter themselves, and anyway cannot benefit from standard solutions.

The heterogeneous associations could not develop any standards, as, e.g., the iron and steel employers' association covers not only very large and small user groups of different trades but also many different IT supplier firms as members.

5   The Trade Associations' Different Patterns of Involvement in Information Technology

The 31 trade associations represented in the survey that have worked with IT for their members, have handled the task very differently and their mediating efforts have materialised in a wide range of trade solutions. A few examples illustrate this diversity.

A few very centralistic trade associations, which are interfering in many aspects of the life and business of their members, saw a standard IT solution specifically designed for their members as both a new product and an important service to their members (The Pharmacies Association, The Authorized Electricians).

Most trade associations were fairly late at adopting IT. Only in a few cases the trade solutions have been developed for the "pioneers" among the enterprises. This has been the case if the trade as a whole faced loss of markets and the development of an IT solution could be one way of fighting the threat and survive. In most other trades the IT solution offered by the trade association was not designed for pioneers, as they had already been using IT for several years when the trade association was able to offer an alternative.

The effect of attempts to promote the use of IT is hard to measure. Many firms and other mediators, such as auditors, however, are referring to the impact of information about and the promotion of solutions from the trade associations.

Especially *the Pharmacists' Association* has engaged in the development of a collective IT solution for their members. They started out already in the early seventies by establishing a central service bureau in the IT department of the association. In the late seventies a minicomputer based solution was launched, but being complicated, expensive and very much delayed, it was strongly questioned. The delay implied, that a competitor was able to offer alternative PC based solutions. The competitor had developed a small configuration. It was not a real computer, but a typewriter with a limited memory for labels. But as he was developing new solutions and already had established good contacts with the pharmacies in other service functions, the centrally designed solution offered by the association's IT service bureau was not competitive. However, the competitor turned out to have promised more than he could fulfil, and at some point when the firm was facing economic difficulties, the trade association seized the chance to buy the firm. But the association was still facing the need for developing a new and more advanced system including better hardware and software.

The idea of having only one solution never materialised, and the larger and more prosperous pharmacies seemed to push for a larger system, which would be much too expensive for the smaller pharmacies.

To sum up, the development in-house by the computer department of headquarters has been very expensive, and many different models have been developed. It has been heavily subsidised by the trade association.

A few other trade associations have invested in the development of a standard system designed for the trade, such as the painters and the association of construction firms. *The Painters' Association* has developed a relatively simple system based on a DOS-steering system. Both associations started out by designing a PC solution, and they seem to have been able to maintain the same solution with few adjustments.

The Electricians' Association (ELFO) holds a strong position vis-à-vis its members partly because they have no true alternatives, and partly because the trade association offers important courses relate to authorisation, legal regulation, new materials, etc. In 1983 the association decided to engage actively in the role as mediator of IT to their members and signed a contract with a hardware and software supplier. Three solutions were exclusively developed for ELFO members and the association was in charge of sales:

1. A solution based on modem. A centralised system based at headquarters.
2. A PC based solution for small firms.
3. A PC based solution for larger firms.

The central solution implied, that the trade association handled all invoicing, a situation which most of the firms found unacceptable.

The first PC solutions were well received, but they were small and not based on a DOS steering systems. It was either difficult, expensive or impossible to run other programmes on the hardware. The service of offering up-dated price diskettes was seen as the chance of obtaining monopoly on this service. But within a short time, competitors emerged offering the same service.

Hence, ELFO has developed new solutions of larger capacity, but is challenged by competitors. The trade is, however, one of the most computerised trades, about 60% of the members are using IT. About half of these are using the trade association system.

In terms of authorisation the position of the plumbers' association is in many ways similar to that of the electricians' association, although it does not enjoy the same monopoly. Not all plumbers are organised in *the Plumbers' Association*. Some have joined the blacksmiths' association, or other related associations.

The plumbers' association negotiated with one supplier firm, identified and defined the needs of the trade and secured the specifications. The development of the system took place outside the association, whose role was more of a negotiating intermediary. But the system could only be sold to members of the trade association. The trade association engaged in the development and testing of the solution, and supported it in terms of providing regular up-dated price diskettes for the plumbers, as a service they thought to be unique. In the beginning the solution was marketed and sold by the association, but later on this function was taken over by the supplier. As in the case of the Electricians, other suppliers have developed trade specific solutions including price diskettes. Only half of the plumbers with IT have implemented solutions developed and recommended by the plumbers association.

In general, trade specific IT solutions are only used by 10% to 30% of trade association members – the plumbers are ranging low while the electricians are ranging relatively high. The two trade associations estimate that only half of the firms using IT are using the trade associations' systems. The remaining part has invested in others competitive trade specific systems. The savings banks and pharmacies are significant exceptions. Here, more than 80% of the members use the trade associations' service bureaus.

94% of the pharmacies are stated to use the trade association's IT solution. This includes, however, members who used the competing trade IT solution at the time when the trade association took over the competitor. Thus the 295 users are using 7 different systems. The latest system, which was developed in 1986, is currently being used by 8% of the pharmacies. The association is aiming at 80% of the pharmacies using this system by 1990.

6   Trade Associations' Changing Role as Mediators of IT

Trade associations that have engaged in the IT field primarily argue that the field is too complex to be handled by the members individually. The firms have little knowledge of the solutions available, what supplier to use and how to deal with IT. In this respect the trade associations have viewed their role as one of securing their members a safe introduction to the "world of IT".

The associations have emphasised different aspects of entering the "world of IT". Some associations have primarily focused on minimising the costs of investment and maintenance (negotiated reduced prices for members), while others have been more concerned about securing the members a stable and independent supplier.

Viewed from the perspective of time, the role of specific trade association solutions seems to be changing. Today, none of the trade associations imagine that they will be able to enjoy "monopoly" as suppliers. After a few years the Plumbers' Association, for example, no longer cooperates as closely with the supplier as in the beginning but has to a larger extent taken on the role of consultant and advisor.

The trade associations seem to become increasingly aware of the fact that it is impossible to cover the whole range of firms in a trade by one small and one large configuration. The members are too heterogeneous to fit into a standard trade solution. If an electrician, for instance, contracts an agency for a specific type of machinery, it is extremely complicated for him to fit this into the standard trade system. There is an increasing need for larger systems covering combined retail business. Carpenters, who aside from working as such also deal in wood, find that none of the systems developed either for construction firms or for the timber industry cover their range of business.

Even if the "security" of trade specific systems may seem to be advantageous, this notion may prove to be false. If the firm is not very representative of the trade, configurations other than the standard trade specific solutions should be considered.

Some trade associations try to avoid these problems by merely specifying criteria or recommending supplier firms. These associations have neither invested money nor too much energy in the development and maintenance of systems, they merely act as advisors.

Those trade associations that have developed their own IT solution may face problems as their status vis-à-vis the members changes from being exclusively an industrial body to also comprising the role of supplier. This situation may cause problems in two ways.

First, the trade association may be tied to a specific system that may become obsolete or outdated. It is difficult to change system if the management has "invested" much prestige in its development and, moreover, has committed itself to the members already using the system in terms of keeping it up-to-date. This is what happened in the pharmacy trade.

Second, the trade association can no longer act as an independent advisor to its members in IT matters.

In some trades (architects and surveyors) where the competitive situation has caused loss of markets, the trade associations have used their IT solution as a means to regain markets and increase membership. In the case of the surveyors, the trade has over the years lost an increasing share of its market to the consulting engineers and in an attempt to restore its position, the association has decided to invest approximately 300,000 US dollars over a three-year period in a collective IT solution for the members.

As to the trade associations' motives for offering a trade solution, it is quite evident that a number of trade associations have used their trade IT solution to attract new members. If only members can acquire the trade IT solution, then it can be used as an incentive for the free riders of the trade to join the trade association. Many of the services provided by a trade association, such as rates and negotiations with political agencies, are based on collective action, but the outcome is not always exclusively to the benefit of the members.

In this group no new members can be attracted and the risk of investing on behalf of all members is high (as in the case of the Pharmacists' Association). In the case of the lawyers, trade association membership is compulsory by law and thus there are no free riders which the association needs to attract. This may well be the reason why the Lawyers' Association is the only association that has pursued an IT strategy implying that the association "blue stamps" IT solutions developed by suppliers. Here, *any* enterprise in the trade can benefit from the trade association's mediating efforts whether or not it is a member.

As far as the hardware and software is concerned, several of the associations have changed hardware and/or software for their IT solution. This has often been complicated because the association has committed itself to firms using the system and is obliged to keep the solution up-to-date to attract new users. This problem has especially been encountered by the associations which have tied the IT solution to a specific type of hardware, such as the pharmacies and the electricians.

No trade associations have undertaken to develop systems for their members since the mid eighties. The variety of standard packages did not motivate other trade associations to venture into the role as technological agents.

7 Advantages and Disadvantages from the Enterprises' Point of View

To the small enterprises the *advantage* of a trade IT solution is primarily the feeling of security it offers. When the IT field seems to be a "jungle" of systems, suppliers, hardware and software, the "package" IT solution offered by the trade association might help to overcome the fear of entering this jungle. Trusting their own trade association to safeguard the interests and needs of its members, both the enterprises and their auditors are often more confident with implementing an IT system that has been developed by or in co-operation with the association.

Whether the IT solutions offered by the trade associations in general are better or easier to implement than other customised or standard IT systems is beyond the scope of this discussion. But on the basis of interviews with the trade associations, they seem to have been very much concerned with getting the systems to work and to avoid failure stories which might have a negative effect on the association itself resulting in, e.g., reduced financial support and/or loss of members. The trade associations are thus more committed toward the enterprise than the suppliers. The trade IT solution is in this way dependent on and concerned about the customer.

All of the trade associations have emphasised user support, and have designed introductory courses to ensure a gradual and successful implementation of the IT solution. Trade associations have also expanded courses and training activities, such as linking courses in economic management and accounts to IT (The Painters' Association). Once IT is bought, the courses should aim at expanding the application area. This changes their role more towards that of a mediator and away from that of a supplier.

The role and function of those persons communicating with the member firms have changed considerably over time. The first representatives to talk IT with the members were very technically minded and did not know anything about the application area. Also, many of them were incapable of communicating with non-specialists. The trade associations reacted quickly to this problem and stressed slow and careful (i.e., successful) introduction through a combination of courses and instructions in the member firm, and the establishment of "hotline"-services.

In general the trade associations lacked in-house competence in the initiating phase of building up a solution. Most trades referred members to the supplier firm, with whom they had a contract.

The disadvantage of trade specific IT solutions is that they have a tendency to result in large "package" solutions. IT solutions marketed by trade associations very often cover virtually all administrative routines but in terms of separate modules. In order be able to operate the whole range of modules in firms of all sizes within the trade, a large hardware installation is often required. Usually the modules can be purchased individually, but in order to get a maximum discount, the enterprise often buys the complete "package". Consequently, the introduction to computerisation becomes a giant step for the enterprise and a gradual step-by-step adaptation becomes difficult. This favours the medium sized firms and disfavours the small enterprises.

Many of the trade systems have bundled hardware and software. There are two reasons for doing so. First, the trade association may want only to deal with *one* supplier of both software and hardware making it easier to place the responsibility for the solution. Second, the trade associations can often negotiate a favourable discount on hardware if the enterprises buy additional equipment and software from the same supplier.

The bundling of hardware and software, however, also has some serious draw backs, as the trade association becomes dependent on one particular supplier and the enterprises dependent on one particular piece of hardware. Thus the risk of being stuck with an obsolete system increases.

The pattern of the trade associations acting as mediators of IT deviates on two major points from the predictions made in the early seventies (EDB-Rådet, 1975).

First, only a few trade associations have established a service bureau solution (savings banks, dentists and the electricians; the latter gave up the service bureau solution in favour of a decentralised solution). The "white book" was written in 1973 and the outlined structure was adapted to the existing technology (mainframes). Most trade associations have entered the field at a later stage (after the emergence of the minis and the PCs) and have based their solution on a decentralised model.

Second, the concept of trade specialised IT solutions, which the experts mentioned as a concept for the large industrial firms, has not been pursued by the trade associations of the large industries. But rather by the trade associations of artisans and small industry.

The early developed systems suffered from various types of "growing pains". Financially, the task of developing trade specific solutions also proved to be difficult for the associations to handle as the number of users increased much slower than expected. This situations has also changed the market for trade association solutions.

So far the application area seems to be limited and not much dependent on trade specific issues, such as stocks. Most trade association solutions include storage control. Most small firms that have tried to introduce such a system discover, however, that there is a considerable gap between what should be in stock according to the storage control, and what is actually there. Construction workers, for instance, or other skilled workers have not yet accepted the importance of keeping track of and reporting all items used. The issue of storage control, however, has prompted some wholesalers to venture into competition with the trade specific systems (e.g., within plumbing). To secure permanent delivery relations some wholesalers offer to deliver price diskettes listing all the necessary product numbers. The diffusion of these systems, however, is very limited.

The pharmacists' systems included many more aspects than economic calculations, such as stocks and orders. The plumbers and electricians, operating with a large number of products, could benefit from trade specific price diskettes. Most types of trades, however, are not sufficiently homogeneous to benefit from standard solutions but need flexible systems.

Currently few of the small or medium sized retail businesses have adapted to IT. Some of these, e.g., paint shops, could benefit from trade specific solutions. But today the trade associations are, in many cases, facing competition from small software suppliers who have designed a programme to one customer which they then try to market to other potential customers as a trade specific solution.

Even though there is a need for standardisation, too, standardised trade association programmes may prove only to fulfil the needs of a minority of members. A more feasible long term strategy aiming at the majority of members would be to offer to assist the members in defining criteria and in selecting appropriate hardware and software. But this requires that the staff involved has some kind of knowledge about the field and the issues to be computerised.

Chapter VIII
Purposive and Potential Networks in Small Firms' Adoption of IT

Andrew Lloyd Friedman and Mette Mønsted

1   Introduction

In this chapter we develop a network approach to interfirm relations. This approach is then used to explore the ways computer services and equipment have been diffusing to small Danish businesses in recent years.[1]

We define network relations as transfers of goods or services (including information or emotion), whether or not they are directly paid for, between an organisation (or member within an organisation) and external individuals and/or organisations. These transfers must occasion some personalised contact (though it may only be written or via the telephone) and must be repeated or at least potentially repeatable. A key feature of network relations is that information, beyond that conveyed by the price of goods exchanged, is a critical element.

Computerisation of small firms provides a particularly good example of the importance of network relations. This phenomenon cannot be analysed simply as the diffusion of a well defined and well known product in a competitive market of sellers. The purchase of a computer system is not a straight forward matter for a small firm even though fairly basic computer systems for doing accounts, inventories and other standard procedures have been available for several years at a price the smallest of firms can afford. This is because computer systems are not solutions in themselves, but rather means to solve problems. Therefore, some expertise is required to convert them into something useful.

Implementation is not straight forward, the systems need to be maintained and enhanced. This expertise is rarely available within small firms. Hiring a full-time computer specialist to carry out this work is too large an investment for most small firms contemplating the use of computers solely for administrative and financial purposes. Therefore, the use of computer based systems in most small firms necessitates a continuing relationship with individuals or firms beyond the organisation boundaries of the firm.

However, empirical evidence indicates that information which is critical for these small firms will often come to them along lines other than those between the actual suppliers of the computer system and the small firm. Advice, not only on which system to purchase, but also on both the logically prior issue of whether to purchase a computer system and the consequent issue of how to work with the system once purchased, will not usually come from the suppliers. This is partly because until now there have been very few suppliers with sufficient interest in the small firm market to provide such services. In part this is because small firms cannot or will not pay separately for these services. A complete "unbundling" of these services from hardware purchase has not only occurred, but is highly advertised. Trade magazines advertise and retail outlets offer a bewildering array of hardware and software. Items such as keyboards, monitors, disk drives, disks, operating software and applications packages are priced separately. However, it is difficult to evaluate quality and compatibility. In case of bundling it is mainly in groups of hardware and software.

PC vendors abound who are selling hardware alone at what appear to the non-specialist as very attractive prices. It is easy to be misled into believing that this hardware, combined with some standard packages, will provide useful facilities to small businesses. It is easy to underestimate implementation requirements. On the other hand, pure advice on computer systems and expertise in their use is available from a wide range of sources which are not formally set up as suppliers. Much of this potential advice is available along network lines which have nothing to do with business connections, (such as through the children of small firm owners, or through friends of their children, through colleagues etc.).

Therefore, when we examine network relations, we must distinguish between the different kinds of networks. By this we mean that some personal networks by which quite different "things" are transferred, (emotions, information, articles purchased, articles borrowed) and which contain quite different agents, may become connected when small firms are searching to establish new network relations – i.e., they are potential networks. In fact we would argue that it is the ability to connect and utilise different types of networks which can be a major contributor to the success of small firms. In this the purchase of a computer system is but one example. Rich potential networks can be particularly useful when evaluating any complex or poorly understood action.[2]

In the following we will present some background theory on networks and contracts as well as a model. This model will then be applied to a number of representative cases of small firm experiences with computer systems introduction. The chapter concludes with an evaluation of the contribution of network relations to the success of small firm computerisation and suggestions for future research directions.

2   Theoretical Background

We wish to combine three sorts of theory in order to analyse network relations between suppliers and users in the computing field. These are: social network analysis, the business network approach and relational contract theory.

Social network analysis emphasises effective relations among individuals, such as friendship or clique membership (Alba, 1973, Seidman and Foster, 1978, Hallinan, 1979; Lincoln and Miller, 1979).[3] Even though we are primarily interested in the form and consequence of network relations between computing suppliers and user organisations, this tradition bids us to consider interpersonal networks which are separate from inter-organisational networks, but which affect network relations between organisations.

The business networks approach has recently been developed by researchers at Swedish business schools, (Hägg and Johanson, 1982; Håkansson, 1982; Johanson and Mattsson, 1987). They study linkages between business firms for the purpose of securing resources.[4] These linkages involve repeated exchange of goods and services. Two features interact with exchange linkages. First, the repeated exchange allows mutual trust to build up between firms. Second, an adaptation process occurs within each firm to accommodate repeated exchange.[5] The adaptation process is viewed as an investment in networking by firms. The return on this investment is access to resources controlled by other firms, either as suppliers or as customers.

Viewed this way, the network becomes an alternative to the market as a representation of exchange relations between firms. In the market view of exchange the relative size and number of competitors and customers are treated as the key (but exogenous) factors, determining prices and quantities at which exchange occurs. The connection between these exchange relations and the profitability of firms is also assumed to be exogenously given, by prevailing technological conditions, as long as firms are profit maximisers. With the network view of exchange, the number of customers and suppliers, and the connections between exchange relations and profitability are assumed to be interdependent. Both depend on investment decisions by the firm; investment in search, and investment in adaptation. The degree of trust built up among network members, and forms of mutual adoptions, become critical factors for investigation.

From this business network tradition we draw a number of items. First, certain network relations are the result of strategic investment activities by firms. The trust which develops as a result of mutual adaptation and successful exchange in the past is a necessary condition for current and future successful exchange. This, in turn, is necessary for the very existence, (as well as the success) of business firms. However, all network relations enjoyed by a single firm do not emerge from direct investment by that firm. Some of the relations are developed on a social basis, and may in any community have a strong influence on business relations, influencing support structure, product development, and marketing (Johannisson, 1987). According to Swedish network research the most important characteristic developed is that of firms being connected to others via intermediaries. Network connections between two firms may be indirect, via more than one step. By connecting with one firm, access to many others may be gained, because of network connections which have been made by others. Therefore, an environment exists for firms which contains more than individual firms with whom network connections may be made.

One problem with the business network approach is that it is too positive about networks, at least the version espoused by Swedish business school researchers. Repeated exchange is assumed to generate trust in a positive cumulative fashion. All parties benefit from exchange. It is always a "positive-sum game". This makes the dynamics of networks analysis difficult. It implies that networks never harm a firm's economic position, and therefore that networks never decline, unless firms (mysteriously) disappear. The content of the network relations becomes important to analyse more than merely calculating the volume of connections. Therefore we include some other perspectives on network relations.

The final tradition we will draw on, relational contract theory, takes a less positive view of the outcome of repeated exchange relations.

Contracts may be defined as a set of factors that determine the distribution of rights and responsibilities associated with an exchange. Rights are the benefits arising from an exchange, while responsibilities refer to the obligation to bear the consequences of decisions taken in the process of exchange. Responsibilities relate to what Fama and Jensen (1983) call residual risk, that is, unforseen or not explicitly accounted for situations associated with the exchange. This definition embraces what are known as discrete contracts as well as relational contracts, that is, it covers single exchange situations and also repeated exchange situations (Macneil, 1978). The latter we are calling network relations.

Parties generally try to maximise their rights and minimise their responsibilities. In principle it should be possible to identify who has more of the rights and who more of the responsibilities in a contractual relation. The vagueness of most contracts allows to exist overlap of rights and responsibility gap to exist. These are the stuff of conflicts over contracts. An interesting asymmetry is that responsibility gaps need never come to light as unforseen outcomes need not occur.

One advantage of a contract theory view of network relations is that it explicitly anticipates that network relations may have negative outcomes. Exchange may be necessary for both parties, but it may not be mutually beneficial. Exchange processes are embarked upon, are contracted for, without certainty as to how they will turn out. Not only may unforseen circumstances result in one or both of the parties being disappointed, but this possibility is

		Informal	vs.	Formal Factors
		Informal		*Formal*
	individual	norms and		selfenforcement
	party	values		mechanisms
	relation	culture of		private ordering
		the relation		
Level				
of	*environment*	business		court
Factor		practice,		ordering
		potential		
		network		
		relations,		
		alternative		
		network		
		layers		

Figure VIII.1   Factors influencing the Behaviour of Parties in a Contractual Relation

generally recognised. Various arrangements are made to ensure against negative outcomes or to reduce the possibilities of such outcomes, (for example, the courts or the development of a parallel source of supply). Explicit recognition of these arrangements, and their importance for the likelihood of exchange occurring make analysis of contextual factors influencing the behaviour of parties to a contract particularly interesting. These factors are summarised in figure VIII.1. adapted from Noorderhaven (1987, p.9).

Self-enforcement mechanisms are transaction-specific investments which lock the party into the relationship (Telser, 1981). This is the same thing as the Swedish researchers' adaptation process. Private orderings are arrangements made by the parties which discourage non-performance, such as exchange of hostages or agreed recourse to arbitration (Galanter, 1981; Williamson, 1983; Williamson, 1985, p. 164-166). Business practices refer to the "culture" of the branch or field, or network (Meyer and Rowan, 1983; Meyerson and Martin, 1987, Sales and Mirvis, 1984). Court ordering refers to the legal enforceability of contracts as well as ease of access to the courts. In the analysis of cases of small firm computerisation presented in section 4 we will show how important the personal potential networks are in the world of small firms. We will also show that differences in the norms and values of computer systems suppliers compared with small firms have led to unsatisfactory exchange relations in this field. Potential network relations and alternative network contacts are discussed in detail below.

The main problem with relational contract theory is that it does not analyse how contracts are generated in a satisfactory manner. This stems from a negative view of contracts shared by most of the economists working in this field. They see contracts as constraints on the freedom of choice of parties. It is as though contracts are a necessary evil. This view makes it difficult to analyse why anyone would want to enter into a contractual relation. The economists' overly negative view of contractual relations and the overly positive view of the Swedish business network tradition must be combined and modified for our purposes.

3   A Network Model

3.1   Directed Graphs

Network relations are typically represented in the social network literature by directed graphs. A graph is a set of points, or nodes, some of which are connected by lines indicating the presence or absence of a relation. A directed graph is one in which the lines also indicate the direction of the relationship, that is providing information. In figure VIII.2. a directed graph is presented.

Let us take the node labelled 1 to represent a small firm, and the other nodes to represent individuals or organisations from whom the firm may receive information about computer systems. In this situation the firm receives information directly from two sources (2 and 3). Each of these receive information from 4, though there is an interchange of information between 2 and 4. Two paths, each of two lines in length connect the small firm with 4.

3.2   Potential Network Relations

The lines in figure VIII.2. represent actual flows of information. However, we also wish to represent potential flows, or at least connections which are easily activated because they require 'low' investment by the small firm. 'Low' must be thought of in terms of time and money which the firm can easily afford. This value will depend on the size of the firm, the potential gain they expect from the investment and their perception of the likelihood that the investment will pay off.

Potential network connections are characteristics of a firm's environment. There are two quite different aspects to this environment. First, there are the network connections which connect firms with whom a particular firm has direct links to third-party firms with which the first firm has no direct links. Second, there are the network connections between firms in the same "area" as the first firm, but with which the first firm has, as yet, no connections.[6] In both cases a

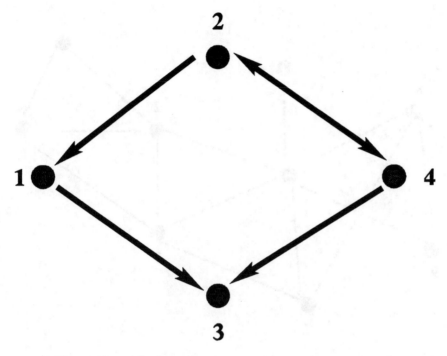

Figure VIII.2   A Directed Graph

set of direct long-term exchange relations may be developed without a very great investment in networking. Of course, the availability of these network relations is a matter of degree. The investment in networking required to turn potential into actual connections will vary. We will represent a potential network connection by a broken line, (see figure VIII.3.). The potential network relations may be of high interaction, but with another social content, i.e., the content is usually not transferring this kind of information, for example, family relations, leisure time activities etc.

There are many different ways that a potential network relation might occur. Organisation 5 may become indirectly connected with the small firm (3) because both 5 and 3 are directly connected with the common node 6.

Another reason for potential connections to exist is that they are already indirectly related to firm 1 in other ways. For example, node 5 may be connected to 1 via ties of friendship. There may be kinship ties. There may be business ties other than ones concerning computer systems. It is clear that if firm 1 were to establish an actual relation with say 2 or 3, this would allow them access to a wider information network than if they related to 8 or 9. Information about networks may be an important adjunct to information about computer services.

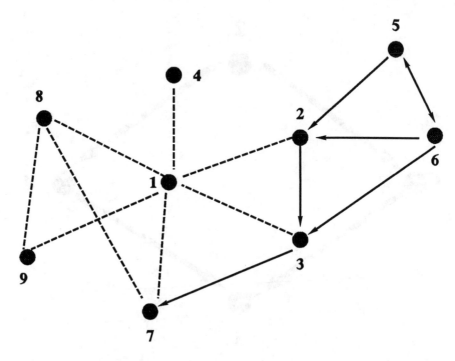

Figure VIII.3   A Potential Network Graph

Bengt Johannisson stresses that the contact network of small entrepreneurs (new firms less than two years old) is characterised by people with a large network. The personal contacts used as "sparring partners" represent a large potential network (Johannisson, 1987; Monsted, 1987).

3.3   Purpose Versus Other Types of Potential Linkages and the Time Dimension

In order to emphasise the different roles of networks which are not specifically about the transfer of goods or services for computerisation, we will draw graphs which distinguish purposive from other potential connections. Purposive connections are those which are specifically made in order to gain access to information, services or materials relevant to computerisation, typically to computer firms. These will be formal and often also contractual relations.

The potential connections are linkages which are formed for other purposes such as friendship, kinship, general business interests, non-business interests. However, the importance of these connections for the process of computerisation is that they can, at a later date, either transform into direct linkages which

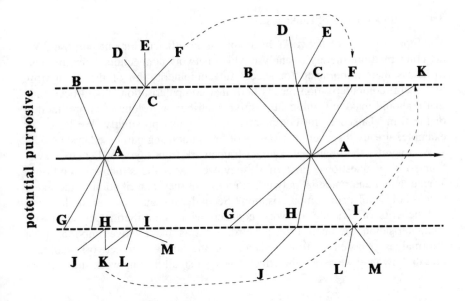

Figure VIII.4   Computerisation Graph

are formally about computerisation or they can lead to the introduction of third parties into direct purposive linkages. In order to illustrate these concepts we will construct graphs as demonstrated in figure VIII.4.

The solid line represents the locus of positions of the firm whose computerisation is being analysed through time. Above the line are the purpose linkages defined in the previous paragraph, below the line are potential connections. Above and below the solid line are broken lines. On these lines are represented the individuals and organisations with which the firm being analysed has linkages. Above the top line and below the bottom one are third parties, those whose connections with the firm being analysed is indirect, via others with which the firm does have direct linkages.

All these linkages are drawn with solid lines. Network changes between time periods are represented by broken lines with directional arrows.

It is important to note that over time some contacts break off. Either they are unfruitful or have fulfilled their purpose. This may be directly attributed to computing or it may have been to give access to a third party who was more relevant.

3.4   "Importance" of Linkages

The representation of networks by graphs is insufficient for our purposes. We are concerned not merely to analyse which network connections exist, but also to assess their importance for successful computerisation of the small firm. Successful computerisation means both that computerisation should occur and that it should make a significant positive contribution to long-term profitability of the firm.[7] Unsuccessful computerisation is a real possibility. We have, for example, already discovered instances of firms not using purchased systems.

We may use the relational contract framework from figure VIII.1. to answer four sorts of questions. First, how may we assess the structural conditions around actual and potential networks in terms of their contribution to the likely success of small firm computerisation? Second, how may we assess the costs and benefits of existing network connections in contributing to successful computerisation of small firms? Third, what is the relative importance of informal as opposed to formal factors of the small firm network ecology? Fourth, how may we assess the effectiveness of small firm network strategies?

4   Evidence

4.1   National and Branch Levels

Let us begin with the first question. Figure VIII.1. presents a scheme for ordering an assessment of the context of the Danish computer information network. At the environment level we must decide whether court ordering and current business practice are conducive to a successful computerisation of small firms.

Court ordering does not seem to be particularly helpful in relation to small firm acquisition of computer systems. A contract is not made for a useful system, that is to say, something that will reduce bookkeeping time or tax calculations by so many hours. Unfortunately, many small firms cannot specify what they want from a system and then make a contract based on the specification, because they do not know enough about what they could get on the market and because the resources required to write up a useful specification are too great. So it is difficult to see how a small firm could benefit from going to the courts to enforce a contract, or how they could benefit from the threat to do so. On the other hand, the cost of going to court in terms of time lost by the firm's owner as well as in court costs is likely to be high.

Current business practice is much more interesting for our cases. First, the practice of the computer field is important. Here no standardised product for small firms is available. There are many competing solutions coming from different sources. This is complicated further by the practice of selling different elements of hardware and software, as well as software services and advice, either separately or in various combinations. Often it is difficult for a small firm to assess which combination of products and services they require and which combination they are in fact acquiring from any one source. Often general advice on systems is provided by nominally independent sources which are, in fact, tied to the supplier of a particular brand of hardware or software.

A second characteristic of the computer field is that few firms have specialised in providing advice or systems to small firms although this field is developing rapidly. At the moment opportunities among medium and especially larger firms are much more lucrative. This means that traditional sources, hardware manufacturers and software houses, are not particularly careful about what they provide for small firms. To put it in terms of the contract definition, traditional computer suppliers are unwilling to accept responsibility in contracts with small firms.

These two factors lead small firms to explore and invest in information relations unconnected with material supply of systems and to activate potential relations available to them. Therefore, the potential network relations become important. In particular friendship relations and other networks of trust are relied upon, (note figure VIII.4.).

Four alternative potential network relations have been important for small firms in their attempts to compensate for what they view as unsatisfactory business practice on the part of traditional computer suppliers. First, in many branches of the Danish economy trade associations exist. Several have invested in computer systems which they then sell or lease to their members (see Chapter VII). Therefore, trade associations also represent both systems and advice suppliers. Trade associations might have been expected to provide independent advice. However, in many cases they are viewed with the same suspicion as advisors peddling a particular brand. This is because trade association solutions generally are geared to their most important members. Trade associations often have not developed separate advice or systems geared to their smaller members. We found dissatisfaction among several small-size firms with the trade association-backed system for their trade.

A second source of advice and solutions for small firms are the auditors. In Denmark auditors play an important role.[8] Not only do many of them specialise in dealing with small firms, but also several have developed the capacity to advise on computerisation. All small firms have an auditor, at least for the annual accounts. However, to which extent the auditor is used as an advisor to economic management or other issues beyond the tax laws, varies.

To many small firms, however, the auditor is perceived as the "natural" advisor, because he knows the firm. As administrative IT is closely related to the field of the accounts, it would be natural to discuss the problem with the auditor.

It is an obvious issue in assessing advice from auditors whether computer systems will replace auditor services and if so, whether auditors will be biased against advising small firms to purchase such systems. However, it seems that the advice most small firms are getting (both from traditional suppliers and trade associations) is to buy larger systems. Auditors advise for small systems that may complement rather than replace traditional auditor services. This seems a welcome antidote to many small firms. However, just because small firms do in fact choose to go slow, does not mean they have made the right decision.

Third, there are professional sources of advice, the technological institute, the TIC[9] and others offering courses such as the large union of white collar employees, HK[10] and the business schools. These have grown substantially during the past few years. The TIC seems particularly relevant for small firms.

Finally there are informal relations through relatives and friends. These networks have been very important for several small firms, though they often coincide with other sources of advice. Small firms often have friends or relatives who are professional suppliers of computer systems or advice, or may draw upon the experience of other small firms which they know.

In order to assess structural conditions at the individual and relations levels, and to judge costs and benefits to small firms, we now must turn to particular cases of small firm computerisation. These cases will also provide examples of how alternative networks have compensated for unsatisfactory network relations with traditional suppliers.

4.2   Individual Firms and Individual Relations Level

We have investigated a number of networks concerning computerisation of small firms. The five cases presented represent a wide range of experiences which we believe have been common to the computerisation of small firms.

Left-it-on-the-shelf: Firm T
Firm T, a small tinsmith firm, had decided to introduce IT for administrative purposes, because it would have to come some time anyway and they might as well jump into it. Seeing the tempting cheap solutions in one of the large supermarkets, the owner bought a package solution. He could not find out how to implement the machinery and after a week, he gave up and decided to wait until he had more time. It has now been standing unused for three months. He does not have the time to start it up and finds the instructions too poor. It takes too long to get into it when you are inexperienced. The machine stands in the corner collecting dust, "until I feel I have the time to work on it".

The Trade Association Solution: Firm E1
Firm E1 is active in the electricians' trade association, ELFO, and "bought" their system late in 1983. Both husband and wife are owners and active in networks

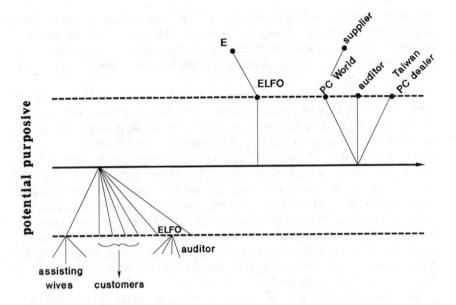

Figure VIII.5.   Electrician: E1

associated with their firm. The husband is active in ELFO and the wife in the association of "assisting wives in small enterprises". They were interested in IT as the future way of managing stock, prices, invoices and accounts. They bought the ELFO PC-system when it was offered at an introductory ELFO-meeting in December 1983. The system, a package including hardware and software developed by a service bureau, firm S, was delivered in February 1984. The delivery also included service and instruction. All of E1's accounts have been computerised since 1984.

The owners have made adjustments to the ELFO system. The husband tried to add separate systems for technical drawing. He bought the software, but the capacity of the hardware was not large enough to run it. He had to give up and bought another PC for the drawing system. The wife has worked with the auditor on adapting E1's previous accounting system to the system purchased from ELFO. The network relations are demonstrated in figure VIII.5.

E1 represents the case of a very small firm (2 employees plus husband and wife) with a lot of resources invested in searching for information and developing networks with high potential for supplying useful information. Their "below the line" social and professional connections before computerisation were rich in that they led to highly webbed potential contacts.

Their initial formal computerisation linkage came from the husband's strong informal connection with the trade association. E1's norms and values in relation to the contract with ELFO included a positive and open attitude. This helped them to develop alternative sources of information as well as own expertise, when they realised the inadequacy of the trade association's solution. They limited their transaction-specific investment by concentrating on continued investment in search.

ELFO is marketing a range of systems including an on-line invoice service as well as separate large and small systems. However, they have "captured" a market and are able to sell systems to clients who are likely to be unaware of alternatives or unwilling to subject ELFO to critical judgement by comparing it with other alternatives. As an association, ostensibly serving its members, ELFO has a paternalistic attitude to members. ELFO has substantial transaction specific investments in links with members who buy their system. On the other hand, ELFO is likely to distinguish between active and passive members. As far as firm E1 goes, it is likely to be considered as an "important" or active member. In the relationship ELFO has taken responsibility to the extent of offering a fixed price on set up service and they have made an agreement with a software house to provide free user support in the first year. However, their up-date service is relatively expensive.

The case of firm E1 can be judged as a success because the system purchased is being fully utilised, and E1 has continued with the system for several years. However, E1 is critical of the ELFO PC solution. It is too small (capacity based on 64K) and not compatible with IBM. The husband was disappointed that the system could not handle technical drawing applications, or at least had the capacity to develop them. Therefore, he bought a separate Taiwan PC and an American drawing programme he had seen advertised in the trade magazine PC World. Hence, figure VIII.5. shows a further development of the network in the case of E1. Formal connections related to the system were developed with the auditor, the trade magazine, the dealer who supplied the Taiwan PC, and the Danish dealer who supplied the technical drawing package.

In the case of E1 informal network connections were unimportant once the trade association solution was purchased. Rather the owner has become an IT specialist himself, learning from the trade magazines and from his own experiences.

Happy-buy-and-use-case: Theatre Equipment
A husband and wife firm producing and marketing equipment for small toy theatres and adapting plays for these. When they started out, they needed a typewriter. They discovered that a good one was almost as expensive as a cheap PC that could carry out many more tasks. They went to one of the large supermarkets in September 1986 and bought a small Taiwan PC off the shelf for 1,000 US dollars inclusive of a word processing programme and a printer. They implemented the system themselves and spent one month learning it.

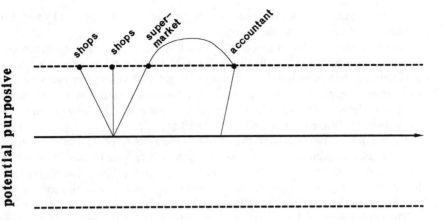

Figure VIII.6   Theatre Firm

Once they had the system, they contacted their accountant who assisted them in working out the plan of accounts for the firm. The auditor has not been giving much other advice, but agrees to the solution. The few times problems have arisen, they have contacted the software firm, but they have not yet been charged for any services rendered.

They subscribed to Armstrad News in the first period in order to acquire some insight, but after a year they cancelled the subscription.

They have had no courses and have had no friends to help. One friend (neighbour to the firm) pushed to have a "proper" IBM solution, but they have been very satisfied with the one they bought and it has still surplus capacity.

The-supplier-trade-alternative: E1-Service

A small electricity service and repair firm with 3 skilled labourers, 5 apprentices, and a part time book-keeper. For two years they had contemplated introducing IT, because it would facilitate pricing and invoicing. The owner attended a course at the Technological Information Centre (TIC) in 1985. He had been considering the ELFO solution, but decided not to buy it mainly because it was not very developed and did not contain enough 'numbers' for his electrical items. The small version was too small with only 700 numbers, and the large one (6-7,000 numbers) was too expensive and geared to larger firms. For comparison the wholesaler has nearly 28,000 numbers. When consulting colleagues at ELFO's regular courses he had often been recommended the "ELKAS" system, a trade specific electricians system developed by a software firm as an alternative to ELFO's system. The auditor, who he had used for many years, also recommended this system. Together with the auditor he visited one of his colleagues, who had the system and found it satisfactory. He bought

"ELKAS" from K-data. An important argument was the price (13,500 US dollars including a Sperry machine).

A consultant from the software firm installed the machine and gave instructions. The consultant is practically doing a 24 hours service, or at least he is available for help, which is free of charge for the first year. After one year, the maintenance contract will amount to 30 US dollars a month. Even if it is not a trade association solution, it is developed as a trade specific solution and new price disks are offered at the same price as ELFO.

By the time of the interview, they had had the system for 9 months and were still exclusively using it for invoicing and orders. The owner found it important to proceed slowly, and the auditor had been very helpful. The introduction does, however, imply solid changes in the workshop and a socialisation of the employees to exert greater discipline with the numbers.

The book-keeper had been somewhat reluctant to use the system, but was now about to start on the accounting system assisted by the auditor and a consultant from the software firm. But the book-keeper still found it laborious to get through the manual.

The Failed Traditional Supplier Case: Firm El-Trade
El-trade is an interesting case of a firm that clearly rejected the trade association solution. They have 2 sections, an electrician business and one selling Swedish warm air regenerators. They found the trade association's (ELFO) solution too standardised. The on-line solution was also rejected because they did not want to supply ELFO with information on their operations. This suggests that the general level of trust in ELFO is limited. For ideological reasons, too, El-trade never seriously considered the ELFO solutions. In principle El-trade has been against any centralised, bureaucratic organisation that might limit their freedom. ELFO is considered a centralistic trade association which supports electricians in their traditional role of electrical installation and repair and tries to maintain the separation of this work from related activities, such as El-trade's involvement in the more mechanical field of warm air generator supply. El-trade resented ELFO spending membership fees on developing a computer system only suitable for members involved in purely traditional electrician's jobs.

El-trade began their own search for a computer solution in 1985 when they attended a course at their local TIC. The staff at TIC helped El-trade to formulate their requirements for computerisation. El-trade visited a trade exhibition at the large exhibition centre in Copenhagen (the Bella Centre), but the conflicting information from trade representatives left them confused. Advised by the TIC, El-trade decided to "play safe" and purchased an IBM Piccolo. They bought their machine from a dealer, C-data who also sold El-trade a software system designed by H-Data, but sold and serviced by C-data. Soon after this transaction C-data went bankrupt and H-data took over the servicing of the system.

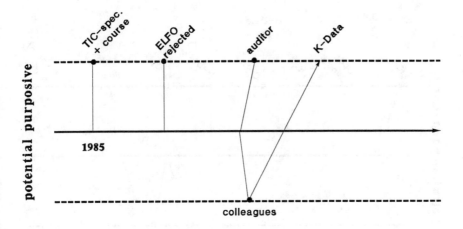

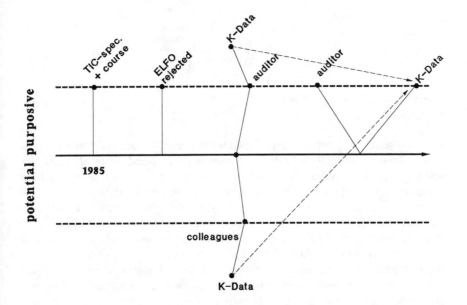

Figure VIII.7   Trade-specific Supplier Solution: El-Service

H-data is a one-man company. El-trade was satisfied with the system and the firm until the system accidentally was damaged in December 1986. For some time they had considered expanding the system as more capacity was needed to cope with the trade section of their firm. They found that H-data and his systems

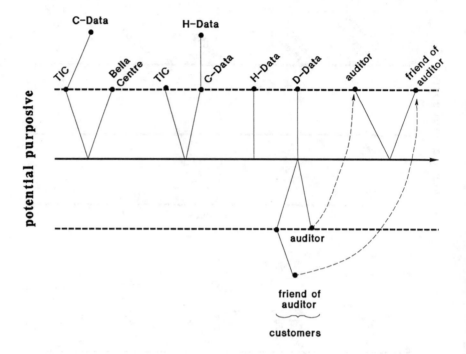

Figure VIII.8   Electrician El-Trade

were too small. A group of people from the bankrupt C-data had formed a new professional software firm, D-data. El-trade was contacted as an old customer and they signed a contract with D-data for an Albatross system including both hardware and software. This was disastrous. A continual process of new investments ensued, as the system could not handle what D-data had promised. Furthermore, the service was slow and incompetent.

In this kind of small firm cultural milieu people talk about such problems with the customers. One of El-trade's local customers was an auditor, who had worked with the Albatross. He offered to help and had a friend who could manage the programming and testing. They immediately changed auditor, and his friend began to function as a 24 hour trouble-shooter. He has now installed another hard disk, as the original one was too small and he has corrected many errors. The friend earlier had a service firm himself. He is now employed, but is willing to assist (against payment) in the evenings and weekends. Figure VIII.8. shows the network supporting El-trade's computerisation.

The norms and values of the owners of El-trade are very much against large organisations. They have the values of craftsmanship, "when you buy a system, you buy a solution and it is not delivered before it works". The husband has worked with steering systems and his wife is an educated accountant. As service people in this sector, they have experienced emergency cases. They understand that often service has to be rendered urgently, and they expect software firms to share this attitude. H-data was revealing clear craftsmanship norms, but D-data did not. They recommended systems which were almost obsolete. The wife saw the new DSI-programme advertised shortly after they made the contract, but nothing could be changed. The system never really functioned, there were many problems, but the leasing contract was signed and the firm had been paid. The expected professionalism of D-data was only visible in the attitude that "time is money, I have to be paid per hour no matter what I do during that time".

The nature of the relationship was, from El-trade's point of view, based on trust and this had worked well with H-data. Therefore, they admitted to have been naive in their relationship with D-data. They should have made sure that no money was paid before the system worked and that the formal contract made this point clear.

The break down of formal assistance came at a time when El-trade had no formal contacts who they could ask for advice. But then they started talking with people and found assistance via their potential network. The accounting system was either not functioning or only partly functioning for half a year. When the promised assistance did not come after many calls, they gave up and finally got support from their informal sources. The auditor and the 24-hour trouble-shooter have become a part of El-trade's formal and purposive network. El-trade has not tried to follow up on the contract with D-data. Going to court would not help as much of the software and hardware facilities required during the implementation process to make the system fulfil the requirements were not clearly specified in the contract. Also El-trade feels they have neither the time nor the energy for such an enterprise, which may not lead to anything.

Firm Carpentrade: A Cautious Late-Comer
The firm Carpentrade works within both carpentry (kitchen renovations) and the timber trade. They also sell kitchens and cupboards retail from a shop. This small firm, employing 15 people on a full time basis, is unusually vertically integrated. Consequently, they are very small suppliers within several different fields. Investigations of the offered standard solutions led to a rejection of the trade solution from both carpentry and timber trades associations. These were criticised for being too big, too expensive, uncoordinated and not IBM compatible. Just before Christmas 1986 Carpentrade bought a Taiwan computer from HS, a friend of their son, and began to use word processing in order to get some experience in working with a computer. They received a lot of guidance from their son and his friends. Carpentrade has hired a new clerk for 32 hours per week to put the accounts into the computer based on a standard package, but by October 1987 the package had not yet been chosen. The auditor's advice is being used and the clerk has experience with some accounting systems. HS, the

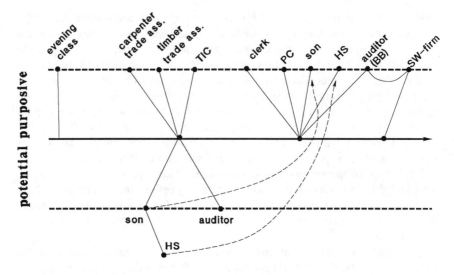

Figure VIII.9   Firm Carpentrade

friend of the son, promised "to make a programme for order deliveries" (invoicing system) free of charge. He thought this would only take him a few days, but by the time of the interview (mid March 1987) nothing had come out of it. The computerisation related network for Carpentrade is represented in figure VIII.9.:

Carpentrade has taken a long time to introduce IT. The owners, however, have been aware of the technology and attended courses since early 1983. In a Danish context they are not a very small firm. In 1986 they had a turnover of 2,5 million US dollars. Nevertheless, they had no computer-based system by the time of the main interview, March 1987. There are two ways of viewing this case. Either we can regard it as a case of failing computer networks or as evidence of the lack of effective computer systems at reasonable prices.

The latter view is part of the answer. Neither of the two relevant trade associations' solutions were appropriate enough for the firm to justify the high cost. Carpentrade has actively sought information to be able to assess the systems, but the easiest potential information source, the trade associations, did not offer broad enough information. Rather than advising on which system to buy in order to fulfil the requirements, they pushed their own system. The value of the trade association network was probably that it prevented Carpentrade from making the mistake of buying one of those systems. Carpentrade would have introduced IT a long time ago, if "the right solution" had been available. The problem is the boundaries between the different trades they are in: production, repair, and sales.

Carpentrade's knowledge of problems in firms that have bought trade solutions has made it wary of buying any system as long as nobody in the firm or the family is an expert on IT. When the offer came from HS, their son was accustomed to the equipment, and HS often visited the owners for social reasons.

Until recently, Carpentrade has rejected using an auditor as the source of general advice on IT. They did not want to pay extra for the limited services of the auditor. However, they happened to meet a good auditor (BB) whom they hired a year before the interview, and he is being used as a resource person who also gives advice on IT solutions for the accounts.

Carpentrade could find no standard solutions for their accounting systems. In the end they "chose" to purchase equipment from a professional hardware supplier, because: a) the price was very low and could be compared with a new typewriter, b) this supplier also had a friendship relation with the owners' son. Even compared with a standard accounting system, Carpentrade will get a very cheap system because HS is providing advice and some software for free.

Let us use the categories from figure VIII.1. to evaluate the "contract" between Carpentrade and HS. The norms and values of HS are not known. Carpentrade appears to have a very cautious but positive attitude towards IT. Though they have considered introducing IT for years, they have rejected available solutions because of the price and capabilities of the solutions. However, apart from paying for the equipment from HS and buying both for their home and office, there is a reluctance to treat the software, advice and maintenance services provided by HS as part of a financial transaction. Naturally, they are pleased because they believe they are finding an informal path to computerisation. However, they are paying for computer services in the form of both a sophisticated user, the new 32 hours clerk, and the extra advice contract with their auditor. With the clerk Carpentrade is making transaction specific investments, though they are covering themselves (making an alternative, though not parallel investment) with the auditor, and with their own and their son's computer training. The invoicing system is complicated in a business covering different trades. But the introduction of this system is not a precondition for the accounting system. It may be easier for them to delay the accounting system. The conclusion seems to be that it has to be custom-made, and that this will be very time-consuming.

The nature of the relationship is one of friendship mixed with exchange. HS is building up his competence through a learning process in the firm. However, there seems to be no private ordering. This, and the lack of any quid pro quo for the software, leaves a huge responsibility gap. On the surface HS has taken all responsibility upon himself, but there is no private ordering involved. It already seems likely that the system will be substantially delayed, if delivered at all. If HS does not deliver, not only is no court discipline possible, but also the absence of financial exchange reduces the moral authority with which Carpentrade might press HS. When a friend is doing you a favour, it is difficult to complain if the favour does not meet your expectations.

The case is a success in the way that the slow introduction has actually resulted in the final purchase of a system which works and which they are satisfied with. The problems of introduction have been few due to the gradual adjustment to the machinery.

5   Conclusion

Looking at the different networks of assistance, the dominat features seem to be: the long time sequence to get the systems to work, and the lack of capacity to solve problems in the networks contacted for assistance. The demands of the small firms in their first contacts with supplier firms are not specified in such a way that they can be easily dealt with. This may often create a crisis in the decision-making, delaying the decisions and increasing the feeling of insecurity. There are several cases of long periods, both for the decision to buy IT and for the choice of what to buy. This period is characterised by confusion and seems to last long, and the firms are stuck because nothing happens.

But when the system is purchased there is still a long process to get it to work properly. If the introduction of IT is assessed within the first half year, it is likely to be judged a failure either because it is not working, or because only a fraction of the capacity is utilised.

When blocked in the purposive network of assistance, potential network relations seem to be activated. The use of these networks may in the first round be interpreted as functionalistic, a good and solid way of solving problems. But they leave a lot of security problems and variety in access to these networks. The networks are disjoined and do not to any large extent open the possibilities of leading to other resources and networks.

Those networks that provide new sources of information are the social/friendship relations. When the straight professional or formal contractual relations fail or prove insufficient, other social contacts such as colleagues, friends, or other professional consultants are used in order to try to solve problems, to give information or to obtain contact for assistance in decision-making or problem solving. Some of the contacts established this way may change and become the new purposive or formal contractual network relations. These may include professionals, but fundamentally they are based on personal trust, common norms and friendship. The assessment of the expert in such relations is not linked to professional knowledge, but to the person in his social capacity.

The strength of these informal or potential networks to solve problems created in the formal contractual system is useful but not ideal. It should be no excuse for neglecting the formal network and support structure. The lack of a formal functional support structure increases the emphasis on other network relations. Either the firms have to develop expertise internally as is the case of E1, where the owner himself developed expertise, or the firms have to develop relations with others who may assist in solving the arising problems. All the trade associations' systems are developed to provide this support structure, but if firms are outside the typical core of firms, the solution may not fit, and "neutral" advice from the association cannot be obtained. Then the field is very open for decisions.

The problems of the formal networks may be related to discrepancies in the expectations of the relationship. The small firms demand an immediately functional solution, and the supplier offers standardised equipment, demanding some installation adjustments. This may be the basis for the use of other network relations.

Access to other contacts and sparring partners becomes important every time new types of problems arise. To most of the firms the computing field is new, and new supplier networks have to be developed within this field in which skills are difficult to evaluate.

Small firms cannot employ expertise in all new fields, but are dependent on external expertise. Some Scandinavian studies (Andersson, 1979; Vikoren, 1979) have concluded that partner firms, and firms in collaboration with others are more successful than isolated small firms. "The problem is not to be small, but to be isolated" (Vikoren, 1979). Network relations break some of this isolation and are less demanding than other forms of real collaboration.

Among small firms, the electricians have a very active trade association providing many courses on technical development, law etc. This implies that more electricians have a richer network to draw upon than other small firms. They know "colleagues" from courses and may use these contacts in other contexts.

We may conclude that firms with a wide and strong network are more likely to succeed in solving new problems and therefore also in solving the problem of introducing IT. The strong networkers, however, invoke network relations at an early stage and may not have to activate their potential network at the trouble-shooting stage in the same way as described above. The capacity to deal with the introduction of IT may easily reflect the general capacity to deal with new types of problems by using the network relations.

Notes

1   Small firms in Denmark are defined as less than 20 employees in official Danish statistics. This compares with a definition of less than 50 employees in the major European countries

(Great Britain, France, West Germany). This reflects the comparative domination of the Danish economy by small firms.

2   Such as a move into a new market, as well as purchases of other large inputs (including labour).

3   Other kinds of relations have been examined using social network analysis, such as awareness between members of a scientific community (Breiger, 1976) or co-worker relations in a bureaucratic organisation (Lincoln and Miller, 1979). The nodes of networks in this literature have not always been confined to individuals. They have sometimes been organisations (Sonquist and Koening, 1975; Galaskiewics, 1979; Burt, 1980) or even nations (Snyder and Kick, 1979; Breiger, 1981).

    Scott (1988) has recently traced the "first true formulations of social network analysis" back to the 1930s. Though the field's major expansion occurred in the 1970s.

4   During the 1980s the term networks has been used explicitly in this work. However, earlier Swedish work focused on linkages and analysed both the economic *and* the social dimensions of these dyad relations between firms without mentioning the concept of networks (Färnström and Kedström, 1975; Andersson, 1979; Vikoren, 1979).

5   To put this into terms frequently used in labour economics to describe employee behaviour in relation to employing firms: the firms learn how to deal with difficulties by "voice", rather than by "exit" from the network; that is, they allow difficulties with the relation to be acknowledged and dealt with.

6   Area may be thought of geographically, but it is best thought of as social, and particularly economic. An obvious example is of two firms whose outputs and inputs could be linked in a supplier-user relation without major change in technology by either, but which currently do not have such a relation; such as the supplier of a component to a competitor who uses exactly the same component as the potential linking firm.

7   Successful computerisation may also mean a positive decision not to computerise. It may be that after careful, but inexpensive evaluation of the possibilities, a firm decides to wait until more appropriate or cheaper systems are available. It may also simply decide not to computerise.

8   Many auditors/accountants for small firms are the less educated, the registered accountants.

9   Technological Information Centres are established in each county, except in Copenhagen and Aarhus, where the Technological Institutes work. TICs have an engineer, an economist and a few other staff that assist local manufacturing and construction firms in the primary consultancy, defining problems and finding relevant consultants for them.

10 The tradeunion association for shop assistants and clerical staff.

Part C
The IT People
Strategies, Skills and Careers

Introduction

This part focuses on the primary actors in the IT field, those who we label core IT people. They are the people who are identified in occupation statistics as the IT specialists. They are those with job titles in the general occupations of systems analysis, programming and computer operations. We include managers and supervisors for all these occupations, including those identified as EDP managers. Information about data entry staff have been included under the general occupation category of operations in chapter XII, but in the other chapters when we refer to operators we exclude data entry. Also many of the propositions discussed in chapters IX, X and XI refer to systems and programming specialists alone.

Three perspectives on the IT people are presented in this part. *First* in chapter IX the strategies IT people pursued are examined. Danish IT people stand out in comparison with others in the IT field due to their high level of trade union membership. Also the presence of a union solely dedicated to organising IT people (PROSA) is unique to Denmark. These features of Danish IT people are placed in the context of different strategies which IT people could pursue. Six strategies are identified: craftsmanship, trade unionism, professionalism, management traineeship, job hopping, and entrepreneurship. Craftsmanship has traditionally been a very strong strategy among Danish IT people compared with IT people elsewhere. Also trade unionism among IT people in Denmark has been strongly influenced by a strategy of professionalism.

Tight labour markets throughout the history of the IT field has made all six strategies viable alternatives for the vast majority of IT people. Other environmental conditions have affected the relative advantage of these six different strategies. This connection between environmental conditions and relative advantage of different strategies is examined in relation to IT people in general, to IT people in Denmark and to IT people working in one IT community in Denmark, (a community which comprises one large organisation). We present evidence that professionalism and certain more individualistic strategies will become more important among Danish IT people in future.

A *second perspective*, presented in chapters X and XI, emphasises management strategies and the effect of contingency factors on how IT people are treated in organisations. In particular the deskilling hypothesis which dominated analysis of IT people in the 1970s is challenged. This hypothesis was derived from Braverman's (1974) pioneering work on the general degradation of labour in twentieth century capitalism.

In chapter X the CHIPS data is used to refute this hypothesis in relation to the Danish IT people. Flexible division of work, a high degree of autonomy, high wages and good career prospects continue to characterise IT people in Denmark in the 1980s. The evidence suggests a need to go beyond Braverman's Taylorist approach. Following Mintzberg (1979) a contingency theory approach is offered to explain the position of the IT people in Denmark. Organisations in the IT field must be viewed as open systems and factors such as the environment, the technology, management ideology and power relations between management and employees must be taken into account.

In chapter XI a more recent restatement of the degradation hypothesis by Kraft and Dubnoff (1986) is criticised. It is argued that during the 1980s a shift away from Taylorist or Direct Control management strategies and toward Responsible Autonomy types of strategies has occurred in the United States as well as in other countries. In particular the development of career ladders, preference for generalist skills, and the recombining of analysis and programming job functions has occurred. These are explained, in part, by a new emphasis on user relations in the IT field. It is argued that Kraft and Dubnoff's own data, as well as data from other projects, supports this hypothesis, rather than their own degradation hypothesis.

Finally, in chapter XII a more empirical perspective is provided on the IT people in Denmark. In recognition of the dynamic character of the IT field, this chapter provides detailed data on the historical development (1970-1988) as well as the present situation of IT people. Characteristics described include: the distribution of job titles; the level and types of formal qualifications held and those preferred by employers; the age, gender and geographic distribution of the population; salary distribution by job title, age and gender; and career and mobility patterns.

The population of IT people has been growing steadily, but the distribution of job titles has changed substantially in the past two decades. Analysis and programming, the "higher level" jobs, multiplied four and a half times between 1970 and 1988, but the operations categories declined by 12%. Also within the analysis and programming group, the higher level job categories (other than management) grew much faster than average.

The IT field continues to be dominated by young people, but there is a substantial minority above 40 years of age. It also continues to be male dominated, though women increased their share of analysis and programming jobs from 13% to 22% between 1981 and 1988. Women are particularly under-represented in managerial positions.

Salaries are high. Women are paid less than men. There is a clear correlation between age and salary up to and including the 40-44 age category for men, but only up to the 35-39 age category for women in most job categories. This falling off of salaries for IT people in their fourties also applies to those in management job categories.

The IT field continues to be dominated by those without formal IT qualifications. It has always been common to recruit people with practical experience outside the field. However the importance of the EDP-assistant qualification for entry level jobs in systems and programming has been growing rapidly in the recent years.

Finally, the IT field shows some career patterns. It is common to enter the field as a programmer or analyst/programmer and then move either into systems programming, or to the analysis job categories of systems consultant or systems planner. It also appears that IT management is primarily recruited from those with experience in IT job categories.

Chapter IX
Strategies of IT People in Denmark – Trade Unionism, Craftsmanship and Professionalism

Andrew Lloyd Friedman

1   Introduction

What distinguishes IT people in Denmark is their strategic use of trade unionism to further their material conditions.[1] Danish IT people are remarkable because the density of their trade union membership is very high compared with membership in other countries (around 70% in Denmark in 1988). Though trade unionism is also high among IT people in the other Scandinavian countries, Denmark stands out further in that a substantial proportion of IT people in Denmark belong to a particular union, PROSA, which is entirely dedicated to organising IT people and which is not connected with a more general trade union. PROSA appears to be the only substantial trade union in the world which completely specialises in organising IT people. However unionisation among Danish IT people is not high compared with the general level of unionisation in Denmark. Denmark is one of the most highly unionised countries in the world. It is this combination of features of the Danish IT people that we will be analysing in this chapter.

In the sections below, the origins and development of PROSA and of IT unionisation in Denmark will be described and analysed. Then the particular strategies IT people pursue through PROSA and other Danish trade unions will be analysed with reference to a model of strategies for IT people. We shall argue below that IT people stand out from many other groups of employees because of the wide range of strategies available to them. Their relatively substantial freedom of action derives primarily from labour market shortages which IT people have enjoyed in all countries for almost the entire history of the field. This has encouraged a rather unusual sort of trade unionism among IT people in Denmark, one which has strong elements of other strategies, particularly of professionalism. In succeeding sections a general model of strategic possibilities for employees is presented. This model will then be related, first, to the general position of IT people, second, to the situation of IT people in Denmark, and third, to a particular IT community in the Danish IT field, the people working in a large public sector service bureau, Datacentralen.

2   Trade Unionism among IT People in Denmark

2.1   ship

Measured by the density of union membership, trade unionism appears to be a particularly important strategy for core IT people in Denmark. Two features of unionisation among IT specialists in Denmark stand out. First is their high trade union density.

According to our figures of 1987 unions membership among IT specialists was distributed across different unions as follows.

SAMDATA	6,500
PROSA	5,000 (1986 figure)
DBLF	1,550
DFLF	779
DSLF	500
DIF, DJOF	500
	14,829
	− 350[2]
	14,479

Based on an estimated population of core IT specialists of 20,000, this gives a unionisation density of 72%.[3] Unionisation is particularly high in the large public sector service bureau (Datacentralen and Kommunedata), in the national and municipal government offices and in the large private banks.

2.2   Historical Background

Unionisation among IT specialists appears to have been negligible in Denmark before 1967. According to PROSA, no one organised IT specialists before 1967. It is likely that some belonged to unions in organisations where unionisation of white collar workers was very high, such as in the post office, or the railway, or the large private banks. In the early 1960s the main white collar union (HK) treated computer programmers as some type of office workers rather than as something special according to a SAMDATA source. At this time the general level of white collar unionisation was high in Denmark, 55% compared with a rate of 69% for blue collar workers[4]. At that time white collar unionisation was much lower in Great Britain (less than 30% in 1964) and in the United States (11% in 1968). However it was much higher in Sweden (70% in 1968).

In 1967 about 25 programmers and systems analysts at Scandinavian Airlines (SAS) decided they wanted their own agreement with the company. At that time it was SAS policy only to negotiate with unions on a national basis, so the group of programmers and analysts decided to create a national union for IT specialists. This was the beginning of PROSA. Originally PROSA meant PROgrammers and Systems Analysts. The next group to join were operators at Datacentralen. Soon there were two groups at Datacentralen, which formed separate local branches, one for operators and one for programmers and analysts. In the early 1980s these groups joined together. After the group at Datacentralen joined the union, the name PROSA came to represent PRogrammers, Operators and Systems Analysts. Now PROSA organises anyone working with computers according to it's legal registration for the right to state benefits.

PROSA grew steadily from 1967. It grew to a membership of 1,000 in 1976, and to 5,000 in 1986. By 1988 this figure had grown to 6,800 (Bjorn- Andersen et al, 1988).

During the late 1960s and early 1970s the number of white collar workers grew very quickly in Denmark. The number of white collar workers belonging to trade unions grew even more quickly.[5] The two main white collar unions are HK[6] (composed mainly of private sector employees in shops and offices and municipal employees) and the FTF (a federation of white collar unions, mainly in the public sector and in the financial sector).[7] Both HK and FTF were growing rapidly during this time. However, the rapid growth of white collar unions did not occur automatically. HK and FTF were competing hard for new members. Early in the 1970s HK launched a massive recruitment campaign. Posters and advertisements appeared on buses and trains and in other public places stressing the benefits to be gained from joining a large organisation (Blum and Ponak, 1974, p.75).

Soon after its formation PROSA became part of FTF. During the period from 1968 to 1971, when PROSA was making steady progress with recruitment, few programmers joined HK. HK still did not make special efforts to recruit IT people. In 1971 this changed. As part of HK's general recruitment drive, SAMDATA, a special branch for IT specialists was created. SAMDATA grew quickly, particularly during the first few years. It had 4,000-4,500 members by 1980. SAMDATA was most successful at recruiting operators and data preparation staff, rather than programmers and systems analysts.

The other important unions recruiting core IT specialists are the financial sector unions, DBLF (private commercial banks), DFLF (insurance companies) and DSLF (savings banks). All these unions belong to FTF. Of these DBLF is by far the most important. IT specialist membership of DBLF grew slowly during the 1960s and early 1970s. DBLF did not appear to have made special efforts to recruit IT specialists. By 1973 DBLF had recruited 20-30% of its potential IT specialist members. At that time some IT specialists began to try to establish their own union within the commercial banks. Some tried to set up their own section within DBLF. Some joined PROSA. Our DBLF interviewee described the period from 1973 to 1976 as one of open warfare between DBLF and PROSA. In 1973 PROSA withdrew from FTF (or was thrown out), because PROSA did not accept the jurisdictional demarcation defined by FTF by which

PROSA was excluded from recruiting IT specialists in the jurisdiction of other established unions within FTF.[8]

In 1973/74 DBLF was stimulated to take a more active recruitment policy toward IT specialists for several reasons. First, it was the time when PROSA, responding to the challenge of newly created SAMDATA, began actively to recruit IT specialists in the financial sector. Second, it was the time when on-line systems were being established in larger banks. At that time DBLF (and DSLF)[9] began to respond to the demands of the membership, many of whom were becoming direct end users of computer-based systems. However the unions' new concern with IT from the users perspective generated bad feeling among IT specialists in the banks. From DBLF's perspective "DP people always took offence if we said anything was wrong with new technology." (DBLF interview, 1987) From the IT specialists' perspective DBLF was dominated by members who were hostile to new technology and who did not understand their needs.

By 1975 DBLF had set up seminars between IT shop stewards and shop stewards representing other bank employees. This helped to ease the communication problems between the two groups of DBLF members. IT staff became more aware of employment and deskilling consequences of IT on users. During the next few years it became clear that the introduction of new technology was coinciding with financial sector growth. DBLF was aided in its fight with PROSA by the employers, who wanted to negotiate with a single union. Therefore 1977/78 was the boom time for organising IT specialists into DBLF. By 1980 DBLF had organised about 60% of potential IT specialist members.

The most significant date in PROSA's history, after 1967, was 1976. In that year, after a series of strikes, PROSA won a collective agreement with the Danish state sector. That agreement transformed PROSA into a "real trade union, and not just a bunch of people interested in trade unions and education." (PROSA interview, 1986)

The agreement marked a turning point in PROSA's fortunes. During the five years leading up to 1976, the established unions came to undercut PROSA's appeal. It was SAMDATA and DBLF that were expanding most quickly. After 1976 PROSA's growth accelerated. At that time PROSA had 1,000 members to show for its first decade. In the next decade four times that number were added.

Unionisation growth has continued into the 1980s. The union density of IT specialists for DBLF has grown from 60% in 1980 to 75-80% in 1987 in spite of continued growth in the number of IT specialists employed in the private commercial banks.[10] During the 1980s DBLF established a special IT staff committee and has been employing people at its HQ with IT education and experience. There still appears to be grumbling among ordinary IT specialists and IT shop stewards in DBLF. Nevertheless the success of the union at achieving high wages and good working conditions compared with other white collar workers, as well as certain special treatment for IT members, has "kept PROSA at bay".[11]

During the 1980s PROSA and SAMDATA have also flourished. SAM-DATA's membership has grown from 4,000-4,500 in 1980 to 7,000 in 1988. Prosa's membership has grown to 6,800 in 1988.

Thus there has been substantial growth of unionisation among IT specialists in Denmark, but this growth has not been steady, it has occurred in spurts. These spurts may be associated with the following series of important events, which are deduced from the previous historical account. However, each of these events has to be understood as reflecting more long-term changes in the position of IT specialists in Denmark and in the general economic and social situation of white collar workers in Denmark.

1. Establishment of PROSA	1967
2. Active Recruitment by Established Unions	1971-75
3. PROSA's first collective agreement	1976
4. Unemployment Threat to New Entrants	1982-83 + 1988-?

At first, before the late-1960s, IT specialists in Denmark did not join trade unions. It is likely that they considered themselves to have little in common with other workers. They were not employed in large numbers at individual sites. They were well paid, had good working conditions, and had good opportunities to improve their employment positions by moving to other employers. New sources of employment were continually arising with the spread of computers. To put it in the language suggested by A.O. Hirschman (1970), IT specialists were either satisfied with their position (loyalty) or they could easily alleviate their dissatisfaction by leaving their employer for another (exit). They did not believe that they needed a collective voice.

The beginning of PROSA in 1967 changed this. Why was PROSA formed at that time? First, the mid 1960s, was the time when the overall level of white collar unionisation began to grow. It is likely this was stimulated, in part, by the success of blue collar workers at achieving wage rises in a time of growing inflation, when white collar workers' traditional wage differential above blue collar workers was therefore being eroded. A second reason for the growth of white collar unionisation was the sheer growth in numbers of white collar workers, who would now find themselves in larger offices, increasing the numbers in a common situation where grievances could more easily resonate, and making it easier for trade unions to contact them. Both of these reasons for unionisation also applied to IT specialists in the mid- 1960s.[12]

The second major change occurred between 1971 and 1975 with serious efforts to recruit IT specialists exerted by established white collar trade unions. Arguably this change of attitude may be directly attributable to the success of PROSA at organising IT specialists working within the jurisdictions of these established unions. The positive effect of competition among unions recorded by Hannan and Freeman (1987) is in evidence here. In addition the growth of on line systems in the financial sector stimulated DBLF to embrace IT specialists in order to influence the effects of these systems on many of its members who were becoming direct end users.

It seems clear that the development of unionisation in the early 1970s occurred more because unions changed their attitude toward IT specialists, than because IT specialists changed their attitude toward unionisation. With the establishment of SAMDATA and with DBLF's new policy of attempting to recognise the special needs of IT specialists, the cost of collective bargaining and of participating in national decisions about the education of IT specialists fell. Joining SAMDATA or DBLF would allow IT specialists to join collective groups which were both recognised by employers *and* which had a new found commitment to improving their specific employment position.[13]

On the side of the IT specialists themselves, the knowledge that some had joined PROSA without adverse consequences, and the general growth of white collar unions during the 1970s, would have increased the attraction of this strategy by making it more familiar to them (contagion effect). Some of the reasons for the general growth of white collar unionism during the 1970s were the growing rate of inflation, the positive attitude toward white collar unionisation of the Danish government and the subsequent willingness of Danish employers to negotiate with white collar unions. This would also have applied to IT specialists.

However one other reason for general white collar union growth, the threat of unemployment, had little effect on programmers and analysts (though it was likely to have been an important reason for operators and data preparation staff joining unions). We argue that recent IT union growth has been stimulated by the threat of involuntary unemployment during the 1980s. The threat of unemployment has been noted as a strong incentive to unionisation, even if the actual experience of high levels of unemployment is associated with declining unionisation. In addition the operation of the unemployment insurance fund (which is administered by trade unions, rather than the state, in Denmark) has meant that unionisation tends to rise during periods of high unemployment in Denmark, instead of falling, as it does in most other countries (see Pedersen, 1978; and Scheuer, 1984).[14] Unionisation of operators has traditionally been higher than for programmers and systems analysts. The longer period under which operators have lived with the prospect of redundancy (due to the spread of minicomputers and advances in the automation of certain operator functions) goes some way to explaining their higher unionisation rate. Though the real probability of long term unemployment may have been lower for computer programmers, the fear of unemployment among newly qualified programmers was easily expressible in terms of joining a trade union.

This encouraged students training to become programmers (especially those students taking the EDP-assistant course), to join a trade union. Both SAM-DATA and PROSA have been able to recruit substantial numbers of students.[15] The threat of unemployment on graduation largely disappeared for EDP-assistants after 1984, but it has returned in recent years. According to a survey carried out by SAMDATA in June, 1988, 69% of new graduates from the EDP-assistant course had no job when they finished their examinations.[16] This compares with results of earlier surveys by SAMDATA which found that 47% of those graduating in January, 1988 had no job and 43% of those graduating in June, 1987.[17]

2.3   Distribution of Membership

The most highly unionised occupational group of core IT specialists are the operators. There was a higher proportion of operators in PROSA than other categories. Programmers came next, followed by systems analysts. There were less than 100 keyboard operators in PROSA. Also operators and key punch operators were the most numerous groups within SAMDATA. Systems programmers were the least represented group. DBLF organises all EDP- staff, from project leader down, roughly in proportion to their numbers, except for higher grade engineers (i.e., systems programmers and network specialists), who remain largely unorganised. Therefore the overall occupational distribution appears to be that operators and key punch operators are most highly organised, followed by applications programmers. Systems programmers and network specialists appear to be the least organised groups.

The distribution of union members by firm and industry sector is strongly related to the size of computer installations and the public/private sector divide. PROSA has agreements primarily in the public sector, for example, at Datacentralen and Kommunedata and in the State bureaucracy. While half of PROSA's members are in the private sector, union density in the private sector was far lower. About a third of PROSA members were not working under an agreement, mostly in the private sector, where most of PROSA's members are spread thinly (often only as single individuals), in some 600 organisations. SAMDATA has agreements through HK in most large organisations. It has about 25% of its members in the public sector, mainly at Kommunedata, in municipal government officers and in the state tax office. SAMDATA's private sector members, are mainly in small private firms, though there are large numbers at Jutland Data Centre, a private software centre, and at LEC (a milk marketing association). DBLF membership among IT specialists is concentrated in the more traditional union areas of the financial sector, the five big commercial banks. It is lower in the newer areas, the multinational banks and at the PBS (the central clearing house for banks).[18]

The age distribution of union members largely reflects the young age of IT specialists. It appears that until 1982 IT specialists who were trade union members were somewhat older than average IT specialists. It normally takes time to appreciate the benefits of trade union membership, especially for employees in a tight labour market. However, this has changed since the widespread success of the main unions at recruiting students in the EDP-assistant courses. Note from chapter XII that the annual output of the EDP-assistant course had grown to 750 by 1988 representing some 4% of the total core IT specialist population.[19]

Finally, the gender distribution of membership is about 2/3 male to 1/3 female for both PROSA and SAMDATA according to estimates by their respective chairmen. This ratio of 2:1 represents a substantially higher proportion of women in the unions than in the population of IT specialists in Denmark. The ratio for the whole Danish IT population is 3:1 and for all systems developers it is 4:1 (see Chapter XII, Table XII.7.).

2.4   Education: The Key Issue for Unions in the IT Field

Note the statement by PROSA cited above (section 2.2), that the achievement of a collective agreement in 1976 meant that PROSA became a real union, no longer just a bunch of people interested in trade unions and *education*. PROSA has an active education policy. It is their policy to fight for their members to have 10% of their working time allotted to further training. It is also PROSA policy that employees should be able to choose for themselves which training they receive. In addition PROSA, along with the other relevant unions, sits on tripartite committees to design formal state education for IT specialists.

SAMDATA's recruitment rate, which was very rapid in the early 1970s, revived again in the early 1980s. Both Hans Sorensen and Erik Lykke Jensen attributed this to a change in the officers of SAMDATA, which occurred in 1980. The new officers were more active in their recruitment and they were especially more active in their education policy.[20]

"The first thing we did (on taking over in 1980) was to offer members free courses in anything, like expert systems. We hired teachers for weekends. This helped recruitment. Education is the best way to get recruitment and to increase activity levels of the members" (SAMDATA interview, 1987).

Education of IT specialists is not a contentious issue for DBLF members because of the positive attitude of the employers toward education. Though training is covered by local agreements, the banks want to keep up with the latest technology. Competition among the banks based on IT-related services is keen. Therefore, while for many IT-specialists covered by HK agreements the union has to pay for training, for DBLF members the employers pay.

IT specialists have a high regard for training. In part their positive attitude to training arises from an intrinsic desire to be "in the know", to keep up with the latest developments in a field where available technology is changing rapidly. Many programmers leave jobs because they believe them to be technically boring. For example, one programmer at the PROSA conference stated that he left the state sector because "they always used the same language, there were no new languages and no good education development. It was boring, so I left".

The importance of both the intrinsic character of the work and of opportunities to train in new techniques have been noted as important motivating factors for computer programmers elsewhere, (Mumford, 1972; Couger and Zawacki, 1980; Couger, 1988). In Denmark trade unionism is seen as an effective means for achieving this aim. The union negotiates for better training from the employers or the union organises and provides training itself. This does not only increase the quality of IT-specialists working life, it also increases their value on the labour market. This makes it easier for individual IT-specialist to switch jobs in pursuit of higher wages or better working conditions. In this sense trade unionism and job hopping strategies may be complementary in Denmark. Normally we would think of these two strategies as alternatives: trade unionism as a collective strategy, the expression of voice rather than exit, and job hopping as a purely individualistic strategy. However, when job hopping often occurs due to search for better working conditions, and when trade unionism is seen as a way not only of improving current working conditions through collective bargaining, but also as a way of increasing the individual's bargaining position on labour markets, then the two strategies can complement each other. When they leave one IT job for another, IT specialists leave their employer and their work mates, but normally they would not leave their union, in the case of SAMDATA and PROSA members. PROSA in particular defines itself on an occupational basis.

The education issue relates to the strength of unionisation among different occupational groups of IT specialist. There is a strong positive relation between the amount of education you have and the training which employers will fund of their own accord. It was described as a pyramid with systems programmers at the top, operators at the bottom, and applications programmers in the middle (PROSA interview, 1986). Education opportunities from employers is therefore in an inverse relation to the degree of unionisation among different occupation groups. Systems programmers see little need to organise themselves in order to gain better education opportunities or better salaries. On average systems programmers receive more than the other non-management job categories among IT specialists; more than systems consultants and more than systems planners. The difference in salaries between systems programmers and other non- management job categories is particularly pronounced for those in the 25-39 age groups (Chapter XII, Appendix D, Table D:3).

2.5   Other Issues of Concern to the Trade Unions

Education is not the only issue that trade unions for IT specialists in Denmark have embraced which allows IT specialists to pursue other strategies for their material improvement via the trade unionism strategy. Three wider issues that have been prominent at PROSA conferences in the 1980s are; first, the problems of registers of information on individuals, and particularly whether public registers should be maintained in private companies, second, ownership and exploitation of copyright over software and third, new technology agreements. By and large PROSA is against the holding of public records in private firms, though half of PROSA's members are in the private sector. On copyright PROSA is in favour of individual systems developers having copyrights, though the problem for the union when members receive a portion of their income in royalties is recognised. In this latter issue PROSA can be seen to be actively supporting a policy which may be more characteristic of a professional association, perhaps even of a trade association, than of a trade union. In this case the trade union is clearly following the path down which the aspirations of its members is leading.

PROSA has generally been supportive of new technology agreements. In this (and the policy on registers), it seems to be following a policy more characteristic of a professional association. That is, a concern for the effect of the product they produce on society. The ethical side of PROSA activity is generally pursued much more in terms of the effect of IT specialists' work on society, rather than on its effect on trade unionism.

2.6   Trade Unionism and Professionalism

IT specialists in Denmark, particularly those belonging to PROSA, appear to regard trade unionism as something akin to belonging to a professional association. Certainly the collective bargaining function is important, but before 1976 almost a thousand IT specialists belonged to PROSA without an agreement. Currently some 3,000 of PROSA and SAMDATA's 12,100[21] non- student members, and more than 20% of all IT specialists belonging to trade unions, belong to unions without having the benefit of a collective agreement.

What do they get from their membership fees? During the 1987 PROSA annual conference (discussing a year dominated by a major strike in the public sector) representatives from the East and West branches (representing primarily members who work without an agreement), emphasised the importance of the services provided to PROSA members.

"Out in the country, East and West do the most trade union work. The rest just make contracts" said one representative from East at the 1987 conference. The "real" trade union work involves keeping members aware of developments in their field through the union newspaper, providing a forum for them to express their opinions about IT-related issues, giving advice on issues where there are grievances, and providing support for their education and training aspirations, including courses directly organised by the trade union.

Notably PROSA's annual conference acts as an important informal job market. As one person at the 1987 PROSA conference noted, "Job advertisements are only a legal formality. Now recruitment companies are in favour. The

PROSA conference is important as a job market". In this PROSA also clearly acts like a professional association.

We are certainly *not* arguing that PROSA is not a "real" trade union. In fact PROSA seems to resemble the most traditional sort of trade unions; the craft unions which emerged as trade unions from medieval guilds in Great Britain, primarily in the early nineteenth century. IT specialists, like traditional craftsmen, have generally been interested in the quality of their working life as well as their salaries, to a greater extent than unskilled workers.[22] Like traditional craftsmen, they have also been concerned with the product of their labour, with its quality and its effect on others, rather more than other workers.

3   Employee Strategies

In order to explore further what is distinctive about Danish IT people, a general model of employee strategies is presented here. This model serves as a context with which to discuss both the behaviour and special position of IT people in general, and the particular behaviour of IT people in Denmark. The strategies distinguished here have been derived from observations of IT specialists during the past 13 years through the Bristol University project on Management Strategies in IT and the ICON projects as well as the CHIPS project.[23] It is therefore likely that these strategies will be somewhat more prevalent among IT specialists, than among employees in general. For this reason, this collection of strategies are offered as a first step towards defining a strategic framework for employee strategies. However, we have more confidence in the framework as a means to compare Danish IT people with IT people in other countries, particularly those in the UK and USA.

3.1   The General Context of Strategic Behaviour

What are strategies? Mintzberg (1987) presents a strong case for eclecticism. He argues for five rather different and valid definitions for strategy. Strategy is often thought of as a plan, as a consciously intended course of action to deal with a situation. This strong definition of strategy has been argued for by Rose and Jones (1985) and Storey (1985). Close to this definition intentionality is a definition of strategy as a ploy, as a specific manoeuvre intended to outwit an opponent or competitor. This is the definition of strategy most commonly used in economics, particularly in game theory. However Mintzberg also notes that strategy may be defined as a consistent pattern in a stream of actions, whether or not it was intended. This Mintzberg suggests is a complementary concept to strategy as plan. Strategy as plan can be labelled *intended* strategy, but plans can go unrealised and need not therefore be identifiable from outcomes. On the other hand, a strategy as pattern can be labelled *realised* strategy. Mintzberg also uses the labels *deliberate* versus *emergent* strategies.

Another definition of strategy Mintzberg distinguishes is strategy as position, a means of locating an organisation in an environment, the mediating force (or match, Hofer and Schendel, 1978) between the internal and the external context. This notion has been called a "root strategy" (McNichols, 1983). It relates to what may be viewed as a logically prior notion of establishing what the entity is that has a strategy. It is an aspect of strategy by which the strategic actor defines itself ("it" because it is likely to be an organisation or other collective entity) or at least its own boundaries.

Finally, Mintzberg defines strategy as a perspective, an ingrained way of perceiving the world. This aspect of strategy is to organisation what personality or ideology is to the individual according to Mintzberg. It is the character of an organisation, ways of acting and responding that are distinctive and integrated.

All these variants may be related to the original military definition of strategy; that is, the art of a commander-in-chief. It is a rather small step to use the term strategy to describe the art of the head of an organisation. We wish to go further. In common with the widespread extension of the concept of strategy in recent years, we wish to extend the application of the term to ordinary people.

We want to use the concept to analyse how a particular population, those we have defined as the IT people, behaves. We want to develop the analysis in a manner which will be applicable to subsets of that population (including particular communities, see Chapter I). We also want to develop the analysis in a way which will allow us to make predictions about the future behaviour of IT people. In order to do this we will attempt to identify distinct strategies and to make connections between identifiable conditions affecting IT people and subsets of IT people and those distinct strategies. Because we are dealing with groups of people, we will not concentrate on psychological factors. We will therefore use a definition of strategy which does not emphasise individual consciousness and deliberation, a definition dealing with what Mintzberg calls realised or emergent strategy rather than intended or deliberate strategy.

We can eliminate strategy as perspective as well as strategy as plan or ploy. We are interested in analysing sets of individuals within the IT field rather than organisations, or other directed collectivities. When dealing with people, as Mintzberg notes, there are other concepts which capture the idea of individual perspective, that is, personality or ideology. One characteristic of strategy as perspective which we do not wish to emphasise is its implied immutability. Once established, perspectives become difficult to change (Brunsson, 1982). While we do not wish to eliminate the possibility of IT people making mistakes, we do not want to analyse mistakes. Rather we wish to emphasise rational connections between changes in environmental conditions and changes in strategies.

Finally, because it is people rather than organisations we will be dealing with, strategy as position is less relevant. This leaves us with strategy as pattern.

We define strategies as patterns in the stream of decisions and actions taken by individuals or groups which can be related to the achievement of long run goals. This definition is similar to those proposed by Miles and Snow (1978) and by Thurley and Wood (1983). We take the hallmark of strategic decisions to be rationality in decision-making rather than consciousness or consistency. That is, they imply that there is a relation between means and ends. These ends can be utilitarian,[24] based on material interests, or they may be value-oriented, based on ethical, aesthetic, religious or political ideals (Poole, 1986). Strategies will be used to link propositions about environmental conditions facing computer people with observed outcomes. This link is not a transparent one, it does not allow a simple transformation of environmental conditions into observed patterns of behaviour because the link has two connections. Here we concentrate on the first connection (A in figure IX.1.), the effects of various environmental factors on the relative efficiency of different strategic paths. Actual outcomes depend on whether or not particular actors take the paths which appear to the outside observer as the most likely to allow them to achieve their goals (B in figure IX.1.). They depend on both connection A and connection B. However, material environmental conditions, strategies and outcomes are embedded in the context of other psychological and social influences.

Differences between actual outcomes and those which may be predicted from the constellation of environmental conditions may occur for several reasons. It may be that environmental conditions favour more than one strategy. Our analysis of connection A may not result in strong predictions, or it may yield contradictory predictions. It may be that environmental conditions are perceived differently by the actors themselves, compared with the external analyst. It may be that actors are unable to pursue certain strategies because of impediments which are not easily revealed to external observers, such as emotional conflicts (D), ideological influences (C) or the views of particular friends or authority figures (E).

Also we must recognise that actors can make mistakes. The link between means and ends is not a simple one. Many paths which would seem to lead toward our heart's desires turn out to be blocked, or to lead away from desired ends, only after several steps along those paths are taken. These problems often can not be foreseen. Experimentation is therefore necessary. Also continual changes in environmental conditions will not only affect the paths available to actors, but also the strength of the connections between those paths and long run goals. Environmental changes are likely to be perceived by actors slowly and imperfectly. Often perceptions of changed environmental conditions may only be improved by stepping along that path.

Inertia is a particularly important reason for actual outcomes to differ from expectations based on whichever strategies are most favoured by environments.

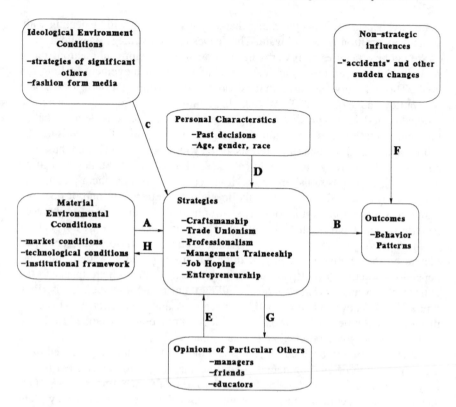

Figure IX.1   Model of Strategic Links between Environment and Outcomes

Clearly most of the time people live with the consequences of strategic choices made in the past (connection D). Altering directions requires considerable energy.

A further sophistication of strategic analysis would be to examine environmental influences on the degree of effort required to make strategic decisions. Environmental factors can not only influence the relative efficiency of different strategies for achieving one's goals, but also the degree of availability of different strategic options. For example, the tight labour market for computer specialists and the assumed national importance of this area encourage organisations and government agencies to publicise opportunities in this field. This can make it easier for individuals within the field to change jobs or to become entrepreneurs because information costs about these options are relatively small.

All the points mentioned above mean that the connection between strategies and outcomes for specific situations (B) can only be analysed with very detailed information. Such an analysis will not be attempted here. Rather we will assess the opportunities for actions which could improve IT people's material position or further their ideals. We will concentrate on connection A. Our analysis will be confined to large groups of people in similar circumstances, in order to avoid the need to predict what any particular individual will do in a specific situation.

Placing strategies at the heart of our analysis helps to guard us against environmental determinism. Though environmental conditions may favour one particular strategy, the choices and actions must still be made by actors. Furthermore strategic choices can affect an actor's environment either directly, by altering specific environmental factors (such as winning particular legislative or other legal changes or building certain institutions, connection H), or by changing the actor's position in the environment (Mintzberg's strategy as position, G and H), or by stimulating reactions by other actors in or out of the field, such as direct managers within IT, top managers of user organisations, IT journalists and educators, or governments, (G and then E).

There is another set of connections which could be shown in figure IX.1. This would run from outcomes "back" to all the other factors. We will not be much concerned with these "reverse" connections. They are more appropriate for studying detailed histories of institutions within the field. We have used some of these connections in our analysis of particular trade unions in the field in section 2.2 above (particularly the establishment of PROSA, the reaction of HK to this challenge and changes in leadership of SAMDATA).

3.2   Six Strategies[25]

Six strategies may be distinguished as having been pursued by IT people:[26]

1) Craftsmanship
2) Trade Unionism
3) Professionalism
4) Management Traineeship (Internal Labour Market Strategy)
5) Job Hopping (External Labour Market Strategy)
6) Entrepreneurship (Product Market Strategy)

3.2.1   Craftsmanship

What makes a craftsman? The material basis for craftsman status is the ability to perform a set of tasks which require considerable on-the-job training. This means that the skills required for the work are available primarily among existing practitioners. Existing practitioners are therefore in a position which allows them to control entry into the job. The requirement of practitioners to train newcomers represents both a material finite limit to how many new entrants can be trained *and* a strategic weapon allowing practitioners to choose to limit the number of newcomers below this material limit.

What kinds of tasks require considerable on-the-job training? Tasks which involve considerable discretion and judgement based on past experience rather than formulae, for example, working with complex tools which must be coordinated very precisely, (a good analogy would be playing a musical instrument). Another way of looking at such activities is to stress the unnatural aspect of this work. Work which requires acting in an unnatural way will often have the appearance of being relatively easy on the surface to try, but very hard to do well. All work of this sort will not stimulate a body of craftsmen. Two other qualities seem important.

First, the ability to complete a wide range of the required tasks individually.[27] If the work requires someone else at crucial stages then it is likely that the tasks will be regrouped. There will be an incentive to strip down jobs which require fine coordination with others. The timing of such jobs can be more easily established and monitored if they are short. However, if people can be left to get on with creating a clear object (which can then be stored, thereby allowing completion to be decoupled from the timing of the next stage in the industry) then the advantages of dividing up jobs[28] will be less likely to outweigh the added costs of coordination and monitoring. Also, technical difficulties in having individuals complete a wide range of tasks individually will allow combinations of only subsidiary tasks into jobs which are even less likely to allow practitioners to regard themselves as craftsmen, for example, nurses. It is possible to imagine small groups of people carrying out complementary jobs acting in concert, but this has not been the most common pattern.

Second, it is important for the body of tasks to remain stable for a long period. If technical change allows the type of craft skill to be avoided by doing the same job differently, the craft-like material conditions are likely to be isolated to individual work sites. This is likely to tie practitioners to particular firms.

What are the likely consequences of craftsmen-type material conditions? There is widespread evidence, particularly from British economic history, that people in these conditions are likely to develop strong independent organisations. Their ability to limit entry into the craft will allow conditions of almost permanent labour shortage. Also, given the difficulty of achieving 'master craftsman' competence, it is likely that craftsmen will be committed to work tasks more than employment relation, committed to their craft more than the enterprise employing them. Limited supply of craftsmen will give them high mobility among firms and so further weaken their ties to any particular employment relation.

3.2.2   Trade Unionism
Significant deterioration in status and working conditions is one important material condition to encourage trade unionism. Note the importance of the unemployment threat to new entrants into IT in the 1980s discussed in section 2.2 above. Growth in white collar trade union membership has been shown to be

strongly related to high levels of inflation (Bain and Elsheikh, 1976). This may be based on recent moves toward Direct Control types of strategies, which in turn could reflect deteriorating product market conditions or changes in IT management. A second condition is a strong union presence elsewhere in the company. This will often be based on large firms size and also on form of ownership; public sector organisations being more likely to be unionized in all countries. For white collar workers, the attitude of the employer has been found to be an important factor explaining trade union membership (Bain and Elsheikh, 1976). The state as an employer, especially when Social Democratic Parties have been in power, has traditionally looked upon trade unions with less hostility than private employers. This factor has been important for explaining the high level of trade unionism in the Danish IT field.

Obviously, closed shop agreements will make this factor of critical importance. A third basic material condition is based on large sized departments, perhaps particularly where there are relatively homogeneous working conditions within departments.

Finally, trade unionism is also affected by what in Britain were known as friendly benefits. Trade unions act as a club to pool earnings in order to provide social benefits for their members. They have traditionally provided pensions, unemployment, sickness and accident insurance and a range of specific benefits such as burial expenses and even housing out of such funds. To the extent that these benefits have come to be provided by the state, independent of the trade unions, one important set of material bases for trade unionism is removed. If provision of such benefits are made by the state through trade union machinery, then this material basis for pursuing the trade unionism strategy is enhanced. The provision of unemployment insurance through the trade unions in Denmark has been an important encouragement for membership among IT people.

3.2.3 Professionalism

Professional attitudes could be thought of simply as modern craft attitudes, but there are some important differences. Typically professional tasks involve some combination of:

a) Command of a body of difficult to acquire theoretical knowledge, though this knowledge may be more important for confirming professional status, rather than actually performing the tasks.
b) Knowledge of bureaucratic procedures – most professions involve dealing effectively with large organisations, usually public bodies.
c) Most professional jobs require the ability to place people for whom work is done into a client type relation. Formal qualifications, jargon and certain social and interpersonal skills can all help to create this sort of relationship.

The essential difference between the material basis for craftsmanship and for professional status is the ability to adjudicate competence in the set of skills required for tasks by formal examination procedures. The hallmark of a profession is the professional qualification. Merely to become a candidate for such qualification requires many years of general education, usually at a high academic standard. Therefore potential professionals have undergone years of careful socialisation before entry to the profession. This, along with screening during the qualifying period, acts to limit the supply of professionals and thereby increases their bargaining power. Because the models for professionalism are all people who carry out work tasks which mainly act in a professional capacity directly with the public, a major role of the professional association is to establish and police working standards. To act 'professionally' is usually taken to mean to act according to standards set by a professional body, thereby to demonstrate competence.

What is the material basis for professional status? It involves performing a set tasks which require a high degree of moral weight. The tasks need to be complex enough to justify years of training, but the emphasis is not on excellence in their execution, but rather competence, which thereby inspires confidence that task execution will not fall below some standard. Tasks concerning health, legality, morality and honesty or esoteric knowledge, are most likely to fall into this category.

What are the consequences of professional organisations and attitudes? Even more than with craftsmen, professionals are likely to develop strong independent organisations and professional qualifications are likely to give holders as individuals a fair degree of independence from employing organisations. Professionals will be concerned with work tasks and develop loyalties to performing those tasks to professionally regulated standards as opposed to employer expediency.

3.2.4   Management Traineeship

Here we are thinking of careerists who look to job ladders within organisations in which they are currently employed to fulfil their aspirations. The way internal labour markets are designed generally means that, beyond the lowest levels, individuals must take on at least some managerial functions if they are promoted. This is a particular problem for specialists. Some will look to moving up grades within specialist departments. Some will concentrate on up-grading the whole specialist department within the company. Some will see the need to move out of a specialist department into general management as the key to their career development.

What are the material conditions for these attitudes? First, the existence of well developed internal labour markets within firms, which in turn is based on a combination of

– Large installation size,
– Large company size,

– Responsible autonomy management strategies within firms[29],
– Performing tasks which require a high degree of firm-specific knowledge.

Firm specific knowledge is the stick – meaning that it is difficult for individuals to move out of the firm and get "credit" for past experience and on-the-job training. Responsible Autonomy-type strategies and well developed job ladders are the carrots tempting people to stay with firms. It is notable that in Japan, the fact that well developed internal labour markets are so widespread among the higher paying companies means that this acts as both a stick and a carrot because 'good' companies are reluctant to hire people from other firms. In the West people can come off a high rung of a job ladder in one company and join another in a high position either because not all high paying firms have strict job ladders or because most firms do not enforce the ladder so strictly.

3.2.5   Job Hopping
Normally we would think of this in negative terms. People who change jobs often are likely to do so because they are in unstable occupations, or because they find it hard to "fit into" any particular organisation, or perhaps because their personal lives are unstable. Managers would normally be suspicious of people who have been job hoppers. However, there are circumstances when job hopping can be a positive strategy. This is when external labour markets are tight because labour demand is rising, but when internal labour markets are characterised by a combination of seniority rules for internal promotion and several entry ports for outsiders at different points in the hierarchy of internal positions.

3.2.6   Entrepreneurship
This we define as setting up a new organisation to supply some computer- based product. Wide access to resources required to start up new businesses has long been viewed as one of the most positive aspects of capitalism according to liberal thought. However, economies of scale (and other entry barriers) and conservatism of financial institutions ("imperfections" of capital markets) have meant that the liberal ideal is rarely observed in practice. However, in the IT world, especially in software production, economies of scale are weak. Rapid technical change is an important material basis for entrepreneurship, especially if it is capital saving rather than labour saving. If the industry is generally growing rapidly, this can ameliorate technical limitations.

4   Environmental Conditions and the Relative Advantage of Different Strategies for IT People

4.1   Environmental Conditions for IT in General

Certain features have characterised the international computing field throughout its history. The most important of these features is the continual state of shortage in the labour market. Rapid technological change and the relative ease of generating new technology are also particularly important features.

A *Tight Labour Markets* – The most important effect of this is that it allows a number of the strategies outlined above to be considered as realistic options for computer people. Options such as entrepreneurship, job hopping and management traineeship are not such clear or common options for other workers. However, tight labour markets reduce the risks of leaving a job either to take another or to set up one's own business. Also tight labour markets encourage employers to try to retain staff by internal labour markets which increases the feasibility of pursuing a management traineeship strategy. Tight labour markets do not stimulate individual strategies alone. Tight labour markets can also enhance the power of professional associations and trade unions (trade union membership normally rises in boom times, though many associate this with inflation rather than improved bargaining power, Bain and Elsheik, 1976).

B *High Technology* – This will encourage craftsmanship in that high technology jobs may be associated with highly skilled jobs. It can also encourage professionalism where formal qualifications are applicable. That is, a collective body of practitioners will have more incentive to translate required skills into a form which is examinable in a formal way if required skills are substantial, because employers will find certification useful to judge prospective employees. High technology may also discourage management traineeship in organisations where the primary techniques used are not "high-tech". For example, there may be a negative attitude towards IT specialists in organisations primarily providing personal services, or in small organisations which do not trade on their technical sophistication (see chapter II-4).

C *Rapid Technological Change* – The effect of technological changes will depend on whether those changes have occurred from within the organisation or from outside (see D below). If the changes come from outside the organisation and if it involves really drastic changes, then the effect may well discourage craftsmanship. On the other hand, trade unionism or professionalism may thereby be encouraged, as a defense, (professionalism if the defense is to be more in terms of protecting a formal qualifications base, trade unionism if the defense is more in terms of resisting deterioration of existing employment conditions). The changes will also encourage entrepreneurship if those technological changes involve product innovations. As the computing field has become so large rapid technological change is increasingly likely to affect different groups of computer people differently. Certain skills have remained "valid" in spite of rapid technological changes, while others have been deskilled or their skills have been automated away. Systems programmers and operators are examples of these two different tendencies.

D *Strong potential for procreation of new techniques and new products in computer installations* – The computer has always been more of a bundle of potential new technology looking for applications rather than a specific innovation. This has meant that user organisation installations, even very small ones, have been capable of developing new things. In other fields organisations using a technology are rarely capable of developing that technology except for minor adjustments. However entrepreneurship in IT is a possible strategy for a substantial proportion of computer people in user organisations as well as those in the more glamorous hardware and software specialist firms. The ability of practitioners to develop new techniques also favours craftsmanship. Developing ones own techniques increases the discretionary content of the work and allows people to concentrate on developing skill–enhancing new techniques to maintain craft status.

E *Strong Autodidactic Element in the Population of Computer People* – In part this follows from A and C above. Formal education institutions have not been able to keep up with the demand for computer people, nor have they been able to keep up with the rapidly changing technical requirements of new recruits to the field. However, this is not the whole explanation. Computing skills, particularly those of programming are best learned on the job. Learning by doing is important because what is required is not merely to know the rules, but also to know how to apply them and to know how to get out of trouble or how to find and correct mistakes which are inevitably made. This encourages the management to value experience rather than education. It also means that the best way to pick up skills is to work with or near someone who is already skilled, the classic apprenticeship model and the foundation of craftsmanship, as opposed to professionalism.

4.2   Mapping Strategies by Relative Advantage

The strategic implications of the environmental conditions described above are mapped out in figure IX.2.

Compared with other employees, environmental conditions for IT people in general seem particularly to favour strategies of craftsmanship and entrepreneurship. Trade unionism and job hopping strategies are also favoured.[30]

Craftsmanship is an important strategy among IT people. Osterman describes internal labour markets for computer programmers and analysts in Boston in the early 1980s as a craft structure (Osterman, 1984). We believe the basis for a

	Crafts-manship	Trade Unionism	Profession-alism	Management Trainee	Job Hopping	Entrepre-neurship
Tight Labour Markets	+	+	+	+	+	+
High Technology	+		+(?)	−(?)		
Rapid Exogenous Technical Change	−	+ (in defense)	+ (in defense)		+	+
Strong Technical Procreation	+					+
Strong Autodidactic	+		−			
Overall	very strong	strong	strong(ish)	weak	strong	very strong

Figure IX.2   Strategic Implications of Features General to the IT Field

successful craftsmanship strategy has been eroded somewhat since the early years of IT. Systems programming is still an area where conditions for craftsmanship as a primary strategy continue.

In that IT has developed a mysterious jargon and to an extent that IT jobs involve tasks which require certain standards of accuracy, some of the material conditions for *professionalism* exist. The problem is that as IT descends deeper into private organisations, the essential public nature of the work recedes. IT staff who regard themselves as professionals are more likely to be found in public sector departments. Also in the computer services sector they will be more likely to deal with the public directly. Recent increase in concern with user relations and with systems which deal directly with clients and suppliers may in fact encourage professional organisations among IT staff (see Friedman, 1990).

Management Traineeship appears to be a relatively recent strategy among IT specialists. When an IT department is set up in a company with pre-existing patterns of internal labour markets and responsible autonomy types of strategies, the commitment to the company by IT staff is likely to be high. Nevertheless, this is critically affected by the ability of top managers to incorporate IT staff into internal labour markets in a way which relates to staff aspirations. Given the perpetual tight labour markets for IT staff relative to most other staff, consider-able flexibility must be shown. Obviously, this attitude is most likely to develop among IT staff where other staff are of a similar level of technical sophistication and face a similar labour market. IBM is the classic case, but large electronics or telecommunications firms such as Plessey in the UK or General Electric in the US may be further examples.

The existence of large programming pools may encourage *trade unionism* through the traditional notion of homogeneity of working conditions among many people encouraging collective empathy with grievances. We would expect trade unionism to be high in organisations with large numbers of trade unionists elsewhere in the firm.

The computing field is characterised by a tight labour market. People *job hop* without generating as much suspicion on the part of managers as in other occupations. Also a range of labour market institutions have developed in order to facilitate easy movement between jobs. Headhunters, body shops and temp agencies specialising in IT people exist in many countries.

Entrepreneurship is particularly important as a strategy among IT people because the IT field is unusual in that economies of scale and other entry barriers have been conspicuously absent since access to hardware capacity has become rather easy. The computer service sector contains a rapidly growing number of small successful firms.

5 Environmental Conditions and Advantaged Strategies for IT People in Denmark

The following features seem to distinguish the IT field in Denmark. These features are in addition to the general features outlined in the previous two sections. Evidence for these features has been provided in other chapters of this book. The features are:

(i) High concentration of computer people in *large organisations*. In part this is due to the huge service bureaus (which by themselves account for about 20%-25% of computer people in Denmark). It is also due to the high concentration of banking in Denmark. The effect of this concentration may be to increase the management traineeship strategy, to reduce the entrepreneurship strategy and to increase the trade unionism strategy. Large service bureaus will be biased toward the more technical aspects of computing. This will contribute to the craftsmanship strategy (see Chapters I and IV).

(ii) The two points mentioned above help to explain why there seems to be *few large software houses* in Denmark. A related factor would be the *high proportion of small firms* in Denmark (see Chapters VI and VII). This may mean relatively few packages being used which would affect the occupation distribution. Applications programmers would be spending their time developing systems from a more primitive state. This means more technical work for the average applications programmer and would favour craftsmanship.

(iii) Few large software houses in Denmark also mean a *greater reliance on foreign software suppliers, particularly IBM*. IBM appears to have a greater influence in Denmark than elsewhere (see Chapter I-2). Note that Sweden and Norway also have had stronger traditions of independent hardware than Denmark. The IBM community is strong on management traineeship and professionalism.

(iv) *Strong tradition of trade union membership* in Denmark. This is particularly so for the public sector and for white collar workers. However, this level of unionisation is a relatively recent phenomenon. This helps to explain the presence of PROSA in Denmark, an independent union specialising completely on organising people in computer occupations. In Sweden, where there is also high trade union membership among computer people there is no independent union.

(v) *Strong tradition of craftsmanship* . This helps to account for the plethora of associations of computing specialists as well as the high emphasis on education at PROSA and SAMDATA. These associations have not been able to formulate a common entry requirement. The emphasis on education at PROSA is perhaps an indication that PROSA is a modern "craft" type of organisation, though their policy on education concentrates more on education as a continuing right (10% of work time for all) rather than an apprenticeship requirement of entry.

(vi) Relatively *weak job protection legislation* in Denmark coupled with relatively *good unemployment benefits* are intended to allow easy adjustments to new technology and changes in industrial structure through the labour market. This encourages job hopping.

Strategic implications of the special features of the IT field in Denmark are summarised in figure IX.3.[31]

Thus in addition to the obvious explanation of high emphasis on craftsmanship and trade unionism strategies among Danish IT people as being due to high trade union membership and strong craft traditions elsewhere in Denmark, the size distribution of Danish IT has contributed to advantages for these strategies.

6   Strategies of a Particular Group of IT People in Denmark: the Community at Datacentralen

Datacentralen was set up in 1959 in order to develop and maintain administrative IT systems for the public sector. Together with Kommunedata, Datacentra-

	Crafts-manship	Trade Unionism	Profession-alism	Management Trainee	Job Hopping	Entrepre-neurship
Large Installations	+	+		+	−	
Small User Firms	+		?			
Strong IBM Influence	−		+	+	−	
Traditions: Crafts Unions	+	+				
Weak Job Protection					+	
Overall	very strong	strong	strong (?)	strong	weak	weak

Figure IX.3   Strategic Implications of the Special Features of Computing in Denmark

len distinguishes the IT field in Denmark by its high concentration of specialists working in large public sector service bureau. With about 1500 permanent staff, Datacentralen represents between 5% and 10% of the computer population in Denmark, (see Chapter I).

According to Pedersen and Sorensen (1989), there are five dominant values held by the majority of employees at Datacentralen[32]. They are:

a) Control is Necessary.
b) You do not fire people – stay and you shall be rewarded.
c) Big is beautiful.
d) Craftsmanship is a cornerstone.
e) Union membership is important.

Pedersen and Sorensen use the term values as it is used by Schein, that is, the set of individuals' convictions of what ought to be, as distinct from what is, (Schein, 1985, p. 55). Therefore values in this sense could be thought of as goals or as strategies. They could relate to ends (what an individual believes life ought to be like), but they also could be strategic, relating to means, (how the individual ought to pursue his or her goals, including his or her material interests). Both of these ideas are represented in the five values listed above.[33]

"Big is beautiful" seems most clearly to represent a goal. Some people may be thought of as "big organisation people". Big is perhaps synonymous with important to them. Big organisations allow them to identify with status organisations. However according to Pedersen and Sorensen's discussion, big is beautiful and Datacentralen seems to be a short-hand representation of a collection of goals including employment security, stability, and opportunities to work at a wide range of high technology jobs. Therefore, it could also be interpreted as a strategy in that going to work in a big organisation is a means for achieving that collection of goals. This interpretation would allow us to use their evidence as support for the internal labour market strategy which we have labelled as management traineeship.

Another of Pedersen and Sorensen's values, "you do not fire people – stay and you shall be rewarded", expresses the same strategy in more explicit terms. Stay is the strategy. Behind this precept is the acknowledged practice of internal recruitment for higher level positions by seniority (Pedersen and Sorensen, 1989,p. 140-141).

"Union membership is important" seems most clearly to represent a strategy. What union membership is important for is to achieve good working conditions and protection from arbitrary management. What Pedersen and Sorensen observed was the value, the conviction, the strongly held belief, that member-ship in a union was a good thing. Where did this conviction come from? Did it come from a set of beliefs that the majority of Datacentralen employees brought with them into the organisation: from their innate instincts, or from their families, or their education experiences, or from other activities within the wider community? Most of these factors were likely to have been of some influence. Nevertheless, it is likely that the success of trade unionism at Datacentralen also contributed to this widespread value. Successful strategies are likely to develop into values. Employees at Datacentralen were actively involved in the establish-ment of unions for computer specialists in Denmark. There is a very high level of unionisation among analysts, programmers and operators at Datacentralen (60-70%).

"Craftsmanship is a cornerstone" fits easily into our enumeration of strategies for computer people. Pedersen and Sorensen present various expressions of pride in the quality of work. Though this pride is transferred to the company, it is not automatically transferred to the management. Datacentralen employees expressed the idea that they, the ordinary employees, were responsible for the company's reputation for craftsmanship. They were concerned that management would, if unchecked, destroy that reputation in pursuit of sales. The craftsman-ship strategy would traditionally be pursued through external labour markets. We found that in other countries computer people often mentioned a lack of opportunity to develop their skills as a reason for quitting jobs. Within what is recognised as an organisation where it is possible to develop one's skills, a strategy which would have been pursued on an individual basis can be effectively pursued on a collective basis. This requires a common commitment to craftsmanship. We can interpret the value "control is necessary" in this light, as needed in order to pursue craftsmanship in a large organisation.

	Crafts-manship	Trade Unionism	Profession-alism	Management Trainee	Job Hopping	Entre-preneur-ship
Incumbents (Dominant Group)	+	+	+	+ (internal labour markets within computing)		
New Wave			+	+	+	?

Figure IX.4   Strategic Profile of Different Communities Within Datacentralen

According to Pedersen and Sorensen this value is more of a ritual used to signal efficiency and confidence to the company's customers, than an internally held value. This interpretation accords with viewing craftsmanship and internal labour markets as dominant strategies of computer specialists at Datacentralen. This was confirmed by our CHIPS material for Datacentralen. These two strategies, along with trade unionism are represented in figure IV.4. as comprising the pattern of strategies for the dominant group of employees at Datacentralen.

During the past five to ten years there has been an influx of new recruits who have a different set of values from the incumbents according to Pedersen and Sorensen. New recruits are more likely to enter the company with formal specialist education. They view Datacentralen as a place where they can improve their qualifications in order to increase their salaries and promotion prospects at other organisations (1987, p. 152-154). These people are more likely to have been attracted to the computing field by the recent widely advertised good financial prospects for computer specialists. They do not have the same fears of unemployment as most employees. This allows them to view the external labour market as an arena of strategic opportunities. Trade unions are therefore less important for them, (though their lack of interest in trade unions may also reflect an overall change in social climate in recent years, particularly in education institutions). The strategic preferences of the new wave of Datacentralen employees is represented in figure IX.4.

What primarily distinguishes the two groups at Datacentralen are their orientation to markets and the degree of their collective orientation. Incumbents pursue internal labour market strategies. They rely on trade unions, internal promotion policies and the shortage of people with their sort of skills to achieve their material aims, including good working conditions. Good internal training and a good craftsmanship image for the company allows them status for technical virtuosity. Most of these strategies must be pursued collectively.

The new wave pursues external labour market strategies. They rely on formal qualifications and a curriculum vitae of specific types of experience in order to pursue material goals either in labour markets with other companies or in product markets as entrepreneurs. They enter these markets as individuals.

It is legitimate to view these differences as a clash of values as Pedersen and Sorensen do. With such a perspective the main source of change in an organisation would have to be the influx of people with new values. Changes in the values that dominate a set of people would depend primarily on the relative proportion of people holding the respective values. The strategies framework allows another source of dynamics. This is changes in the relative efficiency of the different strategies as stimulated by changes in environmental conditions.

The product market facing Datacentralen has been changing in ways which reflect the general shift towards the third phase of IT described in Friedman (1989). This has forced the company to become more customer oriented. In 1985 they went through a major reorganisation. The old divisions by function (systems, programming, operations) were replaced by a set of profit centres divided by customer type. These changes were intended to increase attention to sales, profits and knowledge of customer needs. This reduces the relative efficiency of pursuing craftsmanship strategy within the company compared with pursuing professionalism and management trainee strategies.

Another change has been the rise of the independent software sector. This increases the efficiency of entrepreneurial, job hopping and professionalism strategies. Software houses, especially in the 1980s, can be set up with relatively little capital. They increase the number of competitors on the demand side of the labour market. Their small size compared with the service bureau and with the user firms means that a higher proportion of computer specialists in these companies will be working directly with customers.

Therefore we would predict that the strategic mix which the new wave seem to be pursuing would gradually become the dominant one at Datacentralen.

7   Conclusion

There have been three aims of this paper. The first was to examine strategies pursued by IT people in Denmark. The second was to help explain why those strategies have been pursued. The third was to develop a general framework which could be used to understand the behaviour of other sets of IT people and of people in other fields. In relation to these aims we must note that this has been a preliminary analysis which has concentrated almost exclusively on only one of the links to strategies (A) shown in figure IX.1.

IT people are distinguished by a wide range of strategies which are relatively easy for them to pursue because of the severe labour shortages which have characterised the IT field from the outset. Tight labour markets have not only undercut Direct Control strategies by managers (see Chapters X and XI), but also they have opened different strategic paths to IT people which are normally rather difficult for other types of employees to pursue. Of the many strategies open to them, IT people in Denmark have been encouraged to pursue a constellation of craftsmanship, trade unionism, entrepreneurship and professionalism strategies. These strategies have resulted in the development of strong trade unions, occupied primarily with education and training issues, and secondarily with professional and entrepreneurial aims (particularly PROSA).

Of course there are other reasons for high trade union membership and for the particular character of trade unionism among IT people in Denmark. For example, the establishment of an independent trade union itself encouraged high membership throughout the field because of the competitive effect. PROSA stimulated the established unions to organise IT specialists at an early stage in the history of the IT field in Denmark (connection H as well as A in figure IX.1).

Danish IT people are highly unionised compared with international levels of trade unionism among IT people. However, compared with the Danish working population, unionisation rates for Danish IT people are low. This we have analysed in terms of the wide range of viable alternative strategies available to them. In particular job hopping and entrepreneurship are individual strategies which weaken commitments to collective action (figure IX.2.). Furthermore, in Denmark, use of internal labour markets to move into management positions is a strong option available to IT people. Together environmental conditions favouring these individualistic strategies may be predicted to lead to a disposition toward "exit" rather than "voice" when IT people become dissatisfied with their material position (Hirschman, 1970). This will weaken collective voicing of grievances through bargaining and other collective action coordinated through trade unions.

On the other hand, trade unions in Denmark have been able to embrace certain strategies that would normally be considered substitutes for trade unionism. They have been able to support and facilitate tactics related to professionalism such as the provision of education and credentials based on formal education, and even the ideologically difficult issue of individual property rights in software. They have also supported the job hopping strategy, (informally at least) through conferences and word of mouth contacts at smaller gatherings. Though the low membership of systems programmers suggests that they have been less successful at supporting the craftsmanship strategy.

As for the value of the general form of analysis proposed here, concentrating on strategic behaviour opens the possibility of developing testable hypotheses and of predicting future behaviour. For example, analysis of the difference in strategic profile between incumbents and new wave groups at Datacentralen gives us an indication of the future strategic balance, not only at Datacentralen itself, but also more generally in the field because of the significance of

Datacentralen in the field and because the new wave at Datacentralen is representative of new entrants into the field. This would suggest a change from craftsmanship and trade unionism to job hopping and professionalism. Another possibility is that the recent recession, which has hit the IT field, will drive even newer entrants to the field (and incumbents threatened with lay-offs) toward the strategy of trade unionism. As noted above (section 2.2), the threat of unemployment had been a powerful stimulus for EDP-assistants to join PROSA and SAMDATA in 1982-83.

This sort of analysis also allows the possibility for the actors themselves to benefit from the analysis. By examining alternative possibilities for how goals may be achieved and the environmental conditions which favour different routes, IT people may come to develop or alter strategies in response to a reading of those environmental conditions. Particular strategies may be developed by learning from the tactical moves made by other groups once the similarities of conditions are recognised. Also the danger of continuing to follow a traditional, deeply rutted, path when conditions favour a change of route, may be ameliorated by analysis which clearly admits alternative routes.

Notes

1   The IT people referred to in this paper will be identified as the core IT people. They correspond to the occupational groups described in Chapter XII. They are core IT people as distinguished from certain peripheral groups who work with IT, but who would not consider themselves to be specialists in IT, such as sophisticated users of IT or IT journalists.

2   There were about 300-400 who belonged to both PROSA and SAMDATA, mostly in the banks and the coops. There is an agreement between FTF and HK that all grades of people employed in the private banks should be organised by DBLF alone. There is no agreement with PROSA. Prosa has few members in the private banks, but in the savings banks DSLF, HK, PROSA and a local staff association all compete. (PROSA interviews)

3   According to Bjorn-Andersen et al (1988), 1988 figures for SAMDATA and PROSA are 7,000 and 6,800 respectively. This would give an estimated total union membership for 1988 of at least 17,129. The number of potential members for PROSA was estimated by PROSA to be 30,000 in 1986. This figure includes data preparation staff, as do most of the unionisation figures. According to PROSA there have very few data preparation staff in the union. It is likely that there are only substantial numbers of data preparation staff included in the SAMDATA figures.

4   1965 figures cited in Blum and Ponak, 1974, p.65.

5   In the three years from 1969 to 1972 the number of white collar workers rose from 850,000 to 973,000, by 14%. The number of white collar trade unionists rose from 399,000 to 493,000, or by 24% (figures calculated from those provided in Scheuer, 1984, based on official statistics).

6   HK is affiliated to the national federation of manual workers, the LO.

7   See Blum and Ponak (1974) for a comparison of HK and FTF. In 1970 HK had 141,000 members and FTF had 161,000. Together they represented 65% of white collar trade unionists.

8   In 1969 and in 1972 FTF and HK made jurisdictional agreements which would have severely limited PROSA's recruitment potential.

9   Joint talks about IT staff took place between DBLF and DSLF in 1974/75 because the unions began "to see the need to organise dp staff because their jobs were important" (DBLF interview, 1987).

10 This is a very high unionisation rate for private sector IT staff. It is not far off the overall white collar unionisation rate in Denmark. However, in Denmark the large private commercial banks are highly unionised. DBLF had achieved an overall membership density of 96% by 1987.

11 Of course, high wages and good working conditions in the private banks are also attributable to high and steady profits in this sector. In the 1987 agreement IT staff got an extra hour of free time per week above what other bank staff enjoy.

12 Bain (1970) found that the growth of white collar unionisation was related to only four factors; the density of white collar unions, the degree of employment concentration, the degree to which employers are prepared to recognise unions representing white collar workers, and the extent of government action promoting union recognition. However this study was carried out before the major growth of white collar unionisation occurred, before the rapidly growing inflation of the late 1960s and 1970s, and before the substantial white collar redundancies of the 1970s and 1980s.

13 As Scheuer (1984) has pointed out, enforceability of collective agreements is easier in Denmark than in Great Britain due to stronger legal backing for implementation. See Gospel (1983) for a comparison of agreement enforcement between Great Britain, Sweden and the USA.

14 It also rises in Sweden where there is a similar arrangement for unemployment insurance (see Kjellberg, 1983).

15 Students join either East or West branches of PROSA. In 1987 there were 300-400 student members in East branch (PROSA interview, 1987). Also 600- 700 SAMDATA members were students and this represented about 50% of the students (SAMDATA interview, 1987). This suggests that almost all students are organised, about half in PROSA and half in SAMDATA. In 1987 there were 1,345 students in courses leading to IT qualifications. Of these 750 were taking the EDP-assistant course.

16 The survey was based on a sample of 130 students taking the two-year course. This represented 61% of the population of relevant students (SAMDATA, 1988).

17 Most of these graduates would have found a job within a matter of months after their graduation.

18 PROSA has 2,000 members without an agreement, SAMDATA has 1,000. DBLF seems not to have any without an agreement.

19 Note that 63% of IT people were between the ages of 25 and 39, compared with 46% for all white collar employees in Denmark (Chapter XII, Appendix D, Table D:2).

20 In 1980 the leaders of SAMDATA were replaced. Hans Sorensen became vice-chairman.

21 The figure of 12,100 is 13,800 minus 350 joint members and 1350 students.

22 In part of course because they have been able to afford to divert their energy from renumeration issues.

23   The Bristol University project ran from 1979 to 1985 (see Friedman and Cornford, 1981; 1987). ICON (International Computer Occupations Network) is a group of IT specialists and academic researchers joining together to study and discuss the organisation of the work of IT specialists. It has regular conferences, the first was held in 1982. It has produced a number of newsletters and working paper collections. Further information about ICON can be obtained from the author.

24   The term utilitarian was originally used by Jeremy Bentham and his followers, to describe any action which has a net tendency to augment the happiness of the community, (the community was taken, by and large simply to mean the collection of individuals comprising it). However, as Williams points out (1976, pp.275-277), utilitarian is now more associated with a more limited class of goals than happiness. It usually refers to practical or material goals. This is the sense in which the term utilitarian is used here.

25   These strategies must be distinguished from the typology constructed by Lockwood (1966): deferential traditional, traditional proletarian and modern privatised workers. Their typology is of worker *attitudes* and it is Lockwood's contention that these attitudes are generated largely by the types of communities in which workers live. Essentially, Lockwood tries to explain why certain groups of workers are more or less militant than others. By using attitudes as the link between environment and outcomes Lockwood falls into the trap of simple determinism. There is a presumed straight forward link between attitudes and behaviour when comparing workers in similar industries.

26   The strategies distinguished below are all, more or less, active. They imply some effort on the part of IT people. The concept of a strategy implies purposive decision-making and action. However, many people do not take decisions concerning their working position very frequently in order to further their aims. Many regard their private lives as more important. We could distinguish such people as primarily pursuing a passive strategy at work, but this is a rather clumsy and contradictory construction. Rather we should accept that actors will all pursue strategies with a varying degree of ardour, that inertia is a general feature of behaviour. Therefore, the degree of inertia should be considered for each strategy, as well as for the whole collection of strategies relating to work. This issue will not be examined in this chapter.

27   Whether tasks can be done individually or not is not simply a technical matter. It depends on custom and management strategy as well as available practical knowledge or techniques. While techniques can change with effort, existing techniques and customary practice still act as a groove to shape the way jobs are formulated, even if there are other factors which can lead the formulations to break out of customary grooves.

28   Lower costs because all round craftsmen do not have to be hired for the jobs made up of tasks requiring lower skills – the Babbage effect (Babbage, 1832).

29   Responsible Autonomy and Direct Control are general two types of managerial strategies. Responsible Autonomy strategies involve managing workers by trying to take advantage of their flexibility. This will involve trying to motivate workers with such practices as responsible jobs, good working conditions and a secure employment prospects. Direct Control strategies are based on the philosophy that workers should be managed as other types of inputs are coordinated. This will involve designing standardised work tasks, detailed monitoring and other deskilling techniques. A general description of these strategies may be found in Friedman (1977). An application of them to computer specialists may be found in Friedman and Cornford (1987) and Friedman with Cornford (1989).

30 As presented above the map implies an equal weighting for all environmental factors. This is a simplification which is unlikely to be upheld with more detailed analysis. Certainly we would expect different environmental conditions to affect specific communities in the field differently. In later sections we discuss the IT people in Denmark and the IT people at a particular organisation which has been identified as a separate community within the Danish context. One way to build a better weighting system would be to identify those environmental conditions which most strongly affect particular categories of IT people, say by job category. Then the proportions of different job categories could be aggregated to give a weighting for the population.

31 Note that these are features which distinguish IT people in Denmark from IT people elsewhere, rather than distinguishing IT people in Denmark from other people in Denmark.

32 In Pedersen and Sorensen this public service bureau is referred to as "Goliath".

33 Normally we might think of values as codes of behaviour. As procedural factors which guide action in particular situations.

Chapter X
Beyond Taylorism: The IT Specialists and the Deskilling Hypothesis

Finn Borum

1   Introduction

It is not very often that we have the opportunity to revisit a field of study after ten years and be confronted with the early perceptions and forecasts of colleges and oneself. In connection with the CHIPS-project I have had that privilege and will use this experience to confront the expected deskilling process of the IT specialists (programmers and analysts) with the actual development in Denmark.

In line with Braverman's deskilling hypothesis (1974) several authors (among others Greenbaum, 1976; Ehn and Sandberg, 1979; Borum, 1977) have assumed that also the specialists employed within the planning functions related to information technology (IT), would also in due time fall victim to a vertical and horizontal specialisation. The planning and design of new information systems would gradually end up being controlled by management, and the specialists hence reduced from craftsmen to dequalified workers who carry out defined tasks.

To illustrate this line of thought the following diagram from Ehn and Sandberg (1979, p. 191) shows the division of work that was developing within the computer departments. The diagram is to be read as a description of a diachronic process where the initial craftsman is replaced by increasingly specialised workers. This does not mean that the craftsmen completely disappear, but that their relative number and importance are drastically reduced over time.

In this chapter, we will focus on the right side of the figure – the IT specialists of programmers and systems analysts, look into the actual development and discuss why it has turned out to be so different from what was expected.

The difference between expectations and the actual development is summarised in section 2. In section 3 possible reasons for this development are discussed from an organisational perspective (Scott, 1981); more specifically,

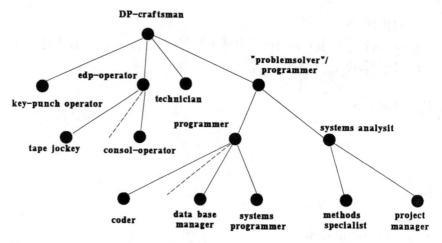

Figure X.1   The Deskilling of DP-workers (after Ehn and Sandberg, 1979)

the Taylorist perspective on organisations will be contested with regard to both its utility for the understanding of work organisation in the IT field, and its empirical validity as a description of management practice.

The empirical basis is primarily research within the Danish computing field, and the theoretical basis is organisation theory. The analysis is operating at a meso level: above the micro level of tasks/jobs and the individual's responses to this, and below the labour market macro level. Although, admittedly, it is hard, and perhaps not desirable, to avoid excursions from one level into the other ones.

2   Deskilling Questioned by Empirical Findings

Data from the CHIPS project indicate that the classical *division of labour* between systems analysts and programmers has been eroding. Specialists that are labelled "programmers" in many cases actually turn out to be working with both programming and systems analysis. The first observations of this phenomenon were made in small and medium-sized DP departments and software houses. My immediate reaction was to explain it as a consequence of the division of labour being too inflexible for that size of organisations.

However, later on the same observations were made in large installations as well as in the case of a very large service bureau (Datacentralen), furnishing the Danish public sector with data processing and software. This does not mean that the division of labour is not more elaborate in large than in small organisations.

In fact, in the large organisation just mentioned, all the job categories depicted in the figure from Ehn and Sandberg (1979) can be found. However, this organisation abandoned the strict division of labour around 1980, subsequent to a re-organisation of the planning functions along customer-oriented criteria, that replaced a traditional functional one.

This shift apparently reflects another dominant trend within the *organisational structures* of the IT field: project organisation or customer- based departments are the standard organisational responses to the task environment. These project groups comprise a mixture of programmers and programmers/planners – the distinction between these two groups mainly being one of seniority or formal qualifications: many of the specialists start as programmers, and then in a couple of years they move into mixed programming/planning functions.

Thus, job enlargement and flexible division of tasks, and not deskilling, is the impression of the development of the Danish IT specialists.

Looking upon the *qualifications* of the IT specialists a certain increase in formal qualifications has taken place, although a 1981 survey revealed that two thirds of the specialists had no formal IT education (Hingel, 1985). The modest fraction possessing a higher education (university degree or the equivalent) has, however, been increasing.

Most important has been the establishment of a public "EDP-assistant" education, which one third of the 1981 population possessed (Hingel, 1985) and which is now held by perhaps more than half of the specialists. But the most important qualifications still appear to be developed through on-the- job-training. Learning by doing, and learning from senior specialists seem to be the core mechanisms, which gives allusions to craftsmanship, not to deskilled workers.

Recruitment to IT specialist functions is increasingly based upon the intake of individuals who are skilled within the application area or trade. Thus individuals are often recruited from user departments to internal computer departments, and supplier organisations often acquire individuals with formal education or practical skills within customer areas.

Thus flexible recruitment patterns have co-existed with a very strict distinction between IT specialists and users: the latter distinction is, however, losing out to the former. Individuals are increasingly moving across this borderline, and in user departments one find former IT specialists as managers or serving as important intermediaries between the DP departments and the user departments. Or you find users who, in fact, spend most, or an important part of their time, on functions that you would label as IT functions.

Finally, the *itineraries* within the Danish IT field further support flexibility as the characteristic of IT specialists occupying positions as programmers and planners. Even if there is a tendency to recruit persons with higher formal qualifications to positions as planners, it is not possible to establish any strong correlation between the individuals' initial qualifications and positions, and their positions and functions after three years within the IT field.

To sum up, there is not much evidence for the deskilling hypothesis[1]: flexible division of work, a high degree of autonomy, high wages, good career opportunities are some of the traits of the IT specialists' work situations within a field that is still expanding.

In the following section some explanations of this development are discussed primarily from a contingency theory approach as formulated by Mintzberg (1979) who stipulates the existence of different structural configurations, each emphasising different methods of coordination and each contingent upon several factors. Without necessarily accepting the totality of contingency theory, it, nevertheless, offers a line of thought which can be employed as a tool to get beyond Braverman's (1974) occupation with Taylorism only.

3   Deskilling Questioned by Contingency Theory

3.1   Organisational Structures as Responses to the Environment

According to Mintzberg (1979) one of the important factors upon which the organisational structure[2] is contingent is the environment of which the dimensions stability and complexity are assumed to be particularly important. The following figure summarises the basic assumptions about what organisational structures that represent "fits" to given environmental conditions (adapted from Mintzberg, 1979, p. 286):

A Taylorist organisation is essentially characterised by machine bureaucracy, and the figure above reveals a fact that is often neglected in relation to the Taylorist mode of organisation: that even though it is based upon a closed, rational perspective (Scott, 1981) the actual organisation is, in fact, an open system, dependent upon a stable and simple environment. In other words: machine bureaucracy is geared towards mass production.

Thus, the figure limits the applicability of the Braverman type analysis to very specific environmental conditions, that are quite different from the dynamics of the IT field. What might explain the erroneous perceptions earlier cited is the fact that they were made around the end of the "main- frame-era", just before the minis had acquired importance. Thus the forecasts projected the features of existing large installations, at that time operating in stable environments, into future tendencies. The technological development in terms of the minis and subsequently the PCs, and the "post-industrial" societal development, however, led to quite different environmental conditions: dynamism and complexity.

Characteristics of environment	stable	dynamic
complex	Professional bureaucracy (standardisaton of skills)	Adhocary (mutual adjustment)
simple	Machine bureaucracy (standardisaton of work processes)	Simple Structure (direct supervision)

(The brackets indicate the basic method of coordination for each structural configuration)

Figure X.2   Fits between Organisational Environments and Organisational Structures

3.2   Information Technology as a Contingency Factor

The above line of reasoning leaves us with a need for understanding the information technology itself as a contingency factor. How does it shape the work situation of the IT specialists, and what pressures does it exert towards certain modes of division of work and coordination? To answer these questions, Woodward's (1965) distinction between unit, mass and process production is useful.

Woodward found that *unit production*, which comprises production of customers' requirement, prototypes, and small batches essentially represented a craft culture, built around skilled workers, working in small groups in close contact with their supervisor. In short, the structures found were organic. In contrast to this, *mass production* of large batches was structured along the lines of machine bureaucracies, characterised by a high degree of formalisation and unskilled workers. The picture shifted again significantly when moving to *process production*, where an organic structure was found, manned by skilled workers maintaining the system, and by specialists surveying the production. The production process per se had been automatised, i.e., the heavy, routinised operations removed from the domain of the workers.

If we compare the work of IT specialists with these categories, its tasks and structural characteristics come closest to that of *unit production*. Production to customers' order has been the main feature of Danish IT specialists, both when employed in internal DP departments, software houses and service bureaus. No mass production of software has yet developed, and craftsmanship, described as the skills you develop through around two years of practical work as a programmer/analyst, is the core upon which the organisational structure is based. In larger installations and service bureaus a certain resemblance with process production is found: surveillance, maintenance and modification of the systems in operation require the employment of skilled programmers/analysts and specialists in terms of systems programmers, lan (local area network) specialists etc., that in many cases hold a university degree.

This picture can be supplemented with the development of increasingly powerful software (operative systems and fourth generation's tools and languages) and easy test and debugging facilities, that to a certain extent remove the more routine task elements from the programmers/analysts. The resulting future development will most likely *not* be one of mass production, but one of skilled workers (programmers/analysts) working within organic- type structures.

3.3   Organisational Structures as Reflections of Management Ideology

Organisational structure is not entirely determined by the environment. Management ideology[3] intervenes in two ways: first in that management does react to its perceptions of environment, not to objective environmental factors, next in that the structural responses chosen to perceived environmental demands represent what management believes to be adequate measures.

That management ideology is important and that it has been changing over time, is recognised by several authors, including Mintzberg (1979), who labels it fashion and deals with it as "the structure of the day" (p. 292-296): new structural arrangements appear from time to time and become fashionable. Examples of "cultural imports" from the US to Denmark after World War Two are MBO schemes (*m*anagement *b*y *o*bjectives), and more recently project organisation and divisionalisation, all three of which are much favoured within the IT field.

Taylorism is not only a label for structural solutions chosen by management in a specific historical and spatial context, but also for a managerial ideology that leads management to prefer certain structural solutions to other possible ones. There is ample evidence, as revealed by a recent study of Hull Kristensen (1986) that Taylorism and Fordism no longer exist as a strong managerial ideology in Denmark. The current structural solutions chosen by Danish industry show great variation and often what Hull Kristensen labels schizophrenic traits. The three new structural arrangements mentioned above can be considered as further evidences of this abandoning of the Taylorist ideology.

That Taylorism infected the IT field in the 1960s and the early 1970s is reflected in both the recipes for how to organise your DP department (see, e.g., Brandon, 1963) and the actual solutions chosen by some of the large installations and service bureaus. However, the comparative research of Friedman and Cornford (1987) shows, that not only in Denmark, but also in other countries it is difficult to interpret recent managerial practice as Taylorism. Instead the strategy of "responsible autonomy" appears to be a dominating managerial action towards the IT specialists.

3.4   Methods of Control as a Result of Power Relations

Power relations in and around organisations are an important contingency factor, which contributes to explain the success and failure of management's controlling and coordinating methods in relation to the IT specialists. These control measures, and their efficiency in the light of the power relations, can be analysed by applying Mintzberg's (1979) coordination categories of formalisation and supervision, standardisation of skills, and control of economic performance.

Formalisation and Supervision
The measures employed during the early phases of the IT field's development fall within this category. Methods and standards were implemented (e.g., Brandon, 1963) that both aimed at making the specialists' production process more transparent, and their products more standardised. By imposing standardisation and supervision of the specialists' practice at least two objectives were pursued. One was reduced costs, another reduced dependency on the individual specialist. By adapting the work methods of specialists to certain norms, and their products to certain standards, craft knowledge could be exploited and did not become irreplaceable.

These measures, which reflect quite distinct Taylorist traits, can be regarded as management's immediate efforts to gain control of the new group of specialists through intraorganisational mechanisms. To have a certain amount of control became important as the scope of the information systems grew, data processing costs represented an important budget item and important segments of the firm's core operating procedures were incorporated in the DP-systems. The division of work between programmers and analysts also falls within this repertoire of control measures.

However, these efforts that essentially deskill the IT specialists were resisted by the specialists in several ways. One was to leave the organisations, if control measures that implied formalisation beyond the specialists' threshold of tolerance were imposed. In a tight labour market – and that has characterised the Danish IT field until today – this exit-option has been extensively utilised, as can be read both from actual labour turn-over and the specialists' loyalty that primarily is directed towards their craft.

The second type of resistance was to bypass the rules and regulations imposed. This is a common story from the installations with well-developed methods and standards: that they do exist, but are only utilised to a limited extent. This discrepancy between management prescriptions and specialists' actual practice is also reported by Friedman and Cornford (1987). To enforce the rules and methods is time-consuming, difficult, and in most organisations run counter to the efforts to terminate projects without exceeding the time and resource scheduled.

Thirdly, rule enforcement is complicated by the fact that the DP managers and supervisors most often are IT specialists themselves. Thus they know the problems connected with strict rule adherence, and perhaps share the craft values of the specialists, they are supposed to supervise. This third source of resistance can be labelled lack of internal cohesion of the management system, that tries to control the specialists.

The fourth source of resistance that appears to be specific in the Danish context is the specialists' utilisation of collective strategies. The large public sector service bureaus and important public sector installations formed the platform for the establishment of an EDP-specialists' independent union (PROSA), that later on was followed by the white collar union's establishment of a competing section (SAM-data). These unions include an important share of the IT specialists employed in public organisations, and PROSA has been influential in some of these as to working conditions, wages and participation and has initiated some strikes.

Formalisation and supervision is thus subject to important limitations, which may explain the emphasis put upon the coordination methods mentioned below. However, they have not been completely discarded and are still part of the management's repertoire. Even if they are not very efficient measures, they may still be important from a symbolic perspective. They signal, that even though the IT specialists have important zones of liberty, they are still subject to manage-ment control, and are not constituting an autonomous professional community.

Standardisation of Skills
The introduction of methods and standards described above was intimately linked to the establishment of internal educational systems by which manage-ment tried to develop skills in accordance with organisational requirements. However, the core of the education remained in the craft-like on-the-job-train-ing, that was only partly controlled by management, and neither solved the problem of supply of IT specialists, nor the creation of a labour force with more generally applicable qualifications.

The Danish educational institutions showed a surprisingly low interest in the establishment of supplier-independent IT education, and were not pushed by the IT specialists. However, around 1970 important private users and employer associations that wanted to reduce supplier-dependencies and to ease the tight labour market, took the initiative to launch public courses in systems analysis and programming. This has led to the establishment of a one year education (EDP-assistant) which currently is the one most important input to the IT labour market, and which constitutes the normal basis for the on-the-job training of programmers.

Even though this education has been criticised for being poorly geared to the actual tasks of the specialists in large installations, it has secured an important and increasing input of individuals since the mid seventies.

As to the contents of the education, management has until now exerted a considerable influence. This was reflected in the recent revision of the EDP-assistant education, in which the unions' representatives were outvoted by management and governmental representatives. In the absence of trends to professionalisation, standardisation of skills through the public educational institutions may both be an accessible and efficient way of assuring a certain control of the IT specialists.

Control of Economic Performance
This method of control implies that IT specialists' output is measured in terms of economy which is equivalent to resorting to (quasi) market mechanisms. It represents a standardisation -or rather translation – of the output of the IT specialists to economic terms. It is a crude, but in many contexts efficient control measure, which avoids the problems and costs involved in examining production process or products of the specialists more closely.

In the Danish context, this control method has become very popular in management circles since the mid-seventies, as it can be seen from the increasing number of EDP-departments that are separated into profit-centres or independent companies, which are supposed to compete with other possible suppliers of services, both inside and outside the mother corporation.

This method of control is not necessarily an alternative to or a substitute of those previously mentioned, but may very well be supplementary. In relation to a grouping of specialists, that controls a complex technology, but does not constitute a collectivity, this may be one way of allowing them autonomy, but at the same time securing management profitability.

4   Conclusion

Revisiting forecasts made on the basis of a Braverman type analysis has demonstrated how the actual development of the Danish IT specialists' skills have contradicted the deskilling hypothesis. It has also been demonstrated how, by replacing the Taylorist perspective on organisations with a contingency perspective, we have been able to reach a more satisfactory understanding of the actual development.

With the reservation, that within the social sciences it is always easier to produce ex-post explanations than ex-ante predictions, the exercise of this chapter shows some important deficiencies of the Braverman type analysis.

Firstly, the Taylorist perception of organisations is essentially what Scott (1981) labels a closed, rational perspective on organisations, and thus poorly geared to the analysis of a field like information technology, within which organisations face complex, dynamic environments. As such the chapter demonstrates how the researchers' perspective on organisations creates limits to the understanding of that field, which may result in poor predictions.

Secondly, the chapter has demonstrated how a simplistic perception of management ideology and strategies assuming that these are stable and un-changed over time, is contested when engaging into a meso-level analysis. Both management ideology and strategies towards the IT specialists have been changing through the three decades considered, and require more complex interpretative schemes than the Taylorist one to be grasped.

Another example of an analysis that goes beyond the simple Taylorist analysis is that of Friedman and Cornford (1987). It demonstrates that the trend towards a more flexible division of labour identified in Denmark is not only an exotic one, but international. Friedman and Cornford's analysis, which focuses solely upon internal computer departments, is also arguing in favour of a contingency analysis, although their theoretical frame of reference differs from that applied here.

The introduction of the contingency-perspective on organisations have allowed us to progress in the understanding of the IT field, as it operates with more realistic assumptions about organisations: that they are *open* systems. This has made it possible to point out the influence of the contingency factors of

– environment,
– technology,
– management ideology,
– power relations between management and employees.

In fact, the analysis has sustained the Child et al (1984) analysis of the consequences of micro-electronics for the quality of work of service providers, that also refuted the deskilling hypothesis.

Still, the contingency view assumes that organisations are rational systems, which leave us with an unsatisfactory understanding of some of the important traits of the IT field. Turbulence is equivalent to uncertainty and ambiguity, and as such loose couplings between individual beliefs (ideology), individual action, and organisational and environmental responses (March and Olsen, 1976). This points to a quite different possible perspective on the IT field – that of loosely coupled systems (see Chapter IV).

Notes

1   In line with Friedman and Cornford's (1987) finding that "responsible autonomy" has been replacing "direct control" as a management strategy towards the IT specialists from the mid seventies.

2   Structure is defined as the combination of the organisation's division of labour and methods of coordination.

3   Ideology in this context denotes a set of beliefs, true or false, about what represent important environmental stimuli, and what are adequate responses to perceived environmental conditions. Ideology in this sense reduces uncertainty and complexity for management by offering a perceptual filter to environmental stimuli and behavioral rules-of-thumb concerning what structural solutions to consider.

Chapter XI
Understanding the Employment Position of Computer Programmers: A Managerial Strategies Approach

Andrew Lloyd Friedman

1   Introduction

Several studies have purported to show that computer programmers have been steadily deskilled (Braverman, 1974; Kraft, 1977; Greenbaum, 1979; Borum, 1980; Kraft and Dubnoff, 1986). This has been interpreted as strong evidence for the general work degradation thesis as proposed by Braverman. Even for new high-tech categories of employees, according to these researchers, the separation of conception from execution in work tasks and the degradation of a large and growing proportion of employees into the category of almost pure executors is a fundamental trend.

In this paper the degradation hypothesis as applied to computer programmers is challenged. Though there have been serious attempts to degrade computer programmers in the past, these attempts have often *failed*. Furthermore recent changes in the employment position of computer programmers have been in the opposite direction, towards a recombination of tasks and towards developing internal labour markets which aim to retain these employees.

It is argued that the employment position of computer programmers can be understood in terms of a framework which specifies several different strategies for managing employees. A key feature of this framework is that actual employment positions arise out of a dynamic interaction between managerial initiatives and the environmental context of those initiatives. Market forces, technological conditions, employee reactions and employee initiatives are critical environmental features. These conditions affect the success of managerial initiatives *and* they can push managers to alter their strategies. In this framework the degradation path is regarded as only one direction along which managers can move.

In the following sections the case for the degradation of computer programmers is presented and then criticised on empirical grounds. This critique is based on the proponents' own data as well as data both from an international survey organised by the author and from other sources. All of the empirical results are then interpreted in terms of the managerial strategies framework.

2   The Case for Degradation of Computer Programmers

Braverman distinguishes two manifestations of the degradation hypothesis associated with computer specialists. First, when computers were first introduced into data processing they were accompanied by a new division of labour. Data processing craftsmen, who had been familiar with all types of tabulating machines, were replaced by a hierarchy of specialists including systems managers, systems analysts, programmers, computer console operators and key punch operators (1974, p. 329). Second, the work of computer programmers has been further deskilled. In early computer installations programmers also carried out analysis functions. Since then programmers have gradually been reduced to "program coders who take as their materials the pre-digested instructions for the system or subsystem and simply translate them mechanically into specialized terminology " (p. 330).

Phil Kraft has taken up this second manifestation of the degradation hypothesis. Kraft concluded that the work of computer programmers was becoming more and more like assembly line work in a car factory (1977, p. 61). This was because the separation of conception from execution was continuing during the 1970s with the bulk of systems developers (the programmers) losing much of the creative aspects of their work through the introduction of packaged programmes, chief programmer teams and especially structured programming techniques.

Recently this position has been reiterated by Kraft and Dubnoff (1986). Their evidence comes from a survey of 667 individuals in the Boston area who defined themselves as employed in a job which involved the design, production, or maintenance of computer software (p. 187). Respondents were asked if they spend a "small amount", a "moderate amount", "a lot" or "most" of their working time on each of 32 named tasks. A correlation of time spent on each task was analysed by a technique called smallest space analysis by which correlation coefficients were mapped onto a two-dimensional map. The closer any two points are on the map, the higher the probability that the same people carry out both tasks.

According to Kraft and Dubnoff, "a textbook diagram of a chain of command emerges" (p. 189), when boxes are drawn around "the most obvious clusters" of tasks on the map (figure 1). These clusters show "remarkably little overlap, especially considering the age of the occupation" (p. 191). "The people who make the decisions and set the specifications rarely write code or manuals or test software" (p. 192). They conclude that "the making of computer programmes has been subjected to a process of intellectual industrial engineering, a scientific management of mind work. In every important respect these techniques are identical to those applied in the production of cars and cornflakes." (p. 194).

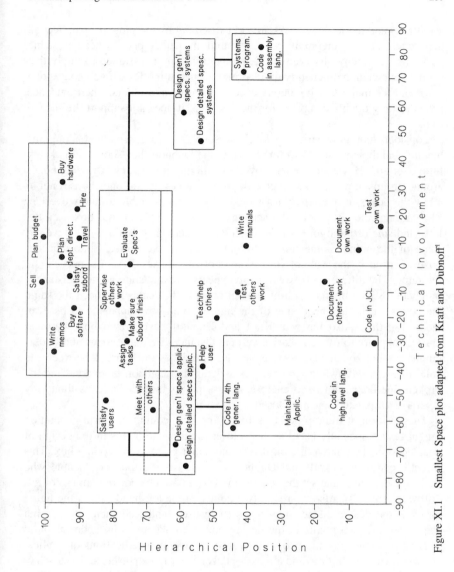

Figure XI.1   Smallest Space plot adapted from Kraft and Dubnoff[1]

3   Reinterpreting Kraft and Dubnoff's Data

Kraft and Dubnoff find a detailed division of labour. They take this to be evidence for the degradation thesis in two steps. First they interpret this division of labour as forming a hierarchy of people carrying out fragmented work. Lower level tasks and higher level tasks are not carried out by the same people. Second they interpret this hierarchy as a pyramid in which people occupy stable positions. Hierarchy observed at one moment in time is assumed to imply that people have been permanently divided into a small minority who do conceptual work and the majority who merely execute the orders of others. Their evidence provides only qualified support for the first step. It does not support the second step.

Consider first how strictly the clusters of tasks are separated along the hierarchical dimension. According to Kraft and Dubnoff they show "remarkably little overlap". However, the term overlap is highly misleading. Drawing boxes around groups of points in a graph will produce no overlap if one chooses not to allow the boxes to overlap, but it would not be unreasonable to allow overlap. The data has merely produced a scatter of points. In fact all four boxes on the left hand side of the figure almost touch each other. They could easily have put some of the points at the top or bottom of any of these boxes into adjacent boxes. Curiously the scale of vertical and horizontal axes does not appear to be the same. The difference between them appears to exaggerate vertical distances by about 18% compared with horizontal ones. If the scales had been the same the boxes on the left hand side of the figure would have appeared to be even closer together. Also the way Kraft and Dubnoff have drawn boxes around clusters appears to overemphasise vertical distances between boxes and under-emphasise horizontal distances. Note the differences on figure 1 between the solid line boxes drawn around clusters as Kraft and Dubnoff have done and the broken line boxes drawn to enclose all task points in their boxes without any "extra" extrapolated space enclosed.

The position of the top point in the coding box, coding in fourth generation languages is especially peculiar. It is closer to all of the points in the design of specifications box above it than it is to any other point in the coding box. This directly contradicts Kraft and Dubnoff's primary thesis that the "people who make the decisions and set the specifications rarely write code or manuals or test software" (p. 192). Also, there are two points on the left hand side of the figure *between* the design and coding boxes (help users and teach/help others), but there are only two points in the design box itself. People who code in fourth generation languages and people who design general specifications of applications software are highly (and almost equally) likely to help users and to teach or help others. This hardly squares with Kraft and Dubnoff's claim that neither coders nor applications programmers are "likely to see the ultimate user of his or her work" (p. 191).

Kraft and Dubnoff's hierarchy is one of control and rewards. Hierarchy of control, which they take to be represented by the vertical axis of figure one, is correlated with earnings, measured by the geometric mean annual earnings of those spending a moderate amount of time or more on each task. Kraft and Dubnoff present a graph of these two variables which does show a roughly positive relation (p. 193). However, evidence for this double hierarchy is limited.

There is what Kraft and Dubnoff call the "apparent anomaly" that coding in fourth generation languages has relatively high earnings, higher than either of the tasks in the design of specifications box. Their explanation is that fourth generation languages "were designed to be used by middle level managers without the assistance of skilled software specialists" (p. 192). However, Kraft and Dubnoff's sample was prescreened to include only those in a job which involved the "design, production, or maintenance of computer software" (p. 187). This should exclude middle managers who may use software, but who would not define their job as to design, produce or use it. Though fourth generation languages were designed to be used by ordinary managers, they have in fact most often been used by specialist computer department staff (Friedman and Cornford, 1984). It is more likely that this apparent anomaly is associated with higher wages for all computing staff in organisations where there has been higher investment in more up-to-date technology.

Coding in high level languages and coding in JCL (Job Control Language) are far lower along the hierarchical axis of figure one and have much lower earnings. The reason for this is that they are associated with older technology. Kraft and Dubnoff do not distinguish between people working in different organisations. This is a problem if there is a systematically different mix of tasks in organisations paying different salaries. The small distance between coding in fourth generation languages and the design of specifications box compared with the very substantial distance between coding in the older languages and the design of specifications box actually provides evidence for a reduction of hierarchy, a recombination of tasks and an upgrading of programmer work (to include more design work) in recent years, *precisely the opposite conclusion to that of Kraft and Dubnoff.*

Even if a hierarchy of tasks can be observed by taking a snap-shot of the jobs as Kraft and Dubnoff have done, by itself this does not mean that the observed pattern represents a permanent pyramid in line with Braverman's long term fragmentation thesis. If the proportion of people carrying out high level tasks is not much smaller than the proportion carrying out lower level tasks, and if people begin with low level tasks, but have a good expectation of moving into higher level tasks, then fragmentation in Braverman's sense has not really occurred.

Interpreting the degree of hierarchy that Kraft and Dubnoff find in terms of a pyramid of people is weakened by the relatively high proportion of people carrying out "high" as opposed to "low" tasks. There are a number of items in the top box which a remarkably large number of software specialists carry out. For example, 17.1% spend at least a moderate amount of time hiring others, 30.7% supervise others and 28.7% make sure subordinates are satisfied. This latter task carried the highest geometric mean annual earnings according to Kraft and Dubnoff's data (p. 188)[2]. The task of making sure users are satisfied "is in practice a major part of only the role of upper- level managers and upper level design specialists..." (p. 191). However, according to their own data 55.3% of the sample spend a moderate amount of time or more performing this task. It was the task on which more of the sample spend at least a moderate amount of time than any other task except one (p. 188)[3].

The small spaces between all the boxes on the left hand side of the figure suggests quite the opposite of Kraft and Dubnoff's claim that "although there are many occupational rungs in software work, there is little evidence that today they are all on the same ladder" (p. 195). Their data gives little direct evidence of one way or another. However, these tasks appear to line up rather well into a single career structure, especially compared with the systems design and coding groups who appear, from the figure, to be on a separate ladder. Evidence to support the claim that there is a strong career structure is provided below.

4   Further Evidence on Computer Software Work: The Data

The primary data upon which this challenge to the degradation hypothesis for software workers is based comes from a survey of 378 data processing departments and computer services firms in six countries. The research instrument was a face-to-face interview with data processing managers and computer services firm managers (all will be referred to as DPMs). A stratified random sample for the US interviews was drawn mainly from the Directory of Top Computer Executives. The sample was stratified by industry (Financial Institutions, Public Sector, Computer Services, Other Private Firms) and by size of computer department (number of analysts and programmers: 10, 10-29, 30-49, 50-99, 99) in order to allow comparability of results with surveys in the other countries. Sample sizes were: US, 95; Japan, 42; Denmark, 42; Norway, 29; Sweden, 28; Great Britain, 142. Interviews were based on a questionnaire which contained open ended as well as multiple choice questions. Interviews lasted between two and four and a half hours and were carried out by country nationals. Researchers from the countries have formed the International Computer Occupations Network (ICON) to continue the work. Results reported here will be referred to as the ICON survey[4]. Most of the US sample (65 sites) were in the same area as the Kraft and Dubnoff study, the Boston area. Also this survey was carried out around the same time as Kraft and Dubnoff's survey (Kraft and Dubnoff: Fall and Winter of 1982-83; ICON survey: February to July 1983).

5   Master/Apprentice System

According to Kraft and Dubnoff it is "given" that software work in the early years of the occupation had a "relatively non hierarchical" task structure (p. 186); that "early programming work developed more or less by default as a master/apprentice system. Specialists in every field were expected to learn and master all aspects of their trade" (p. 185); and that programming was "originally" the preserve of "artisans who responded mainly to their own visions." (p. 194). This is false. While programming work did develop as a master/apprentice system from the outset, this did not mean that they completely responded to their own visions, or that they mastered all aspects of their trade if "all aspects" is meant to include management functions. Programmers did not work for themselves in the early years of the occupation. As Kraft notes elsewhere, early in the history of computing, users and programmers became separated (1977, p. 27). This meant that computer programmers in user organisations would be "directed" by users from the outset. Also what was sold on the market was computer hardware, not software in the early years. That is, programmers were employees, not entrepreneurs. From the outset, they were managed by others. Even in a master/apprentice system we would expect management tasks to be restricted to the masters.

According to Kraft the original master/apprentice system in programming has long disappeared, but there is considerable evidence to suggest that substantial training is given to programmers, that most of the training valued by management is on-the-job experience of a variety of tasks, and that it is experience, rather than formal qualifications which is the major criterion for promotion to higher level jobs in this field. In the ICON survey in the US 63%-81% of DPMs reported that senior level positions among analysis and programming jobs were always or usually filled internally, from lower positions (Table XI.1.).

Another survey carried out in the Boston area in the early 1980s also revealed that the majority of top programming jobs (60%) were usually filled from within computer departments and that many firms had established internal training programmes for computer programmers (Osterman, 1984, p. 172-173).

6   Division of Labour: Analysts and Programmers

As Braverman notes, a clear division of labour developed between systems analysts and programmers in the early years of commercial computing. Studies conducted in the late 1960s and early 1970s attest to this strong fragmentation. Hebden concluded on the basis of a survey carried out between 1969 and 1971 in England, that systems analysts and programmers were sufficiently separated

Table XI.1   Internal Labour Market: Likelihood of Internal Promotion of IT People

	Always Internal %	Usually Internal %	Sometimes Internal %	Never Internal %
Senior Systems Analyst	18	45	37	0
Systems Analyst	23	52	19	6
Trainee Analyst	18	59	10	13
Senior Programmer/Analyst	12	69	19	0
Programmer/Analyst	8	56	36	0
Trainee Programmer/Analyst	19	38	35	8
Senior Programmer	26	53	21	0
Programmer	12	39	42	7
Trainee Programmer	21	30	40	9

to be regarded as two distinct occupations, rather than two segments of a single occupation (1975, p. 127-130). Programmers were more concerned with the technical side of software work, particularly with the hardware configuration, analysts more with users and senior management. Mumford (1972) and Computer Economics (1972) also note this strong separation. However in the Computer Economics survey, carried out early in 1972, a movement *away* from organisation structures which separated analysis and programming functions was reported. Between 1970 and 1972, 34% of organisations surveyed (110 user organisations were surveyed) reported switching from structures which kept programmers and analysts in separate groups to project teams containing both.

Though these surveys were carried out in England, we have no reason to suspect that the American situation in the late 1960s and early 1970s was any different. In fact if Braverman (1974) and Kraft (1977) were correct, as well as several American computer management consultants who wrote more normative accounts at that time (Weinwurm, 1971; Brandon, 1970; Weinberg, 1971), then analysis and programming were even more strictly divided in the US during the late 1960s and early 1970s than elsewhere.

The results of the ICON survey on organisation structures for the US show how few installations were using organisation structures which separated analysts from programmers (table XI.2.). Almost half the sample considered most of their staff to be programmer/analysts, rather than separate programmers from analysts even in name.

Organisation structures which separate analysts and programmers were in a minority in all countries surveyed. They were most common in Japan and England (36% of the sample in each country) and least common in the Scandinavian countries (4% to 12%). Distinguishing analysts and programmers

Table XI.2   Organisation Structures

	Total %
Teams of analysts & pool of programmers	5
Pool of analysts & pool of programmers	5
Teams of analysts and team of programmers	0
Teams of analysts and programmers	37
Matrix of analysts and programmers	4
Pool of programmers/analysts	10
Teams of programmers/analysts	8
Structures separating analysts and programmers	15
Structures denoting analysts and programmers as separate roles	52
Structures denoting programmers/analysts	48
Structures involving project teams (including matrices)	79

as separate jobs in the general organisation description characterised the majority of installations in England (72%). In the other countries the proportion was under half (Japan, 44%; Sweden, 43%; Denmark, 40%; Norway, 10%).

Along with Kraft and Dubnoff's own evidence against their proposition that the people who set the specifications rarely write code, the ICON survey produced similarly contrary evidence. In the US sample 100% of DPMs that used written specifications admitted that the person who codes *actually writes their own specification* at least sometimes and 28% said this usually occurred.

It is likely that recombination of analysis and programming will continue in future. In the ICON questionnaire DPM's were asked about the education attainment they expected of trainees for different job categories (table XI.3).

A clear majority of organisations required some university degree of a trainee for analysis and programming job categories (69%-86%). Note the high proportion of organisations requiring a general university degree. For programmer/analysts and programmers the proportion of organisations preferring general university degrees outnumbered those wanting computer science qualifications by more than two to one. Several DPMs made a point of stating that it was business or liberal arts degrees they wanted. Also many wanted computer staff to have experience or qualifications relevant to the overall markets user organisations were supplying. As one DPM said, "It is easier to teach programming to someone who knows banking, than banking to a programmer". That this DPM should want to teach banking to programmers is some evidence against the degradation thesis. The desire to hire programmers with all round education, and especially to find ones with experience of user areas, suggests that Kraft and Dubnoff's conclusion, that programmers are not likely to see the ultimate users of their work, will be even less true in future.

Table XI.3   Preferred Education for Trainees by Job Category

	Systems analysts %	Prog-rammer analysts %	Prog-rammer %	Systems progs %	Ope-rators %	Data Entry Staff %	Sec. & Adm %
None	13	12	21	18	22	25	29
High school or less	2	3	5	4	55	63	58
Low level Comp. Sci	2	0	2	4	5	2	2
Beyond high school	0	1	3	0	3	0	2
Comp. Sci degree	38	27	19	43	2	0	0
Other univ. degree	47	59	50	31	14	10	9
Any comp. sci requirement	39	27	21	47	7	2	2

DP is coming more and more to provide systems which will be used in the market place directly, either because they are used by customers or used by employees who deal with customers directly, (particularly in the financial sector). Two consequences are; first, the DP function is being upgraded, and second, the product of the DP department is coming to be related more closely with the sort of business the organisation is conducting. The two consequences have been pushing DPMs to look for more highly educated and more business-oriented staff. Though an exaggeration, another DPM summed up the trend aptly as follows. "We need Renaissance people, who can think and act with an open mind" (Friedman and Greenbaum, 1984, p. 132).

7   Division of Labour: Applications and Systems Programmers

In the US, 67% DPMs reported that applications development and systems software development were organised as separate functions. This accords with Kraft and Dubnoff's evidence. Rather than two separate boxes on the systems side of their figure, casual perusal shows that the most clearly separable cluster in figure 1 is the systems group of tasks. The people who carry out the four tasks in this cluster are not likely to carry out other tasks. However, systems tasks are, on average, slightly better paid than the other tasks (p. 193), in spite of systems people being rather unlikely to carry out management functions. Apparent biases in the way Kraft and Dubnoff have scaled the axes and drawn boxes around their clusters of tasks, camouflages both the separation of systems tasks from management tasks and the rather high hierarchical position of systems coding tasks.

Separation of applications and systems software into separately managed groups was common in all countries surveyed except Japan, (Denmark, 87%; England, 79%; Sweden, 71%; Norway, 57%, Japan, 36%). The low percentage in Japan reflects the high proportion of all programming work which is carried out by outside subcontractors.

8   Deskilling Techniques

The Kraft and Dubnoff paper rests on earlier work in which Kraft documents how he believes the degradation of programmers was being achieved. As one American DPM stated, "in the 1970s rules and regulations ruled DP". Kraft picked this up in his research carried out in the mid-1970s (Kraft, 1977). We also found that packaged programmes, chief programmer teams and structured programming techniques were being used in the early 1980s. However, they had not diffused so widely as Kraft had predicted. In places where they had been introduced they were most often operated on a piecemeal and an almost voluntary basis. They were sometimes introduced by the programmers themselves, and they were sometimes abandoned.

According to Kraft the introduction of *packaged programmes* would lead to a division of labour between programming staff in user organisations and superprogrammers in supplier firms. The former would modify and maintain programmes, while only the latter, much smaller group, would carry out the highly skilled original programming. The net effect would be to reduce the overall demand for programming staff as well as average skill requirements.

DPMs and managers of services firms in the ICON research were asked to estimate the proportion of development spending over the last two years on four methods of obtaining a system, (table XI.4.).

Almost half (47%) still design and build their systems almost entirely (90% or more), in house. Though about half of the installations do modify packages, for most of these this work represents only 25% or less of the cost of obtaining systems. For 20% of installations, modifying packages internally represented more than a quarter of the cost of systems. For a further 9%, packages modified externally represented more than a quarter of development costs. Therefore, the

Table XI.4   Methods of Obtaining a System by Industry Group

	Computer Services Firm %	Public User Orgs %	Private User Orgs %	Total %
Designed and built entirely internally:				
100%	30	24	20	23
90-99%	40	17	26	24
51-89%	0	24	17	17
26-50%	10	19	12	15
1-25%	10	11	15	13
0	10	5	10	8
Designed and built for you by an outside firm:				
100%	0	3	2	2
90-99%	0	3	0	1
26-89%	0	11	6	7
1-25%	20	36	12	23
0	80	47	80	67
Package Modified for you by an outside firm:				
100%	0	0	0	0
90-99%	0	6	5	5
26-89%	10	5	2	4
1-25%	0	25	20	20
0	90	64	73	71
Package Modified for you internally:				
100%	10	0	5	3
90-99%	0	0	2	2
26-89%	10	11	23	15
1-25%	40	64	41	51
0	40	64	41	51

most common pattern is to obtain a majority of systems in the traditional manner, by internal staff carrying out both design and programming. On the other hand, most also have a minority of their systems bought in from outside, though most who buy-in packages still carry out modifications internally.

The industry pattern of methods of obtaining systems was remarkably similar. Certainly computer services firms designed and built more of their systems internally, 70% obtained 90% or more of their systems this way compared with 41% of public sector and 46% of private sector user organisations. Nevertheless, a substantial proportion of computer services firms (60%) buy in packages and modify them internally. For 20% this represented more than a quarter of their work. In part this reflects a division of labour within the computer services sector. Service bureaus are more likely to use packages while software houses are more likely to build systems from scratch. Also some firms which call themselves software houses are really what are known as OEMs (Original Equipment Manufacturers). These firms do not manufacture anything. They put together both hardware and software manufactured and written elsewhere, and market it to users. However, the use of packages by other firms in the services sector reflects something quite different. Many packages are development tools, intended to be used by serious programmers. The use of packages should not be equated with automation of the development process. Though this may be what many applications packages do, there has also been substantial progress in creating packages for developing software, such as programmer tool boxes. Kraft's prediction that supplier firms would only build systems and user firms would only use or modify them receives only very limited support from the ICON data.

Chief programmer teams are organisation structures which are intended to concentrate conceptual aspects of programming activity on one person, the chief programmer. The chief programmer works with a backup programmer, who acts as insurance against the chief leaving the project. The team nucleus is completed by a programming librarian. Around this nucleus there is a large number of additional programmers who code under the supervision of the chief and backup programmers. According to Kraft chief programmer teams were being rapidly introduced in large organisations and they were acting as models for the rest (1977,p. 61). Only 22% of the ICON sample in the US reported using Chief Programmer Teams, (though there was a correlation with size of computer installation). If Chief Programmer Teams were diffusing as rapidly as Kraft believed in the early 1970s, and if that trend had continued throughout the 1970s and early 1980s as Kraft predicted, then we would have expected more organisations to have adopted this technique. More damaging to Kraft's position is that several DPMs stated that they had been using Chief Programmer Teams, but they had disbanded them. They were too expensive. The backup programmer had to be a highly skilled programmer who spent most of his or her time acting as a relief for the Chief Programmer, rather than getting on with new work.

Chief programmer teams have been largely confined to the United States. None of the DPMs in Sweden or Norway said they used them. Less than 10% used them in the other countries. It is unlikely that this reflects a diffusion lag to other countries. DPMs in Europe and Japan had heard of Chief Programmer Teams.

The key technique for deskilling programming work during the 1970s according to Kraft was *structured programming*. There are three aspects to structured programming. The first is that the use of a given language (usually COBOL) will be structured so that the resulting programmes will be easier to read and maintain. The usual restriction is to avoid GOTO statements, particularly ones which refer the computer backwards in the programme. A lot of such statements can result in what one DPM disparagingly called "spaghetti code". If programmes are easier for others to read managers will be less dependent on individual programmers. If a programmer leaves, the consequences will be less severe. However, it will take longer for better programmers to write programmes using structured methods. A second feature of structured methods is that they impose an overall structure to programmes. For example, most break up programmes into sections, normally called modules, and only allow the computer to enter and leave a module at single entry and exit points. This makes it easier to read complex programmes and easier to subdivide programming tasks among different programmers. This also reduces the chances that any one programmer will corrupt the work of others. Third, many structured methods include formalistic requirements that the surface appearance or format of the programme and the output, should be standardised.

We first asked DPMs if they use a recognised methodology for system design and programming. To this 72% of DPMs in the US said yes, slightly fewer than those saying yes in other countries (73% to 88%). When asked about specific named methodologies, it turned out that most who said they were using a methodology only used parts of methodologies. For many structured programming only meant modular programming and this only meant that large programming jobs were broken up. Only half of the sample said they used recognised methodologies (41% Structured Design associated with Yourden; 12% Structured Analysis Design Technique; others were used by less than 5% of the sample). In a more detailed question DPMs were asked if they imposed specific restrictions which were common to the methodologies. Here even fewer responded affirmatively. For example, the strict requirement of limiting statements to sequence, selection and iteration was imposed by only 33% of the sample.

Structured methods usually were introduced by DPMs or other higher level DP management but in a few cases they were introduced by ordinary programmers and analysts or by project leaders. Top down design was introduced by project leaders in 16% of cases and by analysts and programmers in 8%, modular programming by project leaders in 23% and by analysts and programmers in 5%. Even Yourdon was introduced by project leaders in 13% of cases.

Even these few cases where structured methods were introduced by low level development staff seems puzzling if these techniques really are primarily ways of deskilling development work. One explanation which would accord with Kraft's thesis is that new staff are taught these techniques in universities and other training establishments. They do not know any better. They have not experienced the craft-like manner of working without such restrictions and they have been "brainwashed" into believing that these techniques are part of professional competence, in spite of them being inherently against ordinary analysts' and programmers' own interests. A different interpretation can be made. These techniques are not inherently deskilling, even though they may have been designed to deskill programming work, and though they may be used in this way in some computer installations. It may be that these techniques can be used as tools to increase programmer productivity without deskilling the work if they are applied flexibly, especially if they are applied *at the programmer's discretion*. Also making one's programmes more legible to others, as well as to oneself, will not represent a significant weakening of programmer bargaining power if the external labour market represents little threat to programmers. This seems to be the case because demand for experienced staff far outweighs supply and because of strong policies aimed at staff retention by management.

We have evidence that use of these techniques is discretionary. "We have had exposure to all the structured methods, but we have not made a commitment to them" said one DPM at a bank. A DPM at an electrical engineering firm said, "There are published guidelines to adhere to design and coding standards. Informally, they are more flexibly enforced". A DPM at a university installation was even more emphatic about flexibility, "All the methodologies are used by some people. Nothing is imposed. We discuss good practice. There are preferred ways of doing things, but everyone is free to choose". Several DPMs gave us the impression that standards were mainly a display for senior management and perhaps for user managers. To them they were a hindrance. "There are certain expectations" one DPM in the financial sector said darkly. Another in an insurance company was much more forthright, "GOTO's are allowed, but we don't want spaghetti. Here is our standards" he said, showing us a thick book. "We have many standards that are imposed by outside groups, but I don't like to be that rigid. I hope no-one checks."

Besides those who used methodologies, but only flexibly, there were others who believed they should not even have formal standards relating to structured methods. "Avoiding GOTO's? There is a programmer art, it depends on the programmer's personality" stated a DPM in the financial sector. "Even our book of standards is informal" said a DPM in an electronics engineering firm.

The really outstanding feature of the use of standards and methodologies was the overwhelming impression we received that even where they formally exist, they are applied flexibly and informally. The way these techniques are sometimes introduced, the risk of labour turnover if they are imposed for all work, the flexibility with which they are imposed and the strong attitude against these methods among some DPMs; all encourage the belief that these techniques are no longer diffusing rapidly in the computing community. Certainly some

DPMs did feel they should impose more standards, more strictly. Some said they had quite recently introduced methodologies. Nevertheless, the evidence for a disenchantment with these techniques and for a withdrawal from them was stronger.

9   Understanding the Employment Position of Computer Programmers

It seems clear that attempts to divide and degrade the work of computer programmers have been made in the past. Moves toward a strict division of labour between programming and analysis functions, and toward formal methodologies have been widely championed since the 1960s. They would increase the visibility of development work, reduce dependence on volatile development staff, allow better cost estimation and maintenance of systems, and deskill programming work (Canning and Sisson, 1960; Brandon, 1963; Reynolds, 1970; Weinwurm, 1970; Brooks, 1975). However, these initiatives have, on balance, been unsuccessful. Certainly some deskilling has occurred, but by and large computer programmers are still highly skilled, highly paid, have a high degree of control over their working procedures and are highly satisfied with their jobs[5]. In order to understand this situation it is necessary to employ theoretical concepts which allow analytical space for managerial failure. An approach which specifies different managerial strategies for maintaining authority over labour is needed. Such an approach, derived from Friedman (1977), is outlined in the following section.

9.1   Managerial Strategies: A General Framework

The maintenance of control over labour is an essential function of management. It should not be assumed to occur in the most efficient way possible. This is because the employment of labour, or rather the purchase of labour time, is not the purchase of an input with fixed specifications. It is no simple technical matter to transform labour time purchased into work as required by employers. Labour time is a peculiar input: first, workers are particularly malleable, you can get somebody to do something once employed beyond what was specified in the original employment contract. Second, workers are ultimately controlled by an independent and often hostile will. These two peculiarities of labour time may be thought of as stimulating two general types of strategies which top managers use toward employees, responsible autonomy and direct control.

With responsible autonomy, managers try to accentuate the positive peculiar aspect of labour time, its malleability. Workers are given responsibility, status, light supervision, and their loyalty towards the firm is solicited. With direct control, top managers try to reduce the amount of responsibility on each individual worker by close supervision, and by setting out in advance and in great detail the specific tasks individual workers are to do. Ultimately, the direct control type of strategy treats workers as though they were no different from other inputs, assuming they can be forced by financial circumstances or close supervision, to act in a predetermined fashion. Ultimately, responsible autonomy treats workers as though they have not sold their labour time, by trying to convince them that the aims of top managers are their own. Both types of strategy involve a contradiction. People do have independent and often hostile wills which cannot be destroyed, and the aim of top managers is to make steady and high profits, rather than to tend to their employees' needs[6].

These contradictions make management vulnerable to failure in two ways. First, the pursuit of either strategy will generate costs and reduce flexibility in particular directions. Direct control strategies will encourage employee resistance. This may stimulate managers to develop even more restrictive working procedures which will be costly and which may exacerbate resistance. With a high degree of direct control managers will find it relatively difficult to move workers around factories or to change work organisation. Each change will require complex and time-consuming planning, communication and implementation of new detailed work tasks. Responsible autonomy strategies may encourage employees to become involved in the profit-making aims of management, but this can also generate bad will over specific policies if employee views are overruled. With a high degree of responsible autonomy, top managers will find it difficult to fire or to degrade employees without undermining the ideological structure upon which responsible autonomy is founded.

Neither strategy is "correct" or "efficient" or represents "best" practice from management's point of view. However, managers will be pushed in particular directions by internal and external pressures which will affect the relative efficiency of different strategies. When faced with a volatile, declining product market which is characterised by severe price competition, managers will be pushed toward direct control types of strategies. The need to cut costs, especially by periodical layoffs, will undermine responsible autonomy strategies. Similarly, direct control strategies will be encouraged if external labour markets are over-supplied (perhaps because required skills are easily acquired and not firm-specific), because the motivation of any particular employee can be more easily assured by the threat of lay-off, rather than the promise of participation.

These environmental influences on strategies stimulate the second source of managerial failure. There are many different influences on managerial strategies directed toward any particular group of workers. Product market, labour market, technical conditions and the history of labour relations for that work group as well as labour relations elsewhere in the company, and in the society as a whole, can be important influences. It is quite possible that different environmental conditions push managers in opposite directions. For example, it is possible for firms to face unstable and highly competitive product markets along with tight external labour markets. As will be shown below, this is just the situation which many firms have faced in relation to their computer departments. Another side to this problem is that environmental conditions are continually changing, but it is difficult to change strategies quickly. Direct control strategies require well-defined lines of control and a high proportion of white-collar staff. Responsible autonomy strategies require an elaborate ideological structure as well as a credible commitment to employment security. To switch suddenly from strong responsible autonomy to direct control, or the other way round, would cause severe disruptions[7].

9.2   Managerial Strategies and Computer Programmers

The broad drift of change in computer departments from the mid-1960s until around the late 1970s may be interpreted as moves toward direct control strategies from a position of extreme responsible autonomy. This was mainly because of rising computer department staff costs. The dramatic fall in hardware prices during the 1950s and 1960s meant that computer department budgets were no longer dominated by machine costs. This was not matched by software cost reductions and so the chief element of software costs, salaries, became the focus of managerial attention. Pressure was particularly acute from top managers who saw the whole computer department budget expanding very rapidly as more and more applications for computerization were attempted.

New user-friendly languages, which would remove the need for programmers altogether, as well as methods for degrading existing programmers received widespread attention. Nevertheless, such techniques were not pursued as vigorously as might have been expected from the literature largely because severe labour shortages had not substantially abated. Demand for more and new types of applications grew substantially. The difficulty of training computer specialists off the job hampered growth of supply. The resulting tight labour markets have allowed computer specialists to resist unpopular management strategies simply by changing jobs. In general, we may assume that employees will prefer responsible autonomy to direct control strategies. In other industries responsible autonomy strategies have been introduced as a positive response to worker demands (Lutz, 1982). Direct control strategies are also expensive and this limited the value of techniques such as chief programmer teams. Another problem with introducing direct control strategies in the 1970s has been a change in the basic technology of computer programming. The operating environment under which systems were developed became more sophisticated with the development of sophisticated operating systems, database and data dictionary software. Automation has occurred, but not of the most skilled aspects of programming. Rather the more repetitive and technical programming tasks have been automated. Increasing sophistication of operating and programming environments also made it easier to establish compatibility between the work of different programmers. For example, the cost of changes in one part of a system in terms of changes required in other parts of the system was reduced. This in turn reduced the need for a strong hierarchical organisation structure in which all coordination between programmers occurred at the top level. The availability of minis and later micros made possible the complete separation of programming from operating environments. This meant that errors occurring in the development of new systems were not so critical to the running of existing systems. Thus less control over the development process was required. In a sense, by the time direct control strategies had become well known, the technical basis for some of these strategies was already being eroded.

During the 1980s, increasing user demands have partly been stimulated by inadequate computer department supply. The problem is not simply that computer departments have not grown fast enough to meet an increasing volume of demands, or that users have not been involved in the system development process. The problem has also been an inability of computer departments to react quickly to changing demands with the staff they already have. This is due largely to increasingly inappropriate direct control strategies pursued within some computer departments.

When computers are to be applied to unstructured problems which will interact more intimately with relatively demanding and politically powerful users, when programming development can be carried out interactively, and when user environments are changing rapidly, direct control strategies within computer departments can become the major reason for system failures (see Markus (1983), for a clear example). What is needed are responsible autonomy strategies.

Why then do many computer departments seem, at least formally, to be pursuing direct control types of strategies? In part they are a carry-over from the 1970s. Though environmental conditions have changed, inertia is still a factor. In part the problem is that environmental influences are pushing DPMs in different directions. Senior managers are influenced by product markets for the organisation as a whole and by rising computer department budgets. They are being pushed toward structured methods to control computer department budgets, as well as to bring computer staff controls into line with the work of other white-collar staff. However, the labour market for computer staff is generally much tighter for computer staff than for other white collar employees. DPMs are more sensitive to this as they must deal directly with the consequences of high labour turnover. This has led to what has been labelled the "plight" of the DPM (Nolan, 1973). The plight may be analysed as a contradiction between the technology and labour market conditions pushing DPMs to pursue responsible autonomy strategies, but senior managers pressing them towards direct control. Several of the DPMs interviewed said that their predecessors had been fired because they were too "soft" with staff. A rather high proportion of DPMs (38%) were recruited from outside the organisation. Also turnover of DPMs seemed high, 23% had been in post for 12 months or less.

In part the reluctance to enforce structured methods, or the flexible enforcement of such techniques, reflects the opinion of many DPMs that they slow up programming work, ("Use of methods depends upon how much of a hurry we are in"), or that they get in the way of the programmer's art. However, it is likely that if the labour market was less tight, DPMs would be less responsive to the programmer's art.

10   Conclusion

The degradation hypothesis postulates progressive separation of conception from execution and a growing proportion of employees who only perform execution tasks. This is a dynamic hypothesis. Kraft and Dubnoff attempt to show that this hypothesis applies to computer programmers with static data, data which presents a snap-shot of their task distribution. It is possible to interpret this data in a way which is completely different from the degradation hypothesis. The hierarchical structure of tasks which Kraft and Dubnoff have found can indicate a standard path of increasing responsibility and status which most computer programmers pass through, rather than a sharp break between whose who only carry out conceptual tasks and those who are relegated to execution. A much wider range of information is required to throw substantial light on the degradation hypothesis.

The evidence presented here does not directly contradict the Braverman/Kraft hypothesis of fragmentation and degradation of programming work. We can confirm that there have been moves toward direct control of programmers. Instead, we conclude that by itself this thesis is too crude. What is required is a more sophisticated analysis that recognises that the degradation route is not the sole path available to management. It may be pursued successfully in relation to some employees, but for others it may be too difficult and costly to implement[8]. This does not mean that it will not be attempted. Managers can and do make mistakes. Also the limited introduction, lenient imposition and subsequent tendency to withdraw from direct control of computer programmers should not be taken simply to contradict Kraft and Dubnoff's claim that managers of programmers use techniques which "are identical to those applied in the production of cars and cornflakes". Responsible autonomy strategies have also been used for car workers (Friedman, 1977). Rather this should be interpreted as a caution against looking for some one best way that managers do (or should) manage any group of employees.

Notes

1   The top box (in terms of hierarchical position) performs upper-level management and control tasks. The next box Kraft and Dubnoff associate with middle-level supervisory workers. The two boxes directly below this involve designing applications specifications and applications programming. The two boxes on the right involve designing systems specifications and systems programming. Adapted from Kraft and Dubnoff (1986, p. 190).

2   Curiously, elsewhere in their paper this task carried the 9th highest earnings out of the 32 tasks, (Kraft and Dubnoff 1986, p. 193).

3   Admittedly some upper-level tasks, such as selling and buying software, are performed by relatively few people for at least a moderate amount of time (9.2% and 12.7%, respectively). However, the wide divergence in proportions of people performing tasks which cluster closely together suggests that there is overlap of tasks within different clusters among people.

4   The ICON sample was based on the population of organisations, Kraft and Dubnoff's on the population of computer software specialists. The ICON figures are therefore likely to be biased toward software specialists in smaller installations. It is likely that division of labour and fragmentation are greater in larger installations. While Kraft and Dubnoff have what they believe to be a representative sample of the population of specialists, in ICON the intention was *not* to get a simple random sample of organisations. Stratification by size allowed a substantial proportion of large installations into the sample.

5   That programmers enjoy a high degree of job satisfaction was a clear conclusion from Mumford's study (1972). Kraft and Dubnoff also found high job satisfaction among the programmers they interviewed. This they regarded as an oddity (communication at seminar presented by Kraft at University of Bath, England, 1985).

6   These types of strategies are labels for two ends of a continuum, rather than a simple dichotomy (Friedman, 1986).

7   One way of alleviating these inflexibilities is to divide the labour force into at least two different groups, central and peripheral workers. Responsible autonomy types of strategies would be used with central workers, direct control types with peripheral workers (see Friedman,1977; Osterman, 1987).

8   The Braverman/Kraft hypothesis of task fragmentation in computing *does* seem to apply to the separation and deskilling of operators and data entry clerks. Note from table XI.3. that the most striking difference in education requirements was between operators, data entry staff, secretaries and administrative staff, on the one hand, and development staff, on the other hand.

Chapter XII
The IT People – Historical Development and Present Characteristics

Finn Borum and Marianne Risberg

1 Introduction

In the early phase of the CHIPS project we were struck by the absence of statistics and factual descriptions on the historical development and composition of the Danish IT people. From a *practical* perspective it is problematic not to possess a better knowledge of trends and progress in manpower within what is commonly regarded as a future growth sector (see, e.g., Social Europe, 1986). More so, when the field in question perhaps is facing a major challenge: that of the transformation from an artisan to an industrial mode of production (OECD, 1985, Kraft and Dubnoff, 1986). Such a transformation, made possible by the present state of hardware and software, will require changes in the qualifications and skills of the IT people. In this context it is interesting to take an historical overview of the development of the IT people in order to identify trends, which might have significance for the future.

From a *theoretical* perspective we are lacking an understanding of the IT people as an occupational group, and of their historical development. The other chapters of this reader are intended to remedy this through different conceptualisations and interpretations.

This chapter is factual in its approach and has provided data for the other analyses. Its initial intention was to examine all available statistics related to the Danish IT people. It is evident from the references that quite a few sources exist which all have been investigated. However, they turned out to be based upon such different sub-populations and samples that even simple comparisons and combinations were impossible.

The only feasible approach turned out to be to draw on statistics from Danmarks Statistik (Denmark's Statistical Bureau) covering the period 1970-1988 as the main data base. The other statistics, then, have been attributed supplementary and correcting roles. Appendix A lists all the statistics consulted.

This approach is not unproblematic, as we have identified three problems of validity connected with the official statistics. The first is a shift in the principle of reporting between the three surveys in 1970, 1973 and 1975 and the yearly salary statistics established from 1981 and onwards. Next, the coverage of the official statistics is not complete, and biased towards the larger enterprises. Thirdly, the principle of reporting based upon job titles introduces ambiguities. These problems are dealt with in more detail in Appendix B.

With these problems in mind this chapter addresses five characteristics of the IT people. First, we look at the *historical development* of the primary job titles comprising the central groups of the IT people. This discussion will lead us to identify how quickly the field has been growing as well as some of the mechanisms behind this developed, particularly since 1970. We note that new job titles have evolved reflecting both further division of labour within the field and changes in the borderline of the field.

Second, we examine the *level and types of qualifications* of new recruits to the IT people, and of the current incumbents. By "qualifications" or "formal qualifications" we refer to curricula acquired at educational institutions. "Skills" is used as a term for what is learned on the job. "Competence" is used as a term for the totality of the individual's knowledge and capabilities, no matter where or how they have been acquired.

Third, we look at the two important *demographic characteristics* of the IT people: Age, gender and geographical distribution.

Fourth, we examine the *distribution of salaries* by job titles and also relate salaries to the age and gender distributions.

The fifth characteristic of the IT people we examine in this chapter is *career patterns and mobility*.

2   Historical Development and Distribution of Job Titles

From the table below, it appears that the number of IT people has more than doubled between 1970 and 1988. The DS statistics, however, do not include all the Danish IT people (see Appendix B), and an adjustment of the figures points towards 25.000 as a more realistic number of IT people (see Appendix B). However, the union Prosa estimates the total number to be substantially higher – and in 1986 it operated with 30.000 (Bjorn-Andersen et al., 1988) as the number of potential union members.

The growth between 1970 and 1988, however, has been uneven. IT specialists occupied with "analysis and programming" have almost multiplied by five, while the category "operations" has been reduced by more than 10% over the period – after a slight increase during the first five-year period.

Table XII.1   The Development of the IT Population 1970-1988. Private Sector

	1970	1988
EDP-manager	236	600
Systems manager	137	278
Programming manager	113	99
Systems consultant	*	3.104
Systems planner	702	1.236
Systems programmer	*	1.278
Analyst/programmer	*	1.935
Programmer	1.190	2.300
Analysis & programming	2.378	10.825
Operations manager	154	236
Operations planner	124	778
Operator	1.032	1.998
Data entry supervisor	187	94
Data entry operator	2.283	699
Other	567	–
Operations	4.347	3.805
Total	6.725	14.630

Another way of looking at the figures presented in table XII.1 is to note that within both the category of analysis and programming and that of operations, the "bottom" of the job hierarchy, grew substantially less (or declined most). While programmers accounted for roughly half of the analysis and programming category in 1970, they only accounted for about a quarter in 1988. Data entry operators accounted for roughly half of the operations category in 1970. They accounted for less than a fifth in 1988.

Thus the IT people were improving their job status, measured by job categories. The composition of the IT specialists gradually became dominated by those holding high status jobs such as managers, planners and consultants.

For a more detailed table covering the period 1970-1988 see Appendix D, table D:1.

2.1   Analysis and Programming

Returning to the growing fraction of the IT people: within *analysis and programming* three new job titles have appeared since 1970. The first one appeared in the 1973 statistics – systems programmers – indicating a technical specialisation of a segment of the programmers in operative systems, data bases, communication networks, etc. It is within this "technical centre group" that we still find programming of special parts of the system in low-level languages, whereas the programmers today use problem- oriented languages.

The second new job title was "systems consultants" (1981) that may have two explanations, of which one relates to the need to create a possibility to promote systems analysts, and to circumvent obstacles to salary increases by the creation of a new job title. The other explanation is a differentiation of systems analysis into more consultancy/sales oriented functions, and into genuine programming (specification) functions. Data from previous studies (e.g., Borum and Enderud, 1981) point to the latter explanation, whereas our observations support both.

Third, the new mixed category of "analyst/programmer" (1982) reflects a trend to depart from the classical division of labour between systems planning (analysis) and programming (see Chapters X and XI). This development is supported by both the more powerful programming tools available today, and the mixed experiences with the more classical, "Taylorist-inspired" work organisation.

The *managerial group* within analysis and programming has increased less than the average growth rate. This may partially be due to the general trend within the IT field to rely more upon project/team organisation and ad-hoc leadership than upon classical hierarchical forms of organisation (e.g., Friedman and Cornford, 1987, and Borum and Enderud, 1981). Another complementary as well as competing explanation might be that the categories of systems consultants and systems analysts conceal an intermediary managerial layer: that of senior people with managerial positions and permanent project management responsibilities.

The group *systems consultants/planners/analysts* shows the most important growth rate indicating the growing importance of analysis, advice and other 'soft services' related to IT.

Programmers come out below average. This in part indicates that the expected automation of programming functions is becoming effective. However, the growth index of this category has increased, if we add the proportion of the mixed group of analyst/programmers to the programmers. Furthermore, the number of systems programmers has also been growing particularly rapidly (quadrupled since 1973). Therefore, though part of the relative decline in numbers of programmers may be attributed to automation, much is also due to an elaboration of this job category into systems programmer and analyst/programmer. There is some evidence that the job category of programmer is being used as an entry level job title, leading on, either to analyst/programmer or to systems programmer. Therefore, the pattern observed may in part be explained by a desire to formalise career ladders by increasing the number of different job titles individuals would normally pass through.

Table XII.2 Growth Rate within the Categories "Analysis and Programming" and "Operations"
Index: 1970 = 100

	1970	1981	1988
Manager:			
EDP-manager	100	114	201
Systems manager			
Programming manager			
Systems consultant/			
planner/analyst:			
Systems consultant			
Systems planner	100	237	893
Analyst programmer			
Systems programmer[1]	100	156	394
Programmer	100	123	193
Analysis and programming	100	176	455
Operations manager	100	51	153
Operations planner	100	316	627
Operators	100	113	194
Data entry supervisor	100	76	50
Data entry operator	100	49	31
Operations	100	66	88
Total	100	105	218

[1] The index figure for systems programmer is from 1973 as none exists from 1970.

2.2   Operations

Turning to operations, two new groups have appeared during the period examined: console operators and operators assistants. However, in table XII.1 these have been truncated in the *operator* category. Two groups have disappeared: the shift supervisors (included in operators in the table) and "other" personnel. The shift supervisors can be regarded as replaced by operations planners and console operators, while the group "other" seems to have disappeared, as we take this category to cover data preparators and technicians.

The reduction by 12% of operations staff generally reflects the automation effect and the integration of certain functions in the user jobs. The group *"other"* has been eliminated from the installations, and the *data entry personnel* has been reduced to less than a third of the initial population size. The group "operators" has increased by factor two (and slightly decreased since 1986), which is a modest increase if compared with the number of installations and the amount of data processed.

Somewhat surprisingly the highest growth rate within operations belongs to the *operations planners* (more than factor six). This could partly be caused by a changed staff composition in line with the increased automation of the operators' functions, and partly caused by senior operators being attributed this job title as a reward.

3   Formal Qualifications

In relation to a new field of which individual competence is a key factor to the development of software and systems implementation, it is interesting to examine the formal qualifications of the actors. By examining the development hereof, we get an impression of the relative importance of the educational institutions and the job situation in relation to acquiring IT competences.

Below we will identify the patterns and trends of the IT people's formal qualifications in three steps. First, we identify the historical development in qualifications between 1970 and 1988 for persons within both development and operations. Then we examine the qualifications from the supply side, i.e., the number of graduates with IT oriented qualifications that have been produced by educational institutions. Finally, we study the qualifications of development people (analysis and programming) by means of a recent survey.

3.1   Formal Qualifications 1970 and 1988

1970 figures for formal qualifications are provided by DS (1970), but since 1970 neither the statistics of Denmark's Statistical Bureau nor those of the Association of Danish Employers provide information about the qualifications of IT people. The only recent statistic on IT people's educational background is produced by Sam-Data, HK's union for IT people (see Chapter IX), comprising its own members only, and thus not representative of the IT field. Thus, the 1988 figures are an estimate based on different sources.

Two characteristics of this table are important: The variety of formal qualifications and the low proportion of academics within IT in the early years. The variety may be explained as the consequence of the educational system's inability to provide obvious candidates for vacant positions within this new occupational field, and the absence of established norms and traditions for recruitment and selection of applicants. "The DP-field has been a mess from an educational point of view for as long as I can remember" as one of our informants from a large supplier put it. The low proportions of academics may be regarded as a consequence of the general lower number of academics

Table XII.3   Educational Background of the IT Population 1970 and 1988

	1970 (DS)	1988 (estimate)
High School	22%	20%
EDP-assistant	–	20%
"Bachelor" in business economics (HA/HD)	3%	5%
Short business educations (HH/Merkonom)	1%	15%
Engineers or other technical educations	4%	5%
University degree or equivalent (inclusive of computer science)	0%	10%
Other (i.e. formal qualifitions below high school exams)	70%	25%
	100%	100%

The 1988-estimate (rounded to multiply of 5) has been produced as follows:

High School exam only: Almost unchanged (evidence Antonsen & Strandgaard Pedersen, 1988).

EDP-assistant: The 5.179 educated throughout the period in % of 25.000.

Bachelor in economics: Adapted from Sam-Data 1986

Short business educ.: –

Engineers: Slight increase.

University degree: 93 datalogs + 603 exam.scient + other universityeducations + candidates from Business Schools of Economics (cand.merc.) = 1600-2000 in % of 25.000.

Other: 100% - above categories.

produced by the educational system then, and the educational institutions' orientation towards more traditional types of jobs. In addition to this, many firms have been inclined to attach little importance to theoretical competence and thus not trying very actively to attract academics.

Computer programming is basically a creative process. Even applying computers to problems for which systems have already been developed involves creating something new. No two information systems (of any substance) are exactly the same, even if they are supposed to perform the same functions. The development, (also the enhancement and even the maintenance) of a computer-based system therefore affords the opportunity to develop new techniques. This aspect of the IT field has been called the autogeneration of new technology (Friedman with Cornford, 1990). The strength of this autogeneration of new technology has devalued academic knowledge and academic qualifications in the IT field.

Though internationally there has been a general devaluation of academic qualifications in the IT field according to a recent study Denmark has, compared to other countries, had a relative small number of IT people with a university degree. For example, in the UK 35% had a non-computer science degree and in the Netherlands 37% had non-computer science degrees, (Friedman et al., 1988, p. 11).

Finally, according to several of our informants, *recruitment* to IT functions is increasingly based upon the intake of individuals possessing social or communication skills, or skills within the application area or trade. Thus, individuals are often recruited from user departments to internal IT departments, and supplier organisations often acquire individuals with a formal education or practical skills within customer areas.

These flexible recruitment patterns coincide with the eroding of the former very strict distinction between IT specialists and users. Individuals are increasingly moving across this borderline, and in user departments one finds former IT specialists as managers or serving as important intermediaries between the DP departments and the user departments. Or users can be observed spending most, or an important part of their time, carrying out IT functions.

3.2   The Supply Side: Output from Educational Institutions

Another way of approaching a statistical description of the IT people's formal qualifications is from the perspective of the supply side of the labour market and see how many individuals acquire the different qualifications. Based upon the following figure from the union PROSA (1984) some statistical information can be given in relation to the 'inner circle' of the figure – educations that aim directly at the IT field. These are described in more detail in Bjorn Andersen et.al. (1988).

EDP-Assistant
The EDP-assistant education started in 1973 and is a basic education aiming at programming and planning functions. If the student's background is a high school exam (Studentereksamen) or the equivalent, exams can be passed after one year, otherwise two years of study are required. According to DS 5.179 students have graduated during the years 1974 – 1987.

The increasing number of graduates is a result of decisions to expand the capacity of the edp schools from about 200 (1975-77), via about 300 (1978- 80) to around 600 (1983). The fall in number of candidates in 1979/80 and 1981/82 can be related to experienced unemployment amongst EDP-assistants.

The table shows, that women account for the relatively most important rise in number of candidates, namely a nine-doubling over the 13 year period from 24% to 40% of the annual output of candidates.

Datanom
As a main rule only EDP-assistants are admitted to this study but students that have acquired some of the necessary basic knowledge through other studies may

Figure XII.1   IT-Educations and Adjacent Educations

apply for admission. The study is composed of a number of individual courses, which the part-time student attends outside working hours. All courses must be passed before writing up the final thesis. Many have started, but only approximately 20 students a year graduate. There is no time limit as to how many years may pass between the various courses and the final thesis.

Datamatiker
The first 30 students graduated in June 1987. It is a 2 1/2 years study admitting graduates from high school (Studentereksamen), or the equivalent. The study aims at qualifying the student to carry out analysis, evaluation, construction, and implementation of larger IT systems.

Table XII.4   Number of EDP-Assistants Graduated during the Years 1974-87

	Male	Female	Total	Index figures		
				Male	Female	Total
1974/75	102	32	134	100	100	100
1975/76	142	46	188	139	144	140
1976/77	135	38	173	132	119	129
1977/78	191	58	249	187	181	186
1978/79	212	89	301	208	278	225
1979/80	214	73	287	209	228	214
1980/81	269	109	378	263	341	282
1881/82	215	132	347	211	413	259
1982/83	372	161	533	365	503	398
1983/84	435	162	597	426	506	446
1984/85	396	201	597	388	628	446
1985/86	449	268	717	440	812	535
1986/87	406	272	678	498	850	506

Data Engineer

The electro-engineer study at The Technical University (Danmarks Tekniske Hojskole) consists of four lines at MA level, one of which exclusively focuses on data processing. It is primarily aiming at hardware. Approximately 40 students graduate each year.

Computer Scientist

During the period 1984-1987, 93 students (MA-level) graduated from the universities of Copenhagen and Aarhus. Computer science is primarily software oriented and aiming at programming, implementation and maintenance of new systems for research and technical-administrative purposes as well as assessment of new EDP-equipment.

Exam.Scient.

This title covers persons with a bachelor degree in computer science, i.e., they have passed the first part of the computer science study. Although it is not a final degree the students have been given the above title because many of them have been unable to complete their study owing to insufficient capacity at the second part of the study. During the years 1980 -1986, 603 students passed the first part of the study. However, we know that a small number of them by now have also passed the second part and thus are included in the above group of computer scientists. But many of them never complete their studies. After having obtained a bachelor degree, they often find a job in IT organisations and stay there.

3.3   The Total Supply of Persons with a Formal IT Education

The account above allows us to arrive at a crude estimate of the total number of individuals with a formal IT education that the educational systems has produced so far:

EDP-assistant, datanom, datamatiker	approx.	6.600
exam.scient, datalog	–	900
data engineer	–	600
total	approx.	8.100

Thus the observed low proportion of the IT people with a formal IT education can be traced back to the limited supply provided by the educational system, which of course is not independent of the recruitment policies of the IT firms. However, it must be taken into consideration that several of the non-IT educations include IT related elements (programming, systems analysis, use of relevant systems etc.). This is the case of the following part-time diploma educations as well as the MA-level degrees at the Copenhagen Business School:

HD Organisation/datamatik (established in 1974)
Cand. merc. datalogi/economics (established in 1986)
HD Informatics and managerial economics (established in 1987).

Other universities have recently established this type of educations combining IT with other substance areas.

Nevertheless, the development of more IT specific competence has by and large been the task of the IT suppliers and the IT user organisations. In this connection the EDP-assistant education is the result of user organisations' efforts to establish a general IT education independent of suppliers. A major motivation behind this was the fact, that in the early years the relevant courses were all offered by the hardware suppliers.

Later on, private educational institutions entered the market as well, and Datacentralen and other large intermediaries/user organisations established their own curricula, partly based on internal courses. As appeared from Chapter I, some of the large communities (IBM, Datacentralen, Kommunedata) have played, and still do, an important role as providers of courses and developers of IT competence.

Even within the few large organisations that have developed an internal formalised education for planners, programmers etc.[1], learning-by-doing still appears to be the primary mode of acquiring IT skills. Our data indicate that the process resembles that of an artisan mode of production. Thus, the more experienced IT specialists pass on to the less experienced their knowledge about how to diagnose and solve problems through collaboration on concrete projects. This apprenticeship system is controlled by the specialists, who form a semi-autonomous body outside the control of management. Thus, the formal educational system and the formalised curricula and courses of the suppliers,

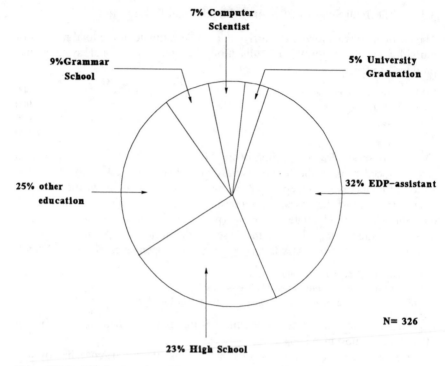

Figure XII.2   Distribution of Qualifications

intermediaries, and users only provide a partial understanding of the processes by which the IT competence and skills are developed.

3.4   A Survey of IT Specialists

A 1988-survey (Antonsen and Pedersen, 1988) of 328 systems planners and programmers from internal DP departments and software houses brings further support to the observation that there is no single itinerary or education leading into IT. The IT specialists in this sample possess very different educations and backgrounds.

From the figure it appears that 'EDP-assistant' (32%) is the most common background for a person working within the IT companies studied. 'Other education' (25%) is the second most popular and 'High School' (student) (23%) the third most common. Among the IT specialists only 12% hold some kind of *academic degree* (Computer Science 7% and other University degrees 5%). 39% of the entire population in the study, have a *formal IT education* (EDP-assistant 32% and Computer Scientist 7%). However, figures from previous studies and

Table XII.5

Population		Formal qualification % distribution				
Years of Seniority within IT	No. of respon- dents	Computer science	EDP-ass.	Other univ.	High school	Other edu- cation and grammar- school
0-5	107	3%	49%	6%	20%	22%
6-10	100	10%	39%	4%	23%	24%
11-15	53	13%	13%	8%	21%	45%
16-29	66	5%	6%	3%	30%	56%
Total	326	7%	32%	5%	23%	34%

other research indicate, that the proportion of IT specialists with a formal IT education has been increasing for several years.

When relating "Qualifications" to "Seniority" within the IT field, we find that the proportion of IT specialists with formal IT education ("Computer Scientist" and "EDP-assistant") has been increasing over time. Within the group of "Oldtimers" (with 16 to 29 years of seniority) the proportion of individuals with a formal IT education is as low as 11%. However, in the group with 11 to 15 years of seniority, 26% hold a formal IT education and this proportion rises to 49% for the group with 6 to 10 years of seniority. Finally, in the group of 'Youngsters' (with 0 to 5 years of seniority), 52% hold a formal IT education, mainly a short non-academic education.

The table furthermore supports the major trends estimated in table XII.2, i.e., a decrease in "other educations", and the declining but continued importance of high school exam.

This must be seen in the light of the changing role of the high school exam over the years. In the 1950s less than 10% of a generation passed this exam, which gave direct access to the university. During the 1960s the figure increased to more than 15%, and in the 1970s to 25%. The mathematical line of high school was considered an indication of a potential that also was appropriate within the IT field. With the increasing proportion of high school exams, the value of the exam in itself has decreased, and it has more and more become the entrance to further studies. Thus a tendency towards a higher level of formal qualifications can be observed. This tendency does not only apply to the IT companies studied. It also reflects both a trend within the IT field at large as a consequence of the creation of IT qualifications (Computer Science, 1969, Computer Engineer 1972, and EDP-assistant 1972), and a general tendency within the Danish society towards a higher level of formal labour market qualifications.

The picture of IT specialists with the background "Computer Scientist" is more complex. The figures show that the majority of computer scientists in this sample is to be found in the "middle experienced" groups with 6-15 years of seniority. Among the very experienced IT specialists and the relatively unexperienced IT specialists, the proportion of computer scientists is low.

The reasons for the relatively low number of computer scientists with 0-5 years of seniority observed in the present sample could be that computer scientists are not as much in demand among the IT companies studied as they used to be, or that computer scientists have become relatively scarce and go elsewhere.

Another likely explanation for what seems to be a recent decline in the proportion of computer scientists could be that "Computer Scientist" students have IT jobs alongside their studies. If they have labelled themselves as "high school diploma", all those holding an "exam. art." degree are included in this category, as they have not completed their study.

4 Demographic Characteristics

In this section we will examine the age and gender distributions of the centre of IT specialists in order to discuss whether the common conception of the field as dominated by young males holds true. We will also compare gender, age and seniority.

4.1 Age

Table XII.6 below shows that the IT centre is young. The main differences between the age distribution of the IT centre and that of all full-time employed white collar workers are

(1) an over-representation of the age groups 25-39 years;
(2) an under-representation of the age groups below 24 and above 45 years, in particular those over 49 years.

This age distribution can be explained by both the recruitment practice within the field (to take in relatively young persons), the expansion of the IT field that keeps the average age down, and by the favourable career opportunities outside the IT centre once a certain seniority and competence has been acquired. The underrepresentation of the very youngest age group (below 24) may be explained by the fact that some prior experience or formal education is increasingly requested by employers.

Table XII.6 Age Distribution of IT People and White Collar Employees, 1988

	I IT people %	II all white collar employees %	Difference (I-II)
- 24	10	13	− 3
25 - 29	22	16	+ 6
30 - 34	23	15	+ 8
35 - 39	18	14	+ 4
40 - 44	15	16	− 1
45 - 49	6	10	− 4
50 -	5	16	− 11
	99	100	

(Source: DS, 1989, p. 1)

The age distribution does not support a commonly held opinion that one cannot keep up with the work demands of the IT field beyond the age of forty ("finished at forty"). In fact 26% of the IT people are 40 years old or more. It may, on the other hand, indicate a "finished at fifty" syndrome, with those above the age of 49 accounting for only 5% of IT specialists, less than one-third of the category over 49 years among all white collar employees. However, this is impossible to determine, as the age distribution also reflects the young age of the IT field. If people in general enter the field in their mid-to-late twenties those entering in the late 1960s and early 1970s would only be in their fifties in the 1990s.

On the other hand, we know from interviews that many entered and left the IT population as defined above. Some have moved on to other positions within IT firms, for instance, staff or managerial positions, while others have moved to positions on the borderline or outside of the IT field. There may be several reasons for this behaviour: Some may leave voluntarily because of career prospects or promotions (cf. Chapter IX). Others may lose interest in IT, find it too demanding, or may be forced to leave.

A comparison of the age distribution between "analysis and programming" and "operations" (see Appendix D, table D:2) shows one important difference: that the age group of 20-24 years accounts for 13% of the operations personnel, while it seems to be extremely rare to recruit people below 25 years to analysis and programming (1%). This reflects recruitment policies that allow people to enter operations with lower formal qualifications than is the case of analysis and programming.

In Table D:2 (in Appendix D) the italicized figures of the categories position and gender show the two or three age groups that account for at least 50% of that population. It appears, that for each of the categories "analysis and programming" and "operations" the age increases upwards in the table, indicating the career ladder that the positions represent. Female data entry operators and supervisors are an exception, here recruitment has dropped due to the technological development.

4.2   Gender and Position

According to Danmarks Statistik, the distribution of the IT population according to gender was in 1981 and 1988 as shown in table XII.7.

Not surprisingly the table shows that the majority of IT people are men – 75% in 1988. This has to be compared with men accounting for only 55% of the total labour force in DS's 1988 statistics. Although the overall percentage of men employed within the field has increased by 2% from 1981 to 1988 there is a tendency towards a larger representation of women within the growth category of "*analysis and programming*". In 1988 they held 22% of the jobs within this category against 13% in 1981. This pattern is also supported by the survey of Antonsen and Strandgaard Pedersen (1988).

This may be linked to the changing pattern of qualifications within the IT field, and in particular that of persons with less than 10 years of experience. One hypothesis could be that the "EDP-assistant" education combined with the general tendency towards a higher level of education has improved the females' possibilities of getting into analysis and planning jobs.

As the category "*operations*" in table XII.7 shows the overall reduction of the female proportion of the IT population is evident: while operations in 1981 was almost fifty-fifty male/female, 65% were men in 1988. The number of women within operations has remained almost unchanged over the five year period, which is the product of a reduction of data entry personnel (primarily comprising women) and a growth within the other operations positions. In fact women's proportion of the latter has been growing more than men's (tripled against increase of 50% from 1981 to 1988), but from a much lower base figure (204 against 1429).

In table XII.7a and 12.7b, a distinction is made between

– managerial positions, i.e., IT managers, systems managers, and programming managers;
– senior positions, i.e., systems consultants, systems analysts, and systems programmers;
– first level positions, i.e., analyst/programmers and programmers.

The distinction between the latter two categories is based upon information about recruitment practices and career patterns. But admittedly it is somewhat

Table XII.7   The IT Population 1981 and 1988 Distributed by Gender

	1981			1988		
	Male	Female	Total	Male	Female	Total
EDP-manager	291	16	307	552	48	600
Systems manager	158	-	158	259	19	278
Programming manager	92	-	92	94	5	99
Systems consultant	403	60	463	2.359	745	3.104
Systems planner	1.062	142	1.204	990	246	1.236
Systems programmer	476	30	506	1.118	160	1.278
Analyst/programmer	*	*	*	1.422	513	1.935
Programmer	1.172	294	1.466	1.705	595	2.300
Analysis & planning	3.654	542	4.196	8.499	2.331	10.830
	87%	13%	100%	78%	22%	100%
Operations manager	79	-	79	204	32	236
Operations planner	358	34	392	647	131	778
Operators	992	170	1.162	1.545	453	1.998
Data entry superv.	18	124	142	22	72	94
Data entry operator	52	1.070	1.122	54	645	699
Operations	1.499	1.398	2.897	2.472	1.333	3.805
	52%	48%	100%	65%	35%	100%
Total	5.153	1.940	7.093	10.971	3.664	14.635
	73%	27%	100%	75%	25%	100%

* job category not existing at that time.

debatable, as the position analyst/programmer in some cases is equivalent to that of a systems analyst.

With this reservation, the index in table XII.7a shows that even though analysis and programming is still male dominated, women have career possibilities, as they are found at all three levels, and in 1988 accounted for a higher proportion of the two upper level positions than in 1981.

The interpretation of the tables, however, is complicated by a lower representativity of the 1981 survey. This makes it difficult to see whether a proportion of the women in senior and first level positions in 1981 actually have been moving upward – as the 1988 figures seem to indicate – or whether it is because organisations, that already in 1981 had a higher proportion of female leaders, have been included in the 1986 statistics.

Table XII.7a   Analysis and Planning: Men and women in % of 1981 and 1988 Population

| | 1981 | | | 1988 | | |
	Male	Female	Total	Male	Female	Total
Managers	97	3	100	93	7	100
Senior positions	89	11	100	80	20	100
First level positions	80	20	100	74	26	100
Analysis and planning	87	13	100	78	22	100

Table XII.7b   Analysis and Planning: % Distribution of Men and Women on Hierarchical
               levels in 1981 and 1988

| | 1981 | | | 1988 | | |
	Male	Female	Total	Male	Female	Total
Managers	15	3	13	11	2	9
Senior positions	53	43	52	52	49	52
First level positions	32	54	35	37	48	39
Analysis and planning	100	100	100	100	100	100

Table XII.7b which contains index figures showing the percentage distribution of the male and female population, respectively, within the three layers offers some even not a very strong support of the hypothesis of a change in the upwards mobility of the two groups: in 1988 a lower percentage of men in managerial positions, but a higher percentage in first level positions. For women a larger percentage occupy senior positions, and fewer first level positions.

4.3   Gender, Age and Seniority

As to *gender*, table D:2 (Appendix D) shows that women within the IT people are younger than the males: while the overall proportion of men:women is 3:1, it is 2:1 for the age groups below 30, but 4:1 for the age groups of 35-49 years. It also appears that the average age of women is lower for all job categories except data entry operators and supervisors. This may be the result of women entering the labour market at an earlier age. However, our observations indicate that the men's military service is outweighed by women's higher educational level. Other explanations may be shifts in recruitment practices of the firms towards employing more women for IT positions, and an increased propensity of women

Table XII.8   Geographic Distribution of the Danish Labor Force. 1986

	Copenhagen		Outside Copenhagen		Total	
	no.	%	no.	%	no.	%
Total labour force (age: 16-66)	800.111	23	2.662.316	77	3.462.427	100
Total white collar labour force	172.691	46	205.767	54	378.458	100
IT specialists	7.833	61	5.033	39	12.866	100

(Source: DS 1987 and information from DS).

to go into IT jobs. Finally, women may have a higher exit-rate from the IT field due to family conditions, lack of career possibilities or development of other career strategies.

A comparison of gender and seniority in Antonsen and Pedersen (1988) shows, that men account for the majority of all groups of seniority, and that the proportion of women is highest in the lowest seniority group.

4.4   Geographic Distribution

As table XII.8 reveals, the IT specialists are strongly concentrated (61%) in the Copenhagen area – defined as the municipalities of Copenhagen and Frederiks-berg and the country of Copenhagen. This concentration is considerably higher than that of white collar labourers (46%) and reflects both the concentration of large IT users – public as well as private sector – in the Copenhagen area, and the subsequent inclination of IT firms to locate their Danish headquarters here.

5   Salary Distribution

Table D:3 (Appendix D) summarises the DS (1986) salary statistics with regard to job title, age and gender. According to DS' survey, there is a clear connection between *gender and salary*: with only two exceptions (female systems program-mers of the age of 35-39 years, and female operations planners of the age of 20-24 years). Women are paid less than men within the same position and age group.

A second evident co-variation exists between *age and salary* – the older you are, the higher the salary, as it appears from table D:3 (Appendix D). However, there is a tendency to pay the oldest groups less. One explanation could be that the age group above 45 has acquired less formal education and accordingly is paid less. Employees in this group may also have started out at a lower wage level and are thus caught up by the young ones, or they are employed in more traditional companies (banks, insurance companies) which may have modest wages, but high job security and a low turnover of staff. The demand for IT people exceeding the supply may provide another explanation, the younger ones with an up-to-date background being more in demand than the older ones.

It is a commonly held opinion that *compared with other occupational groups* the IT people are better paid. Table XII.9, which compares the average wages from Appendix D (table D:3) with the upper quartile, the average and the lower quartile wages for full-time white collar employees, respectively, supports this in the sense that 6.245 of 10.971 male IT people come out above the average, and none come out below the lower quartile male white collar wages.

Female IT people are not in general as well paid as male white collar employees (only 478 out of 3,592 above average male salary). But when compared with *female* white collar employees, the picture changes drastically to 2,566 above the upper quartile of 17.056, and only the operators and the data entry operators are below. This illustrates how the previously identified salary differentiation between men and women within the IT field must be seen in relation to an even more significant differentiation within the white collar labour market as a whole.

If we take into consideration the previously identified fact (table XII.6) that the IT people are younger than the white collar employees in total, the evidence for high salaries is strengthened.

6   Career Patterns and Mobility

Our interviews indicate that it is a widespread practice to recruit actors with previous practical experience outside the IT field. This, however, has to be contrasted with the prevailing practice of recruiting young persons to IT positions. To most persons entering the IT field it is their first job experience, very few of them have more than one or two previous jobs behind them.

With these observations in mind we will now investigate the career patterns within the IT field based upon two data sets: DS' salary statistics, and the "IT specialist survey" by Antonsen and Strandgaard Pedersen (1988) .

6.1   Salary Differentiation as an Indicator of Career Patterns

The data shown in Appendix D, table D:3 indicate a strong correlation between position and average monthly salary. Based upon the two assumptions that

Table XII.9   Comparison of IT Peoples's Average Salary 1988 with Total White Collar Population Salaries (DS, 1989)

	Male IT-people	(no.)	Female IT-people	(no.)
IT people with average salary > upper quartile for male white collar workers	EDP-manager	(552)		
24.550	Systems manager	(259)		
	Programming manager	(94)	Systems manager	(19)
	Operations manager	(204)	EDP-manager	(48)
	Systems programmer	(1118)	(total	67
	(total	2227		
IT people with average salary > average for male white collar workers	Systems planner	(990)	Programming manager	(5)
21.243	Systems consultant	(2359)	Systems programmer	(160)
	Operations planner	(647)	Systems planner	(246)
	Data entry supervisor	(22)	(total	411
	(total	4018		
IT people with average salary > lower quartile for male white collar worker	Analyst/programmer	(1422)	System consultant	(745)
	Programmer	(1705)	Operations manager	(32)
	Operator	(1545)	Analyst/programmer	(513)
*) 17.056			Operations planner	(131)
			Programmer	(595)
			Data entry supervisor	(72)
	Data entry operator	(54)	Operator	(453)
	(total	4726)	(total	2541)
IT people with average salary < lower quartile for male white collar workers			Data entry operator	(645)
15.867				

*) Upper quartile for female white collar employees.

careers lead upwards in the salary system, and that careers are characterised by gradual wage increases more than "giant steps", we can sketch the following picture of the itineraries between the IT positions as shows in figure XII.3.

"Data entry" jobs are the lowest paid positions for both men and women, and the position "operator" seems to be the most likely career prospect. The next step might be "data entry supervisor", "operations planner" and "operations manager". But the wage steps between these categories are so great for men that this conclusion seems dubious.

"Operations planners" are remunerated at roughly the same level as "programmers" and "analyst/programmers". This is compatible with our observation that many persons recruited to operations have the same educational background as the programmers – namely the one-year "EDP-assistant" education or a high school exam. The categories of "programmer" and "analyst/programmer" are so close to each other, that they seem to represent two start positions which as next step may lead to positions as "systems consultant" or "systems planner". On the other hand, the distance to "systems programmer" is so important, that we may assume that "systems programmer" is not only a position to which programmers advance, but also a position to which persons with other formal qualifications are recruited.

When we focus upon the managerial positions, "EDP managers" and "systems managers" somewhat surprisingly receive salaries on the same level. This may reflect that "EDP managers" mainly is used as a title for the top position in smaller installations/firms, whereas in larger installations/firms it is either not used, or used as a title for the head of data processing – i.e., the equivalent of operations manager. Thus the female EDP managers supposedly are responsible for small installations/data processing departments – which leads to a more pessimistic interpretation of women's career possibilities than the analysis of tables XII.7a and XII.7b that was only based upon job titles and gender.

As to career paths to and between the managerial positions we would expect systems programmers as the most likely ones to advance to the position as programming manager. The position as operations managers we expect to be accessible from both programming and systems positions – depending on the importance attributed to technical and general managerial skills, respectively, in the individual organisation.

We would also assume IT people with a technical oriented career path to be tied closer to a career within the IT positions, whereas the more application/ managerial oriented systems analysts/consultants have a better basis for careers leading out of the IT field. This interpretation would lead us to claim the career paths as indicated by the lines in figure XII.3. One important reservation has to be made: the statistics are based upon salary statements from one year, and thus does not represent an "IT generation's" experience of promotion and income development. However, supportive evidence of these itineraries are contained in

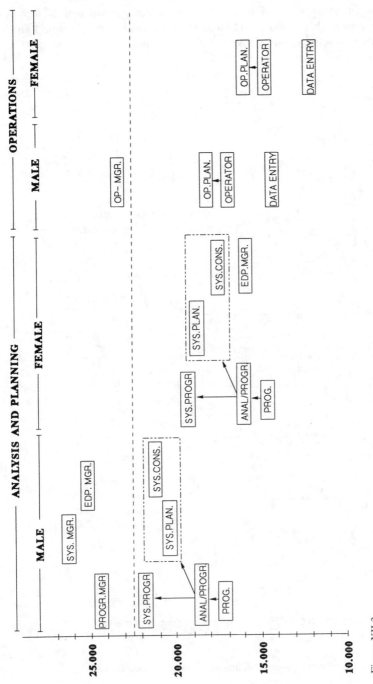

Figure XII.3

some of our informants' own interpretations of career patterns that, however, stress variety more than standardisation as the rule. Take as an example figure XII.4, which represents an encodement of a central informants' statements.

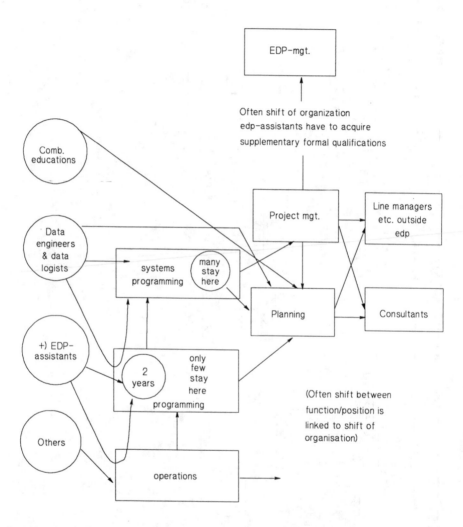

+) A short period of oversupply 1980–81 until employers had geared themselves to this new group.

Figure XII.4   Career Patterns: Large Installations (80% of the specialists)

6.2 A Survey of IT Specialists

Antonsen and Strandgaard Pedersen's (1988) survey carried out among persons working with software development brings further support of the diversity of career patterns. The models of career patterns are tentative and based on information about job function in the first as well as in the present job of the IT specialists, and information about the total number of jobs, which the IT specialists have occupied over time.

Data about first job function indicate that "Programming" and "Programming/ Systems Analysis" are the main entry positions to the IT field. More than two-thirds (69%) of the IT people in the sample (n = 326) have held one of these two positions as their first job.

The figures are 30% for "Programming" and 39% for "Programming/Systems Analysis", respectively. This is sustained by the figures concerning the total number of job functions, which the IT people in our sample have possessed over time. Here, we find that 54% of all the jobs have been either "Programming" or "Programming/Systems Analysis" jobs.

The third most common entry position is "Systems Consultant"'-13% have started in this job function. In contrast few persons start as "Project Leader" (4%), "Systems Analyst" (5%) or as "Systems Programmer" (8%) in their first job function.

Turning to the distribution of present job function, it appears that "Programming/Systems Analysis" is still the most common job function (39%) of the IT specialists studied. The second most frequent job function is "Systems Consultant" (19%), while "Project Leader" is third in rank (16%). Based on this information we can tentatively depict the general career pattern for the IT specialists to be as follows.

When the connections between "Qualifications" and job functions (first and present) are further specified, it appears that there is a significant, positive correlation between both "University Graduate", "Other education" and "High School" and "Systems Consultant" as first job function. Regarding present job function only "University Graduate" and "High School" showed positive correlations of significance with "Systems Consultant".

Another significant, positive correlation appeared between "EDP-assistant" and "Programming/Systems Analysis" for both first and present job function. Furthermore, the "EDP-assistant" appears to be negatively correlated with "Systems Consultant". This is not surprising as EDP-assistants is negatively correlated with age, whereas the position of "Systems Consultants" is positively correlated with age. For the other categories of "Qualifications" no correlations of significance to job positions could be identified. Based on these findings the general model presented in figure XII.5 can be qualified in the following model.

Qualifications   1st job   Present job

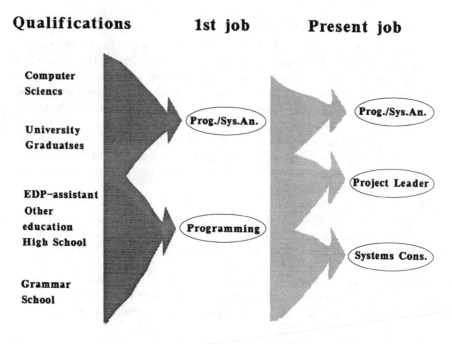

Figure XII.5   General Career Pattern

7   Conclusion

In spite of the growing number of IT people the population has remained an exclusive one. In 1986 the total number of persons employed on the Danish labour marked amounted to 2.662.000. Thus, the IT people only amounts to a little more than 1% of the Danish labour force. This small population is strongly concentrated in and around the Copenhagen area. Here, 61% of the IT people work, while the same area only accounts for 23% of the total labour force, and 46% of the white collar work force.

This reflects the distribution of administrative and service activities in Denmark, but perhaps also centralised systems solutions necessitated by the early information technology – from which it is now possible to deviate.

The *composition* of the IT people has been changing in that "operations" has been slightly declining, while "analysis and programming" (development) has almost quadrupled.

The explanation behind the fall within operations staff is the automation and integration of data entry into other non-IT-jobs. The number of operators has doubled over the period in spite of automation of many functions, but this is

Qualifications   **1st job**   **Present job**

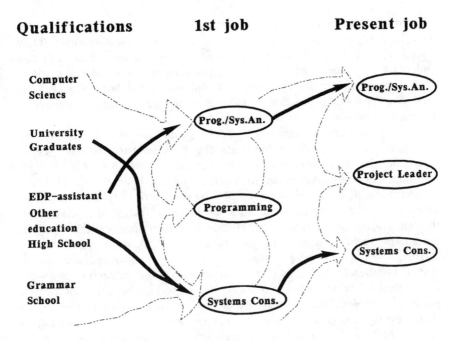

Figure XII.6   Expanded Career Pattern Model

modest in relation to the important increase in the number of computer installations. But within operations a very strong growth in the number of operations planners has been identified (more than factor five).

Within development, the categories systems consultants and planners have grown most significantly (increased by factor 5), whereas systems programmers and programmers account for a lower, but still important growth rate (almost tripled). These different growth rates may be interpreted as reflecting the automation of many traditional programming functions, the integration of some programming and systems planning functions, and the increased importance of advisory and consultancy functions both within and between organisations.

The *qualification* aspect of this analysis shows that the level of formal qualifications within the IT field has been increasing over time. This reflects both a general societal trend, and the fact that specific formal educations aiming at the IT field have been established since the early years. The most important of these (in terms of the number of persons provided to the IT field) is the EDP-assistant education which is geared towards programming. In the light of the slower growth of the programming functions it may be important to evaluate this education in relation to a more 'industrial production' scenario.

The over-all picture, however, shows that the IT field is still characterised by great flexibility as to the formal qualifications of the persons recruited. Only around 30% of the IT people possess a formal IT education, and there is a tendency to rely more upon the recruitment of persons with an education within a substance area, for instance, economics. But still "autodidacts" seem to have good career possibilities within a field that emphasises on-the-job- training in line with the present craft production mode.

The *age distribution* shows that the IT people are young. This can be explained as a consequence of the young age of the industry, the field's heavy expansion, the recruitment practice, and the labour force available. The age distribution does not give support to an often expressed belief that the IT field is so demanding that one has to get out of it by the age of forty. 10% in fact are above 45 years old, and the mean age is 34-35 years. Taking into consideration the career opportunities outside the IT field once a certain experience has been gained, this age distribution is not surprising.[2]

The *gender* of the IT people clearly reflects a male domination much stronger than that of the total labour market in this period. To what extent this reflects the recruitment behaviour of the firms and/or the job seeking behaviour of men and women is not elucidated by the statistics. The increasing percentage of women within the development functions may indicate an ongoing change process, but women both account for a lesser percentage of managerial positions, and generally occupy lower managerial positions than men within the IT field.

As to *wages*, the statistics confirm that IT people are well remunerated, but that pretty clear wage hierarchies exist. This may be seen in relation to the rather high level of *unionisation* among the Danish IT people (see Chapter IX), combined with the concerted actions of some of the important employer organisations such as exchange of salary statistics and informal "codes of conduct" concerning recruitment. The managerial level represents the top of the wage hierarchy. Next comes systems programmers, leading before the systems consultants and systems planners. Data entry positions are the lowest salaried, below the "entry positions" of operators and planners, that are on the same salary level.

Gender is an important dimension: Even if women within the IT field are better paid than women in general, they systematically are paid less than men for the same job within the same age group.

There is a positive correlation between age and salary with the qualification that there is a tendency to somewhat lower wages for the oldest groups.

Finally, our analysis of career patterns revealed some patterns, in particular with regard to the entry-positions of the IT field which turned out primarily to be the positions as operators, programmers and analyst/programmers, but also systems consultant reflecting the diversity of the formal qualifications of new entrants. The further patterns of advancement within the field still seem to be characterised more by variety than by formalised trajectories. This both reflects the relatively young age of the IT field, but also its continued development in response to shifting contingencies.

Notes

1   As examples of the most comprehensive formalised internal training systems in IT organisations can be mentioned:

IBM – that on top of recruiting of persons with long educations operate with 12- 18 months of basic training that includes 10x2 weeks courses in Stockholm.

DC – that has relied heavily upon EDP-assistants that go through individual educational plans which for systems planners include three months of basic training.

KMD – that also has recruited many EDP-assistants who are recruited in 'batches' and go through a one year educational programme including 4-5 courses, laboratory work, and project group work.

2   The actual age distribution can be compared with the following small simulation: Assuming that the 1970-population was 100 with an average age of 25, and that each of the subsequent years 7 at the age of 25 have been recruited (equivalent to a growth to 202 by 1986), and that none have left the field, the average age in 1986 would have been 38 years.

Appendix

Appendix A: Statistical Sources Consulted

Administrationsdepartementet (1982 and 1987): *Statens EDB til Administrative Formål*. Finansministeriet. Copenhagen.

Antonsen, Helge and Pedersen, Jesper Strandgaard (1988): *Computer Specialists – A Survey*. CHIPS Working Paper 1988. Copenhagen.

Civilokonomen: Lonstatistik 1984, 1985, 1986, 1987.

Civilingenior-studiet ved DTH.

Commission of the European Communities. Directorate General for Employment, Social Affairs and Education (1986): The Software Industry. Social Europe, Supplement 6/86.

Computer Personnel Salary Survey. Computer Economics Ltd, October, 1987. London

Danmarks Statistik (1972): *EDB-tælling 1970*.

Danmarks Statistik (1974): *EDB-tælling 1973*.

Danmarks Statistik (1975): *EDB-tælling 1975*.

Danmarks Statistik (1982:1, 1982:1, 1984:1, 1985:1, 1986:1, 1987:1, 1988:1, 1989:1): *Lon- og indkomststatistik*.

Datamatiker uddannelsen. EDB-Skolen. Copenhagen.

Datanom uddannelsen 1986-87. EDB-skolerne.

EDB-Assistent uddannelsen (1986/87). Copenhagen.

Hingel, Anders (1986): "Social Change in the Software and Computer Service Industry" in *Social Europe. Brussels*.

Moller, Michael Nielsen (1984): *Hvad laver civilokonomer*. Rapport 84-1. HA-Center. Copenhagen Business School. Copenhagen.

OECD (1985): *Software: An emerging industry*. Paris.

Politikens EDB Bog 1985. Copenhagen.

Prosa (1986): *EDB-fagets Fremtid. Michael Lund-Larsen: Edb-branchens struktur og kvalifikationer*, p. 59-66. Forlaget Probog. Copenhagen.

Prosa (1984): *Note on the edp-manpower*. Copenhagen.

Prosa (1987): *Lonstatistik*. Copenhagen.

Sam-Data (1986): *Lonstatistik*. Copenhagen.

Scheuer, Steen (1988): *Udviklingstræk i strukturen i de faglige organisationers medlemstilslutning*. Working Paper. Institute of Organization and Industrial Sociology. Copenhagen Business School. Copenhagen.

Appendix B: The Validity of the Statistics

In the years 1970, 1973 and 1975 Danmarks Statistik (DS) carried out special EDP surveys of the IT field (Danmarks Statistik: Edb-tælling 1970, 1973, 1975). Data were collected by means of a mailed questionnaire to preselected companies that were supposed to have introduced EDP. In 1970 94% of questionnaires were returned, in 1973 98%, and in 1975 100%. The surveys covered companies with a main installation amounting to more than DKK 250,000 and with a CPU capacity corresponding to at least 1,000 bytes. After 1975 no special surveys of the IT people have been conducted but from 1982 onwards DS has, in cooperation with Dansk Arbejdsgiverforening (DA) – The Danish Employers' Association – and other trade associations, conducted annual salary surveys on private sector employees. Once a year

- Dansk Arbejdsgiverforening (DA) (The Association of Danish Employers),
- Danske Bankers Forhandlingsorganisation (The Association of Danish Banks),
- Sparekassernes Forhandlingsorganisation (The Association of Danish Savings Banks),
- Danske Forsikringsselskabers Forhandlingsorganisation (The Association of Danish Insurance Companies),
- Slagteriernes Arbejdsgiverforening (The Association of Butchers),
- Danske Vognmænd (The Association of Danish Haulage Contractors) and
- Hovedorganisationen af 1985 (The Association of 1985)

collect questionnaires from those members employing a staff of more than 10 full time employees and pass on the information to DS.

DS collects similar information from companies not covered by the trade organisations mentioned, using the same questionnaire as DA. Within production and construction industries data are only collected from companies employing more than 50 full time employees. As to the remaining trades, data are collected from companies employing more than 20 full time employees. DS' survey covering 1988 comprises 65% of all white collar employees working within the mentioned trades.

The questionnaire covers the following information: Day and year of birth, gender, time of employment, job title, education, working hours (full time/part time), company's pensions grant etc. It is possible to get more specified information from DS than stated in the survey published.

In its present form the survey goes back to 1982 (covering the income year of 1981) – before that time IT people were not specifically listed. The 1981 survey covered 56% of all employees and the 1988 survey 65%, but the percentage varies considerably within the various trades (Danmarks Statistik: Lon- og indkomststatistik 1982:1 og 1989:1)

From the 10% drop in the IT population between 1975 and 1981 it is evident, that reservations have to be made in relation to the 1981-figures. Nothing supports that this decrease in the population should reflect a real drop in the number of employees within the IT field. Instead, it reflects that the DS 1981 statistics only covered 56% of the private white collar employees. Furthermore, it must be remembered that the 1975-survey was based on all Danish installations above a certain size.

A check of another probable source of error – the possible exclusion of the Danish subsidiaries of multinationals, and of the two large service-bureaus serving the public sector (Datacentralen and Kommunedata) – led to a rejection of this as DS confirmed that they are included in the above figures.

A crude correction of the 1981 and 1986 figures based upon DS' own coverage estimates of respectively 56% and 65% leads to the following adjusted figures

	1975	1981	1988
DS-figures	7,762	7,093	14,630
		(56%)	(65%)
Corrected figures		12,666	22,500
		(100%)	(100%)

The corrected figure is still too low if we take the following factors into consideration. We assume 25,000 to be a not too optimistic estimate of the 1988 IT population.

There is a positive correlation between size of firm (the larger the organisation, the larger its administrative staff) and the employment of IT people, and thus we would expect the coverage of IT people to be above the average white-collar coverage, as the larger firms are the most stable data reporters to DS. On the other hand, DS' exclusion of small firms from the statistics also excludes quite a few IT people working in supplier or intermediary firms (consultants, software developers or free-lancers).

Another important comment to the basis of DS' statistics (that also applies to the other sources consulted) is that they are based upon job titles, as reported by the employers, and not upon standardised job functions. There may in many cases be a discrepancy between job functions and job titles. On a tight labour market, a job title on a level superior to the actual functions performed may be a means to give both symbolic and material rewards, in order to reduce labour turn-over. The job titles may also cover somewhat different functions depending on the size of the company or the EDP installation. Furthermore, IT people with other titles are excluded, even though they work within the job functions carried out by the occupational groups in focus. For instance, highly renumerated IT people may be registered under other job titles, such as chief consultant, of department head. To what extent this is the case, we are not able to sort out. But the information about wage levels we have obtained from interviews, indicates that the upper quartile wages from the official statistics are somewhat lower than we would expect.

To this must be added two trends, that also tend to make the statistical figures too low. One is that the "popularisation" of the IT technology has led to the creation of many jobs on the borderline between the IT community and the user community – for instance, users/planners that serve as change agents or go-betweens. IT has also become a part of many jobs – for instance, data registration in general has been integrated into user jobs (as is reflected in the important fall in the number of data entry operators), and many staff specialists utilise IT in their daily work or even develop their own systems by means of fourth generation tools. None of these two categories enter into the IT statistics.

Appendix C: Job Descriptions

The job descriptions given below (adapted from Computer Personnel Salary Survey, 1987) indicate the functions normally associated with the job titles.

EDP-manager (EDB-chef)
Responsible for day to day management of a single DP installation. Usually responsible for development and operations and has an advisory role in long term development plans.

Systems manager (EDB-systemchef)
Responsible to EDP-manager for all systems analysis activities. Would usually have systems consultants or senior systems analysts reporting to him/her.

Programming manager (EDB-programmeringschef)
Responsible to EDP-manager for all programming activities. Would usually have systems programmers or senior programmers reporting to him/her.

Systems consultant (System konsulent)
This category covers at least two different sets of functions
(a) *project leader*
   Responsible for all phases of design and implementation of assigned project(s). Usually has systems analysts, programmers or analyst/programmers working for him/her.

(b) *senior analyst/programmer*

Responsible for analysis, design and programming of assigned project(s) – often in collaboration with assigned analyst/programmers in relation to whom he/she may undertake some leadership functions.

Systems analyst (Systemplanlægger)

Normally responsible to a project leader (systems consultant) or the systems manager for assigned analysis tasks, but may work on a individual assignment such as a feasibility study or an evaluation exercise.

Systems programmer (Systemprogrammor)

Responsible to either programming manager or operations manager for the installation, modification and smooth functioning of systems software. Would normally work with (application) programmers, operations, hardware manufacturers and software suppliers. May assist in debugging of application programmes and the evaluation of new software.

Analyst/programmer (EDB-planlægger/programmor)

Responsible for analysis, design and programming in assigned section of a project. May have programmers reporting to him/her. Would report to systems consultant/leader.

Programmer (application programmer) (EDB-programmor)

Responsible for writing and testing programmes from a programme specification. Normally works under direction and guidance of a project leader, a senior programmer or an analyst/programmer.

Operations manager (EDB-driftschef)

Responsible to EDP-manager for all aspects of operations, production and control. May have responsibility for technical support in some installations, and thus have systems programmers, network specialists etc. reporting to him/her.

Operations planner (EDB-driftsplanlægger)

Responsible to operations manager for the effective programming of the computer and peripheral equipment operations. May develop and enforce operations standards.

Operator (EDB-operator)

Responsible for effective performance of assigned work in the computing room, "house keeping", setting up of peripheral units, and the monitoring of systems' performance.

Data entry supervisor (EDB-tasteoperatorleder)

Responsible to operations manager for all data entry activities. Assigns tasks to data entry operators and supervises these.

Data entry operator (EDB-tasteoperator)
Responsible to data entry supervisor for efficient and correct data conversion to a machine-readable media.

Appendix D: Statistical Tables

Table D:1   The Development of the IT-Population 1970–1988 (Private Sector)

	1970 Total	1973 Total	1975 Total	1981 Total	1982 Total	1983 Total	1984 Total	1985 Total	1986 Total	1987 Total	1988 Total
EDP-manager[1]	236	228	276	307	321	383	388	512	568	653	600
Systems manager	137	136	129	158	172	186	151	192	237	231	278
Programming manager	113	70	62	92	96	76	71	65	117	92	99
Systems consultant	*	*	*	463	617	818	1.145	1.161	1.961	2.483	3.104
Systems planner	702	593	676	1.204	1.562	1.324	1.200	1.347	1.511	1.391	1.236
Systems programmer[2]	*	324	441	506	594	703	745	920	1.001	1.296	1.278
Analyst/programmer[3]	*	*	*	*	81	782	926	1.027	1.284	1.433	1.935
Programmer	1.190	1.211	1.375	1.466	2.198	1.923	1.947	1.844	2.261	2.462	2.300
Analysis and programming	2.378	2.562	2.562	4.196	5.641	6.195	6.573	7.068	8.895	10.041	10.825
Operations manager	154	161	155	79	95	135	154	171	215	225	236
Operations planner	124	217	300	392	528	553	630	610	651	688	778
Operator[4]	1.032	1.135	1.260	1.162	1.789	1.862	1.897	1.847	2.114	2.043	1.998
Data entry supervisor	187	159	164	142	117	127	120	115	116	119	94
Data entry operator	2.283	1.948	2.087	1.122	908	869	894	858	875	736	699
Other[5]	567	621	837	–	–	–	–	–	–	–	–
Operations	4.347	4.241	4.803	2.897	3.437	3.546	3.695	3.601	3.971	3.811	3.805
Total	6.725	6.803	7.762	7.093	9.078	9.741	10.268	10.669	12.866	13.852	14.630

Table D:1 (cont.)   The Development of the IT-Population 1970-1988 (Private Sector)

The content of each job title is described in Appendix C.

* job category not listed in the statistics at that time.

[1] EDP-managers are in most cases responsible for both analysis and programming and 'operations' functions.

[2] In the actual organigrams, systems programmers often are placed within the 'operations department'.
   This table, however, is based upon a functional grouping of the personnel and not an organisational one.

[3] This group appeared in 1981 with 12 persons, but was only separated as a separate category in the DSstatistics from 1982 and onwards.

[4] This category includes the following job titles that have appeared in the statistics as indicated

	1970	1973	1975	1981	1986
Operator	x				
Machine operator		x	x	x	x
Shift supervisor		x	x		
Console operator				x	x
Operators assistant					x

[5] Technicians, who are not included from 1981 and onwards.

Table D:2 Percentage of Full Time Employees According to Gender and Age. 1986 (DS)

		Below 20	20-24	25-29	30-34	35-39	40-44	45-49	50-54	55-59	Above 60	Total
EDP-manager												
male	(493)	–	0.41	5.88	14.00	23.37	26.37	15.42	7.51	3.45	3.04	100
female	(75)	–	1.33	12.00	20.00	24.00	20.00	10.67	6.67	4.00	1.33	100
systems manager												
male	(224)	–	–	5.36	16.52	25.45	34.82	13.84	2.68	0.45	0.89	100
female	(13)	7.69	–	15.68	30.76	23.08	15.38	7.69	–	–	–	100
programming manager												
male	(117)	–	–	10.26	17.95	29.91	23.08	11.11	4.27	3.42	–	100
female	(0)	–	–	–	–	–	–	–	–	–	–	–
systems consultant												
male	(1558)	0.06	4.69	21.89	24.71	23.49	16.75	5.01	2.25	0.83	0.32	100
female	(358)	0.28	6.98	30.17	26.26	19.55	12.57	4.19	–	–	–	100
systems planner												
male	(1225)	0.08	2.86	17.80	26.78	23.27	18.29	6.94	2.37	1.14	0.49	100
female	(286)	0.35	3.50	28.67	30.77	22.03	9.79	3.50	1.05	0.35	–	100
systems programmer												
male	(904)	0.11	3.54	21.02	27.32	24.78	15.04	5.75	1.55	0.55	0.33	100
female	(97)	·	13.40	28.87	22.68	23.71	9.28	2.06	–	–	·	100
analyst/programmer												
male	(966)	0.62	13.35	26.92	26.09	17.49	11.70	2.28	0.93	0.52	0.10	100
female	(318)	–	24.21	39.30	20.44	10.06	5.03	0.63	0.31	–	–	100
programmer												
male	(1701)	1.00	22.87	31.45	19.58	11.35	9.00	2.23	1.83	0.29	0.41	100
female	(560)	1.07	30.18	37.32	19.82	7.14	3.21	0.89	0.18	0.18	–	100
Analysis and planning												
% of total (8.895)		0.39	0.74	24.28	23.28	19.07	14.11	4.92	1.98	0.78	0.45	100

Table D:2 (cont.) Percentage of Full Time Employees According to Gender and Age. 1986 (DS)

		Below 20	20-24	25-29	30-34	35-39	40-44	45-49	50-54	55-59	Above 60	Total
operations manager												
male	(195)	–	2.56	8.21	15.38	24.10	28.72	11.79	5.13	3.08	1.03	100
female	(20)	–	–	20.00	25.00	15.00	25.00	10.00	–	5.00	–	100
operations planner												
male	(545)	–	3.85	14.68	22.39	22.57	20.18	7.89	3.85	2.75	1.83	100
female	(106)	–	12.26	22.64	16.98	20.75	17.92	4.72	2.83	1.89	–	100
operator												
male	(1702)	1.00	14.75	22.97	21.39	15.57	12.16	5.05	2.64	2.47	2.00	100
female	(412)	2.18	23.79	26.70	15.29	11.41	11.89	4.85	2.43	0.97	0.49	100
data entry supervisor												
male	(29)	–	–	24.14	20.69	24.14	6.90	10.34	–	3.45	10.34	100
female	(87)	–	1.15	8.05	18.39	14.94	22.99	13.79	11.49	5.75	3.45	100
data entry operator												
male	(69)	1.45	27.54	36.23	14.49	2.90	8.70	1.45	1.45	4.35	1.45	100
female	(806)	0.62	12.16	17.01	16.50	18.11	15.88	8.68	6.45	3.40	1.24	100
Operations												
% of total	(3.971)	0.81	12.74	20.17	19.32	17.00	15.16	6.67	3.83	2.67	1.64	100
% of total	(12.866)	0.52	11.35	23.01	22.06	18.43	14.43	5.46	2.55	1.36	0.82	100
male		0.34	7.43	16.45	17.13	14.70	11.68	4.28	1.89	1.02	0.69	75.61
female		0.18	3.92	6.56	4.93	3.73	2.75	1.18	0.66	0.33	0.13	24.40

Table D:3 Average Monthly Income According to Age and Gender (DS/1986)

	20-24	25-29	30-34	35-39	40-44	45-49	50-54	55-59	60-	Average
EDP-manager										
male	–	22.014	23.402	25.975	26.977	26.460	24.703	23.728	18.683	25.303
female	–	16.628	15.813	16.846	16.175	16.316	–	–	–	16.244
systems manager										
male	–	22.827	23.745	27.174	27.133	26.393	–	–	–	26.217
female	–	–	–	–	–	–	–	–	–	–
programming manager										
male	–	22.765	21.554	26.485	26.710	23.232	–	–	–	24.485
female	–	–	–	–	–	–	–	–	–	–
systems consultant										
male	15.104	18.407	20.503	22.675	24.153	24.973	23.583	24.739	–	21.234
female	14.385	16.324	17.887	18.973	20.130	19.946	–	–	–	17.770
systems planner										
male	15.275	18.554	20.370	21.907	22.801	23.411	22.553	20.969	–	20.969
female	14.083	17.163	19.210	20.350	20.136	21.849	–	–	–	18.867
systems programmer										
male	15.836	19.344	21.591	23.193	23.562	23.435	23.662	–	–	21.742
female	15.001	18.009	20.423	23.405	23.131	–	–	–	–	19.992
analyst/programmer										
male	13.936	17.013	19.665	21.103	21.983	20.998	22.775	–	–	18.622
female	13.631	15.764	17.627	19.159	19.747	–	–	–	–	16.192
programmer										
male	13.768	16.984	18.547	19.511	20.360	20.005	18.818	–	–	17.208
female	13.295	15.606	16.632	17.498	17.400	–	–	–	–	15.330

Table D:3 (cont.) Average Monthly Income According to Age and Gender (DS/1986)

	20-24	25-29	30-34	35-39	40-44	45-49	50-54	55-59	60-	Average
operations manager										
male	–	18.491	21.840	24.374	24.164	23.571	23.969	–	–	22.890
female	–	–	–	–	–	–	–	–	–	–
operations planner										
male	13.843	17.023	18.146	19.162	19.463	18.035	17.544	17.216	15.682	18.207
female	14.403	15.241	16.148	16.465	16.883	–	–	–	–	15.971
operators										
male	12.873	14.627	15.973	15.837	16.418	15.589	16.018	14.538	14.903	17.208
female	12.200	13.345	14.605	14.690	14.023	–	–	–	–	15.330
data entry supervisors										
male	–	–	–	–	–	–	–	–	–	–
female	–	–	14.038	15.681	15.121	15.152	14.463	–	–	–
data entry operators										
male	12.063	13.648	16.472	–	–	–	–	–	–	14.196
female	11.045	11.967	2.008	12.260	12.359	12.649	12.281	12.800	12.884	12.079

Data and Methods of the Study

The strength of the arguments in this study does not rest on quantitative data, even though a *102 interviews* were conducted. The CHIPS research project has been relying primarily on qualitative data and methods, and secondarily on quantitative data and methods.

One of the challenges the qualitative researcher faces, is to show that he or she has not made up the results. Critics of qualitative research hold an image of qualitative research as "fuzzy" and "unscientific" (Jones, 1988). A problem therefore is to achieve credibility, trustworthiness and textual authority. According to Smircich (1983a, p. 165), the researcher is "scientific" in that the collection and reporting of data are done systematically, with care and discipline. This appendix is our attempt to make explicit the data of the study and what methods have been used to generate the data.

1   Approaching the Field

This study took place over a three year period, from September 1986 to October 1989, and the project has gone through several phases in approaching the subject matter.

First a pilot study was conducted in the form of a round of interviews with informants, many of whom were *'pioneers'* within the Danish IT-field. These informants provided general information about historical developments as well as the trends and 'state-of-the-art' within the *Danish IT field* today. Partly on the basis of these interviews and partly on the basis of other material – books, previous research, articles, etc., an overview of the Danish IT field was gradually developed. Based on this pilot study, trends and cases within the field that appeared to be interesting and significant, were selected for more focused studies. Significant cases refer to IT firms that seemed to be of importance for the understanding of the Danish IT-field (see chapters I and IV). For instance, cases were selected because of their size and dominance (e.g., IBM), age (e.g. 'pioneers' like RCI and Datacentralen), type (e.g. the software house 'Total' and the IT consultancy firm 'Advice'), unique representation of Danish characteristics (the IT unions, trade associations and the SMEs) or because they reflect a contemporary trend within the Danish IT field (the Unisys merger).

After having selected cases for more focused studies, a preliminary interview guide was constructed together with an observation guide. The interview guide was semi-structured, in the sense that it, on the one hand, used an open-ended format in the questions and, on the other hand, was structured and thematised in order to cover and capture the different themes and research questions of the participating researchers involved in the project. Consequently not all of the questions in the guide were equally relevant for all members of the research project. However, some information, which was initially thought not to be particularly relevant for one's 'own' specific study, later on proved to be quite useful. The first version of the interview guide was tested in practice, and adjusted and corrected according to the experiences we had using the guide during the first two or three interviews.

Based on these interviews some of the initially selected cases were left out, as they appeared to be less interesting than expected. Other cases were left out for more pragmatic reasons, such as, because we could not get access to the company at all or at the time we wanted.

2   Collecting Data in the Field

A round of interviews was arranged with the IT firms that were selected on the aforementioned terms. Access to the company was typically made through a contact person, who agreed to act as *'motivated insider'* (Schein, 1985). This resource person assisted in the selection of the informants, created the necessary contacts and paved our way in the organisation. The internal contact proved to be very helpful throughout this very long process, as this person, for example, also participated in discussions concerning results from the analyses of the data at a later stage of the research.

The next step in the process was to *select the informants* for the interviews. The criteria for selection were based partly on our general knowledge of the field, acquired through the first round of interviews with the 'pioneers' and from other material on the field (e.g., other studies, articles, etc.) and, partly on the specific information we had gained on the firm in question – typically from written material (articles and newsclippings) and a brief, unstructured interview with the resource person. The informants were then chosen on the basis of the following criteria:

– occupational position (e.g., IT or sales)
– hierarchical position (e.g., Manager or employee)
– departmental position
– seniority
– educational background
– gender

The relative weight put on each of the various criteria was balanced according to the particular case – in cooperation with the contact person – when selecting the informants. Apart from these more traditional sociological criteria, which aim at securing representativeness and reliability of the sample, another guiding principle for the selection of the informants was their *'information value'*, as suggested by Enderud (1987). The idea behind this principle is to maximise the information content of the sample, and is based on the idea of a '80-20 rule', that is to say, that 20% of the interview data in a given study, contains 80% of the information (Enderud, 1987, p. 146). 'Information value' was achieved by securing the following qualities of the informants: high level of information (e.g. cross-organizational overview, many contacts), ability to 'think' and reflect in organizational terms, capability to express him- or herself verbally, and willingness to participate in an open dialogue (Enderud, 1987, pp. 148-152).

This is an attempt to select a sort of *'elite respondent sample'* in order not to waste time on poorly formulated, unwilling, uninformed and non-reflective informants. This effort is also an attempt to trade quantity for quality and, an example of fighting one of the myths of organisational research, which Van Maanen has pointed out to be that, 'Organizational research reports are convincing because of their facticity', (Van Maanen, 1988, p. 6). It is likewise an attempt to reduce the likelihood that the interview will develop into one of many perverted forms of interviews like 'absurd theatre', 'examination', 'ritual of politeness', 'catharsis', 'poker game' or 'routine work' (Borum and Enderud, 1981).

One criticism that could be raised against our approach is that, if these considerations and criteria were the only ones guiding the selection of infor- mants, the sample was likely to get somewhat biased (you get the 'enlightened elite' and miss the 'silent majority'). However, the elite respondent criteria were counter-balanced by the other, more traditional criteria for selection. So first we selected informants from the perspective of representativeness, and then within this group we went for the 'elite respondents'.

Each of these *in-depth interviews* lasted approximately from an hour and a half to two hours, and were conducted by two interviewers, using the semi- structured interview guide with open-ended questions, described earlier. The prime interviewer was responsible for asking the questions and securing the flow of the interview, whereas the other person was responsible for taking notes and making sure that relevant information was not left out. This person occasionally asked questions, too, in order to make sure that an answer was correctly understood.

This procedure was chosen instead of using a tape recorder for similar reasons as Yin (1989) gives: people become uneasy speaking with it on, it is time-consuming to transcribe the tapes, the investigators are not 'technical wizards'- they 'fumble' with the equipment – and often tape recording becomes a substitute for listening closely throughout the interview.

After an interview the procedure was as follows. Notes from the interview were transcribed and handed over to the other interviewer, who would make corrections and additions to the text. The next step was to send the written interview to the interviewee in order to make corrections, in case some information was erroneously recorded, and to corroborate the information we had recorded (as suggested by several authors, Enderud, 1984; Schein, 1985 and Yin, 1989). This procedure actually proved to be quite useful as several facts, features and some numbers almost always were wrong one way or another. Another benefit from this procedure was that, after the interview, the informant often came to think of further information. This was added to the interview text. Finally, from a methodological viewpoint, the corrections made through this process are likely to enhance the accuracy of the case study, and thereby increase the construct validity of the study (Yin, 1989).

In this way, *a total of 102 in-depth interviews* were conducted.[1] Of this number of interviews, 76 in-depth interviews were carried out with organisational insiders in 24 case firms (see figure 1. in this appendix for the distribution of interviews by cases). Apart from these 76 in-depth interviews with organisational members, 26 in-depth interviews were conducted with informants from IT unions, trade associations, professional associations and the aforementioned 'pioneers' in the field. Finally, 7 telephone interviews were conducted as follow up to a survey of the trade associations.

A file on each case was established, which included interview reports as well as other written material (internal documents of various sorts, articles from journals, annual reports, case study notes, tabular materials, etc.). Thus, by creating *a case study data* base the documentation and reliability of the study were enhanced (Yin, 1989, p. 45).

Concerning the *question of case identity* (i.e., real or anonymous?) this issue can be raised at two levels, namely at case level and at individual level (Yin, 1989, pp. 142-143). The following arrangement was made concerning anonymity: All individuals were promised full anonymity and the process we set up for approval of the interview, as described above, aimed at securing the interviewees the option of correcting the information in the interviews. With regard to the case identity we also promised anonymity in general, and made the agreement with the companies involved that, if we wanted to publish something using their real identity, they should approve of the material in question before

	Interviews	Special Surveys	Other Data Sources
The IT Field	6 interviews with 8 pioneers	Survey of 328 IT people in 13 companies	All available statistics on the Danish IT field (IT people and IT firms)
IT Institutions			
a) Unions	6 interviews in 3 unions		Participation in PROSA Conference
b) Trade ass.	10 interviews in 6 trade ass.	Survey on 70 trade ass. + telephone interviews	
c) Prof. ass.	4 interviews in 2 prof. ass.		
International Suppliers	14 interviews in 3 int. supl.		Participant observation one week in an int. supl.
Danish Suppliers	25 interviews in 9 Dan. supl.		
Large Service Bureaux	27 interviews in 2 LSBs		participation in internal seminars
Small Users	10 interviews in 10 SMEs	7 telephone interviews in 6 SMEs	

Figure 1   Overview of Sources of Data for the Study

publication. Thus, individuals are anonymous, but most of the case identities are revealed.

3   Data from the Field

As stated earlier, this study relies primarily on qualitative methods and, *multiple sources of data* have been gathered (figure 1 gives an overview and the various sources of data are summarised). The use of multiple sources of evidence in a case study is one way of producing more convincing and accurate conclusions (Yin, 1989).

The main source of evidence for this study has been the interview data (cf. figure 1.). However, this is not the only source of data for the analyses. During our field visits we collected other data material like *archival material* (written reports, internal documents, news-clippings, company journals, etc.). We also conducted *direct observation* (noting the condition of buildings and work

1986	1987	1988	1989
Document analysis Literature search	Informant Interviews Case studies Interim report	Expanded analysis Statistical analysis Survey Network analysis Final analysis	Final report

Figure 2   Overview of the Main Phases in the Project

spaces, the reception of outsiders, physical artifacts, etc.) using an observation guide.

To supplement this data two quantitative studies were also conducted. One survey was made of 328 IT people in 13 IT firms. The sample consisted of 7 internal IT departments, 3 IT suppliers (hardware as well as software) and 3 service bureaus. In total 670 individuals were employed in these companies and 534 questionnaires were distributed as only IT people (software developers) were included. 347 IT people responded, but only 328 were valid responses. For more details on this survey, see Antonsen and Strandgaard Pedersen (1988) and chapter XII by Borum and Risberg in this reader.

Another quantitative study has been made of the trade associations and their role as mediators in relation to the introduction of IT in their member organisations. A questionnaire was sent out to all trade associations in Denmark, in total 150. 70 trade associations responded to the questionnaire and 60 responses were valid. Interviews were conducted with 6 informants in 5 trade associations and additional telephone interviews were made to follow up on the results. For more details on this study, see chapter VII by Mette Monsted and Frans Boch in this reader.

Finally, all available sources of statistics on the Danish IT field (concerned with IT people as well as IT organisations) have been gathered, sorted and analysed. The results from this work are presented in chapter XII by Borum and Risberg in this reader.

These main sources of evidence – in-depth interviews, archival material, observation, surveys and statistics – all contributed as input to the analyses of the study. In figure 2 the main phases of the project are depicted.

The general approach of the study consisted of a "peddling" between theoretical considerations, data collection and data analysis. This "peddling" meant that certain phases were devoted to data collection in the field. Data were analysed subsequently and this gave rise to phases devoted to adjustments of existing theoretical considerations. This in turn required that we returned to the field and new data were collected and analysed. Through this "peddling" between data and theory, the focus of the project was intensified, the analyses were currently adjusted and, data were currently up-dated.

Notes

1   Three of our informants have been counted twice owing to the dual nature of the information they provided ('pioneers' and cases). Some informants have been interviewed twice and during some interviews two persons were interviewed. The number of individuals interviewed amounts to exactly a hundred.

References

Alba, R.D. (1973): 'A graph-theoretic definition of a sociometric clique'. *Journal of Mathematical Sociology*. Vol. 3.

Aldrich, Howard (1971): 'Organizational boundaries and inter organizational conflicts'. In: *Human Relations*. Vol. 24, p. 279-293.

Alvesson, M. and P.O. Berg (1988): *Företagskultur och organisationssymbolism – utveckling, teoretiska perspektiv och aktuell debatt*. Lund: Studentlitteratur.

Andersson, G. (1979): *Samverkan mellem småföretag. En fallstudie av inledningsskedet i en samverkansproces*. Lund: Studenterlitteratur.

Antonsen, H. and J. Strandgaard Pedersen (1988): 'Computer specialists – a survey'. CHIPS Working Paper. Copenhagen.

Argyris, C. and D.A. Schoen (1978): *Organizational learning: a theory of action perspective*. Reading Mass.: Addison-Wesley.

ASQ (1983): 'Special issue: organizational culture'. In: *Administrative Science Quarterly*. Vol 28. No. 3. p. 331-496.

Athos, A.G. and R.T. Pascale (1982): *The Art of Japanese management: applications for American executives*. New York: Warner Books.

Babbage, C. (1832): *On the Economy of Machinery and Manufactures*. London.

Bain, G.S. (1970): *The growth of white collar unionism*. Oxford: Clarendon Press.

Bain, G.S. and F. Elsheikh (1976): *Union growth and the business cycle*. Oxford: Blackwell.

Barley, S.R. (1987): 'Technology, power and the social organization of work: towards a pragmatic theory of skilling and deskilling'. In: S. Bacharach and N. DiTomaso (eds): *Research in the Sociology of Organizations*. Vol.6. Greenwich, CN: Jai Press.

Berg, P.O. and K. Kreiner (1987): 'Corporate architecture: turning physical settings into symbolic ressources'. Conference Paper, 3rd international SCOS conference. Milano.

Berger, P.L. and T. Luckmann (1966): *The Social Construction of Reality*. New York: Doubleday and Company, Inc.

Beyer, J.M. and H.M. Trice (1987): 'How an Organization's Rites Reveal Its Culture'. In: *Organizational Dynamics*. Spring. p. 5-24. American Management Association.

Bjorn-Andersen, N.with F. Borum, M. Broch, B. Due-Thomsen, A.L. Friedman, O. Kudsk, M. Mønsted, J. Strandgaard Pedersen and M. Risberg (1988): 'Labour market for information technology professionals in Denmark'. EPOS Thematic Report. Copenhagen Business School.

Blum, A.A. and A. Ponak (1974:) 'White collar unions in Denmark'. In: *Industrial Relations*, Vol. 29. No. 1, p. 65-82.

Boch, F. (1989): 'Trade associations as mediators of technological adaptation. An empirical study of the strategies pursued by Danish trade associations and a case study of the decision process which led to the formation of a unique strategy'. Thesis. Copenhagen Business School.

Bødker, K. and J. Strandgaard Pedersen (1991): 'Workplace cultures: looking at artifacts, symbols and practices'. In: Greenbaum and Kyng (eds): *Design at Work*. Lawrence Erlbaum Association Inc. Publication. p. 121-136.

Boguslaw, R. (1965): *The new utopians*. Englewood Cliffs: Prentice Hall.

Borum, F. (1980): 'Systems design and scientific management'. In: *Acta Sociologica*, Vol. 23. No. 4, p. 287-296.

Borum, F. (eds) (1977): *Edb, arbejdsmiljo og virksomhedsdemokrati*. Copenhagen: Nyt fra Samfundsvidenskaberne.

Borum, F. and H. Enderud (1981): *Konflikter i Organisationer – Belyst ved studier af EDB-systemarbejde*. Copenhagen: Nyt Nordisk Forlag.

Borum, F., A. Friedman, M. Monsted, J. Strandgaard Pedersen and M. Risberg (1989): *The information systems field – the structuring of experts and expertise*. Copenhagen Business School, Institute of Organization and Industrial Sociology. Copenhagen.

Borum, F. and J. Strandgaard Pedersen (1990): 'Understanding the IT People, their subcultures, and the implications for management of technology'. In: Borum and Hull-Kristensen (eds): *Technological innovation and organizational change*. New Social Science Monographs. Copenhagen. p. 219-248.

Bourdieu, P. (1984): *Questions de Sociologie. Paris. Les Editions de Minuit*.

Bourdieu, P. and J.C.Passeron (1970): *La Reproduction. Elément pour une théorie du système d'enseignement*. Paris. Les Editions de Minuit.

Brandon D.H. (1970): 'The economics of computer programming'. In: G.F. Weinwurm eds. *On the management of computer programming*. New York: Auerbach, p. 3-16.

Brandon D.H. (1963): *Management standards for data processing*. New York: Van Nostrand Reinhold.

Braverman H. (1974): *Labor and monopoly capital*, New York: Monthly Review Press.

Breiger, R.L. (1976): 'Career attributes and network structures: a blockmodel study of a biomedical research speciality'. In: *American Sociological Review*. Vol. 41.

Breiger, R.L. (1981): 'Structures of economic interdependence among nations'. In: P.M. Blau and R.K. Merton (eds): *Continuities in structural inquiry*. Beverly Hills, California, Sage.

Brooks F.P. (1975): *The mythical man-month, essays on software engineering*, Reading, Mass: Addison-Wesley.

Brunsson, N. (1986): 'Organizing for inconsistencies: on organizational conflict, depression and hypocrisy as substitutes for action'. In: *Scandinavian Journal of Management Studies*.May. p. 165-185.

Brunsson, N. (1985): *The irrational organization*. Chichester: John Wiley.

Brunsson, N. (1982): 'The irrationality of action and action rationality: Decisions, ideologies, and organizational actions'. In: *Journal of Management Studies*, Vol: 19. No. 1, p. 29-44.

Burt, R.S. (1980): 'Cooperative corporate actor networks: a reconsideration of interlocking directorates involving American manufacturing'. In: *Administrative Science Quarterly*. Vol. 25.

Canning R.G. and R.L. Sisson (1960): *The management of data processing*. New York: Wiley.

Child, J. (1988): 'On Organizations in Their Sectors'. In: *Organization Studies*.

Child, J. (1987): 'Managerial strategies, new technology and the labour process'. In D. Knights et al. (eds) *Job redesign: organization and control of the labour process*. London: Heinemann.

Child, J., R. Loveridge, J. Harvey, and A. Spencer (1984): 'Microelectronics and the quality of employment in services'. In: Pauline Marstrand (ed.): *New technology and the future of work and skills*. London: Frances Pinter. p. 163-190

Christensen, S. and J. Molin (1983): *Organisationskulturer*. Copenhagen: Akademisk Forlag.

Christensen, S. and K. Kreiner (1984): 'On the origin of organizational cultures'. Paper prepared for The First International Conference on Organizational Symbolism and Corporate Culture. Copenhagen: Institute of Organization and Industrial Sociology.

Christiansen, J. (1988): 'Implementering og pervertering af projektstyringssystemer'. Ph.D. Thesis. Copenhagen Business School. Institute of Informatics and Management Accounting.

Clark, B.R. (1972): 'The organizational saga in higher education'. In: *Administrative Science Quarterly*. Vol. 17, No. 2. p. 178-184.

Cohen, M.D. and J.G. March (1974): *Leadership and Ambiguity*. New York: McGraw Hill.

Collinson, D.L. (1988): 'Engineering humour: masculinity, joking and conflict in shop-floor relations'. In: *Organization Studies*. Vol. 9, No. 2. p. 181-199.

Commission of the European Communities. (1986): Directorate General for Employment, Social Affairs and Education: The software industry. In: Social Europe, supplement 6/86.

Computer Economics (1972): *The Economics of Computing*, London: Computer Economics.

Computer Personnel Salary Survey. Computer Economics Ltd, October 1987. London

Couger, J.D. (1988): 'Motivating is personnel'. In: *Datamation*. p. 59-64.

Couger, J.D. and R.A. Zawacki (1980): *Motivating and managing computer personnel*. New York: Wiley.

Cronin, J.E. (1979): *Industrial conflict in modern Britain*. London: Croom Helm.

Cyert, R.M. and J.G. March (1963): *A behavioral theory of the firm*. Englewood Cliffs, N.J.: Prentice-Hall.

Dahlgreen, G. and P. Witt (1988): *Ledning af fusions förlopp – en analys av bildandet av Ericsson Informations System AB*. Stockholm: EFI, Economiska Forskningsinstituttet.

Dale, A. (1976): 'Adaptive capacities in human systems'. Mimeo, Institute of Organisation and Social Studies. United Kingdom: Brunel University.

Deal, T.E. and A.A. Kennedy (1982): *Corporate cultures*. Reading. Mass: Addison-Wesley.

Dyer, W.G.jr. (1982): 'Culture in organizations: a case-study and analysis'. Working Paper. Massachusetts Institute of Technology, (MIT).

EDB-Rådet (1975): *EDB-rådets hvidbog. Status for edb-sektoren 1974 – et debatoplæg*. Bind 1-4. Copenhagen: Edb-Rådet.

Ehn, P. and Å. Sandberg (1979): *Företagsstyring och löntagarmakt*. Falköping: Prisme.

Enderud, H. (1984): Konflikter i de mintzbergske strukturformer. In: E. Enderud and H. Roed-Thorsen (eds): *Artikler til organisationsteori*. Vol. II. Samfundslitteratur. Copenhagen.

Enderud, H. (1987): Dataindsamling i organisationssociologien: en note om informationsorienteret respondent-udvælgelse. In: Broch et al (eds): *Kvalitative metoder i dansk samfundsforskning*. Nyt fra Samfundsvidenskaberne. Copenhagen.

Färnström, B.O. and C. Kedström (1975): *Makt och beroende i samarbetsrelationer. En studie av mindre och medelstora underleverandörsföretag*. Lund: Ekonomisk Forskning.

Fama, E.F. and M.C. Jensen (1983): 'Separation of ownership and control'. In: *Journal of Law and Economics*. Vol. 26.

Foy, N. (1974): *The IBM World*. Wyre Methuen.

Freeman, R.B. (1981): 'Individual mobility and union voice in the labor market'. In: *American Economic Review*. Vol. 66.

Friedman A.L. (1977): *Industry and labour*. London: Macmillan.

Friedman, A.L. (1986): 'Defending the managerial strategies approach to the labour process'. In: *Capital and Class*. Vol. 30. p. 97-124.

Friedman, A.L. (1987): 'The means of management control and labour process theory: a critical note on storey'. In: *Sociology*. May, p. 287-294.

Friedman, A.L. (1990): 'Four phases of IT – and their implications for forecasting IT work'. *Futures*. pp. 787-800.

Friedman, A.L. and D.S. Cornford (1981): *The pursuit of productivity in U.K. data processing installations*. Bristol: WOC.

Friedman A.L. and D.S. Cornford (1984): 'Choosing an installation as a base for a dp career'. In: *Computing*. June.

Friedman, A.L. and D.S. Cornford (1987): 'Strategies for meeting user demands: an international perspective'. In: *International Journal of Information Management*, No. 7. p. 3-20.

Friedman A.L. with D.S. Cornford (1990): *Computer systems development: history, organisation, and implementation*. London: Wiley.

Friedman A.L. and J. Greenbaum (1984): 'Wanted renaissance people'. In: *Datamation*. September. p. 134-144.

Friedman, A.L., J. Greenbaum and M. Jacobs (1984): 'The challenge of users and unions'. In: *Datamation*, September 15, p. 93-100.

Friedman, A.L., J. Horlück, B. Reiswijck and H. Regtering (1988): *Work organization and industrial relations in data processing departments: a comparative study of the United Kingdom, Denmark and the Netherlands*. Brussels: EEC.

Frost, P. et al. (1985): *Organizational culture*. Beverly Hills: CA. Sage Publications.

Gagliardi, P. (1986): 'The creation and change of organizational cultures: a conceptual framework'. In: *Organization Studies*. Vol. 7. No.2. p. 117-134.

Gagliardi, P. (eds) (1990): *Symbols and artifacts: views of the corporate landscape*. Berlin; New York: De Gruyter.

Galanter, M. (1981): 'Justice in many rooms: courts, private ordering, and indigenous law'. In: *Journal of Legal Pluralism*. No. 19.

Galaskiewicz, J. (1979): *Exchange Networks and Community Politics*. Beverly Hills, CA.: Sage.

Gospel, H.F. (1983): 'Trade unions and the legal obligation to bargain'. In: *British Journal of Industrial Relations*. Vol. 21. No. 3.

Greenbaum, J. (1976): 'Division of labour in the computer field'. In: *Monthly Review*. Vol. 28. No. 3.

Greenbaum J. (1979): *In the name of efficiency*. Philadelphia: Temple University Press.

Gregory, K. (1983): 'Native view paradigms: multiple cultures and culture conflicts in organizations'. In: *Administrative Science Quarterly*. Vol. 28. No. 3. p. 359-376.

Gregory, K. (1984): 'Discovering multiple organization cultures and culture conflicts using native-view paradigms'. In: *The Study of Organizational Cultures*. NUPEPP Occasional Papers No. 22. Northwestern University, Dept. of Anthropology. p. 1-13.

Hägg, I. and J. Johanson (eds) (1982): *Företag i nätverk*. Stockholm: Studieförbundet Näringsliv och Samhälle. 1982.

Hallinan, M. (1979): 'Structural effects on children's friendship and cliques'. In: *Social Psychology Quarterly*. Vol. 42. March.

Hannan, M.T. and J. Freeman (1987): 'The ecology of organizational founding: American labor unions, 1836- 1985'. In: *American Journal of Sociology*. Vol. 92. No. 4.

Hatch, M.J. (1991): 'The Danamics of Organizational Culture'.In: *Papers in Organization*. No. 4. Institute of Organization and Industrial Sociology. Copenhagen: Copenhagen Business School. p. 129-146.

Hatch, M.J. (1987): 'Physical barriers, task characteristics, and interaction activity in research and development firms'. In: *Administrative Science Quarterly*. Vol. 32. p. 387-399.

Hatch, M.J. and Sanford B. Ehrlich (1991): Spontaneous Humor as an Indicator of Paradoc and Ambiguity in Organizations. Paper presented at the 8th SCOS Conference, June. Copenhagen.

Hebden, S.E. (1975): 'Patterns of work identification'. In: *Sociology of Work and Occupations*. p. 107-132.

Hingel, A.J. (1985): Software and Social Change in Denmark. Working Paper. Institute of Organization and Industrial Sociology. Copenhagen Business School. Copenhagen.

Hingel, A.J. (1986): 'Social change in the software and computer service industry'. In: *Social Europe*. Supplement 6/86. Brussels: Commission of the European Community.

Hingel, A.J. (1988): 'The computerization of public administration'. In: *Social Europe*. Supplement 4/88. Brussels: Commission of the European Communities.

Hirsch, P.M. and J.A.Y. Andrews (1983): 'Ambushes Shootouts, and Knights f the Round Table: The Language of Corporate Takeovers'. In: Pody et al (eds): *Organizational Symblism*. Greenwich, CT: JAI Press. p. 145-156.

Hirschman, A.O. (1970): *Exit, voice and loyalty: responses to decline in firms, organizations and states*. Cambridge, Mass.: Harvard University Press.

Hofer, C.W. and D. Schendel (1978): *Strategy Formulation: Analytical Concepts*. St. Paul; MN West Publishing.

Hofstede, G. (1980): *Culture's Consequences: International differences in work-related values*. London: Sage Publications.

Håkansson H. (ed) (1982): *International marketing and purchasing of industrial goods: an interaction approach*. Chichester: Wiley.

Jernets Arbejdsgiverforening (1984): *Behovsanalyse blandt mindre virksomheder vedrorende informationsteknologi*. Copenhagen: Jernets Arbejdsgiverforening.

Johannisson, B. (1987): 'Beyond process and structure – social exchange networks'. In: *International Studies of Management and Organization*, Vol. XVII. No. 1.

Johanson, J. and L. Mattsson (1987): 'Interorganizational relations in industrial systems – a network approach compared with the transaction-cost approach'. In: *International Studies of Management and Organization*. Vol. XVII. No. 1.

Jones, M.O. (1988): 'In Search of Meaning: Using Qualitative Methods in Research and Application'. In: Jones, Moore and Snyder (eds): *Inside Organizations – Understanding the Human Dimension*. California: Sage Publications.

Jørgensen, T. Beck (1977): *Samspil og konflikter mellem organisationer*. Copenhagen: New Science Monographs.

Juhl, H. and O. Engberg (1985): *Politikens EDB-bog*. Copenhagen: Politikens Forlag.

Kidder, T. (1977): *The Soul of a New Machine*. Boston: Brown, Little.

Kilmann, R.H., M.J. Saxton and R. Serpa (1986): 'Issues in understanding and changing culture'. In: *California Management Review*, Vol. 28. No. 2. p. 87-94. University of California.

Kjellberg, A. (1983): *Facklig organisering i tolv lander*. Lund: Arkiv Forlag.

Kluckhohn, F.R. and F.L. Strodtbeck (1961): *Variations in Value Orientations*. New York: Harper and Row.

Kochan, T.A., R.B. McKersie and P. Cappelli (1984): 'Strategic choice and industrial relations theory'. In: *Industrial Relations.* Vol. 23. No. 1. p. 16-39.

Kraft P. (1977): *Programmers and managers: the routinization of computer programming in the United States.* New York: Springer-Verlag.

Kraft P. and S. Dubnoff (1986): 'Job content, fragmentation, and control in computer software work'. In: *Industrial Relations. Vol. 25.* No. 2., 184-196.

Kristensen, P. Hull (1986): *Teknologiske projekter og organisatoriske processer.* Roskilde: Forlaget Samfundsokonomi og Planlægning.

Kuhn, T.S. (1970): *The structure of scientific revolutions.* Second edition. Chicago: University of Chicago.

Kunda, G. (1991): *Ritual and the Management of Corporate Culture – A Critical Perspective.* Paper presented at the 8th International SCOS Conference, Copenhagen, June 26th – 28th, 1991.

Lakatos, I. and A. Musgrave (eds) (1972): *Criticism and growth of knowledge.* United Kingdom: Cambridge University Press.

Lancaster, K. (1966): 'A new approach to consumer theory'. In: *Journal of Political Economy.* Vol. 74. p. 132-56.

Larsen, J. and M. Schultz (1984): *Bureaukrati og videnskab – organisationskulturer i centraladministrationen.* Kobenhavn: Politiske Studier.

Larsen, J.K. and E.M. Rogers (1984): *Silicon Valley fever: growth of high technology culture.* Basic Books.

Lawrence, P.R. and J.W. Lorsch (1967): *Organization and environment: Managing integration and differentiation.* Boston: Harvard University.

Levitt, B. and J.G. March (1988): 'Organizational learning'. February 1988 version of paper prepared for *Annual Review of Sociology.* Stanford University.

Lewin, K. (1952): In D. Cartwright (ed): *Field Theory in Social Science: Selected Theoretical Papers.* London. Tavistock.

Lincoln, J.R. and J. Miller (1979): 'Work and friendship ties in organizations: a comparative analysis of relation networks'. In: *Administrative Science Quarterly.* Vol. 24. No. 3.

Lockwood, D. (1966): 'Sources of variation in working-class images and society'. In: *Sociological Review.* Vo. 14. p. 249-67.

Lorrain, J. (1979): *Concept of ideology.* United Kingdom: Hutchinson and Co.

Louis, M.R. (1983): 'Organizations as culture-bearing milieux'. In Pondy, Frost, Morgan and Dandridge (eds): *Organizational symbolism.* Greenwich: JAI Press. p. 39-54

Louis, M.R. (1985): 'An investigator's guide to workplace culture.' In: Frost et.al. (eds): *Organizational Culture.* Beverly Hills: Sage. p. 83-93.

Lundberg, C.C. (1985): 'On the feasibility of cultural intervention in organizations'. In: Frost et al. (eds): *Organizational Culture.* Beverly Hills: Sage Publications. p. 169-195.

Lutz, B. (1982): 'Social endogeny of technical progress and the question of human labour'. In: O. Diettrich and J. Morley (eds): *Relations between technology, capital and labour.* Brussels: EEC.

Lysgaard, S. (1961): *Arbejderkollektivet.* Oslo: Universitetsforlaget.

Macneil, I.R. (1978): 'Contracts: adjustments of long-term economic relations under classical, neo-classical, and relational contract law'. In: *Northwestern University Law Review,* Vol. 72. p. 854-906.

March, J.G. (1981): 'Footnotes to Organizational Change'. In: *Administrative Science Quarterly.* Vol 26. No. 26. p. 563-577.

March, J.G. and H.A. Simon (1966): *Organizations*. New York: Wiley.

March, J.G. and J.P. Olsen (1976): *Ambiguity and choice in organizations*. Oslo: Universitetsforlaget.

Marks, M.L. and P.H. Mirvis (1986): 'The merger syndrome', Psychology Today October. In: *American Psychological Association*. October. p. 42-47.

Markus, M.L. (1983): 'Power politics and MIS implementation'. In: *Communications of the ACM*. Vol. 26. p. 430-444.

Martin, J. and C. Siehl (1983): 'Organizational culture and counter culture: an uneasy symbiosis'. In: *Organizational dynamics. American Management Association*. Autumn. p. 52-64.

Martin, J. and D. Meyerson (1988): 'Organizational cultures and the denial, channelling and acknowledgment of ambiguity'. In: Pondy, Boland and Thomas (eds): *Managing ambiguity and change*. New York: Wiley. p. 93-125.

Martin, J. (1988): 'Symbolic responses to layoffs in a software firm – managing the meaning of an event'. In: Jones et al.(eds): *Inside Organizations – Understanding the Human Dimension*. Sage. p. 209-225.

Martin, J., M.S. Feldman, M.J. Hatch and S.B. Sitkin (1983): 'The uniqueness paradox in organizational studies'. In: *Administrative Science Quarterly*. Vol. 28. No. 3. p. 438-453.

Martin, J., S. Sitkin and M. Boehm (1985): 'Founders and the elusiveness of a cultural legacy'. In: Frost et al. (eds): *Organizational Culture*. Sage. p. 99-124.

Maurice, M, F. Sellier and J.J. Silvestre (1982): *Politique d'éducation et organisation industrielle en France et en Allemagne*. Paris. Presses Universitaires de France.

McGregor, D. (1960): *The Human Side of Enterprise*. New York: Mcgraw-Hill.

McNichols, T.J. (1983): *Policy-Making and Executive Action*. New York: Mcgraw-Hill

Meek, V. Lynn (1988): 'Organizational culture: origins and weaknesses'. In: *Organization Studies*. Vol. 9. No. 4. p. 453-473.

Meyer, J.W. and B. Rowan (1977): 'Institutional organizations: formal structure as myth and ceremony'. In: *American Journal of Sociology*. Vol. 83. No. 2. p. 340-363.

Meyer, J.W. and W.R. Scott (1983): *Organizational environments – ritual and rationality*. Beverly Hills: California.

Meyerson, D. and J. Martin (1987): 'Cultural change: an integration of three different views'. In: *Journal of Management Studies*. Vol. 24. No. 6. p. 623-647.

Miles, R.E. and C.C. Snow (1978): *Organization strategy, structure and process*. New York: McGraw- Hill.

Mintzberg, H. (1987): 'The strategy concept I: Five Ps for strategy'. In: Carroll G.R. and Vogel, D. (eds): *Organizational Approaches to Strategy*. Cambridge Mass.: Balinger.

Mintzberg, H. (1979): *The structuring of organizations*. Englewood Cliffs: Prentice-Hall.

Molin, J. (1987): *Beyond structure and rationality*. Copenhagen: Akademisk Forlag.

Monopoltilsynet (1988): *Markedet for databehandlingsudstyr*. Redegorelse fra Monopoltilsynet. Copenhagen.

Mønsted, M. (1985): *Små virksomheder i rådgivningssystemet*. Copenhagen: Nyt Fra Samfundsvidenskaberne.

Mønsted, M. (1987): *Flexibility and growth in small manufacturing enterprises – the case of Denmark*. Copenhagen School of Economics, the Entrepreneurship Group.

Mønsted, M. (1990): 'Skills and overview in SMEs'. Recontres de St. Gallen.

Mønsted, M. and P. Neergaard (1986): 'EDB i mindre virksomheder'. In: P.Neergaard (ed): *Okonomisk styring i mindre virksomheder*. Copenhagen: Civilokonomisk Forlag.

Mønsted, M. and M. Risberg (1989): 'Små virksomheder og edb-service'. In: E. Maaloe and N. Thorsen (eds): *Teknologiens muligheder – og menneskets.* Copenhagen: Industri- og Handelsstyrelsen.

Morgan, G. (1986): *Images of organization.* Beverly Hills: Sage.

Mueller, R.K. (1986): *Corporate networking: building channels for information and influence.* London: Macmillan.

Mumford, E. (1972): *Job satisfaction: a study of computer specialists.* London: Longman.

Nahavandi, A. and A.R. Malekzadeh (1988): 'Acculturation in mergers and acquisitions'. In: *Academy of Management Review.* Vol. 13. No. 1. p. 79-90.

Napier, N.K. (1989): Mergers and Acquisitions, Human Resource Issues and Outcomes: A Review and Suggested Typology. *Journal of Management Studies.* Vol. 26. No. 3.

Neergaard, P. (1989): *Microcomputers in small companies. Benefits achieved and problems encountered.* Mimeo, Institute of Informatics and Economic Management, Copenhagen Business School, Copenhagen.

Nolan, R. (1973): 'Plight of the EDP manager'. *Harvard Business Review,* May-June. p. 143-152.

Noorderhaven, N.G. (1987): 'Contractual relations and the interorganizational quest for control'. Paper presented at the 8th European Group for Organization Studies Colloquium. Antwerp, Belgium.

OECD (1985): *Software: An emerging industry.* Paris.

Organization Studies (1986): 'Special issue on organizational symbolism'. Vol. 7. No. 2.

Orton, J.D. and K.E. Weick (1990): 'Loosely Coupled Systems. A Reconceptualization'. In: *Academy of Management Review.* Vol 15. No. 2. p. 203-223.

Osterman P. (1984): *Internal labor markets.* Cambridge Mass: MIT Press.

Osterman P. (1987): 'Choice of employment systems in internal labor markets'. In: *Industrial Relations.* Vol. 26. No. 1. p. 46-67.

Ouchi, W.G. (1980): 'Markets, bureaucracies, and clans'. In: *Administrative Science Quarterly.* Vol. 25. pp. 129-141.

Ouchi, W.H. (1981): *Theory Z: How American Business Can Meet the Japanese Challenge.* Addison-Wesley.

Pascale, R. and A. Athos (1981): *The art of Japanese management.* New York: Warner Books.

Pedersen, J. Strandgaard (1991): *Continuity and change – cultural perspectives on organizational change and transformation in information technology firms.* Ph.D. Thesis, Copenhagen: Samfundslitteratur.

Pedersen, J. Strandgaard and J.S. Sorensen (1989): *Organizational cultures in theory and practice.* Aldershot. Avebury: Gower.

Pedersen, P.J. (1978): 'Union growth and the business cycle: a note on the Bain- Elsheikh Model'. In: *British Journal of Industrial Relations,* Vol. 16. p. 373- 377.

Peters, T.J. and R.H. Waterman (1982): *In search of excellence.* New York: Harper and Row.

Pettigrew, A.M. (1973): *The politics of organizational decision-making.* London: Tavistock.

Pettigrew, A.M. (1979): 'On studying organizational cultures'. In: *Administrative Science Quarterly,* Vol. 24. p. 570-581.

Pfeffer, J. (1981): 'Management as symbolic action: the creation and maintenance of organizational paradigms'. In: B. Staw and L.Cummings (eds): *Research in organizational behavior.* Vol. 3. p. 1.52. Greenwich, CT: JAI Press.

Pfeffer, J. and G. R. Salancik (1978): *The external control of organizations. A resource dependence view.* New York 1978: Harper and Row.

Poole M. (1980): 'Managerial strategies and industrial relations'. In: M. Poole and R. Mansfiels (eds): *Managerial roles in industrial relations*. Farnborough: Gower.

Poole M. (1986): *Industrial relations: origins and patterns of national diversity*. London: Routledge and Kegan Paul.

Prosa (1986): EDB-fagets fremtid. Michael Lund-Larsen: *Edb-branchens struktur og kvalifikationer*, p. 59-66. Copenhagen: Forlaget Probog.

Reynolds C.H. (1970): 'What's wrong with computer programming management?' In: G.F. Weinwurm (eds): *On the management of computer programming*. New York: Auerbach. p. 35-42.

Ritzer, G. (1975): *Sociology – a multiple paradigm science*. Massachusetts: Allyn and Bacon.

Robbins, S.P. (1988): *Essentials of organizational behavior*. Englewood Cliffs, N.J.: Prentice-Hall.

Rogers, E. (1962): *Diffusion of innovation*. 2nd revised edition. Free Press. London.

Rogers, E. and F.F. Shoemaker (1971): *Communication of innovations. A cross cultural approach*. 2nd edition, Free Press. London.

Rose M. and B. Jones (1985): 'Management strategy and trade union response in plantlevel reorganization of work'. In: D. Knights et al. (eds): *Job redesign: organisation and control of the labour process*. London: Heinemann.

Salaman, G. (1974): *Community and occupation. An exploration of work/leisure relationships*. Cambridge: Cambridge University Press.

Sales, A. and P.H. Mirvis (1984): 'When cultures collide: issues in acquisition'. In: Kimberley and Quinn: *Managing organizational transitions*. Homewood, Illinois: Irwin. p. 107-133.

SAMDATA (1988): *SAMDATA's job analysis for June, 1988*. Copenhagen: SAMDATA.

Schein, E.H. (1983): 'The role of the founder in creating organizational culture'. Organizational Dynamics. Summer. pp. 13-28. *American Management Association*. Summer. p. 13-28.

Schein, E.H. (1985): *Organizational culture and leadership. A dynamic view*. San Francisco: Jossey-Bass.

Scheuer S. (1984): 'The impact of unemployment on union density in Denmark'. Mimeo, Copenhagen School of Economics and Social Science.

Scheuer, S. (1988): 'Udviklingstræk i strukturen i de faglige organisationers medlemstilslutning'. Working Paper. Copenhagen: Institute of Organization and Industrial Sociology.

Schultz, M. (1990): *Kultur i organisationer: funktion eller symbol*. Copenhagen: Nyt Nordisk Forlag.

Scott, J. (1988): 'Social network analysis'. In: *Sociology*, Vol. 4. p. 109-127.

Scott, R.W. (1981): *Organizations: Rational, Natural and Open Systems*. Englewood Cliffs. NJ, Printince Hall. Inc.

Scott, R.W. (1987a): *Organizations. Rational, natural and open systems*. Englewood Cliffs, N.J. 2nd edition: Prentice-Hall.

Scott, R.W. (1987b): 'The adolescence of institutional theory'. In: *Administrative Science Quarterly*. Vol. 32. pp. 493-511.

Scott, R.W. (1990): 'Institutional analysis: variance and process theory approaches'. Paper prepared for the Scancor symposium on institutionalism. Stockholm, Sweden, August 29th-31st.

Seidman, S.B. and B.L. Foster (1978): 'A graph-theoretic generalization of the clique concept'. *Journal of Mathematical Sociology*. Vol. 6.

Selznick, P. (1957): *Leadership in Administration – A Sociological Interpretation*. New York: Row, Peterson and Company.

Shrivastava, P. (1986): 'Post-merger integration'. In: *Journal of Business Strategy*. Vol. 7. No. 1. p. 65-76.

Siehl, C. and J. Martin (1989): 'Measuring Organizational Culture: Mixing Qualitative and Quantitative Methods'. In: Jones, Moore and Snyder (eds): *Inside Organizations – Understanding the Human Dimension*. California: Sage Publications. p. 79-103.

Smircich, L. (1983a): 'Studying organizations as cultures'. In: G. Morgan: *Beyond method. Strategies for social research*: Sage. p. 160-172.

Smircich, L. (1983b): 'Concepts of culture and organizational analysis'. *Administrative Science Quarterly*. Vol. 28. No. 3. p. 339-358.

Snyder, D. and E.L. Kick (1979): 'Structural position in the world system and economic growth, 1955- 1970: a multiple network analysis of transnational interactions'. In: *American Journal of Sociology*. Vol. 84. March.

Social Europe – the software industry (1986): Supplement 6/86. Commission of the European Communities. Directorate General for Employment, Social Affairs and Education.

Sonquist, J.A. and T. Koening (1975): 'Interlocking directorates in the top U.S. corporations: a graph theory approach'. In: *Insurgent Sociologist*. Vol. 5. Spring.

Storey, J. (1985): 'The means of management control'. In: *Sociology*. Vol. 16. p. 251- 269.

Svejstrup, P. (1976): *Niels Ivar Bech – en epoke i edb-udviklingen i Danmark*. Copenhagen: Data.

Telser, L. (1981): 'Theory of self-enforcing agreements'. In: *Journal of Business*. Vol. 53. February. p. 27-44.

Thompson, H.S. (1979): *The great shark hunt*. New York: Warner Books.

Thompson, J.D. (1967): *Organizations in action*. New York: Mc Graw-Hill.

Thurley, K.E. and S.J. Wood (1983): 'Business strategy and industrial relations strategy'. In: K.E. Thurley and S.J. Wood (eds): *Industrial relations and management strategy*. Cambridge: Cambridge University Press.

Van Maanen, J. (1988): *Talæes From the Field*. The University of Chicago Press. Chicago and London.

Van Maanen, J. and G. Kunda (1989): 'Real Feelings: Emotional Expressions and Organizational Culture'. In: Staw and Cummings (eds): *Research in Organizational Behavior*. Vol. 11. Greenwich, CT: JAI Press. p. 43-103.

Van Maanen, J. and S. Barley (1985): 'Cultural organization: fragments of a theory'. In: Frost et al: *Organizational Culture*. Sage. p. 31-53.

Vikøren, B. (1979): *Samarbeid for mindre industriforetak*. Vol. 5.

Walter, G.A. (1985): 'Culture collisions in mergers and acquisitions'. In: Frost et al (eds): *Organizational Culture*.

Waterman, R.H. jr. (1987): *The Renewal Factor*. Bantam Books.

Watson, T.J. (1963): *A business and its beliefs. The ideas that helped build IBM*. New York. McGraw-Hill.

Weick, K.E. (1976): 'Educational organizations as loosely coupled systems'. In: *Administrative Science Quarterly*. Vol. 21. No. 1.

Weick, K.E. (1979): *The social psychology of organizing*. Reading Mass: Addison-Wesley.

Weinberg G. (1971): *The psychology of computer programming*. New York: Van Nostrand Reinhold.

Weinwurm G. (ed) (1970): *On the management of computer programming*. New York: Auerbach.

Whitley, R. (1990): 'The comparative analysis of business recipes'. Manchester. Manchester Business School.

Wilkins, A., M.P. Thompson and W. Gibb Dyer (1991): 'A Consumer's Guide to Stories about Cultural Change'. Paper presented at the 8th International SCOS Conference, Copenhagen, June 26th – 28th, 1991.

Wilkins, A.L. and W.G. Dyer jr. (1987): 'Toward a theory of culture change: a dialectic and synthesis'. Working Paper, presented at the 3rd International SCOS Conference, Milan, 86-2 Brigham Young University, US.

Williams R. (1976): *Keywords a vocabulary of culture and society*. London: Oxford University Press.

Williamson, O.E. (1983): 'Credible committments: using hostages to support exchange'. In: *American Economic Review*. Vol. 73. September. p. 519-540.

Williamson, O.E. (1985): *The economic institutions of capitalism*. New York. Free Press.

Woodward, J. (1965): *Industrial organization: theory and practice*. Oxford: University Press.

Yin, R.K. (1989): *Case Study Research – Design and Methods*. Applied Social Research Methods Series, Vol. 5. Newbury Park: Sage Publications.

Bibliographical Notes

Finn Borum
Born in 1942. MBA from Copenhagen Business School 1970 (Organisation theory). 1975 Ph.D (dissertation on organisational change). 1964-1971 systems planner and head of planning department in private enterprises. Since 1971 positions at the Institute of Organization and Industrial Sociology, Copenhagen Business School. Since 1977 associate professor in organisational change and systems development.

Research Activities Comprise
- action research in hospitals and private enterprises
- studies of planning and change processes in connection with the implementation of EDP systems
- evaluation and implementation studies in developing countries (WHO and DANIDA)
- management consultancy in public and private organisations.

Books
Finn Borum (1976) *Organisation, magt og forandring* (Organisation, power, and change). Nyt Nordisk Forlag, Copenhagen.
Finn Borum (1977) *Edb, arbejdsmiljo og virksomhedsdemokrati.* (EDP and Quality of Working Life). Nyt fra Samfundsvidenskaberne, Copenhagen.
Finn Borum and Harald Enderud (1981) *Konflikter i organisationer – belyst ved studier af edb-systemarbejde* (Conflicts in Organisations: Studies of Systems Design and Implementation). Nyt Nordisk Forlag, Copenhagen.
Finn Borum (1986) *Organisationssafari* (Organisational Safari). Nyt fra Samfundsvidenskaberne, Copenhagen.
Finn Borum and Peer Hull Kristensen (eds.) (1990) *Technological innovation and organizational change – Danish patterns of learning, networks, and culture.* New Social Science Monographs, Copenhagen

Andrew Lloyd Friedman
Born in 1948. Senior Lecturer Department of Economics, University of Bristol. Founder of ICON (International Computer Occupations Network). Visiting professor during the past ten years at Boston College, USA; Chuo University, Japan; Linkoping University, Sweden; and Copenhagen Business School, Denmark.

Books
Andrew Lloyd Friedman (1977) *Industry and Labour* Macmillan, London.

Andrew Lloyd Friedman and Dominic S. Cornford (1981) *The Pursuit of Productivity in U.K. Data Processing Installations,* WOC, Bristol.
Andrew Lloyd Friedman and Dominic S. Cornford (1989) *Computer Systems Development: History, Organization and Implementation,* Wiley, London.

Some Key Articles Concerning the IT Field
Andrew Lloyd Friedman and Joan Greenbaum (1984) "Wanted Renaissance People", *Datamation,* September 1st, p. 134-144.
Andrew Lloyd Friedman (1987) "Specialist Labour in Japan: Computer Skilled Staff and the Subcontracting System", *British Journal of Industrial Relations, 25/3,* p. 353-369.
Andrew Lloyd Friedman and Dominic S. Cornford (1987) "Strategies for Meeting User Demands: An International Perspective", *International Journal of Information Management, 7,* p. 3-20.
Andrew Lloyd Friedman (1990) "Four Phases of IT – and their implications for forecasting IT work", *Futures, 22/8,* p. 787-800.

Mette Mønsted
Born in 1945. Master in Sociology. 1985 Ph.D. in Business Economics (dissertation on a project on small enterprises and the technological service system). Associate professor at the Centre for Innovation and Entrepreneurship, Copenhagen Business School.

Research Activities
– small enterprises
– the growth and flexibility of SMEs
– the SMEs and the service systems, entrepreneurship and innovation.
Earlier research has been on development research on population and trade in East Africa. More recent research is more dealing with different forms of networks for different purposes, and stimulation of entrepreneurship for regional development.

Publications Related to the Subjects of This Reader
Mønsted, Mette (1985) *Små virksomheder i rådgivningssystemet* (Small Enterprises in the Counselling System). Copenhagen.
Mønsted, Mette (1987) *Flexibility and Growth in Small Manufacturing Enterprises. The case of Denmark.* Centre for Innovation and entrepreneurship, Copenhagen Business School, Copenhagen.
Mønsted, Mette (1991) *Different types of Regional Networks – Methodological considerations.* Paper presented at the ICSB conference in Vienna, June.

Jesper Strandgaard Pedersen
Born 1959. Assistant Professor at the Institute of Organization and Industrial Sociology at the Copenhagen Business School.
General research interests focus on Organisational Culture and Symbolism, Organisational Change and, the Information Technology Industry. Specific research interests have concerned cultural transformation processes in information technology firms, occupational subcultures and, the role of culture in mergers and acquisitions.
He is currently working on a project on mergers and acquisitions, studying the relations between motives, processes, organisational forms and outcomes of mergers and acquisitions.

Publications Related to the Subject:

Borum, F., A. Friedman, M. Monsted, J. Strandgaard Pedersen and M. Risberg (1989) *The Information Technology Field – The Structuring of Experts and Expertise*. The CHIPS Project Research Report, Institute of Organization and Industrial Sociology, Copenhagen Business School.

Bødker, K. and J.Strandgaard Pedersen (1991) Workplace Cultures: Looking at Artifacts, Symbols and Practices. In Greenbaum, J. and M. Kyng (eds), *Design at Work*. Lawrence Erlbaum Associates, Inc.Publ., New Jersey.

Pedersen, J.Strandgaard and J.Steen Sorensen (1989) *Organizational Culture in Theory and Practice*. Gower/Avebury, Aldershot, England.

Pedersen, J.Strandgaard (forthcoming): The Unisys Merger – When Lovers Meet or a Well-Arranged Marriage? To appear in: *Mergers and Acquisitions: Learnings from the Practice*. Working Document No.3. Centre for Organizational Studies, Barcelona, Spain.

Pedersen, J.Strandgaard (1991) *Continuity and Change – Cultural Perspectives on Organizational Change and Transformation in Information Technology Firms*. Ph.D. dissertation. Copenhagen Business School, Ph.D. Series 2.91, Samfundslitteratur.

Index